The History of Phoenicia

Josette Elayi

The History of Phoenicia

translated from the French by Andrew Plummer

♆ LOCKWOOD PRESS

2018

The History of Phoenicia

© 2018, Lockwood Press

ISBN: 978-1-937040-81-9

Library of Congress Control Number: 2017952621

Cover design by Susanne Wilhelm. Cover image courtesy of Zev Radovan, Biblelandpictures.com.

Originally published as *Histoire de la Phénicie*, © Perrin, 2013

Printed on acid-free paper

"This audacious Phoenician did not stop pondering in his mind the problem of navigation. In himself, he ceaselessly agitated the Ocean."

Paul Valéry, *Eupalinos or The Architect*, 1923

Table of Contents

Preface

The history of Phoenicia is little known, widely scattered, and fragmented. Narrating it poses a challenge as the Phoenicians were spread out over the whole of the Mediterranean world for roughly a thousand years. The sources of documentation available are multiple, disparate, intermittent, and all in all extremely limited. What a paradox for a people that invented the alphabet to have left behind so few written traces! Archaeological exploration of Phoenician sites is also limited, as they are buried under the modern cities of Lebanon with a few in Syria and Israel. Sometimes construction work or building restorations bring to light some ancient remains, a narrow window on the past. If the Antiquities Authority is alerted in time, it can carry out salvage excavations before the bulldozers move in. This was how, in 1969, the Lebanese archaeologist Roger Saïdah discovered in Beirut, at the bottom end of Martyrs' Square on a building site next to the old Rivoli cinema, some rich Bronze Age tombs and a superb stonework sphinx, engraved with the name of the Pharaoh Amenemhat IV, who ruled around 1772–1764.[*] He wrote, and not without bitterness: "This dig will most likely be the last opportunity for archaeologists to study the history of the ancient city." However, history was to prove him wrong: the civil war which ravaged Lebanon from 1975 to 1985 totally destroyed the city center of Beirut, enabling archaeologists from all over the world to carry out excavations before reconstruction work started. This was how the Phoenician city of Berytus was miraculously resurrected.

Up until now, no Phoenician specialist has risked writing a history of Phoenicia focusing both on historical events and the socioeconomic facets of the civilization.

Only a small number of general books have been published about the trade, industry, religion, art, and writing of this supposedly mysterious people, offering just a few pages of what is, at best, a "historical overview." Despite the difficulty of this task, I have decided to take on

---

[*] The dates mentioned are all BCE (Before Common Era) unless stated otherwise.

ix

the challenge. I wanted to unwind a common thread in this impassable and arcane labyrinth that I have been visiting for more than thirty years now. I think the reader will be able to follow me with the help of the chronological frame of Phoenicia's history that I have endeavored to weave. I have presented the core of this history, based on the most recent research developments, so as to make it understandable and easily accessible. When several interpretations were possible for the same event, I have opted for the one which, to me, seemed the most plausible. I have pointed out the uncertainties when I was simply unable to get off the fence. The history of Phoenicia spans a period of nearly nine centuries, between 1200 and 332. I have centered it essentially on Phoenicia and its colonies, giving a brief mention to the history of the Punic city of Carthage and its colonies.

Which Phoenicia are we talking about? Which region of the globe are we in, and in what era? Indeed, even though the history of Phoenicia started in 1200, what happened in this region before then? We know that it was inhabited since prehistoric times when, around 5300, Byblos was a Neolithic fishing village, and that the site was occupied continuously thereafter. Between 1200 and 883, Phoenicia enjoyed an exceptional period of independence. Our knowledge of that period is very hazy, hence the reference sometimes made to the "dark age," just like the corresponding period in ancient Greece. Yet, this was Phoenicia's golden age, as, it was not again to enjoy another genuine period of independence. After 883, it was continuously dominated by the great powers of the moment and its own history became embroiled in theirs. It fell successively under Assyrian domination from 883 to 610, then under Babylonian domination from 610 to 539, and lastly under Persian domination from 539 to 332, the latter date traditionally marking the end of its history. The region subsequently went through periods of Greek domination, then Roman, then Byzantine, then Turkish, before concluding with French colonization. It was not until 1943 that Lebanon, the principal successor of ancient Phoenicia, finally became an independent state.

Introduction

From antiquity to the present day, the Phoenicians have alternately provoked Phoenico-phobic and Phoenico-philic reactions, never indifference—beginning with the Bible, which, owing to its multiple redactions, reflects diverse traditions. At the time when Solomon, king of Israel and Judah, was closely associated with Hiram I, king of Tyre, biblical texts praised the skills of the Phoenicians, remarkable in all the arts and great entrepreneurs. Yet, from the marriage of King Ahab to the Tyrian princess Jezebel, they were accused of the worst turpitudes, especially idolatry. The prophets, most notably Ezekiel, expressed violent criticism of the Phoenician cities, in particular Tyre, the proudest and most corrupt of them all. These virulent attacks were essentially due to ideological differences and the religious deviance of the chosen people who were attracted by the Phoenicians' religious practices.

The Greeks were also split between two conflicting tendencies. On the one hand, they admired the refinement and practical intelligence of the Phoenicians in the purple dye, precious metals, glass, and wood industries, in canal-digging techniques, in trade, navigation, exploration, and the invention of the alphabet. Thus, in the *Iliad*, Achilles presented a silver crater to the winner of a race, an object of outstanding beauty, made by a talented silversmith from Sidon. On the other hand, the Greeks systematically deprecated Phoenician culture, which was perceived as being antagonistic to their own. They viewed them as everything from slick and petty thieves, unscrupulous adventurers, and slave-traders, to bloodthirsty devils sacrificing children and even indulging in cannibalism. More generally, in their eyes, the Phoenicians belonged to a barbaric and depraved Orient. The concept of "barbarism" plays a major ideological role in their dualistic vision of the world: all non-Greeks were barbarians. In fact, the main explanations for the prejudices that the Greeks harbored against the Phoenicians are commercial competition, as they often competed for the same markets, and political rivalry, as the Phoenicians were on the side of the Persians, hereditary enemies of the Greeks.

1

The Romans held a more nuanced view than the Greeks because they did not tar all non-Roman peoples with the same single brush of negative judgment: each nation was individualized and catalogued according to its system of values. In the Phoenicians they recognized outstanding qualities. According to the Latin author Pomponius Mela, they excelled in writing, literature, in all the arts, in navigation, naval warfare, and politics. However, the judgement offered by the Romans was mainly directed at the Carthaginians, or Punics, descendants of the Phoenicians, with whom they were mainly in contact through trading competition with their merchants, and through military conflict with their army and their fleet during the Punic Wars.

Among the criticisms, two contradictory strains emerge. For some, the excesses of civilization had produced in this people excessive softness, a decline in moral values, and that famous, later proverbial, Punic deceitfulness. For others, conversely, a lack of civilization was responsible for liberating primitive instincts, the inability to control impulses, and pathological instability. From one perspective, the Carthaginians were dangerous enemies, all the more worth subduing: this was the viewpoint held by the historian Florus. From the other perspective, they were cowardly and despicable adversaries, barbarians who had to be squashed at all costs: this was the ideological approach adopted by the historian Titus Livius.

The Fathers of the Church, meanwhile, only remembered the malevolent stereotypes portrayed by ancient authors, and so it was a deliberately negative attitude that stood out in their accounts of the rituals and beliefs of both Phoenicians and Carthaginians.

The Orientalist movement of the nineteenth century reflected a taste for the East, with the Phoenicians finding their place on both a scientific and artistic level. In 1837, the German philologist Heinrich Gesenius published his *Monuments of Phoenician Language and Writing,* and he is considered to be the founder of Phoenician epigraphy. From the time that Phoenician writing was deciphered, archaeologists multiplied the number of excavations of sites recognized as being Phoenician all round the Mediterranean basin. In 1862, the writer Gustave Flaubert, having researched the subject meticulously, published *Salammbô,* a novel that brought Carthage's refined and ferocious civilization back to life. In 1863, the opera *Les Troyens* by Hector Berlioz premiered in Paris: it staged the alliance between the Trojans and Carthaginians in their joint opposition to the Africans.

In 1860, massacres of Maronite Christians by the Druze in Lebanon prompted France's intervention, with an expedition of six thousand troops for a period of nine months. The archaeological mission of Ernest Renan was annexed to the military expedition in order to excavate in Arwad, Amrit, Byblos, Sidon, and Tyre. On his return, in 1864 Renan published his *Mission of Phoenicia*, a valuable archaeological study. Although an outstanding professor of Hebrew at the Collège de France, he remained fascinated by the "Greek miracle," the inspiration for his famous *Prayer on the Acropolis*. His view was that "genius is the lot of Greece alone" and that the Phoenicians were mere intermediaries, having produced only an imitation of art. "The inferiority of the Phoenicians as regards art," he wrote, "seems, in fact, to have persisted to the present day in the country where they lived. The population of the coast of Syria [current day Lebanon], immensely talented in trade, is the least artistic in the world." The fundamentals for this Helleno-centrist current were fueled by the theses of Johann Gustav Droysen, who adhered to a political movement in favor of unifying the two Germanys. The German historian found an example to follow in the conquests of Philip II of Macedonia and Alexander the Great in the face of Asian despotism and Oriental decadence.

The notion of Hellenism's superiority, the reflection of "cultural racism," forms an undercurrent in archaeological research on the Phoenicians. For some Hellenist archaeologists, a Phoenician site is only worth excavating if it has remains dating from the period after Alexander the Great's conquest, or if it had been visited beforehand by the Greeks. Several excavations have been carried out in the Near East in order to study the Greek settlement of the region before the arrival of Alexander. Even before Greek colonization in the first millennium, it is wonderful to be able to go back to episodes of colonization by the Mycenaeans or the Cretans, more presentable ancestors of the Greeks than the Phoenicians. Lastly, the results of excavations are distorted because the emphasis is put on the discoveries of Greek material at the expense of Phoenician material. During a large part of the twentieth century, there was a tendency to see Greeks everywhere.

The results of the different ideological preconceptions are surprising. On the island of Cyprus, which is split between three ancient cultures, Greek, Phoenician, and indigenous, the Phoenicians are insidiously subsumed under the Turks and are consequently ostracized. In Lebanon, whereas some Christians claim to have exclusively Phoenician origins, some Muslims ignore the Phoenicians and claim pure Arab ancestry.

For some quarter of a century now, the Phoenicians have been undergoing a revival and we are seeing an increasing series of important and well-staged exhibitions, supported by glossy catalogs that are extremely useful for introducing this people to the general public. The first, entitled The Phoenicians and the Mediterranean World, was shown in Brussels in 1986. In 1988, the Palazzo Grassi in Venice presented a spectacular exhibition on The Phoenicians, which attracted a substantial audience. It was followed by several others. The last one, The Phoenicians' Mediterranean, was held in 2007 at the Arab World Institute in Paris. Curiously, each of these exhibitions seemed to be blind to the previous ones, thus claiming to reveal a little-known civilization to the public at large as if for the first time. What they overlooked especially was the substantial progress achieved through scientific research over the last twenty-five years, to which they were virtually staking a claim. The history of the Phoenicians cannot rely on gazing at objects alone, nor on a collective imagination, with its infatuations or repudiations, but needs to be rooted in an in-depth knowledge of the results of research work.

Who really were the Phoenicians?

"Phoenicia" and "Phoenicians" are Greek names *(Phoinikè* and *Phoinikes)* designating the country and the people respectively. We encounter them for the first time in eighth-century Homeric accounts, which reference a yet earlier era. The Phoenicians are perhaps even mentioned in the Mycenaean tablets of Crete in the second millennium. The Greeks had very early contacts with populations from the Near East through their trading activities in the Mediterranean. At the outset, they called "Phoenicians" all the trading partners they met in the Aegean islands whose home base was the Near East, a place with which they were unfamiliar. At first sight, the Phoenicians did not stand out from other Near Eastern populations. As a result, they confused them with Carians. Progressively increasing contacts between them led to the emergence of a greater awareness, and they called them "Phoenicians," though for us the inherent defining criteria are not always very clear.

Where does the word "Phoenician" come from? Did the Greeks invent it, based on their own language, to refer to this Near Eastern people? Did they take it from another language in the region? Or does the word come from Phoenician itself? The Egyptians called the Phoenicians *fenkhu*, which sounds similar, but may not have the same linguistic origin. The word "Phoenician" is close to a Greek word meaning "dark red." This has been the starting point for numerous assumptions: did the Greeks refer to the Phoenicians in this way because of their dark skin (compare "Redskins"), or because they had red hair, or even because they were purple-dye specialists? This last suggestion is the most plausible one. The word "Phoenician" certainly has nothing to do with the Greek name for the lyre, nor the palm tree, nor the phoenix, the mythical bird from Ethiopia capable of rising from its ashes. The word "Punic," referring to the Carthaginians, descendants of the Phoenicians, is clearly derived from the Greek word "Phoenician." Initially, the Greeks also called the Phoenicians "Sidonians," possibly because Sidon was the only Phoenician city they had heard of.

The difficulty encountered by the Greeks in distinguishing the Phoenicians from neighboring Near Eastern populations also applied to the Assyrians, Babylonians, and Persians. Yet, they would have known the Phoenician populations better, having subjugated and integrated them into their empires. The Assyrians and Babylonians distinguished three categories of Near Eastern populations: those from the inland areas, those from the coast, and those from the middle of the sea, that is, the islands. The Phoenicians are included in the coastal population, and sometimes in the island population as several Phoenician cities are island sites. This imprecise view of the Phoenicians can be explained by the fact that the Assyrian Empire was primarily a terrestrial empire, and the Mediterranean and its coastline a late discovery, and something that perplexed them. For the Persians too, the Phoenicians did not exist as a people. They were a part of the inhabitants of Transeuphratene, one of their provinces, located beyond the Euphrates. The perspective was that of the central authority in Persepolis, looking westwards to the area east of theriver. Paradoxically, the Phoenicians, who for us are Orientals, were, in the eyes of Persian kings, Occidentals, just like the Greeks, the only difference being that Phoenicia belonged to them, unlike Greece.

To solve all these difficulties inherent in the terms "Phoenician" and "Phoenicia," surely the simplest thing is to know how the Phoenicians referred to themselves and how they referred to their country. But this task is even more complicated. At the time of Saint Augustine, who lived in the fifth century CE, the North African villagers in the region of Carthage called themselves Canaanites. The equivalence between Phoenicia and Canaan can be found in the New Testament, in the Septuagint, the Greek translation of the Bible, and in later authors such as the Greek geographer Stephanus of Byzantium. During the first millennium BCE, the land of Canaan was frequently mentioned in the Bible as being a fertile region with vague boundaries. In the second millennium, the texts from Mari (eighteenth century), Alalakh (seventeenth century), and Ugarit (thirteenth century) mention the Canaanites as being a foreign people living in the south of their territories. In the Amarna

Letters (fourteenth century), the land of Canaan corresponds roughly to the Asiatic province of Egypt, stretching northwards towards Tripoli in present-day Lebanon, where the Homs Gap opens out, encompassing the Phoenician cities of Byblos, Beirut, Sidon, and Tyre. In his letters to the Egyptian pharaoh, the king of Byblos explicitly states that his city is part of Canaan. In other words, at that time the Phoenicians were living like other coastal and inland populations in the land of Canaan, an area of the Near East with imprecise boundaries. In the first millennium, no Phoenician inscription mentions Canaan or the Canaanites, other than coins from Beirut, which was known as "Laodicea in Canaan" at the beginning of the second century. However, the Phoenicians were always used to referring to themselves by their city: Sidonians, Tyrians, Arwadians, and Byblians. Greek authors such as the historian Herodotus follow the usage of each city, while still retaining the overall term of "Phoenicians" as a slightly vague entity.

Although it was easy for other Occidental Semites to distinguish the Phoenicians in this period, non-Semites such as the Greeks probably found it harder to differentiate Occidental Semites from one another. Maybe the Phoenicians' seafaring activities helped identify them. Yet, even admitting that Greeks could, for example, recognize a Tyrian, an inhabitant of a coastal city, from a Judean, an inhabitant of an inland city, were they capable of distinguishing a Tyrian from a Sidonian? That is highly unlikely. It is unclear whether the Phoenicians represented one single entity, as imperfect knowledge of a reality can mask internal differences and lead to a superficial and distorted vision of that reality. There is no question that each Phoenician city had its own character, for example, the dialectal variants of the language, the composition of its religious pantheon, variations in its political system, or its foreign policy. Despite these differences, the perception of basic common features that characterized the Phoenicians cannot be explained, at least not solely, by the distorted and broad-brush view of outside observers to their culture.

These common features are easier to distinguish in Phoenicians of the first millennium than in proto-Phoenicians of the third and second millennia, for historical reasons that will be developed later in this book. The Phoenicians of the first millennium had their own language, Phoenician, which clearly differs from Hebrew or Aramaic, the official language of the Assyrian, Babylonian, and Persian administrations. Phoenician religion, with its own deities such as Eshmun, Milqart, or Baalat Gubal, was also different from that of neighboring peoples. The Phoenician city-states stand out within the West Semitic world because of their unique political institutions. Phoenician art was perhaps a bit more sensitive than others to foreign sources of inspiration, but more often than not it succeeded in assimilating and making an original synthesis of them, compared to the art forms of other Western Semites.

In the absence of appropriate terms to refer to this people and its country—terms that may never have existed—we have no option but to use the Greek terms "Phoenicians" and "Phoenicia." Even if they do not correspond exactly to reality, they are convenient and conform to a well-established tradition.

The origin of the Phoenicians

Were the Phoenicians indigenous or did they come from somewhere else? In the Bible's *Book of Genesis*, Sidon, which referred to Phoenicia, is presented as the eldest son of Canaan, himself son of Ham. Noah, the patriarch, had three sons: Shem, Ham, and Japheth, whom he saved from the Flood thanks to the ark that bears his name. One day, when Noah was drunk and naked in front of his sons, Ham mocked his father. Noah cursed this ungodly son and his descendants, in particular Canaan and Sidon, hated enemies of the people of Israel. It was in their territory that the people of Israel would conquer the land promised by Yahweh.

Greek and Latin authors concur in considering the Phoenicians not as indigenous, but as immigrants. However, the traditions they have amassed about their origins are disparate. The Latin historian Justin wrote that the Phoenicians were forced to leave their territory following an earthquake. According to him, sometime later they settled near a Syrian lake before founding their cities along the coast. He merely said that their original territory was a seismic zone, which offers several possibilities, including Mesopotamia, Syria, Palestine, and the shores of the Red Sea. As regards the Syrian lake, the Dead Sea, the Sea of Galilee, and Hula Lake have all been proposed. Not all of these geographical presumptions can be taken seriously because Justin's text is too vague, even assuming it was correctly documented. According to the Greek geographer Strabo and the Latin author Pliny the Elder, the Phoenicians (Arwadians, Sidonians, and Tyrians) originated from the Persian Gulf. Both based this on information assembled by Androsthenes, an explorer under Alexander the Great. Herodotus, when he visited Tyre in around 450, learned that its inhabitants arrived from the Erythraean Sea, which would have been either the Persian Gulf or the Red Sea, both of which open onto the Indian Ocean. Based on the dating given by Herodotus, the arrival of the Tyrians would correspond with the Early Bronze Age migrations in the whole of the Near East, notably the arrival of the Amorites in Palestine around 2300. Strabo's account of the Persian Gulf theory has been reexamined in the light of excavations carried out on the islands of Bahrain in the 1980s. There was an important trading center there that could correspond to the islands of Arados and Tyros (or Tylos) mentioned in ancient sources. However, no specific find provides confirmation that the Phoenicians settled there before the Hellenistic period, though a Greek funerary stela dating from the second century indicates that the name of the deceased's father was Phoenician.

In sum, the question of the origin of the Phoenicians cannot be resolved today owing to a lack of explicit documents. In any case, the question is badly formulated, since, insofar as the Phoenicians do not tie in with the concept of nation in the modern sense, there is no point in trying at any price to seek out a common origin for all the cities. Archaeology does however provide some certitudes: the Phoenicians were at least partly indigenous, they did receive inflows of foreign populations with the waves of migration from the Near East, and throughout the whole of their history they welcomed foreign peoples in transit, some of whom did settle in their cities, which were very open to the outside world.

The issue of origin needs to be posed in terms of continuity and discontinuity. Phoenician sites were generally occupied continuously, although some were periodically abandoned, or were reestablished, like Tripoli, which was inhabited during the Early Bronze Age and refounded in the fifth century. It also happened that the Phoenicians sometimes occupied a site that was originally Greek, like Al-Mina on the Orontes, or that a Greek community settled in a Phoenician site, like Tell Sukas in Syria. Racial identification of the Phoenicians is not relevant, as physical anthropology studies show that Near East populations, both Semites and non-Semites, were totally mixed as of the fourth millennium. Hence, the most recent fashionable research on the identification of the Phoenicians, by their DNA, is extremely fragile.

Language and writing constitute good markers for continuities and discontinuities, for example, changes in spelling, linguistic development, introduction of foreign expressions (borrowed from Aramaic for example), peoples' names indicating their family origin. The evolution of Phoenician pantheons, with the gradual demise or total disappearance of certain traditional gods, and the introduction of foreign gods and cults, also help to measure the phenomena of discontinuity. Material culture too, in its many aspects, paints a picture of the populations that produced it.

Several dates have been proposed for the beginning of Phoenician history, based on the archaeological discontinuities observed. Some cite its inception around 3000 due to Semite and Amorite migrations and the appearance of so-called "Canaanite" pottery. Others point to its beginning around 2000 by connecting the Phoenicians with the Canaanites; or around 1400, in association with the events described in the Amarna tablets. Another date suggested is about 1200, at the transition between the Bronze and Iron Ages, with the arrival of the "Sea People." A date as late as 1000 has also been put forward on the basis of Greek accounts. The 1200 proposal seems to be the most objective one, even though some observers see it as an ideological choice to obscure the encounters between the ancestors of both Phoenicians and Greeks in the Aegean Sea in the course of the third and second millennia, and with them the Oriental influences on Greek civilization.

The date of 1200 must be taken as approximate, marking the birth of a new historical process. The profound changes that occurred around that date in the Near East sparked the emergence of Phoenician cities as distinct political entities. Can we talk about Phoenician unity? According to our current conception, a people is a collection of individuals distinguishable by race and origin, but whose unity comes from a common territory, a single language, and the same historical and cultural process. This modern definition is not directly transposable, because unity and diversity, continuity and discontinuity represent components of the history of the Phoenicians and of Phoenicia. Continuity with the period before 1200 is indisputable, and for this reason we can talk of proto-Phoenicians, as we shall see later.

Traditionally we end the history of Phoenicia in 332, a precise date this time, as it corresponds to the conquest of Tyre by Alexander the Great. This does not suggest that the Phoenicians disappeared overnight, but the Greeks progressively imposed their Hellenistic culture on them, hence little by little Phoenician culture was eclipsed.

Where did the Phoenicians live?

The Phoenicians lived in the cities located on the Mediterranean littoral of the Syro-Arabian area, known as the "Fertile Crescent." This coastal band, split between Turkey, Syria, Lebanon, and Israel, is bordered by a high mountainous chain dominated, from north to south, by the Jebel el Ansarî, Mount Lebanon, and the mountains of Galilee, Samaria, and Judea. Stretching behind this coastal range is the long gully formed by the valley of the Orontes River, the Bekaa Plain, and the Jordan Valley.

It is bounded in the east by the parallel Anti-Lebanon mountain range, which borders on the Syrian desert. The main routes of communication between the Mediterranean coast and the hinterland are the Homs Gap and the Akko depression leading to the Jordan Valley.

It is impossible to draw a precise map of Phoenicia because its boundaries changed over the course of its history, due to numerous political realignments. At its largest, which corresponds to the description given by Herodotus, it extended from the Gulf of Iskenderun in the north to the town of Ashkelon in the south. Going inland, it barely extended beyond the coastal mountainous chain, some 50 kilometers maximum.

Phoenicia did not constitute a country in the modern sense. It was made up of a juxtaposition of city-states comprising parceled and discontinuous territories. This fragmentation in no way inconvenienced the Phoenicians as it was easier for them to communicate by sea than along the coast road. In fact, communication was interrupted at several points by promontories that were hard to get around, like Ras Chekka (which the Greeks called Theouprosopon, "Face of God"), Ras en-Naqura, and Ras al-Abiad ("The White Promontory"), and by often torrential waterfalls cascading down the mountains. It was this geographical situation that led to political fragmentation and the emergence of urban city-states, whose agricultural land was always fairly limited.

Phoenician cities often had a recognizable look to them: they were built on rocky headlands that could benefit alternately, depending on the season, from the presence of two ports with different orientations. The small islands just off the coast, which could provide mooring facilities, also became urban settlement areas, as it was easier to fortify and defend them in the event of an enemy attack. The natural rocky protections, a characteristic feature of Phoenician ports, were supplemented by the building of seawalls. In reality, the sites of Phoenician cities were chosen not by the Phoenicians but by the proto-Phoenicians, sometimes several millennia earlier, and therefore represent a major point of continuity.

We must now clarify what we identify as being a Phoenician site, as this term is sometimes misinterpreted. A site is not Phoenician just because a few Phoenician vase shards were discovered there: vases were objects that travelled and so are merely evidence of trading activity, not of a Phoenician presence. First we need to identify the major Phoenician cities, which are known thanks to explicit documentation: they are Arwad, Tripoli, Byblos, Sidon, and Tyre. Other towns were dependent on these cities, either on a short-term basis or a more long-term one. Whoever the inhabitant populations were, and whatever their material culture, they were under Phoenician political domination, and hence Phoenician during that period of domination.

The ruins of the major Phoenician cities are buried beneath the succession of towns built on top of them since antiquity: Greek, Roman, Crusader, Arab, and modern. The whole ancient Phoenician coast had a high population density and nowadays constitutes an almost continuous urban area. New buildings are always constructed at the expense of earlier ones, which are covered over or demolished. The damage caused to Phoenician remains has grown sharply since the 1960s, as modern building techniques have enabled deeper foundations to be dug. Agglomerations of secondary Phoenician cities sometimes escaped this excessive urbanization and have left room for fruitful excavations.

Which are the principal Phoenician sites as identified in written sources and archaeology, and which play a role in the history of Phoenicia? Arwad is the large northern city. The main urban conglomeration was located on a rocky island 2.5 kilometers off the Syrian coast. Its coast-facing harbor was divided into two harbors by a jetty. As available construction space was limited, Arwad became known, already antiquity, for its houses on several stories. Entirely covered with modern housing, except for the ruins of its fortifications, no excavation has been possible on the island of Arwad. However, underwater prospecting has been done, revealing the remains of shore installations and neighboring towns. These towns—Jeble, Tell Sukas, Tartus, Amrit, and Tell Kazel—have been excavated. The site of Tell Sukas, ancient Shuksu, has brought to light the ruins of a town with a temple, a necropolis, and a Phoenician period port. Still today, the ruins of Amrit (Marathos) are impressive, and include the sanctuary dedicated to Eshmun, the healer god, the residential areas, the port, the stadium, the necropoleis with their monumental tombs, and the quarries. Tell Kazel is a high tell dominating the valley of the Nahr al-Abrash, ancient Eleutherus, 3.5 kilometers from the sea. Excavations have revealed two housing complexes, a large temple, a huge residential area, and fortifications. Identification with the ancient city of Simyra is possible, assuming that a port, which has not yet been discovered, existed nearby. The neighboring town of Arqa, the ancient Irqata, is an enormous tell bordering on the rich Akkar plain, where excavations have unearthed a small sanctuary, a necropolis, and fortifications. Cheikh Zenad is one of the coastal sites of this plain, and was inhabited during the Persian period.

The Phoenician city of Atri, called Tripolis by the Greeks, was covered by the modern city of Tripoli. Some fortuitous finds and some salvage excavations have however brought to light a few remains.

South of Tripoli, the unexcavated city of Enfeh (Ampi) is well equipped with a sloping rocky beach, which would have enabled vessels to be launched and hauled ashore. While the town of Batroun (Batruna, Botrys) has not been excavated, it features remains of a harbor and a Roman amphitheater.

In the Phoenician city of Byblos, the perimeter of the ancient tell is preserved, but the lower city lies under the modern town. The tell, excavated at length over more than fifty years, has produced numerous Roman monuments, which have been dismantled to give access to the Bronze Age temples and necropoleis. The Phoenician period is poorly represented, apart from the Persian period fortress and the fortifications. The ports are currently being explored.

Beirut (Berytus) has benefited from intensive salvage excavations that occurred prior to the reconstruction of the city after the civil war at the end of the twentieth century; they have uncovered remains from all periods, including a few Bronze Age walls, the fortified Iron Age tell, the harbor district and the harbor dating from the Persian period, the industrial zone, necropoleis, and a dog cemetery. The reconstruction of the city center spared a number of finds. All the others have been cataloged but have not yet been published.

The large Phoenician city of Sidon is also buried under the modern city, but several sectors of the ancient town have been excavated: the royal necropoleis (now inaccessible), the ancient Castle of Saint Louis with a residential area and tombs, the ports, and the sanctuary of Eshmun, the god of healing, located 2 kilometers from the city. Nine kilometers to the south, the fortified site of Tell al-Burak, "little Sidon," has recently been excavated: a Bronze Age building was unearthed bearing mural paintings and also a residential area. The excavations carried out in Sarafand, ancient Sarepta, 13 kilometers south of Sidon, have brought to light a sanctuary, domestic installations, industrial remains of metalwork, purple dye and oil production activities, together with a pottery factory equipped with twenty-four ovens and fifteen workshops.

In the large Phoenician city of Tyre, the majority of the imposing ruins currently visible date to the Roman and Byzantine periods. For the Phoenician era we do however have an area of workshops situated next to the cathedral of the Crusaders, the temple of Jal el-Bahr, and the necropolis of Al-Bass, where more than two hundred burial and cremation tombs have been unearthed. The jetty built in the northern harbor in the eighth or seventh century, more than 12 meters wide, allowed carts of merchandise to maneuver, and ships to be loaded and unloaded.

Several towns located farther south belonged to the large Phoenician cities of Sidon or Tyre, at least for part of their history. They have been excavated to a greater or lesser extent. Umm al-Amed, the ancient Hamon, Akhziv, and Akko were Tyrian possessions. The excavations in Umm al-Amed uncovered the Hellenistic town, whose two temples of Milkashtart and Ashtart date back to the Persian period at least. Akhziv has furnished several buildings and four Phoenician-period necropoleis. In Akko, Saint John of Acre during the Crusades, the residential districts around the tell were excavated, revealing a large administrative building, the fortifications, the necropolis, the Phoenician harbor, and the Hellenistic temple. Tell Keisan was an agricultural center, fortified since the Bronze Age to serve as a place of refuge for the population of the plain.

The excavations at Atlit (Arados, city of the Sidonians) have delivered necropoleis and a double harbor with a very sophisticated layout. The site at Dor has undergone extensive excavations that have unearthed numerous remains dating back to the Middle Bronze Age and covering the whole Phoenician period, including, residential districts, a housing complex, textile industry facilities, temple, fortifications, and harbor. The cities of Dor and Jaffa were given to Sidon at the end of the sixth century by the king of the Persians. Jaffa's ancient tell is buried beneath the modern city, but some excavations were made when reconstruction work was carried out in the old city, revealing continuous occupation from the Middle Bronze Age to the Hellenistic period. Several structures were unearthed there, including a temple, a large warehouse, and a forge. The excavations at Ashkelon, which was a Tyrian possession in the fifth century, brought to light some fortifications, a sanctuary, warehouses, and a spectacular dog cemetery containing more than eight hundred graves.

These are the main sites that made up Phoenicia, or at least were part of it at some point in their history. The territories of the large Phoenician cities varied in size and importance, and were sometimes fragmented. We now understand why it is impossible to trace the overall borders of Phoenicia, in the modern sense of the term, around this discontinuous patchwork that shifted over time. Nevertheless, the notion of a border did exist for each Phoenician city, as evidenced by the king of Sidon who, when receiving the cities of Dor and Jaffa, and the rich wheat fields of the Plain of Sharon, said that he added them to extend the "borders" of his city's territory.

Did the Phoenicians also settle in northern Syria and southern Turkey in the ninth and eighth centuries? In fact, more and more Phoenician or bilingual inscriptions have been discovered there. The Aramaic stela of King Bar-Hadad I, found near Aleppo, is dedicated to the Tyrian god Milqart. That could imply the existence of a Milqart sanctuary and hence a solid settlement of Phoenicians. The Kilamuwa Inscription, from the kingdom of Samal, engraved on the wall of the king's palace in Zincirli and celebrating his reign, is written in Phoenician. Similarly, the inscription of Karatepe, a site north of Zinjirli, written in Phoenician by King Azitawada on the wall of his palace, praises his exploits. Several Phoenician divinities are also invoked. The representation of a Phoenician galley on a bas-relief of the palace in Karatepe, a long way from the sea, is puzzling. These official inscriptions of non-Phoenician kings pose a problem because they imply more than just trading relationships with the Phoenicians. This phenomenon can perhaps be explained by the success of the Phoenician alphabet, which enabled the language to spread in northern Syria and southern Turkey. In any event, it does mean that Phoenicia enjoyed immense prestige at the time, and that in this region ongoing contacts did exist with the Phoenicians. According to ancient sources, Myriandos, on the coast of Cilicia, was a Phoenician city in the fifth century. On the coast of Lycia, the place name Phoinike, nowadays Finike, also preserves the memory of a Phoenician presence.

Between mountain refuge and maritime adventure

For Phoenicia, as for modern Lebanon, the choice between the mountains and the sea was always a difficult one. The high coastal range, which peaks at 3,088 meters on the Qurnat as-Sawda, acts as a natural barrier, rising rapidly in steps above the sea with a lot of cloud cover clinging to its summits. Its steep slopes were covered in antiquity by dense forests. It abounds in natural springs with perennial or seasonal water courses hurtling down to the sea. Consequently, Phoenicia's wealth of forests and water represents something unique in this semi-arid region, once the coast is left behind. The high mountain area of Phoenicia was dangerous, populated by wolves, lions, bears, and other wild animals. At the same time, for the Phoenicians it was an object of veneration. On the mountain tops they established numerous sanctuaries, such as those of Baetocece (Hosn Suleiman) above Arwad, Sfireh above Tripoli, Afqa above Byblos, and Deir al-Qalaa above Beirut. The Bible records how the Canaanites made sacrifices to their gods up in the mountains. From the sea it was very hard to gain access to Phoenicia's high mountain areas because the forests were thick, the slopes steep, the gorges deep, and the torrents dangerous.

Access to the high mountain area of Lebanon was only opened up relatively recently. The upper Nahr Ibrahim Valley, the ancient Adonis above Byblos, is one extraordinary example of this isolation, a conservatory of technological traditions transmitted from generation to generation since antiquity. The architectural technique of the Phoenician ribbed wall has been conserved in some traditional houses in the village of Aqura. In everyday items of pottery (jars, cooking pots, bowls), there has been no change in the technique or the shapes between the Bronze Age and modern times. The Lebanese glazed mezze dishes go back at least to the thirteenth century CE. This high valley, almost cut off from the world, has lived self-sufficiently off its agricultural products, its forest, and its mineral resources. Because of their isolation, the Syrian-Lebanese mountains have always represented a refuge for threatened populations, for example the Maronite Christians or the "hash-smoking" sect of the Assassins.

The Phoenician high mountain region does however retain a link with the sea, to which it is very close. It was a navigation landmark for sailors, who would see it from a long way off. In the opposite direction, it served as an observation point out over the sea, enabling the detection of invaders or looters. Hence the Phoenician god Baal-Saphon was the god of both storm and wind who appeared on the Jebel al-Aqra north of Ugarit, and the god of navigation in the treaty concluded between the Assyrian king Esarhaddon and Baal I, king of Tyre.

Sea and mountains are closely connected in Phoenicia. Were the Phoenicians pushed towards the sea by geographical determinism, because they were cramped for space on the coast, hemmed in by the mountains? That is probably the main explanation. However, they would not have embarked on high sea adventure if they were not able to build ships, using the forest resources provided by the mountains. They would not have been able to shelter their ships if they did not have expertise in fitting out their harbors. They would not have succeeded in their adventure if they had no knowledge of how to open up shipping routes and find welcoming ports of call.

The stereotypical image we have kept of the Phoenicians is that of merchants, which by the way is also that of the Lebanese today. Rightly so: in addition to regional trade, they took part in the important hinterland caravan trade. However, the core of their activity was sea-based—import, export, and transit—over medium and long distances. From the very beginning of Phoenician history, trading covered two sectors: state business and private business. When Phoenician cities fell under foreign domination they had to fulfill trading assignments to order, for example bringing back precious metals, ivory, and exotic animals for the Assyrian kings. The Bible's book of Ezekiel gives an overview of all their trading routes centered on Tyre in the eighth century, from the Mediterranean to Armenia, Mesopotamia, and Arabia. Phoenician trade was based on the exchange of goods, with coins only becoming involved at the end of Phoenicia's history. Herodotus describes the dumb-barter system as employed by the Carthaginians. They deposited their goods on the shore, then went back to their ship and started making smoke. Noticing this smoke, people who lived in the area would come down to the beach, leave some gold in exchange for the cargo, and then retreat. The Carthaginians came back to examine the gold, took it, and, if it seemed the right value for the shipment, went away. Otherwise, they would go back to the ship and wait for the locals to come back and up their offer.

The search for raw materials, especially metals, played a major role in the Phoenicians' trading activities, and determined their itineraries to the sources in Anatolia, the western Mediterranean, and the Arabian Peninsula. The second component of Phoenician trade was the sale of finished goods, often technically and aesthetically of high quality. The third aspect was the ability of the Phoenicians to act as sole intermediaries for exotic and rare goods much in demand on the markets, such as spices and semiprecious stones. On top of these three main sectors, Phoenician trade was driven by all types of goods that have left no archaeological trace. Grain, for example, where the role of the Greeks is well known, involved selling off the Phoenicians' cereal surpluses, especially those from the inland wheat fields. They knew how to adapt their itineraries depending on the best prices they could get for their goods. According to the Greek historian Diodorus, they would buy silver cheaply in Spain in exchange for low-value goods. They also stored goods in warehouses, such as those in the harbor of Beirut, and redistributed them later, at the right moment to optimize their profits. Also according to Diodorus, the fire of Sidon in 347 melted a huge amount of gold and silver, an indication of the wealth of the city's inhabitants.

The Phoenicians were not just merchants, but also explorers. Their far-flung trading routes led them to discover lands that were unknown to their contemporaries. Doubts still subsist regarding some of the sites frequented by the Phoenicians. Tarshish (Tartessos), whence their ships returned laden with gold, silver, ivory, monkeys, and peacocks, seemingly corresponds to the region of Huelva, in the south of Spain.

On occasion they were assigned exploration missions. Around 600, the Egyptian pharaoh Necho II asked them to organize a voyage of discovery to the south. They went down the Red Sea and spent three years circumnavigating Africa. According to Herodotus's account, they sailed during the summer, which was customary ancient practice, stopping off in the autumn to sow wheat and setting sail again after the harvest. Their route back to Egypt took them via the Pillars of Hercules (the Strait of Gibraltar) and the Mediterranean. One particular detail would appear to vouch for the authenticity of this account: on leaving, wrote Herodotus, the sun was to their left. Returning, the sun was to their right, which he refused to believe. In any event, it meant that they could prove that Africa was surrounded by sea, except at its northeastern extremity where it connects with Asia.

On the other hand, the Greek author Athenaeus's account of the Phoenicians or Carthaginians crossing the Sahara is not very reliable, particularly as he maintained that they crossed it three times without drinking. The Latin author Avienus relates the two expeditions undertaken by Himilcon and Hannon. Himilcon allegedly set out from Carthage around the fourth century, crossed the Strait of Gibraltar, continued northwards around the Iberian Peninsula, and sailed up the Atlantic coast of Gaul until he reached the Cassiteride Islands (England), in this way following the ancient tin route. Hannon meanwhile, also having crossed the Strait of Gibraltar, is supposed to have followed the western coast of Africa down to Cameroon or Gabon.

It is possible that the Phoenicians, who knew the Atlantic Ocean well, travelled as far as the islands of Madeira, the Canaries, or the Azores only on an exploratory basis, as the excavations on these islands have revealed no trace of any Phoenician settlement. A few clues like the sign of Tanit on the island of Lanzarote (Canaries) could indicate that they called there. On the island of Corvo (Azores), eight Punic coins and one Cyrenian coin were said to have been found, but the treasure has since disappeared.

Did the Phoenicians discover America? In 1874, the director of the National Museum of Rio de Janeiro published a sensational discovery: a copy of a Phoenician inscription found near Paraíba in the north of Brazil. This copy had apparently been handed to him by a stranger in 1872. According to the inscription, which was well written, a ten-ship-strong expedition was sent by King Hiram of Sidon from the harbor of Ezion-Geber in the Red Sea. Having circumnavigated Africa, the ships were caught up in the Atlantic storms and only fifteen survivors managed to reach the Brazilian coast.

The authenticity of this inscription, which nobody saw, sparked endless debate in scientific circles. Theoretically, assuming they encountered favorable currents, it is possible that a Phoenician ship did cover the 3,500 kilometers all the way to Brazil. But the inscription reflected the level of understanding of the Phoenician language that was current in the nineteenth century CE and which has evolved substantially since then. It is this fact that prevents confirmation of its authenticity. It was most likely the work of a learned man in the court of the Emperor Pedro II who had an avid interest in Semitic languages. Phoenician studies had become very fashionable in the wake of Ernest Renan's archaeological mission in Phoenicia and the discovery of the inscribed sarcophagus of the king of Sidon, Eshmunazar II. The latter was the principal inspiration for the Brazil inscription. Perhaps the counterfeiter was seeking to please his sovereign by inventing for his benefit the origins of South American civilization.

Activities and specialties

The Phoenicians were not just seafarers, merchants, and explorers. They had other sea-related activities, starting with fishing. Indeed, this is how the first Assyrian kings describe them in their annals when relating their amazing discovery of the Mediterranean, charged with all the prestige of the exotic. A fishing trip, organized for them by Arwadian fishermen, is presented as a fabulous adventure. The Phoenicians fished to be able to eat fish and shellfish. Salted fish was one of their specialties, and also perhaps *garum*, a sort of pickled sauce obtained by macerating the fish. Murex fishing was, however, of prime importance, because purple dye, the coloring substance secreted from the glands of these mollusks, was the only indelible pigment known at that time. This particular fishing, which the Tyrians especially excelled at, was done very close to the shoreline. Pliny the Elder explained the process: nets are put in position containing shellfish, which act as bait and which grip when they close up their shells. When the murex approach and extend their tongues to eat them, the shellfish close, capturing the tongue of the murex, whose greed is punished.

It must not be forgotten that the Phoenicians were farmers too. The twenty-eight-tome treatise on agronomy by the Carthaginian Mago acquired such renown that the Roman Senate had it translated into Latin. Was this rural science the legacy of Phoenician farmers? Possibly so, because even if their farmlands were limited, the Phoenicians knew how to enhance the value of any cultivable space, be it the narrow coastal plain, the foothills, or mountain slopes laid out in terraces. Phoenician, Mediterranean-type agriculture is based on the cultivation of cereals, vines, olive trees, and fruit trees. Fine wheat flour and Phoenician wine, especially the wine from Byblos, were highly appreciated in Greece and Egypt. Already in the second millennium the agricultural wealth of the region amazed the pharaoh Thutmosis III: "The gardens are full of fruit, wine streams like water in the presses, and the seeds in the fields are more abundant than the sand on the beach." During the May to October dry season, an efficient system of irrigation was set up, comprising ducts, wells, and reservoirs. Sheep and goats were raised on the higher ground, above 1,000 meters.

Even though their cities did not wield great power, the Phoenicians did master military skills. They had sufficiently strong war fleets for the Assyrians, Babylonians, and Persians to use to strengthen the maritime power of their empires. They called on the Phoenicians for their ship-building expertise and also to constitute their ships' crews. They also engaged their soldiers in their land forces. The Phoenicians were brilliant defense strategists: blockaded within their strongly fortified cities, with the help of their war fleets, their military experts, and defensive techniques sophisticated for the time, they resisted numerous sieges.

In the field of urban planning, they knew how to adapt small housing blocks to the frequently rocky and rugged terrain of their sites, by digging into the rock and building artificial terraces. These blocks were interconnected by means of a tight network of streets, or by steps when the slope was too steep. The Phoenicians would appear to be the originators of the standard urban orthogonal plan, made up of blocks of housing with streets intersecting at right angles. This grid layout, known as Hippodamian, is traditionally attributed to the Greek inventor Hippodamus of Miletus, who supposedly inaugurated it in the city of Olynthus in 432. But the Phoenicians had been applying it to their cities as early as the sixth century. The orthogonal plan of Beirut also included a graduated system of covered sewer lines, from house to alleyway, from alleyway to street, whose main sewer line emptied into the harbor. This system was earlier than the oldest known Greek systems.

The Phoenicians were renowned architects upon whom King Solomon called to build the temple of Jerusalem. Their building techniques were able to resist the pressure of the earth on downward sloping land, as well as the frequent earthquakes that occurred in the region. These included pillared walls to reinforce weak points, alternate mesh casings, and anchorage points in the rock, partly dug, partly constructed. They knew how to raise solid fortifications and high battlement towers. Private houses, generally built in a limited space, often had several floors. Phoenician harbor installations displayed characteristic amenities: partly dug into the rock, the harbors were protected by the construction of artificial breakwater barriers and jetties whose foundations were sunk into the water. They were bounded by quays made of huge blocks, joined together by dovetailed metallic joints, with the ship mooring bitts spaced along them.

Living in a region with such a wealth of forests, the Phoenicians mastered woodworking in all its forms. In their shipyards, warships, merchant ships, and fishing boats were all built using oak and cedar, the most durable woods, for the interior; pine and fir timbers were used for the outer construction. The different elements were assembled using mortise and tenon joints, and fixed with long bronze and iron nails. The ships were then caulked with oakum, coated with pitch, then covered with strips of lead over all the submerged part. The ram of the galley was made of wood covered in bronze or entirely of bronze. The Phoenicians were good carpenters, joiners, and cabinetmakers, because wood was also a major building component.

They were also famous for dyeing. Huge deposits of empty and crushed shells are typical features of the main purple-dye production centers such as Tyre and Sidon. Once they had been fished, the murex were put into large ponds exposed to the sun, where they were crushed. The fragments of shell were removed and the flesh left to rot. Given the smell, this stage of the process was carried out away from the residential areas.

After about a week, the flesh was wetted and kneaded to reduce it to a paste. This product, when dry, constituted the purple dye, whose violet color could be diluted, even turning pink, depending on the quantity of water added to the mixture. The Phoenicians also used the roots of lotus flowers and saffron pollen to obtain the color yellow, and copper oxide for green and blue. The textile industry was coupled with dyeing, and Phoenician fabrics were renowned and exported. Weaving looms were of the horizontal type, with no heddle; the fixed canvas was stretched by terracotta weights, and a shuttle led the thread across the canvas.

The Phoenicians are considered to be the inventors of metalwork. They smelted metals by finely grinding the ores and subjecting them to intense heat in half-buried terracotta ovens. The flame was activated by terracotta piped bellows inserted at the bottom of the ovens. The molten metal was collected in terracotta dishes and then poured into molds. The expansion of Phoenician trade towards northern Syria, Cilicia, and the western Mediterranean guaranteed Phoenicia substantial quantities of raw materials. Its craftsmen knew how to work all metals. Its goldsmiths and silversmiths mastered filigree, encrusting, and graining techniques. Encrusting was known in Egypt, the Levant, and the Caucasus, but fine graining was a feature of the Syro-Mesopotamian world. Monetary die engravers used semi-incuse or relief in the hollow techniques, taking their inspiration from Egyptian bas-reliefs.

Phoenician sculpture is split into three categories: statuary in the round, relief statuary, and sarcophagi. For the choice of stone, preference was given to the kinds of rock that were closest to hand, limestone, and sandstone for example, which in addition were easy to work. However, Greek marble was also imported. The relief was represented by decorative architectural features, votive thrones, and especially votive and funerary stelae. The sarcophagi were anthropoid or illustrated. Seals, in the form of a scarab or scaraboid, could be made from ordinary or semiprecious stones such as steatite, carnelian, jasper, agate, and rock crystal. They replaced the cylinder seal of the second millennium at the same time as clay tablets gave way to media such as tablets made of wax or papyrus. These fragile media have disappeared and all that remains nowadays are the seals for stamping them.

Ivory work was a great Phoenician specialty. Elephant ivory was the most commonly used, but hippopotamus, walrus, sperm whale, and wild boar ivory were also employed. Other similar-looking materials were also worked: for example, bone, horn, and seashells such as tridacnids. We do not know whether the elephant tusks were imported from Africa or India, whether they came from elephants still living in the Syrian steppe, or from animals kept in the royal parks, referred to as the "paradises." Some pieces of ivory were gold-leafed, others painted, inlaid with colored glass paste or semiprecious stones.

Tradition has it that the Phoenicians invented glass. Pliny the Elder related how Phoenician sailors, disembarking on a beach at night, lit a fire and protected themselves against the wind using blocks of saltpeter. The saltpeter apparently fused with the sand, hence giving birth to glass. In reality, vitreous materials had been known since the fourth millennium, and were especially used in Mesopotamia in the second millennium, then in Egypt. The Phoenicians in turn made high-quality products and introduced glass into the western Mediterranean region. Glass was worked on a core of raw clay: the vitreous paste was stretched around the core and shaped into the desired form. Polychrome decoration was obtained by applying threads of colored glass paste, using new pigments and dyes. The Phoenicians were also acquainted with the technique of cold-cut glass. Transparent glass appeared later, replacing glass paste when the technique of glass blowing was developed. The Phoenicians also produced amulets, extremely popular lucky charms, made from semivitreous earthenware, soft faience, and steatite.

There were active ceramic and coroplastic industries in Phoenicia, the workshops generally being located near the clay deposits. The clay was kneaded for a long time with water, with a degreasing agent added when necessary. It was then sometimes hand-modeled, but more often monovalve or bivalve molds were used for figurines, masks, and lamps. For pottery, they used a potter's wheel. Once the items produced had been left to dry, they would be decorated. They were then fired in a kiln consisting of two superimposed chambers separated by a clay panel pierced with holes. The fire was lit in the lower chamber to heat the objects placed in the upper chamber to a temperature between 600 and 800 degrees.

Painting was another Phoenician activity, even though few traces remain today. Phoenician buildings were painted, sometimes with frescoes, in the same way as tombs, statues, sarcophagi, and terracotta figurines, on which some remnants of color have survived. Vases were embellished with painted decorations, even if they were somewhat sketchy, and may bear inscriptions painted in black or red. The decoration of ostrich eggshells is one of the original aspects of Phoenician painting. These shells were large, solid, and waterproof. To empty the egg, a small hole was made at the pointed end. The shell was cut open to render hemispherical sections that could be used as bowls. In the Phoenician era, ostriches roamed the steppes bordering the river valleys in Syria, Mesopotamia, Egypt, and the northern Sahara.

Phoenician art

Was Phoenician art as mediocre as Ernest Renan claimed? "That art," he wrote, "issued originally from troglodytism, was essentially an art of imitation; that art was above all industrial; that art never raised itself, for its great public monuments, to a style that was at once elegant and durable." A judgement as severe as this is a result of Greco-Roman culture, or more precisely, of a certain perception of that classical culture, which was forged by the Renaissance and which we have held onto. It is characterized by a desire for singularity and individualization. In this conception, art represents, above all, the expression of individual genius. People are keen to attribute each work of art to a specific individual, and some Greco-Roman art productions do sometimes bear the signature of the person who made them, such as statues, vases, or coins. But Phoenician art is the very opposite of this conception. Phoenician works of art do not seek particularity. Quite the opposite: they show respect for tradition and continuity with the past. Most of the branches of

Phoenician art have their origin in the third and second millennia, and take their inspiration from earlier works. It would be unfair to devalue Phoenician art on the pretext that the artists did not create a name for themselves and were not idolized in later centuries.

The production of Phoenician art is above all characterized by workshops, schools, and standards. It is here where differences and the originality appear. In antiquity, artists travelled from one workshop to another in order to complete their training, and they shared their know-how. Phoenician art is a composite art that, in exceptional ways, succeeds in producing original syntheses based on borrowings from Egyptian, Syrian, Mesopotamian, Anatolian, and Greek art. Furthermore, Greek art itself, between the mid-eighth and end-seventh centuries, is characterized by what is known as the Oriental phenomenon, influenced by manufactured goods, ideas, and customs imported from the Near East and Egypt.

Areas of expertise are not the same from one culture to another. The Phoenicians were far more skilled than the Greeks in ivory working, whereas they were mediocre in ceramic art where the Greeks were past masters. In addition, whole branches of Phoenician art were lost, such as decorated fabrics and sculpted furniture, or only conserved outside Phoenicia, such as decorated metal bowls. Yet, written sources do preserve the trace of the Phoenicians' reputation in these areas.

Among the branches where they stood out, ivory working, with its golden age in the ninth and eighth centuries, was a domain in which they excelled. They produced pieces ranging from the simplest to the most sophisticated, like items of furniture clad in finely crafted ivory panels. The most beautiful pieces were discovered in the Assyrian palaces, as they formed part of the tributes paid. They were also to be found in some royal tombs in Cyprus and Samaria, the city of King Ahab who was married to princess Jezebel of Tyre, which exported Phoenician luxury goods.

The Phoenicians also executed metal artwork. According to the Old Testament, King Solomon called on a Tyrian bronze maker by the name of Hiram to produce the prestigious bronze items for the temple of Jerusalem. The gold, silver, and bronze decorated bowls, all found outside Phoenicia, are their most famous metallic productions, highlighting the influence of a Syro-Phoenician phase between 900 and 700, and a Cypro-Phoenician phase between 700 and 550.

To the Phoenicians we owe the illustrated and anthropoid sarcophagi. The most ancient example is that of Ahiram, king of Byblos, dating from the tenth century. Production was particularly fruitful in the fifth and fourth centuries, but remained destined for a small minority of Phoenicians with substantial financial means. The most beautiful specimens, partly inspired by Greek art, have wrongly been incorporated in the Greek heritage, on the pretext that the Phoenicians were incapable of conceiving such masterpieces themselves.

As regards terracotta artifacts, it is especially in high-quality coroplastics that the Phoenicians made a name for themselves in the sixth and fifth centuries. The decorated anthropoid sarcophagi, discovered in tombs in the region of Arwad, are unique works of art. They combine both the technique of working pottery in the making of the cylindrical body of the sarcophagus and the combined technique of impression-modeling, well known in terracotta figurines. The faces of the deceased are skillfully represented with their hair or headdress, sometimes bare of ornament, sometimes richly embellished.

Lastly, the Phoenicians distinguished themselves in the so-called "minor" arts, such as jewelry, coins, seals, and glass objects. Some fifth- and fourth-century Phoenician coin engravers turned out genuine works of art. Seals best capture the diversity of influences that had been intertwined from the very outset in Phoenicia. Phoenician glassmakers created new models, such as pendants in the form of masks, sometimes evil-looking ones. All the products manufactured were initially aimed at satisfying the domestic market, but later, as they were very much in demand, they were exported in bulk outside Phoenicia.

In short, despite its detractors, Phoenician art existed and it was original. It synthesized local traditions and numerous influences, its roots delving deep into the cultures that had succeeded each other in Phoenicia since the second and third millennia, and even beyond.

PART ONE

PHOENICIA BEFORE 1200

1

The Prehistory of Phoenicia
(ca. 700,000–3200)

The territory of what would be Phoenicia was occupied continuously over a very long period in prehistory. Knowledge of these earlier periods gives us a better understanding of its history. The position of Lebanon, between the 32nd and the 34th parallels, means damp winters and dry summers. The high mean temperature, sufficient rainfall and the high level of sunshine provided a favorable framework for early human settlement. One of the most ancient testimonies of human activity in the Near East consisted of a handful of sharpened splinters of flint, discovered in Borj Qinnarit near Sidon. They date to the Lower Paleolithic period, around 700,000 years ago, keeping in mind that the exact chronology of the Paleolithic period has not yet been clearly established. In Lebanon, thirteen sites dating from the Lower Paleolithic, period have been documented, forty-five from the Middle Paleolithic and thirty-nine from the Upper Paleolithic. In those times, there were three types of habitat in the coastal area: caves, rock shelters, and open-air sites, especially in the sandy region south of Beirut. Up until around the year 9000 at least, food was for the most part guaranteed by hunting and by gathering seeds and berries. Studying the Paleolithic period in the Near East, especially in Lebanon, is essential for understanding the origins of modern Man (*Homo erectus*), starting with the migration of populations from Africa. Modern man appeared in the Near East around 90,000 to 100,000 years ago and the Neanderthals from around at least 60,000 years ago. However, the arrival of successive waves of Neanderthals coming from Europe does not necessarily imply changes of a technological or economic nature.

Similarly, important cultural transformations could be due to human groups who were morphologically similar, but with different traditions. From about 40,000 years ago, *Homo sapiens* were living in caves

27

or rock shelters, and making objects that were increasingly complex. Near the National Museum of Beirut, tools dated to between 17,350 and 14,650 years ago have been discovered that belonged to the last groups of hunter-gatherers.

What we refer to as the Neolithic revolution took place roughly between 12,000 and 9000, and was characterized by the gradual sedentarization of populations. Fifty-six sites dating from the Neolithic period have been documented in Lebanon. We see the appearance of the first sedentary villages simultaneously with the development of agriculture, especially the cultivation of cereals; with the domestication of animals; with a whole new range of stone instruments; and with the making of terracotta vessels for storing food reserves. Hence, the first houses in Ras Shamra, the future Ugarit in Syria, were built in around 7500 by farmers-livestock raisers from the hinterland who arrived to settle along the coast. Initially the houses were circular, then rectangular and divided into several rooms, bounded by stone walls between 0.50 and 0.70 meters thick; lime-covered floors only appeared after 6000 BCE. At the site of the future Phoenician city of Byblos, a modest village started to grow around the year 5300. Its inhabitants were farmers, fishermen, and hunters. They lived in small rectangular one-room houses; the ground was covered with lime, and the roof, of which no traces were left, must have been made of branches, mud, or animal skins. Sedentary societies of the Neolithic period were profoundly different from the nomadic societies that preceded them. Gradually they managed to organize themselves, as is shown by the increase in population, the nature of their constructions, the installation of places of worship, the implementation of administrative practices attested by the use of seals or the development of systems of exchange. The main features of the Neolithic revolution are probably to be found in the evolution of society and mindset.

During the first phase, or early Neolithic, the range of tools expanded, with arrows, dart shafts, daggers, sickles, scissors, and hooks made of bone. Grindstones and mortars were made of limestone, along with dark-colored luster-painted pottery, and crockery bleached with lime mortar, decorated with shell impressions or incisions, which already reflects a concern for aesthetics. In Byblos, green stone votive hatchets, pendants, engraved pebbles, and terracotta figurines have been found. The dead were buried directly in the ground, either lying on the back or in a folded position. The religious aspect is omnipresent: the skull cult is characteristic of this period. The apsed house in Byblos, which contained well-crafted potteries, anthropomorphic statuettes and ox shoulder blades has been interpreted as a sanctuary. The concentration of individual burials in pits all round this building confirms the sacredness of the site. The disparities in the way in which funerals were handled point to the social hierarchy that already existed at that time.

The second, or Middle Neolithic, period saw the appearance of new tools: axes, adzes, awls, and large augers. This new material is interpreted as being an adaptation to woodworking, in connection with the exploitation of the nearby forests. The discovery of terracotta spindles and bone needles in Byblos and Ras Shamra attests to sewing, spinning, and perhaps also to weaving activities.

In the third or Late Neolithic phase, villages focused more on water sources. The houses no longer had whitewashed floors, and the ceramic was of poor quality. Weaponry and tools changed. The sharp pointed projectiles disappeared, giving way to the first basalt clubs. The multiplication of axes, scissors, and awls indicates a more advanced degree of specialization in carpentry techniques. The domestication of animals became more prevalent, evolving in different ways from one site to another. The coastal societies developed trading activities in raw materials such as obsidian, volcanic glass from the eastern Turkey. The new knowledge and practices that characterized the Neolithic period in the Near East were to spread to western Europe from 6500 BCE.

The Chalcolithic denotes the period when the first metal instruments appeared, around 4500 to 3200 BCE. Small objects such as beads, or hammered native copper pins, were known since the beginning of the Neolithic period however. Instruments made of copper from the Chalcolithic period are different: they were obtained by casting, a process indicative of the presence of genuine metalworking skills. Fifteen sites dating from the Chalcolithic period have been identified in Lebanon. In the early Chalcolithic period, around 3800–3700, the village of Byblos covered an area of 8,000 square meters. Its houses retained the same form as in the previous period, but were substantially bigger, reaching up to 10 meters long and 7 meters wide, which is indicative of progress in building construction techniques, particularly as regards the roofing. New pottery shapes started to appear: we find craters, pitchers, and especially large storage jars for grain more than a meter tall, fitted with handles and decorated with gadroons. Flint tools had not disappeared: hatchets, adzes, scissors, awls, and blades were characterized by a special way of cutting referred to as "Canaanite." These blades, discovered particularly in Beirut, were used as sickles or harrow components, used to separate the grain from the chaff. Evidence of fishing activities has been provided by numerous copper hooks. The new important element in religious customs was burial in large storage jars: an opening was made in the belly of the jar in order to introduce the corpse in a very folded position.

The Late Chalcolithic period, characterized by social complexity and centralization, is represented in Byblos, Beirut, and Sidon. Towards the end of this period, architectural style changed: houses were no longer rectangular in shape, but oval and double-apsed. Alongside were small round constructions, probably granaries, and silos made out of clay. The absidial houses in Sidon were surrounded by an enclosure. One building, used as a sanctuary, was constructed next to the fresh-water spring in Byblos and was protected by an enclosure. Inhumation in large storage jars, some as high as 2 meters, developed. At this site more than 2,000 tombs have been identified, 344 of which were for children, that contained many funerary offerings, probably in preparation for the afterlife. These included objects made of bone, flint, and obsidian; vases; toiletry items; gold and silver jewelry; and weapons. The density of the tombs reflects the importance of this village in the late prehistoric period.

The necropolis is located outside the village, which already indicates a very clear separation between the worlds of the living and the dead. To begin with, pottery was still freely hand-modelled, but standardization of products points to them being made by professional potters. Then the potter's wheel was introduced. Flint tooling evolved, with the appearance of fan-shaped scrapers. Different metals started to be used for making weapons, tools, and jewelry: copper for daggers and hooks, silver for headbands, bracelets and rings, gold for rings and beads. One ceremonial club is in ivory, with a silver handle. From the fourth millennium, Byblos played a central role in the Levant, trading in silver from mines in the Taurus mountains in southern Turkey. It became a regional center on the political, economic, and religious levels.

At the end of the prehistoric period, the villages in Lebanon were already structured, with their communication routes, their religious centers, and their specialized activities. Agriculture had developed considerably: they knew how to cultivate cereals such as wheat, barley, and rye, but also seed crops such as lentils, peas, chickpeas, and vetches. Arboriculture was also practiced, especially that of the olive tree. Full sedentarization of the populations facilitated the development of an efficient agriculture. Substantial concentrations of pollen indicate the presence of fields close to the villages. Sheep, goats, pigs, and dogs were the usual companions of the inhabitants. A funerary jar discovered in Byblos contained the skeleton of a man, and next to it in a small jar that of his dog, to which he must have been attached or else which had been used as a sacrifice. The diversification of activities was the starting point for individual specialization, which, in the following millennia, was to provide each individual with a profession. This would seem to be the beginning of the commercial stage as they began exporting and importing finished goods, and not just rare votive objects.

2

Byblos and Egypt
(3200–1500 BCE)

The first contacts between Byblos and Egypt

The emergence of writing, around 3300/3200, is used as a criterion to mark the end of the prehistoric period. However, it did not appear at the same time in all regions of the Near East. The term protohistory is used for those populations not yet introduced to writing, but who were known through contemporary texts emanating from other populations. This is the case of Byblos where the first local trace of writing is dated around 2600–2300 (Third or Fifth Egyptian Dynasty). It is a hieroglyphic inscription giving the name of Baalat-rum, perhaps king of Byblos, inscribed on a locally made cylinder. The use of hieroglyphic writing in this region is a unique example in the third millennium.

Among the future Phoenician cities, the first to emerge and to develop was Byblos, in the Bronze Age, which emerged in Lebanon around 3300. Local traditions, documented by the historian Philo of Byblos, suggest it is the oldest city in the world. This is not true, because the very first cities were born in the Nile Valley (e.g., Hierakonpolis) and Mesopotamia (e.g., Uruk). Urbanization then spread to Palestine with Arad, Syria, Anatolia, Iran, Central Asia, and the Indus Valley. The unpredictability of archaeological finds plays an important role in the knowledge of these cities. Hence, the recent excavations in Tyre and Sidon have shown that their development came shortly after that of Byblos. The ancient levels of other cities such as Arwad have never been excavated and may still hold some surprises.

How can the spectacular development of Byblos be explained? The first reason lies in the territory's mineral resources, and the second in its forest resources. In the hinterland of Byblos there were some fairly insignificant ore deposits. But—and this is highly exceptional in the Near East—these sites provided a combination of copper and tin ores, both of which are used to make bronze. Exploited on a local scale, the Biblians were able to facilitate the early development of bronze metallurgy and to satisfy the needs of local craftsmanship. However, the essential richness of Byblos lay in its immense forest resources, which is why the prehistoric village gave way, in the Bronze Age, to an enterprising city dedicated to maritime trade.

Of the famous forests exploited in antiquity, only a few minuscule forests, little more than a few groves or isolated trees, remain these days on the Jebel Jaje and at Tannurin in the hinterland of Byblos. Some sparse remains of cedars have been preserved in a dozen or so sites, such as Bsharri, visited by the writer Lamartine. Various species of trees grow on the western slopes of the Lebanese mountains, depending on the altitude. The lower level, between 0 and 1,000 meters, mainly consists of carob, maple, olive, oak, and pine trees, pine-nuts, and Aleppo pines. The Aleppo pines disappear down into the Nahr Ibrahim gorges, at an altitude of some 1,200/1,300 meters, being replaced by cypress and ash trees, with oaks still present. Between 1,500 and 2,000 meters is the territory occupied by cedars, specifically the "Lebanese cedar" variety and fir trees. Above 2,000 meters, the dominant tree is the arborescent juniper.

The cedar, emblem of the current Lebanese flag, was the most prestigious wood in antiquity, with both cypress and pine also being

Cedar trees on a hillside in modern Lebanon. Courtesy of BiblePlaces.com pictorial library.

33

appreciated, and much sought after for shipbuilding. Cedar is the most difficult wood to exploit as it only grows at a very high altitude and is a tall tree whose barrel has an imposing circumference. The tree-felling equipment was rudimentary at that time: the loggers used axes and sometimes, later, saws. However, the main difficulties laid in transporting the wood down to the sea. Before the first millennium, there were no paths in Lebanon's forests, other than dried-up riverbeds, to enable the use of teams of beasts of burden. A large number of porters and oxen were used, but they focused on felling trees that were close to a watercourse. The best time for felling was when water levels were at their highest, when the snow melted. Some of them, such as the Nahr Ibrahim, had a sufficient flow rate to sweep along cedar trunks. This is referred to as "log booming," a very ancient technique.

The urban development of Byblos was intimately linked, from the beginning, to what was to constitute its singularity during the major part of its history, that is, a privileged relationship with Egypt, for whom it was always the major supplier of wood. The city was the focal point for most of the Levantine trade with Egypt and benefited from countless royal gifts offered by the pharaohs. In 1921, the Egyptologist Pierre Montet undertook four excavation campaigns in Byblos and unearthed the most remarkable set of Egyptian objects ever found outside Egypt.

As early as the Egyptian predynastic period, around 3500, Egypt had commercial ties with Syria-Palestine and Mesopotamia. Egyptian texts only mention the timber trade explicitly from the Fourth Dynasty pharaoh, Sneferu, who reigned around 2543–2510. However, exports of cedar wood were attested from the fourth millennium, by the discovery of remnants of "cedar of Lebanon" wood in Egypt. Graves in Abydos, dating from the First Dynasty, around 2900–2730, contained fragments of cedar wood. It is impossible to know whether a timber trade, by sea and direct, existed already during that period. The first contacts between Byblos and Egypt are also documented by the discovery of several Egyptian objects at the site of Byblos. Egyptian objects found in other Syria-Palestine sites are extremely rare, confirming that Byblos really was at the center of Levantine relations with Egypt. Numerous offerings bearing hieroglyphic inscriptions with the name of pharaohs or queens of the Old Kingdom, testify to the antiquity, the intensity, and the continuity of relations between Byblos and Egypt: ten names of pharaohs belonging to the second and especially the Fourth, Fifth, and Sixth Dynasties. At that time, Egypt imported considerable quantities of cedar wood for its ships, and the roof structures and doors of its palaces and temples. Stone bowls dating from the Third Dynasty, around 2592–2544, were imported from Byblos. A coffin discovered at the base of the pyramid of the Third Dynasty pharaoh Djoser was made using four types of wood, three of which, cedar, pine, and fir, must have come from Byblos.

The wood from the forests of Byblos was transported to Egypt on a type of ship known as the "Byblos ship." Why this name? Does it refer to ships constructed in the shipyards of Byblos, ships belonging to it, ships made using the wood from Byblos, or even Egyptian ships used only on the Egypt-Byblos route? These Byblos ships remain a mystery, but some idea can be gained from the weight and quantity of wood transported, which obviously called for enormous cargo ships.

In what form was the wood transported to Egypt? The considerable difficulties posed by the transport of large tree trunks would have meant that, in most cases, they must have been trimmed and sectioned before shipment. The large pieces of timber, once they had been brought down from the mountains, were stored on the seashore. The cargo ships were loaded in one of two ways. Small-sized wood was loaded onto ships and probably properly stowed so as not to move in the event of a heavy swell. The large sections of timber, such as trunks and beams were fastened together using cables. Alternating the placing of one section with a hole drilled in the end next to a nondrilled section, would have formed a raft structure, which was then attached to the ship's stern.

Has the Byblos harbor used for the timber trade with Egypt been identified? The current small harbor, known as the "northern harbor," is the old medieval harbor, but it is wrongly considered as having taken over from the large ancient harbor. This modest creek, 120 meters long and 60 meters wide, with a shallow draught, no doubt provided shelter for small craft during the Phoenician period, but it would not have been able to handle 20 to 30 meter-long cedar trunks or the size of ships required for transporting them. To the north of this small harbor, Saqiet Zaidane Bay, bordered by an 800 meter-long beach, is too exposed to the full force of the southwesterly winds to be used as a harbor. Chamiye Bay, at the foot of the ancient tell, is too small and open, and is equally inappropriate. El Skhiny Bay, to the south of the tell of Byblos, is currently clogged by alluvium and used as a beach. It was from this bay, some 1,500 meters long and 250 meters wide, that the timber destined for Egypt must have been shipped. Two torrents, now dried up, flowed into the sea there. To the north it was protected from the dominant swells by sandstone dune reefs. Navigation was controlled by an ancient lighthouse, 28 meters high, erected to the southwest of the tell. Large ships temporarily anchored offshore, in the reefs, waiting to come and

The coast of Byblos.
From Carayon 2008.

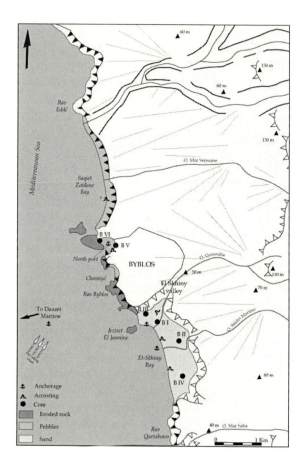

dock in the harbors of the harbor of El Skhiny and to load the pieces of wood stocked close by. Exploration of this bay has shed light on this important timber trading harbor. Activities in El Skhiny Bay were seasonal, because transporting the timber down the torrents or along their dried-up beds was tied to specific periods, and maritime navigation took place between May and September. To go from Byblos to Egypt, it was advisable to wait for September in order to take advantage of the favorable northerly and northwesterly winds.

Even though the timber trade between Byblos and Egypt was conducted by sea, there was also an overland route, that had been used since the fourth millennium. Going from Palestine, it went through the region of Gaza, crossed the Isthmus of Suez and followed the eastern branch of the Nile Delta. But coming from Byblos, the use of the overland route was more problematic, as it was interrupted by several rocky promontories, namely, the Ras el-Abiad, the Ras en Naqura, and Mount

36

Carmel, which were difficult to circumvent, and rivers such as the Nahr Ibrahim, the Nahr al-Kalb, the Nahr al-Awali, and the Nahr Litani. In addition, in southern Palestine, the risk of encountering nomadic tribes who would loot the caravans was real.

The construction of the Temple of Baalat

The temple of Baalat Gubal, "Lady of Byblos," was the most important temple in the whole of the ancient Near East and played a central role in relations between Byblos and Egypt in the third millennium. During the first phase of Byblos' urban development, the city was not yet fortified; the fortifications and the access ramp to the city gate date to the second phase. Once the urban organization was established, the entire site was progressively covered with houses, large residences, and a street network. Around 2800, that the temple of Baalat was built. The tell of Byblos consisted of two mounds separated by a small central depression, sheltering a spring and perhaps a lake, where from the outset the main sacred area was located. The temple of Baalat was built to the north of the spring.

The first phase of the temple was comprised of one room flanked by a large, irregularly shaped courtyard, bordered by two pilasters. It was similar to the almost contemporary temple of Khafaji in Mesopotamia, but it developed along different lines. The second temple consisted of a

View of the Baalat Gubal temple at Byblos. Courtesy of BiblePlaces.com pictorial library.

The "relief de la maisonette" from the third temple of Baalat at Byblos. From Montet 1928, fig. 6.

twelve-columned room, with masonry made of small stones to imitate brickwork. This technique is characteristic of the Netjerikhet complex built at Saqqara under the Third Dynasty. There is no proof, however, that the second temple of Byblos was the work of Egyptian craftsmen.

At the time of the Fifth and Sixth Egyptian Dynasties, around 2435–2118, the L-shaped temple in Byblos, dedicated to an unidentified male deity, and the important third temple complex of Baalat were built. The entrance façade of the previous temple was retained, and a second double-entry façade was added together with a series of apartments for the priests. The influence of Egypt is present in this third temple, which resembles that of the pharaoh Sahure in Abusir, but its features can also be found in the temples of Mesopotamia and Syria-Palestine. Its decoration, on the other hand, is of Egyptian inspiration: the "Renan relief" now in the Louvre showing a pharaoh being kissed by Baalat; the "relief de la maisonette" with two symmetrical scenes showing a pharaoh before a seated goddess with an Egyptian headdress; a stone inscribed with the name of Baalat; and a cornice with a frieze of sacred snakes, which resembles Egyptian models known from the reign of the pharaoh Djoser.

This third temple of Baalat was destroyed in the Sixth Dynasty, during the Amorite invasions between 2300 and 2100. Subsequent temples were made up of one east-facing, sacred room with a porch and entrance columns. The links with Anatolia, Mesopotamia, Syria, and Palestine are obvious. The temple of Baalat continued to function, with multiple changes to the layout and reconstruction work, right up to the Roman period. In its final form the temple may have been flanked by a courtyard containing a baetyl (sacred stone), as represented on a coin issued under the Roman Emperor Macrinus in the second century CE.

Baalat was the supreme goddess of Byblos and protective deity of the kings of Byblos. She was worshipped from the beginning of the third millennium up until the first millennium. The key role she played is underscored by all the royal inscriptions, as well as by the central position of her temple, its antiquity, and its immense size. In Egypt, the name of Baalat of Byblos was a title of the Egyptian goddess Hathor at least since the Middle Kingdom when she became the patroness of foreign lands. In Byblos, the Egyptian goddess Hathor had been venerated since the Old Kingdom. The identification of these two goddesses was therefore very ancient. Hathor was one of the first Egyptian goddesses, where she was already worshipped in the First Dynasty. At the side of Ra, she took part in royal funeral rites under the Fourth and Fifth Dynasties, and retained that role throughout the whole history of Pharaonic Egypt. Her sacred animal was the cow whose form she assumed to breastfeed the pharaoh with her milk. Much later on, in the fifth century, on the stele of King Yehawmilk of Byblos, Baalat was to be represented with the horns of a cow and a sun disk like Hathor, dressed in Egyptian fashion and holding an Egyptian-style scepter. The "relief de la maisonette" that decorated the third temple of Baalat bears the inscription "beloved of Hathor, Lady of Byblos." The text of an Egyptian sarcophagus from the Middle Kingdom reassured the deceased in these terms: "Hathor, Lady of Byblos, is holding the rudders of your boats." Much later, in the third century, under the Ptolemies, she was again mentioned in the temple of Edfu.

The existence of a divinity common to both the city of Byblos and to Egypt was a determining factor in relations between the two states. Veneration of the goddess by the Egyptians in the temple of Byblos from the very beginning of the Old Kingdom is attested by the rich offerings sent by the pharaohs and the Egyptian cult objects used. On a stone reused in the obelisk temple, but which probably came from the temple of Baalat, the hieroglyphs read: "I have made an endowment, I have had her temple built, [that of] Hathor, Lady of Byblos." The presence of a red granite statue of Nyuserre, a Fifth Dynasty pharaoh, does not suffice to prove the existence of a cult of the royal image. The temple of Baalat was not an Egyptian temple practicing the royal cult.

The numerous Egyptian cult objects found in this temple do however reveal the nature of the worship of Baalat. First, round offering tables in alabaster and calcite were used from the Third and Fourth Dynasties, and became more frequent under the Sixth Dynasty. Several bear inscriptions in the name of individuals or pharaohs such as Teti, Pepi I, and Pepi II. Many stone vases played a role in the cult, and their inscriptions mention mainly Fourth and Fifth Dynasty pharaohs. Some of them came from the royal workshops in Memphis and contained luxury products such as oils and ointments. Many other Egyptian stone vases used in worship, familiar through the Egyptian bas-reliefs, have been unearthed in the temple of Baalat. This array of offerings is indicative of the piety of the Egyptians, or rather of the pharaohs and the elites towards Baalat of Byblos.

Religion represents only a part of the relations between the two states. Nothing is known about the kings of Byblos in this period, but as Baalat was their protective divinity, just as Hathor was that of the pharaohs, the temple of Baalat embodied the place where the interests of the two states converged. This common goddess was invested with the same role in the political system of the kings of Byblos and that of Egypt.

Egyptian stone vases, especially when inscribed, were objects of prestige, easy to transport in the trading and diplomatic networks of the Near East. They were long-lasting trade items, which could be conserved, and testified to the establishment of contacts between the two states. So, these ceremonial offerings were not just motivated by piety or the desire for protection in a place situated a long way from the Nile Valley. They represented one of the instruments by which the pharaoh sought to obtain political and economic benefits from the Byblian authorities, knowing that Byblos was a key commercial center in the trading networks of the Near East. Egyptian royal gifts gave the Byblian elites a form of prestige. They were government-funded productions, linked with the crowning of new pharaohs or the jubilee to celebrate the renewal of power.

Byblos was the main source of timber for Egypt under the Old Kingdom. It also supplied the products extracted from conifers, oils, resins, and scents that were essential in Egyptian mummification techniques, which were developing on a wide scale. Forest resources were so precious for Egypt and so profitable for Byblos that, to a large extent, they determined the foreign policy of both states. Byblos also acted as an intermediary on the route between Egypt, Cilicia, and Syria-Palestine in order to procure oil and wine for Egypt prior to the development of Egyptian viticulture, and exotic goods such as lapis lazuli, imported from Ebla or Mari, and from the distant deposits in Afghanistan.

The tell of Fadous-Kfar Abida, some 20 kilometers north of Byblos, revealed two children's graves from the first half of the fourth millennium. Later, it was a small coastal town, fortified from the end of the

Early Bronze Age, around 2750, with narrow streets, some of which intersected at a right angle. Egyptian luxury goods of a somewhat later period, from the Twelfth or Thirteenth Dynasty, were discovered there. It was a small regional administrative center controlled by Byblos that served as a staging post for routes to northern Syria. State-run commercial trade played a dominant role in Egypt under the Old Kingdom, even though this state control did not exclude individual initiative, which emerges beginning in the Fourth Dynasty. In exchange for wood and other products supplied by Byblos, Egypt may have exported to Byblos goods that did not all leave a trace, such as linen, papyrus, gold, earthenware, and seashells.

Even if the temple of Baalat sponsored the relations between Byblos and Egypt, there were probably direct contacts as well between the pharaohs and the kings of Byblos. It was no coincidence that the palace and the royal tombs were then located next to the temple. Lots of Egyptian objects were found there as well. Some of the expressions inscribed on vases should not be taken literally: "The pharaoh Pepi is the possessor of foreign lands." They were high-sounding formulae, but devoid of reality. In that period, the pharaoh had no authority over Byblos, which was not an Egyptian colony, as has sometimes been said. But there were some Egyptian craftsmen working in Byblos, and the influence of Egypt was visible in several fields such as architecture, art, and religion.

Traces of Byblos in Egypt are harder to detect. The bas-reliefs on the funerary monuments of Sahure at Abusir represent the arrival of ships, with Asiatics, among whom there were perhaps people from Byblos. However, it is not known whether they were slaves, prisoners, settlers, or emissaries. A foreigner having a certain court status, perhaps from Byblos, was buried in a tomb at Giza. This site also revealed jars that came from Byblos, as shown by neutron activation analysis, many such jars being identified mainly in Fourth Dynasty tombs.

How did relations between Byblos and Egypt evolve between the First and Third Dynasties? Egypt's growing timber needs for royal monuments and ships transformed its trading patterns with Byblos. This trade, developed on a large scale, called for tremendous resources and a high level of organization and control. It was probably then that the coastal route towards Byblos started being used, with stopovers such as the Bay of Haifa. Second Dynasty Egyptian texts mention the arrival of tribute and goods from Canaan. The commercial network established with Byblos continued to operate, especially in the reign of the pharaoh Khasekhemwy, whose name appears on an offering table. His reign marked the end of confrontations between Upper and Lower Egypt and

the establishment of sustainable economic, religious, and political structures. Paradoxically, the Third Dynasty is less well known than the previous two. Throughout the entire Levant, the number of large cities diminished, but they were all fortified and strategically located. Their structures were linked to a state administration and a more complex social
organization. In the regional geopolitical context, Egypt was interested
in four areas: the northern Levantine coast, north and south Canaan,
and the Sinai Peninsula. Ongoing relations with Byblos are attested by
the discovery, in the first temple of Baalat, of an alabaster offering disc
inscribed with the name of Neferseshemra, the royal carpenters' scribe.
Even though the pharaoh's domination, actual or desired, over foreign
countries was expressed more and more in the iconography, only Sinai,
with its copper and turquoise resources, came under its control.

The expedition sent to Byblos by the pharaoh Sneferu

The end of the Third Dynasty of Egypt is not very clear. Huni appears to
have been the dynasty's last pharaoh and his reign ended around 2544.
The next pharaoh, Sneferu, founder of the Fourth Dynasty, had a complicated genealogy. His mother Meresankh was not of royal blood and
must have been one of Huni's concubines. Sneferu married his half-sis-
ter Hetepheres I, daughter of Huni and mother of Cheops, the following
pharaoh. The aim of these consanguineous marriages was to strengthen
the legitimacy of the pharaoh's power, a custom that the Phoenician
kings were to borrow from them. Sneferu has remained a legendary figure. He was so popular that he was deified during the Middle Kingdom,
as a model of the perfect king whom his successors claimed to follow.
He reigned for more than thirty years and his reign was glorious.

The Palermo Stone, bearing the inscriptions of the annals of the
pharaohs from their origins through the Fourth Dynasty, relates the
most significant events, year by year. Sneferu was, above all, a warrior
king who led an expedition in Egyptian Nubia to crush a revolt. He
brought back seven thousand prisoners and 200,000 heads of cattle.
Nubia had, for a long time, been a reservoir of labor for Egypt, for
major building works and for the maintenance of order. It also enabled
the Egyptian authorities to control the caravan transit of African goods
such as ebony, ivory, incense, exotic animals, and ostrich eggs, not to
mention the control Egypt exercised over gold mining activities in the
Nubian desert.

Sneferu also conducted a campaign against the Sinai Bedouins. In
so doing, his aim was not to contain any unlikely invaders coming from

Syria-Palestine. He wanted to set up copper, malachite, and turquoise mining on a firm basis, operations for which the Bedouins were fighting with Egypt. Nevertheless, this latent state of war did not prevent him from continuing and even strengthening his trade relations with the Syro-Palestinian region, by sea. For the first time, we have the account of an Egyptian expedition to bring back timber. Sneferu needed huge quantities of wood because he was a builder king. He had ships built as well as a palace, fortresses, temples, residences, and three pyramids. To begin with, to differentiate himself from the previous dynasty, he moved the royal necropolis from Zawyet El Aryan to Meidum, where he built his first pyramid. Around year thirteen of his reign, he left it unfinished to start work on two new pyramids at Dahshur.

The text on the Palermo Stone has gaps in it and the name of Byblos does not appear, but it is easy to restore. Three consecutive years of Sneferu's reign were devoted to shipbuilding and to an important expedition to procure timber, doubtlessly in Byblos. The first year, the pharaoh had two ships built, one 52 meters long, the other 32 meters, in cedar or pine wood. The Egyptian language at the time of the pharaohs could sometimes be remarkably subtle and sometimes vague. As a result, identifying the terms used to designate the species of wood is not easy. The text mentions a large-scale expedition: the arrival of forty ships laden with cedar. The term used could designate either cedar wood or cedar resin. In this period Egypt used vast quantities of ointments concocted from conifer resin at various royal or religious events. Analysis of the sediments left in vases shows that it imported conifer resins from Byblos. However, the forty ships of Sneferu's expedition must have transported timber instead, as the following year he had three further 52 meter-long ships constructed using cedar or pine wood. The third year, he had cedar wood doors made for his palace. The name of Byblos also appeared on the false door of a mastaba (a funerary house) from the same period in Giza.

Sneferu's relations with Byblos have left a few traces in the city: in the foundation deposits of the temple of Baalat an alabaster vase was discovered bearing the name of Meritites, one of Sneferu's wives. An interesting clue to a possible link with Sneferu's expedition is a copper axe found near the mouth of the river Nahr Ibrahim to the south of Byblos. It bears a hieroglyphic inscription indicating that it belonged to a logger in an Egyptian expedition.

What type of wood was supplied by Byblos during this period for shipbuilding? The Egyptians needed several types of ships: royal processional funerary boats, boats for navigation on the Nile and seagoing ships. At Giza, next to the great pyramid of Cheops, royal boats were retrieved from inside two sealed pits: one of them, dismantled in 407 pieces, was magnificently preserved, and still gave off a strong smell of cedar. It was 43 meters long and 5 meters wide, equipped with six pairs of oars, composed of 95 percent cedar wood, with wooden joints of sycamore and jujube. Six other royal boats, less than 10 meters long, also almost entirely made out of cedar wood, were found in the pyramid of Sesostris III. The boats used for transport on the Nile are only known from drawings: they were made of wood, equipped with a shallow keel, and are reminiscent of the earliest papyrus vessels. The seagoing ships were the famous "Byblos ships," constructed in the shipyards of Byblos or in Egypt based on Byblos models, like those of Sneferu's expedition. A fragment of one of these cedar-wood ships was found in Egypt. The wreck of a 15 meter-long cargo ship discovered off Uluburum in southern Turkey, dating from the end of the Bronze Age, was also made of cedar wood. In the New Kingdom, cedar became very expensive, but continued to be used for shipbuilding.

Theophrastus, the Greek philosopher and naturalist, wrote in his *History of Plants* that warships were made of fir timber because of its light weight, whereas merchant ships were made of pine wood due it its rot-resistant qualities. He added that the Phoenicians and the Syrians used cedar wood for their ship construction, as the forests of Lebanon had far more abundant supplies of cedar than fir or pine. Nevertheless, the relative light weight of cedar wood, its low shrinkage, the fact that it is easy to work, and its high durability even in a marine environment are qualities that made it a highly suitable wood for shipbuilding. Its pleasant smell made it appreciated as timber for construction and its beautiful finish made it popular for carpentry. The cedars that grow in Lebanon nowadays, not very tall and for the most part twisted, seem different from those that populated the dense ancient forests. Then, they must have been taller and straighter, like the cedars of the Taurus, which still today reach up more than 30 meters. The remains of the conifers found in Egypt, in predynastic or Old Kingdom levels, are of cedar, pine, fir, cypress, and juniper. In Byblos, wood, especially cedar there as well, played a major role in construction, to strengthen structures. Similarly, in Arqa, another Early Bronze Age city north of Tripoli, while the walls of the houses were built using mud bricks placed on a rubble base, the load-bearing posts were made of timber set on stone bases to support the upper floors, as well as for the beams of the ceiling, the floor, and the roof framing.

The development of the city of Byblos was clearly linked to that of Egypt. Sneferu's successor Cheops is known for his pyramid, the largest one at Giza, one of the seven wonders of the world, yet the Egyptians did not remember him fondly. Herodotus presents him as being cruel and unscrupulous: wiped out by twenty years of expenditure for the construction of his pyramid, he allegedly prostituted his daughter in order to extract money from her lovers. After a period of conflict between two rival branches, Khafra reverted to the Cheops tradition and had his pyramid built next to that of his father. The third Giza pyramid is that of his son Menkaure. Several objects discovered in Byblos attest to the intensification of its relations with the pharaohs of the Fourth Dynasty. The name of Cheops appears on a vase in the shape of a monkey. Khafra's name is inscribed on a cylinder, together with the epithet "Beloved of the gods, beloved of Hathor." Menkaure is one of the most frequently attested names, appearing on five vases, a scarab, and a small plaque that reads "The golden Horus, Menkaure, who gives life and all joy, eternally."

The lapis lazuli trade with northern Syria intensified under the Fourth Dynasty, as did that of Anatolian silver. The starting point for these trades was Tell Mardikh, ancient Ebla, where Egyptian stone vases have been found. Egypt's trade with Ebla must have been channeled through intermediary centers like Byblos and perhaps Ugarit, on the Syrian coast. It was via these cities that the Egyptian vases probably transited from northern Syria and southern Turkey. Byblos became increasingly wealthy thanks to its trade with Egypt, taking the whole coast along with it in its dynamism.

The culmination and end of relations with Egypt

Byblos' relations with Egypt, already solid under the Fourth Dynasty, intensified under the Fifth (around 2435–2306). This new dynasty appears to have made Egypt even more outward-looking. The reign of the first pharaoh, Userkaf, was quite short. No object inscribed with his name has been discovered in Byblos, but links between Egypt and the Aegean world have been attested by the discovery in his funerary temple of a vase originating from the Greek island of Kythira.

His successor Sahure represented the countries he had vanquished on the bas-reliefs of his Abusir funerary temple, a common place for exposition that went well beyond historical verisimilitude. However, the representation of the return of a maritime expedition with bears is totally factual: it took place in Byblos' mountainous hinterland. The name of

Sahure is attested on a terracotta cylinder discovered in the city. In his reign, the Egyptians started to take an interest in exotic animals for their royal menageries, including bears from Mount Lebanon, which they received in exchange for royal gifts. From Nubia they imported animal skins and elephant ivory. Hippopotamus ivory was also traded in the eastern Mediterranean, as far as Crete. Tree species were imported to be cultivated in Egypt, such as the Sinai juniper and the unidentified Byblos "hair-tree." "Asiatic copper" imported in this period was either bronze from northern Syria, or copper from Feinan or from the Sinai.

Little is known about the reign of Neferirkara Kakai, Sahure's brother and successor. It is most likely he who had the Palermo Stone engraved. He continued relations with Byblos, where an alabaster vase inscribed with his name was found. His successor Nyuserre is known for the solar temple he built at Abu Ghurab, a temple with a central obelisk that was to influence sacred architecture in Byblos. He maintained mining and quarrying activities in the Sinai, and he too sent an alabaster vase bearing his name and a statue to Byblos. This was the period when provincial and court officials started to gain more power and autonomy, and gradually undermining the authority of the Egyptian central power.

The pharaoh Isesi reigned over forty years. He conducted a vigorous external policy towards the mines and quarries in the Sinai, towards the diorite quarries located west of Abu Simbel and towards the incense from the Land of Punt, on the African shores of the Red Sea. He maintained relations with Byblos where he left his name on several offerings. In his reign, the number of expeditions and journeys to Byblos undertaken by individuals multiplied. The power wielded by Egyptian officials continued to increase and fiefdoms in the true sense of the word started to emerge. Unas, possibly the son of Isesi, the last pharaoh of the Fifth Dynasty, reigned for about thirty years. He was known as a builder in Elephantine and Saqqara, where later he was to have the status of a local divinity. He pursued very active diplomacy with Nubia and Byblos, to which he sent a large number of offerings. Even though the Old Kingdom was at its peak, two threats weighed on Egypt: the emerging fiefdoms, and the absence of a male heir.

Teti ascended to the throne and inaugurated the Sixth Dynasty in around 2305. His role was that of a peacemaker. He married the daughter of Unas so as not to break with the previous dynasty. He issued a royal decree exempting the temples from taxes and was the first pharaoh linked to the worship of Hathor in Dendera. He pursued the international relations of the previous dynasty with Nubia, Punt, and Byblos, where an offering disk bearing his name was found. Teti was assassinated, perhaps by his successor Userkare, head of the opposition. Yet, the latter appeared to act as the mainstay of Teti's widow, the regent Iput, during the minority of Teti's son.

When Pepi I was old enough to ascend the throne, he reestablished the legitimate succession. In his reign of some fifty years, relations with Byblos reached their height. Nineteen vases, lids, and offering trays bearing his name, most of them in alabaster, were discovered in the temple of Baalat. He declared himself to be "son of Hathor, Lady of Dendera who lived in Byblos." In appearance, the Sixth Dynasty maintained its high level of civilization and stepped up its building works, which further amplified its trade with Byblos. However, the pharaoh had to deal with a conspiracy instigated in his harem by his own wife. Subsequently, he married two daughters of a notable from Abydos in order to annex Middle and Upper Egypt, whose ties with the central power had weakened. In the end, he was obliged to bow to the autonomist pressure of the regions, which had steadily increased under his reign.

These events are narrated in the autobiography of Huni, a high Egyptian official under the first three pharaohs of this dynasty. The Sinai tribes threatened to close their mines and their quarries to Egypt. The expansion of the Assyrian Empire towards the Mediterranean and the threat to Egypt from the Amorites were a concern to Pepi I. It was in his interest to consolidate his relations with Byblos in order to tie the city still more closely with his policies. It was in this context that he sent a seaborne expedition led by Huni, which landed on the "northern mountain" coast, probably a reference to Mount Lebanon, to surprise his enemies from the rear instead of making a frontal attack.

His son Merenre I succeeded him and continued his policies, but he was above all occupied by his wars in the south of Egypt. He received the submission of the leaders of Lower Nubia. Only one document bearing his name appears in Byblos. Nevertheless, he did benefit from the military campaigns conducted in Syria-Palestine by Huni on behalf of his father.

His half-brother Pepi II was young when he ascended to the throne. His long reign is characterized by the continued weakening of the central power in the face of strengthening local identities. As regards external policy, despite appearances, pharaonic power was cracking. Pepi II significantly increased the expeditions in the Sinai, in Lower Nubia, and especially in Punt, and to Byblos, where eleven expeditions are mentioned in one single text. "The ships of Byblos" were used more than ever. The intensive official contacts that Byblos established with Egypt resulted in several concepts and symbols being adopted, like the *uraeus*, the cobra rearing up on its tail, the Egyptian royal emblem. At least seven objects bearing the name of Pepi II have been found in Byblos, including alabaster vases, a lid, a vase, and a statuette in the form of a monkey. However, the vulnerability of the Egyptian caravans and the powerlessness of the protection troops were no longer a secret to anyone. The level of insecurity was continually on the rise: Egyptian officials commissioned by the pharaoh were assassinated during the expeditions, one of them in particular in the region of Byblos where he was responsible for having a ship built.

The increase in the power of local officials was an important factor in the disintegration of the Egyptian state. In addition, the exceptional longevity of Pepi II resulted not only in administrative sclerosis but also in a successional crisis. His son Merenre II only reigned for one year. His daughter Nitocris (Rhodopis) was without doubt the last pharaoh of the Sixth Dynasty. It is related how she supposedly avenged her assassinated brother Merenre by drowning his murderers in the room where they were holding a banquet. Egypt's Old Kingdom ended in a period of total confusion. The disintegration of the central administration accelerated, and the external situation became dangerous for the weakened Egyptian power. Byblos was so tied to Egypt that it felt the full force of the consequences of this catastrophic situation.

The end of the third millennium was a chaotic period in the Near East owing to the Amorite invasions. The Amorites were seminomads of Syrian origin, Amurru designating at that time the mountainous region stretching eastwards from Ugarit to the Middle Euphrates. They moved towards Mesopotamia and contributed to the downfall of the kingdom of Ur and the Sumerian civilization. Between the end of the third millennium and the beginning of the second, the Amorite dynasties seized power in most of the Near Eastern cities such as Uruk, Larsa, Isin, Babylon, Mari, Aleppo, and Qatna (modern Homs). They also ruled in the cities along the Syro-Palestinian coast and as far as Egypt. It was a period of immense upheaval, characterized by fires and the destruction of cities, one after the other. In Byblos, stone vases offered by the pharaohs were found under a thick layer of ashes, broken and charred. They were the evidence of the violent fire that destroyed the city's temples after they had been sacked at the end of the Early Bronze Age. Other buildings, such as the pillared residence and the city's northeast gate, endured the same violence. Byblos could not rely on Egypt's protection because it too was plunged in factional struggles, an absence of central power, social unrest, and famine. Nubia proclaimed its independence.

Sinai's mines and quarries were in the hands of the Bedouins, known as "sand-dwellers" or "Asiatics," who invaded the Nile Delta. Relations with Byblos were totally interrupted, prompting bitter complaints from the Egyptians: "We can no longer sail to Byblos these days. How are we going to find cedar wood for our mummies?" This complaint exceeded simple economic and military considerations, as it affected religious concerns, which were crucial for the Egyptians: no cedar meant no mummification, and no mummification meant no life eternal.

Byblos's situation was just as dramatic: its prosperity and its prestige crumbled, and it succumbed to its enemies. The Amorites settled in the city and took hold of power. Its elites became, at least in part, Amorites. For some 150 years, there is no trace, either in texts or in archaeological finds, of the slightest contact between Byblos and Egypt. This period, separating the Old Kingdom from the Middle Kingdom of Egypt is known as the "First Intermediate Period" (around 2118–1980). It was a dark and critical period of Egypt's history about which the Egyptians wrote very little.

Byblos, northern Syria, and Mesopotamia

The Egyptian pharaohs were not the only ones interested in Lebanon's forests. The first-known expedition from Mesopotamia to the "forest of cedars" was that of Sargon of Akkad (or Agade), around 2450. This expedition had immense symbolic value because subsequent kings boasted of similar exploits. His grandson Naram-Sin related that he reached the Amanus, the "cedar mountain," in the southeast of Turkey. In the third millennium, these expeditions were probably targeting the Amanus forests rather than those of Mount Lebanon. Gudea, king of Lagash around 2100, boasted having been the first to penetrate the cedar mountain. He felled the cedars himself with large axes and sent them floating down over the mountain torrents "like enormous snakes."

The forest of cedars played an important role in the Epic of Gilgamesh, composed in the Sumerian period, of which there are numerous versions. Gilgamesh and Enkidu conducted an expedition to this mythical spot, the cedar forest. On arrival, the two friends marveled: "Motionless, on the edge of the forest, they gazed at the height of the cedars which spread out their foliage: delicious was their shade and all embalmed in scents." But they came up against Humbaba, the monster guardian of the cedars, and had to fight him to be able to enter the forest. The first Sumerian versions of the legend appear to locate the cedar forest on Mount Amanus. In contrast, from the beginning of the second millennium, Akkadian versions locate it on Mount Lebanon and Mount Hermon. It was allegedly the titanic fight between the two giants, Gilgamesh and Humbaba, that dislocated and separated these two mountains. In Enmerkar's Sumerian tale, the cedar mountain constituted the boundary of the known world, ruled over by the king of Sumer.

Relations between Byblos and Mesopotamia were established from the third millennium, episodically and on a limited basis to begin with, and in no way comparable to those that the city maintained from the outset with Egypt. Proof of this is provided by a number of similarities in craft productions: for example, an ivory from Byblos representing an animal resembles an ivory from Ur. The earliest mention of Byblos in Mesopotamian cuneiform texts appears in a Sumerian text from Ur's Third Dynasty, dated to the reign of Amar-Sin, around 2046–2038. We learn that Byblos was governed by a certain Ibdati, a name of Amorite origin. Nothing indicates that the city was part of the Sumerian Empire of the Ur III Dynasty at that time, as some have believed. These administrative tablets only vouch for exchanges of gifts between Ur and Byblos, as well as with other cities in the Near East such as Ebla and Mari.

Trading relations between Byblos and Ebla in the third millennium were intense. Byblos imported raw metals, fabrics, perfumes, livestock, and foodstuffs, and exported linen and worked metals. The courts of the two cities also created matrimonial ties between them: a princess of Ebla married a king of Byblos. Texts from Ebla give an insight into Byblos's political institutions and its society, which comprised the king, the queen, the king's mother, the Elders, commissioners, officials, messengers, and citizens.

At the beginning of the second millennium, the kings of Mari, capital of the Middle Euphrates, in turn conducted expeditions up to the cedar mountain. King Yahdun-Lim, whose reign commenced around 1810, undertook an expedition towards the west in pursuit of the Benjaminites, a nomadic tribe. The movements of these nomads were partly linked to seasonal migrations. Having left the Euphrates, they reached the Mediterranean, travelling via Palmyra, Qatna, and the Homs Gap, or via Yamhad and the Amuq Valley. Yahdun-Lim, victorious, reached the Mediterranean coast, where he soaked his weapons to symbolize the combat between the sea and the storm god, with whom the kings of Mari identified themselves. As plunder, he brought back various species of timber from the cedar mountain, in this case certainly Mount Lebanon given the route he had taken. A little while later, his rival Shamshi-Adad I, who ascended the throne of Assur around 1807, repeated the

Cella of the Obelisk Temple at Byblos. Courtesy of BiblePlaces.com pictorial library.

exploit. One of Yahdun-Lim's successors, king Zimri-Lim, also came as far as the Mediterranean, accompanying his father-in-law to Ugarit. The Mari texts mention the city of Byblos on several occasions, as well as "Byblos-style" fabrics. The king of Byblos, Yantin-Ammu, had luxurious gifts sent to king Zimri-Lim of Mari: this king was perhaps Inten, although the chronology of these kings remains approximate.

After the destruction of Byblos at the end of the Early Bronze age owing to the Amorite invasions, the city was rebuilt straightaway, unlike what happened at the same time in Palestine. There is no evidence of the site being abandoned for any period of time nor of ita urban traditions being interrupted. The layout of the city was not modified, even though changes were made in terms of the buildings. The temple of Baalat was rebuilt according to a different plan that the previous period, indicating the undeniable influence of architectural fashions that had entered from the north. The sacred area was supplemented by the obelisk-adorned temple whose rich votive deposits bear witness to significant developments in bronze metalworking.

The king of Byblos Abishemu I and his successors

Despite everything, the history of Byblos remained tied to that of Egypt. Relations between the two states were perhaps not totally broken off during the First Intermediate period. The Egyptian Middle Kingdom commenced around 2080, with the Eleventh Dynasty. The pharaoh Mentuhotep II succeeded in reunifying the two kingdoms of Egypt again, after several years spent pacifying the country. He resumed the Old Kingdom's foreign policy. He pursued the Asiatics and established Egypt's border at the Nahr Litani, between Sidon and Tyre. His major-domo Henenu led an expedition towards the "cedar plateau," meaning Mount Lebanon, and brought back the timber needed to resume the Egyptian construction program. The pharaohs of this dynasty took tough action to reestablish the situation in the cities on the Levantine coast, but it was the pharaohs of the Twelfth Dynasty who were to consolidate relationships with these cities.

In the reign of Amenemhat I, who ascended to the throne around 1939, relations with Byblos and the Aegean world were reactivated. He boasted of having put an end to the Asiatic infiltrations thanks to a sytem of fortifications on the eastern border of the Delta called the "Wall of the Prince." He was assassinated following a conspiracy hatched in his harem, and was replaced by Sesostris I. The affair was sufficiently distressing for official literature to seize hold of it in the Story of Sinuhe, one of the most popular works in Egyptian literature. It is the moral story of an administrator of Sesostris I's harem, aimed at explaining the assassination of Amenemhat I and legitimizing his successor. Sinuhe became frightened as soon as the news of the assassination broke, the starting point having been the harem, and fled through fear of reprisals across the Isthmus of Suez. He got to Syria travelling via Byblos, then went to Qatna, where he was taken in by a prince of Retenu, a region of Syria-Palestine. In the end he was recalled to the court of Sesostris I and bestowed with honors.

The pharaoh intensified the action initiated by his father, conquering Lower Nubia, controlling the oases in the Libyan desert, exploiting the gold mines situated to the west of Coptos, and extracting stones in the Wadi Hammamat. Trade links with Syria-Palestine led the Egyptians to the Bekaa plain and as far as Ugarit. At Tell Hizzin, 11 kilometers from Baalbek, a statuette from this period was discovered bearing the name of a dignitary from Asyut in Upper Egypt.

The Middle Bronze Age was a period of peace and prosperity in the Near East. Byblos was thriving. The treasures offered to the temple and the riches accumulated in the royal tombs of the nineteenth and eighteenth centuries were exceptional for one single city. These riches had no equivalent in Egypt other than in royal tombs. Amenemhat II, a combat sport enthusiast, ascended to the throne around 1878 and pursued his father's foreign policy. Egypt played a major role especially in the Near East. In the foundation deposit of the Egyptian temple of Montu at Tod, four chests were found containing a Syrian "tribute," comprising silver plates and lapis lazuli amulets. The word "tribute" perhaps designated a simple commercial exchange. In any case, Egypt extended its control over a large part of Syria-Palestine: along the coast roughly up to Nahr al-Kabir, the ancient Eleutherus, and inland up to Baalbek and Damascus.

Egyptian royal emissaries travelled across the whole of the Near East, taking hoards of Asiatic riches back to Egypt. In exchange, the pharaohs of the Twelfth Dynasty placed offerings in the temples of Beirut, Qatna, Ugarit, Ebla, and especially Byblos. Egyptian presence is attested by several statuettes dated to this dynasty in Ugarit, Qatna (modern Mishrife), and Megiddo. Relations were particularly close with Byblos, where a sculpture in the name of Sesostris I and a bone cylinder seal in the name of Amenemhat II have been found. Some false notes did however occur during this peaceful period: Sesostris III led an expedition against the populations of Shechem and the Litani River region. Some execration texts (lists of the enemies of Egypt) were directed against the Syro-Palestinian "rebels," particularly those of Byblos, Jerusalem, Shechem, and Ashkelon. The Palestinian towns began to surround themselves with huge walls from about 1850. Yet, Egypt continued to welcomed Asiatics, farmers, soldiers, and craftsmen, who came in search of work, bringing with them new techniques and a whole variety of influences. Conversely, the kings of Byblos and the local elites were highly influenced by Egypt, taking on Egyptian titles, using the hieroglyphic script, and importing objects manufactured on the banks of the Nile. But all of Byblian society was not affected by this process of acculturation. In fact, the temple of Baalat, the obelisk temple, the sacred precinct, and the field of offerings received countless offerings indicating the donors were from a wide diversity of social, economic, and professional statuses. The various oriental and Egyptian influences rubbed shoulders with the ongoing assertion of local features.

The royal necropolis of Byblos, discovered accidentally in 1922, brought to light the kings of the nineteenth and eighteenth centuries. Nine tombs were excavated, formed by a wide rectangular or square pit dug in the rock. The pits were covered by slabs and filled with earth. At the bottom of the pit, to one side, a burial chamber containing a large royal sarcophagus and offerings and closed by a wall was excavated. Only three tombs remained intact, the others had been

N

Above: Drawing of Tomb
I at Byblos, combining
Virolleaud 1922, figs.
2 and 4. From Schiestl
2007, 266, fig. 1.

Below: View of the sar-
cophagus of Abishemu I
from Tomb I at Byblos.
Courtesy of BiblePlaces.
com pictorial library.

plundered in antiquity, or more recently. Tombs I to IV date to the Egyptian Twelfth Dynasty.

Tomb I contained the skeletal remains of the king of Byblos Abishemu I, buried in a white sarcophagus with tenons, together with several animals. It also contained rich presents offered by the pharaoh Amenemhat III, who reigned from 1818 to 1773. This provides the approximate dating of Abishemu I's reign. He was a very rich and refined king, as evidenced by the objects placed in his tomb: for example, a mirror and sandals in silver, a silver "teapot" made by Byblos craftsmen, which exceeded the quality of Egyptian teapots and several bronze tridents symbolizing both his royal power and his warrior function. Abishemu I maintained excellent relations with Egypt and was himself totally under the influence of Egypt's culture. He was a man of contradictions: although under Egyptian domination, at the same time he played at being a little pharaoh, having his Semitic name inscribed in hieroglyphs, a privilege reserved in Egypt for the pharaoh alone.

During the dynasty of Abishemu I, numerous personalities, Egyptian or Egyptianized inhabitants of Byblos, left their names in hieroglyphs on bas-reliefs, vases, and seals. At that time, the prestige of the city of Byblos extended over the whole of the Near East. Its prosperity was exceptional thanks to an economy based mainly on maritime trade, and to its privileged relations with Egypt and other thalassocracies such as that of the Cretans, masters of the Aegean. For forty-five years, the pharaoh Amenemhat III took Egypt to the height of prosperity, which is reflected in his strong policy of construction works. He exploited Byblos's forest resources and contributed to enhancing the city's wealth further.

Tomb II was that of King Ibshemuabi, the son of Abishemu I. It communicated with tomb I, that of his father, via an underground passage. It did not contain a stone sarcophagus, so the king must have been buried in a wooden sarcophagus, which has disappeared due to the high level of humidity of the Lebanese soil. Ibshemuabi had his local title "prince" or "king of Byblos" written on his gold pendant, which was set with emeralds and lapis lazuli. His bronze and gold scimitar bore an inscription mentioning his name and that of his father, with the Egyptian title of "governor." Yet, this title was granted by the pharaoh to governors of Egyptian possessions, mainly large cities and districts, who possessed personal scarabs identical to those of Egyptian officials. One might think that Byblos was a possession belonging to Egypt. But Ibshemuabi more likely enjoyed copying Egyptian titles, including that of the pharaoh, which he would not have been allowed to do if he was merely a governor commissioned by Egypt. In any event, the pharaoh was not offended by this as he offered him a chest of incense and a vase in his name. The king of Byblos appreciated this present immensely given that he had it repaired in antiquity when it was broken. The contents of his tomb were just as rich as those of his father's tomb. The reign of Ibshemuabi corresponded more or less with that of the pharaoh Amenemhat IV, who reigned from 1772 to 1764.

After his death the situation in Egypt deteriorated again, for some of the reasons that prompted the downfall of the Old Kingdom. The last pharaoh of the dynasty was a woman, Sobekneferu, sister or wife of the previous pharaoh, whose very brief reign may have ended brutally. The Second Intermediate period (around 1759–1539) therefore starts with the Thirteenth Dynasty.

Egypt's disarray automatically had repercussions on the history of Byblos. Scarabs mention the names of two Giblite kings of this period: Inten (or Yantin-Ammu), son of Reyen (or Yakin-Ilu). Reyen was perhaps a contemporary of the pharaoh Sobekhotep II, who reigned around 1737–1733 and who left a statue in Tell Hizzin, in the Bekaa plain. As for King Inten, his name, followed by the Egyptian title "governor of Byblos," appears on a bas-relief, with the name of the pharaoh Neferhotep I, who reigned around 1721–1710. The name of Inten is also inscribed on an alabaster vase found in tomb IV where he may have been buried. Three scarabs in his name bear the title "governor of Byblos." Reyen and Inten used epithets normally reserved for the pharaoh alone, such as "king of kings" or "beloved" by such and such a divinity. These two kings of Byblos probably still belonged to the dynasty of Abishemu I, as the way in which they positioned themselves in relation to pharaonic power is identical. Tomb IV also delivered an amethyst scarab inscribed in the name of King Ilimma-yapi, possibly the son of Inten. In this case, his reign would have been close to that of the pharaoh Neferhotep I.

Then came the reign of Abishemu II, probably buried in tomb IX of Byblos. His name is inscribed on an earthenware vase found in this tomb, on an obelisk in the obelisk temple, and on several other objects. He might have been contemporary with the pharaoh Nehesy of the Fourteenth Dynasty (end of the seventeenth century or early sixteenth). After the last Thirteenth Dynasty pharaohs, who only exercised local power, the Fourteenth Dynasty was short-lived and remains virtually unknown. The seizure of power over the north of Egypt by the Hyksos was achieved progressively, over almost half a century. Who were the Hyksos? They roughly correspond to the peoples the Egyptians referred to as the "Asiatics." The Fifteenth and Sixteenth Dynasties were those of the Hyksos. These newcomers fitted into the Egyptian political mold, adopted the hieroglyphic script, and retained the format of royal titles and the official religion, even though their Byblian cultural identity is reflected in their architecture and ceramics, for example.

In Byblos, relations with Egypt under the Hyksos remained good and the kings of Byblos still seemed very Egyptianized. One inscribed limestone slab, found next to the obelisk temple, reveals the king of Byblos Yapa-Shemuabi, son of Abishemu II. A stele dedicated to the goddess Nut mentions King Akery, who was another of his sons. A second stele dedicated to Nut revealed King Akay (Egliya), without any mention of his filiation. Two other kings of Byblos are bound to be contemporaries of the Fifteenth and Sixteenth Hyksos Dynasties in the sixteenth century: Kain, known from a steatite scarab, with a dedication to "Hathor, Lady of Byblos," and Rynty "prince of Byblos," whose name is inscribed on a similar scarab.

The kings of Byblos contemporary with the Second Intermediate period in Egypt—Reyen, Inten, Ilima-yapi, Abishemu II, Yapa-Shemuabi, Akery, Akay, Kain, and Rynty—were still very much influenced by Egypt. From this point of view, nothing appears to have changed in the city of Byblos since the reigns of kings Abishemu I and Ibshemuabi, who were contemporary with the Egyptian Middle Kingdom. However, relations with Egypt were radically different, even though they remained cordial. Byblos was no longer inundated with riches from the pharaohs, who stopped sending prestigious gifts. Once again, Egypt's difficulties had an impact on Byblos, whose prosperity diminished substantially on the eve of the Egyptian New Kingdom.

3

The Other Proto-Phoenician Cities
(3200–1500)

The founding of Sidon

In the book of Genesis, Sidon is presented as the first-born of Canaan. Justin recounts that the city of Tyre was founded by Sidon, who had just been defeated by the king of Ashkelon, one year before the fall of Troy, in the second millennium. These traditions about the founding of Sidon remain problematic. We are also missing inscriptions covering the early period of this city. On the other hand, archaeologists have provided some answers. The first human settlement in the Chalcolithic period was located at Dakerman, 1 kilometer to the south of Sidon. At the beginning of the Early Bronze Age, the inhabitants of Dakerman abandoned this site and settled in Sidon, on the tell of the castle of Saint-Louis close to the north harbor, well protected by a coastal land bar. They were to turn to maritime trade, which would form the basis of their wealth. The name of Sidon appears perhaps in the archives of Ebla, compiled in the third millennium. A residential district from this period has been unearthed, with buildings made of a combination of stone, brick, and wood. Some were grain storerooms, but food supplies also relied on hunting as game was plentiful, including aurochs, wild boars, bears, lions, and hippos. This district was destroyed by a fire around 2600. A deposit of sand 1.4 meters thick covered the third-millennium site, corresponding to a period of abandonment.

For the early second millennium, a necropolis was unearthed with graves of warriors buried with their weapons and of children buried with jewels and weapons. The city developed especially from 1750. The discovery of a cup from the Middle Minoan period (2000–1700) bears witness to trading relations between Sidon and Crete. Two religious buildings, dated around 1600, were unearthed. Their pavement had been damaged by repeated fires, caused by ritual sacrifices. At that time, Sidon may have been in the orbit of the state of Mitanni, before the Asiatic campaigns of the pharaoh Thutmose III. His name appears, with that of Irqata, in the list of names of a Hittite ritual from the first half of the fifteenth century. A tablet in cuneiform writing discovered in Sidon and dated to around 1400 contains an order for wooden objects. This tablet was of local production, indicating that cuneiform was used in that period in the city's trade, and that the city had relations with Mesopotamia. These relations went back to the end of the third millennium at least, as evidenced by a Sumerian tablet, dated to about 2033, discovered in the neighboring locality of Kharayeb.

Sidon developed later than Byblos, and was at that time a city of lesser importance, possessing fewer forest resources. It does not appear to have had as privileged relations with Egypt as did Byblos, nor to have attracted as much wealth. Traces relating to ancient times are tenuous: only a small Egyptian-style pitcher dating from the First Dynasty has been found. A bone box dating from around 1700 contained a scarab with an inscription imitating Egyptian hieroglyphs: it could point to a Sidonian scribal tradition that employed hieroglyphic writing, in Sidon as in Byblos. Relations between Sidon and Egypt are attested beginning in the Second Intermediate period by the Hyksos material, imported Egyptian ceramics, an alabaster vase, and some scarabs. One of the scarabs, in the name of Djed-kheper-re, was found in a temple destroyed by fire in the thirteenth century. In Tell el-Burak, a town in the neighborhood of Sidon, the beautiful paintings decorating a palace of the early second millennium were of Egyptian influence and are evidence of contacts with Egypt.

It is generally thought that Sidon was used as a mere stopover harbor for coastal navigation between Byblos and Egypt. But perhaps the urban excavations in Sidon hold more surprises in store regarding its importance. Byblos is well known because a large, sparsely populated area of the city was excavated before the expansion of the modern agglomeration, but this is not the case for Sidon where preserved plots are scarce in what is today a very densely built city.

The founding of Tyre

Ancient sources are more forthcoming about the origins of Tyre. Its great antiquity is reflected in the biblical book of Isaiah and in classical sources. Strabo wrote that Tyre was "the largest and the oldest Phoenician city, rivaling Sidon, not only in area, but also in reputation and age." When Herodotus visited Tyre in around 450, the priests of the temple of Milqart (Heracles) told him that it had been built at the same time as the city, 2,300 years previously. This is how we arrive at the date of 2750 for the founding of Tyre. According to the Greek historian Flavius Josephus, Tyre was founded 240 years before the construction of the temple of Jerusalem in the tenth century, which gives a date around 1200. The Egyptian execration texts, the first texts to mention Tyre, date to the nineteenth century. The Legend of Keret, a fourteenth-century Ugaritic text, recounts the visit of King Keret to the temples of Tyre and Sidon. All these dates vary too widely to be reliable, and some may even indicate refoundation dates, such being fairly frequent occurrences in antiquity.

What does archaeology tell us? Not a lot, as the city of Tyre is buried beneath the modern urban conglomeration and has only been excavated from Hellenistic-period levels. However, a survey carried out in the more ancient levels shows that the site was occupied from the Early Bronze Age (3300–2000), but that the remains of a large architectural feature set on the rock only appeared at the end of that period. The insular city was originally made up of two islands that were joined by King Hiram I; the island would later be connected to the continent by Alexander the Great. After a hiatus in the occupation of the survey area between approximately 2000 and 1600, the town started to develop. In the beginning it was a second-rank city that was superceded by Byblos, Ugarit, and Sidon in terms of international trade.

Did Tyre have contacts with Egypt? One king of Tyre, whose name is not clear, is mentioned in a nineteenth-century Egyptian execration text. A few Egyptian objects were discovered at the site, whose early levels, let us not forget, have not been excavated. They include a quartz cylinder seal with the title of an Egyptian Old Kingdom official from the Third or Fourth Dynasty, and scarabs, including one from the period of Thutmose III. Under Egypt's Eighteenth Dynasty, in the years 1539–1292, the opening of Egypt to the Near East continued—a prerequisite for the importation of raw materials. A stele from Karnak commemorates the actions of Ahmose, the first pharaoh of this dynasty. He expelled the Hyksos and reconquered the Egyptian Delta, bringing a halt to Canaanite demographic and military expansion. From that point, Tyre and the other Levantine cities were then subjugated to Egypt.

For more than three centuries, the Near East was marked by Egyptian domination, direct or indirect, depending on whether the locations were the pharaoh's garrison towns, like Gaza and Beth Shean, or city-states, governed by kings and retaining a degree of autonomy, like Tyre and Sidon. Thutmose III, son of a concubine of Thutmose II, was only a small child when his father died. His mother, Hatshepsut, supported by the clergy of Amun, became co-regent and monopolized power until her death, in mysterious circumstances, in around 1458. Thutmose III had to confront a new revolt of the small Asiatic states, which had rallied to the prince of Kadesh, who was under the influence of the Mitanni. The Mitanni united the Hurrian principalities of Upper Mesopotamia and then spread from Mesopotamia to Syria, to the cities on the coast and to Palestine. It took seventeen campaigns for the pharaoh eventually to control the situation. It was a difficult period, with the coastal cities caught between the two rival empires of Mitanni and Egypt. Thutmose III was ultimately victorious and Egyptian supremacy was provisionally recognized in the Near East, especially with respect to tribute. Byblos, which is mentioned in the account of his campaigns, was always the most powerful city. It would appear that the pharaoh reserved a royal estate for himself within its forests.

The founding of Arwad and other cities

The origins of the city of Arwad are little known as it is rarely mentioned in the sources and has not been excavated. It is not certain whether its name appears in the Ebla and Alalakh archives in the third and second millennia. Strengthened by its insular position, which protected it against attacks, Arwad was totally focused on maritime trade. It does not appear in the list of Asiatic states under Egyptian domination, established from Thutmose III's conquest. No precise mention of the city is made in the sources before the Amarna Letters around 1350.

Among the maritime cities of the north, Marathos, modern Amrit, was on the Syrian coast, almost opposite Arwad. It was inhabited from the end of the third millennium on a tell situated to the east of the so-called *maabed* sanctuary. The site continued to be occupied in the Middle and Late Bronze Ages. It is possible that it figures in the list of cities mentioned during the Syrian expedition of the pharaoh Thutmose III, under the name of Karat-Marat.

Simyra, probably Tell Kazel, near the mouth of the Nahr al-Abrash, is possibly already mentioned in the Ebla texts. In the second millennium, it was the main center of the kingdom of Amurru. After the conquest of Thutmose III, it became an administrative district, reporting to an Egyptian governor.

Irqata, nowadays Arqa, on the edge of the rich Akkar Plain, was one of the first urbanized centers between the middle of the third millennium and the middle of the second. Later it was no more than a village of no importance.

Tripoli, Atri in Phoenician, has delivered some Late Bronze Age remains in the necropolis of the Crusaders, inside the castle of Abu Samra, the old Mount Pelerin.

Batruna, modern Batroun, between Tripoli and Byblos, perhaps figures in the Ebla texts in the third millennium, but its existence is attested in the second millennium. According to Flavius Josephus, the town was founded by King Ithobaal I of Tyre who reigned around 887–856, but this was probably a refoundation.

Beirut (Berytos), whose name means "wells" in the plural, is possibly mentioned in the Ebla texts as "Baurtu." This would not be surprising because the site was inhabited since the Lower Paleolithic. The town existed since the Early Bronze Age; it was fortified from the Middle Bronze age and has been inhabited continuously down to modern times. The discovery of a sphinx inscribed with the name of Amenemhat IV bears witness to relations with Egypt under the Twelfth Dynasty.

Among the cities of the south, Sarepta, modern Sarafand, situated between Sidon and Tyre, was claimed throughout the whole of its history by the two cities. It possibly figures in the texts of Ebla, then from the second half of the second millennium, it was cited in those of the pharaoh Amenhotep II and of Ugarit. The archaeological remains date to the Late Bronze Age. Akhziv, between Tyre and Akko, possibly figures already in the Ebla texts. The archaeological remains date to the Middle Bronze Age. The city was then encircled by fortifications, which were destroyed in the Late Bronze Age.

Akko, Saint John of Acre to the Crusaders, is mentioned in Egyptian texts from the nineteenth century. The oldest traces of settlement go back to the beginning of the second millennium. The city developed during the Late Bronze Age especially.

Tell Keisan, located in the plain of Akko, is perhaps the ancient Akshaph. The site was occupied without interruption from the Neolithic to the Hellenistic period.

In Dor, a port town 25 kilometers south of Mount Carmel, the oldest remains unearthed date back to the Middle Bronze Age.

Jaffa, a port town south of Tel Aviv, was fortified during the Middle and Late Bronze Ages. It is mentioned in the texts of Thutmose III, which tell how the pharaoh conquered it. As a present to the governor of Jaffa, the pharaoh sent him large baskets in which were hidden Egyptian soldiers who seized the town from within.

Birth and demise of the kingdom of Ugarit

Ugarit, modern Ras Shamra, is located 12 kilometers north of the Syrian city of Lattakia. Excavated systematically since 1929, it is well known today. Occupied since the Neolithic period, it became the capital of a prosperous kingdom during the Bronze Age. Its territory was quite large, encompassing in particular the harbor of Mahadu, now Minet el-Beida 1.5 kilometers away, and Ras Ibn Hani, 5 kilometers away, with its royal residence. The royal palace of Ugarit covered 7,000 square meters just by itself, already comprising a ninety-room ground floor, five courtyards and a garden. Numerous archives, written in Akkadian cuneiform and Ugaritic cuneiform, shed light on the city's history. It is mentioned in the texts of Ebla in the twenty-fourth century, those of Mari from the eighteenth century, and the seventeenth century Alalakh texts.

Ugarit maintained constant relations with Egypt from the nineteenth century (Twelfth Dynasty), as shown by the various objects bearing the names of Sesostris I, Sesostris II, and Amenemhat III. It was an important trading city, controlling part of the traffic between Mesopotamia, Cyprus, the Aegean, and Egypt. For a city that depended heavily on its commercial activities, free access to sea routes was vital. Consequently, it conducted a pragmatic policy of recognizing the supremacy of the major powers of the time in order to obtain the goodwill that was essential for its prosperity and even for its survival. In the eighteenth and seventeenth centuries, the kings of Ugarit first sought protection from the kings of Yamhad, modern Aleppo. During the sixteenth century, they became vassals of the kings of Mitanni. But attacks by Hittite kings and Egyptian pharaohs forced the kings of Mitanni to confine themselves to Carchemish, Aleppo, and northern Syria.

Ugarit's probably voluntary submission to Egypt occurred around 1440, when Thutmose III seized the Canaanite and Syrian coastal region. Peace was reestablished in Asia and, in 1419, the Mitanni reconciled with Egypt through a series of marriages between daughters of the Hurrian kings and three successive pharaohs, who took the Hurrian princesses as secondary wives.

The Late Bronze Age, especially the period between 1365 and 1200, is the best-known of Ugarit's history. Around 1365, the city suffered an earthquake, partially destroying its archives. Ugarit's relations with Egypt reached their peak in the reigns of Niqmepa V and the pharaoh Amenhotep III. Their relations deteriorated in the reign of Niqmadu II, when Tutankhamun occupied the throne of Egypt.

In reality, the king of Ugarit dreaded the Hittite raids in northern Syria. The Hittite state, formed in around 1650, became a true empire in the reign of Suppiluliuma who acceded to the throne around 1353. The king of Ugarit, Niqmadu II, saw fit to rally to the Hittite king in around 1330. His decision was motivated by the weakness of the successors of the pharaoh Tutankhamun; to him the Hittite king Suppiluliuma appeared to be a better protector, as he was capable of maintaining order in the region. Ugarit enjoyed a privileged status, obtaining the right not to intervene in the conflicts between its suzerain and foreign powers or rebellious subjects. But, after the consolidation of Hittite power at the end of the fourteenth century, the Hittite king Mursili II imposed on the king of Ugarit, Niqmepa VI, a true vassalage treaty, including military obligations. He made his cousin, the king of Carchemish, responsible for overseeing his Syrian vassals, starting with the king of Ugarit.

Under the pharaoh Ramesses II, the Egyptians and the Hittites confronted each other in 1274 at the Battle of Kadesh. In 1258, the alliance concluded between the pharaoh Ramesses II and the Hittite king Hattusili III initiated a long period of peace. Over three decades, the pacification of the Near East was complete, except for the discord between the Hittites and Assyrians. It was the golden age of diplomatic and commercial exchanges between the major powers and the small prosperous states like Ugarit. A huge traffic of goods and men was organized by genuine firms between Hatti, Egypt, the coastal cities, Canaan, Cyprus, Emar, and Babylon. But a number of crises unsettled Ugarit's royal family in the reign of Ammishtamru III, to such an extent that the Hittite kings were obliged to intervene on several occasions in the internal affairs of the city.

The reigns of Ibiranu VI and Niqmadu III coincide with a period of international crisis. The Hittite king Tudhaliya IV went to war unsuccessfully against the king of Assur, Tukulti-Ninurta I. The latter would later seize Babylon and the Kassite kingdom. But fairly rapidly a reconciliation between the Hittites and the Assyrians restored confidence. The blockade imposed on the Assyrians by the Hittite king, which had lasted several years, was lifted. International trade resumed even more intensely, to the benefit of Ugarit, Emar, and all the centers of trade in the region. However, Hittite tutelage remained a heavy burden for Ugarit, and Ibiranu VI married a Hittite princess without doubt in an attempt to alleviate its effects. Egypt was now a friendly power, but distant, hence unable to lighten the weight of Hittite domination.

Sharelli, the mother of Ammurapi, acted as regent when her son, only about ten years old, ascended to the throne of Ugarit in 1210. The decline and fall of the city paralleled the decline and fall of the Hittite kingdom. Ammurapi, the last king of Ugarit, and Suppiluliuma II, the last Hittite king, both reigned from 1210 to 1185 approximately.

In many ways, Ugaritic culture heralded Phoenician culture. In the same way as Ugarit, the cities of Arwad, Byblos, Sidon, and Tyre were closely related maritime centers that participated in the same activities and were comprised of mixed populations. The local Ugaritic language was quite close to first-millennium Phoenician and used a thirty-sign cuneiform alphabet, which is generically linked to the traditional Phoenician alphabet. Several items of local Ugarit craftsmanship point the way to Phoenician productions, such as metallic cups with an engraved decoration, and the Phoenician ivories. Most of the gods worshiped at Ugarit, with a few modifications owing to evolution over time, were extremely popular with the Phoenicians. In sum, there was a fundamental continuity between the Ugaritic and Phoenician cultures despite the major historical upheavals that separated them.

4

The Small Vassal States of the Near East (1500–1200)

The small states in the great power arena

The lesser states of the Near East were caught in a vice-like grip by the great powers that confronted one other in their territories, namely, Egypt, Mitanni, and the emerging Hittite and Assyro-Babylonian powers. In practice, they found themselves in a geographical area at the crossroads between Mesopotamia, Egypt, and Asia Minor on the one hand and the eastern Mediterranean littoral on the other, hence giving them strategic value in terms of international trade as well as in the political rivalries between the great powers. The period between 1500 and 1200 is well documented by the archives of the Hittite capital Boghazkoy, by the Assyro-Babylonian Chronicles, by the Ugaritic texts, and especially by the Amarna Letters. In 1887, 382 tablets written in Akkadian, the diplomatic language of the time, were discovered next to the royal palace of Amarna on the left bank of the Nile. They contained the pharaohs' international correspondence with the other major powers and especially with the kings of the small states of the Near East, whose language reflected West-Semitic influence. All these letters were written between the thirtieth year of the reign of the pharaoh Amenhotep III and the third year of the reign of Tutankhamun, roughly between 1360 and 1330.

The small states of the Near East were vassals of Egypt since Thutmose III succeeded in overcoming the Mitanni after sixteen Asiatic campaigns. In year 42 of his reign, around 1437, he regained control of the Phoenician cities in the region of Tripoli, which had switched allegiance back to Mitanni again. The Egyptian provinces in the Near East each had an administrative center and an Egyptian governor: that of Amurru in Simyra (Tell Kazel), that of Canaan possibly in Gaza, and that of Upi in Kumidi (Kamid el-Loz), a Lebanese site that has delivered archival materials and Egyptian objects. The reign of Amenhotep III

66

represents the zenith of the Eighteenth Dynasty. This pharaoh was one of the greatest builders that Egypt had known. He closely involved his queen Tiye in his policy decisions, aided by her strong personality and her longevity. During his reign, Egypt was peaceful and enjoyed a degree of influence in Asia and in the Mediterranean basin. The list of peoples in the temple of Soleb indicates their respective position according to Egyptian ideology of the time, hence signifying their relative importance. Asiatics were divided into two groups: at the top level were Ugarit, Kadesh, Cyprus, Hatti, and Naharina; at the second level were Tyre, Sidon, Byblos, Carchemish, and Assur. The reign of the son of Amenhotep III and Tiye, Amenhotep IV, whose principle wife was the famous Nefertiti, underwent significant upheaval, which was to lead to the Amarna revolution. In year 4 of his reign, around 1349, this pharaoh proclaimed, in the manner of a prophet, that the solar god Aten was his only god. He took the name Akhenaten and had a huge city built at Amarna. The dogma of this new cult resembled a monotheism. The return to Amun orthodoxy took place in the reigns of his successors, notably of the young Tutankhamun, when all traces of the heretic pharaoh Akhenaten were erased. The last two pharaohs of the Eighteenth Dynasty restored the old order: Ay, the former vizier, and Horemheb, the former commander in chief of the army.

After the reign of Amenhotep III, Egypt was no longer a respected power, either internally or externally. The situation deteriorated in Mitanni, but Egypt, its ally, was incapable of providing any assistance. The rising power was that of the Hittites, who gained decisive ascendancy at the juncture of the reigns of Amenhotep III and Akhenaten. The Hittite king Suppiluliuma extended his southern border up to Lebanon.

The international political system of the Near East was then founded on the undisputed existence of two ranks of royalty: the great kings and the small kings, the former wielding power over the latter. Each small king was necessarily the servant of one of the three great kings of Egypt, Mitanni, or Hatti. According to the local ideology, the vassal owed loyalty and military obligation to his lord, in exchange for which he was authorized to reign and he was protected. His basic obligations were to pay tribute, to align his foreign policy, and to submit to his lord's judgment should there be any dispute with the other small kings. This rigorous definition of the reciprocal nature of the protection and loyalty obligation between lord and vassal, or the patron state and the client state, was clearly understood by the Hittite community. Conversely, it went against Egyptian ideology: for the pharaoh, the small king was a peripheral Egyptian official, responsible for protecting the pharaoh's land and for preparing the passage of troops and officials who had come from Egypt. In exchange, the pharaoh merely granted him physical and political survival. Lesser kings, even if they had been tied to Egypt for a long time, like those of Byblos, could not count on the pharaoh's protection in the event of a conflict with neighboring kings because they were all vassals of Egypt. Inside their small states, they retained their authority even though they were restricted by their entourage (members of their family, high-ranking officials, and military leaders) and were fearful of succession crises and conspiracies, as the Phoenician kings were later. In difficult situations, the people could impede royal authority through passive resistance or an uprising. Lastly, the small kings had to take into consideration the groups of nomads who controlled the wooded, mountainous, or steppe areas, and were able to obstruct communications and trade.

Nevertheless, this lord-vassal or patron-client alliance structure was fragile. Some small kings were tempted to change alliance, depending on how the region evolved geopolitically and on their own interests. Sometimes they tried to encourage neighboring kings to change alliances. They could also play a double game with two major powers. Normally, they were not allowed to envisage territorial conquests. Yet, some of them were very ambitious and paid little heed to loyalty. For example, the land of Amurru, situated between the island of Arwad and Tunip in inner Syria, had been an Egyptian province since the Nineteenth Dynasty. But in around 1350, Abdi-Ashirta of Amurru rose up against Egyptian authority. He founded the kingdom of Amurru, establishing a dynasty that was to survive for 150 years. On his death, the pharaoh succeeded in taking back several towns from him. But his sons, especially Aziru, shortly afterwards regained the towns that had been lost and rebuilt the kingdom of Amurru. Aziru played a double game by allying with the pharaoh in order finally to make a pact with the Hittite king, an enemy of Egypt.

How was Egypt able to accept the expansion of the kingdom of Amurru, thereby undermining its own Asiatic policy? To stop that expansion, it would have been forced to commit itself militarily with substantial resources, which it could not do as it was going through a period of weakness and inertia at that time. The pharaoh preferred to turn a blind eye; he let the power of the kings of Amurru grow since they continued to pledge allegiance by paying tribute and claimed to make conquests on its behalf. Faces were saved, even if the solution masked a different reality.

The misfortunes of Rib-Hadda, king of Byblos

Rib-Hadda, king of Byblos, is well known through sixty or so letters, which represent the longest Amarna correspondence. These letters, addressed to the pharaoh or Egyptian dignitaries, spanned a period of about twelve years around 1350. The reign of Rib-Hadda must have been quite long because he presented himself as an old man at the end of his correspondence. Much more verbose than the other small kings of the Near East, he tried to defend himself to the pharaoh who had criticized his verbosity: "You are the one who writes to me more than all the other mayors." The small vassal kings were referred to in this pharaonic correspondence by the terms "mayors" or simply "men."

When Rib-Hadda ascended to the throne, Byblos was still a powerful city, whose territory included the mountain villages and stretched northwards as far as the region of Tripoli. Batruna (Batroun), Shigata (Chekka), and Ampi (Enfeh) were part of its territory, together with the unidentified towns of Burusilim and Ibirta. Some of the other towns in the region quoted in his correspondence, before being included in the kingdom of Amurru, were perhaps also attached to Byblos: Wahliya (Tripoli?), Ammiya (Amiun), Kuasbat (Kusba), Ardata (Ard), and Magdalu (Medjdelia?). The king of Byblos was to lose all of his towns one after the other during his reign. He wrote that his ancestors had always been on good terms with Egypt and placed under the protection of the pharaohs, and he regretted this lost paradise.

Rib-Hadda appeared to be highly literate; he knew how to express himself extremely well and intentionally used literary turns of phrase. His correspondence had a marked autobiographical character: he was giving an account of himself through the eventful history of his time. His account is very egocentric: broadly speaking, the world comprised two elements: himself and those who were his enemies. He was loyal to the pharaoh, upright, and fair, and considered himself superior to the others because, unlike them, he refused to betray him. In his letters he expressed a real psychosis: he was rejected and persecuted by all his enemies and he felt like a bird in a cage; to top it off, he was abandoned by the pharaoh despite his repeated calls and was plunged into solitude and despair. Hoping, for a long time in vain, for an Egyptian intervention, he ended up sinking into the deepest pessimism. At the same time, yet paradoxically, throughout the whole of his correspondence, he gave the impression of being an adept diplomat and a clever manipulator. He tried all the tricks of the trade to get his correspondent to react. The pharaoh was obliged to protect him because Egypt had always protected his ancestors. They were bound by the same cult of Baalat, the divinity to whom the pharaoh owed his throne. The pharaoh had to help him because he was the sole perfect servant. He pretended not to hesitate telling him the truth, even if it was unpleasant, contrary to all the others who shamelessly deceived him. In reality, he himself was capable of skewing the facts to provoke a reaction. He tried to make the pharaoh feel guilty by accusing him of having granted his aid to vassals who had betrayed him. He also tried to frighten him by making him think that Egypt was going to lose everything if Byblos was not given assistance. He flattered his interests and pointed out to him the prospects for profits: "There is a lot of money and gold in Byblos, and the goods belonging to its temples are considerable." He provoked him virulently, in essence saying to him: are you lazy, weak, incapable, powerless, cowardly, and do you allow yourself to be dishonored without reacting? He even issued him an ultimatum: if the pharaoh decides not to help him, he will ally with Egypt's enemies, the easy solution that everyone suggested to him and that would solve his problems. In the end, he tried to make him feel sorry for him, saying that he was old, overwhelmed by illness, and at death's door. Despite the eloquence, the power of persuasion, and all the cunning employed by the king of Byblos, Amenhotep III and Akhenaten did not come to his aid.

Despite Rib-Hadda's exaggerations, due to both his psychosis and his desire to manipulate the pharaoh, the historical basis of his correspondence is authentic, as is shown by the overlaps with the other letters and sources. The first part of his correspondence dates to the reign of Abdi-Ashirta, king of Amurru. In that period, the mountain tribes from Jebel el Ansariye to the north of the Lebanese chain east of Tripoli were attracted by the opulent coastal towns. Led by Abdi-Ashirta, they set out to conquer them, with the support of the Apiru, armed bands hostile to Egypt, who were to help him build the kingdom of Amurru. In this way he directly threatened the territory bordering that of Byblos. He started by seizing Irqata and Ardata. He took advantage of the situations of social unrest and discontent to incite the populations of the towns to assassinate their leaders, with the active involvement of the Apiru. The king of Byblos was conscious of the danger that the conquests of Abdi-Ashirta represented, both for himself and for Egypt. He therefore urged the pharaoh to intervene militarily to stop his advance and restore order in the Egyptian province of Amurru.

In the aftermath, Abdi-Ashirta was coveting the fortified city of Simyra (Sumur), headquarters of the Egyptian commissioner of the province. The correspondence of Rib-Hadda and that of Abdi-Ashirta give two different versions of the fall of Simyra. The latter maintained that Simyra had been attacked by the troops from Shehlali, an unidentified town, and part of its population massacred; he claimed to have saved Simyra and posed as protector of Amurru, in the service of the Egyptian commissioner. According to the king of Byblos, Abdi-Ashirta took advantage of the commissioner's absence to capture the city and set up his quarters there. Whatever the reality, he became a de facto vassal of Egypt as a result.

He then attacked other towns in the region of Tripoli, some of which belonged to the king of Byblos. Following his usual tactics, he incited the populations of the towns he coveted to rise up by sending them this clear message: "Kill your lord, join the Apiru, and you will be safe!" Following which, he forced the towns that removed their leaders to form an alliance with one another, so as to free themselves from Egyptian tutelage as well. The king of Byblos accused Abdi-Ashirta of cooperating with the Mitanni and accused the Mitanni of plotting against Egypt. That was certainly false because the alliance between the Mitanni and Egypt must have been maintained against the Hittite threat. At the same time, Rib-Hadda renewed his submission to the pharaoh, again pledging his loyalty and affirming that all his actions were aimed at protecting the Egyptian province. Whether the pharaoh was convinced or not, he did not intervene. In this same period false rumors were circulating about the king of Byblos's death or the capture of his city.

When all that remained to him was the city of Byblos, Rib-Hadda feared a peasant rebellion. Chased out of the countryside that Abdi-Ashirta's troops had ravaged, the peasants of Byblos took refuge under the shelter of the city's fortifications. Under siege, Rib-Hadda was no longer able to pay for supplies and the residents were forced to sell their sons, their daughters, and the timber from their houses in order to buy grain in Yarimuta, possibly in the region of Beth Shean. Famine threatened. In reality, the king of Byblos did not want to use his personal wealth or the temple's treasures to save the situation.

Rib-Hadda narrowly escaped an assassination attempt backed by Abdi-Ashirta. Fearing for his life, he appealed to his southern neighbors for assistance, the kings of Beirut, Sidon, and Tyre, who had received orders from the pharaoh to give him help. The order reached them too late because they had already rallied to Abdi-Ashirta. In utmost distress, the king of Byblos was on the point of paying him a heavy ransom to buy his freedom and that of his city. He was unexpectedly saved by the death of Abdi-Ashirta, then at the height of his power, in control of Amurru and part of Canaan. The circumstances surrounding his death were never elucidated, but it coincided with an Egyptian expedition being sent to retake possession of the town of Simyra: the Egyptians could have executed him at that point in time.

The second part of Rib-Hadda's correspondence dates from the following period, when the three or four sons of Abdi-Ashirta, led by Aziru, resumed his policy of conquest. It was virtually a return to the earlier situation, at the beginning of Abdi-Ashirta's reign. The king of Byblos had reclaimed his cities and the Egyptian province of Amurru had regained its authority. But it was a rerun of the scenario of the previous reign: Aziru and his brothers progressively captured all the towns in the region of Tripoli and those of the king of Byblos. The whole of Amurru was reconquered except for Irqata and Simyra. Rib-Hadda of Byblos had received orders to go to Simyra to await the pharaoh's arrival. This proved impossible, as all his attempts to get there and to dispatch men and ships to assist him were blocked.

The town of Ullasa (Orthosia), at the mouth of the Nahr al-Barid, was taken by Arwad and its Egyptian officials took refuge in Byblos, which was again plagued by famine. The supply of cereals forwarded from Yarimuta towards Byblos, while transiting via Beirut, was intercepted by the ships of its king Yapah-Hadda in the service of Aziru. Nor could Rib-Hadda continue to ensure his deliveries of timber to Egypt as his ships were blocked. Simyra was besieged by land by Aziru and his brothers, and by sea by the ships of Arwad. The pharaoh wrote to the king of Byblos: "Be vigilant. You must stand guard." But, in response, Rib-Hadda rage about his impotence and reproached the pharaoh for abandoning him.

Aziru and his troops seized Simyra, chased out or killed its Egyptian officials, and largely destroyed it. He wrote a letter to the pharaoh that is a masterpiece of hypocrisy. He explained that he was still loyal, but that he was obliged to take Simyra because its Egyptian officials prevented him from serving Egypt adequately. In addition, he promised to rebuild the city. Using the pretext that he feared a Hittite offensive against Amurru, he had the audacity to ask the pharaoh for military assistance. In the end, in order to consecrate his vassal status, he went to Egypt, after which the Hittites captured several towns in the Amqu region, the Lebanese Bekaa. The pharaoh, too gullible, decided to let Aziru leave, thinking, wrongly, that his new vassal would defend Egyptian interests against the Hittites.

On the contrary, once he returned, Aziru rushed to help the Hittites attack all the pro-Egyptian towns in the region, such as Qatna and Tunip. The last city loyal to Egypt was Byblos, which in turn was also threatened. Its peasants had all left and the city was besieged. Rib-Hadda was vigorously urged by his compatriots, his parents, and his wife to ally with Aziru to at last secure peace, but he still refused to betray the pharaoh. As a last resort, he asked him for ships in order to save them, himself, and his gods, especially Baalat, the divinity common to Byblos and Egypt. He spoke enthusiastically about the riches in the goddess's temple and about his own wealth but in vain: The pharaoh did not even bother to reply.

Rib-Hadda then went to visit the new king of Beirut, Ammunira, to seal an alliance with him. His journey was wrongly interpreted by his fellow citizens as a desertion of Byblos and, when he returned, he was denied access to the city. In the meantime, his younger brother had seized power and handed Byblos over to the troops of Aziru. The latter wrote to the pharaoh, saying that Rib-Hadda had tried to buy him and rally to him in order to regain his throne, but for once, the pharaoh refused to believe this lie. Rib-Hadda was forced to spend at least a year in exile in Beirut old and ill. He sent his son to Egypt to again attempt to persuade the pharaoh to retake Byblos, claiming that half of its inhabitants were pro-Egyptian and that the city could easily be taken. Not only did the pharaoh fail to intervene, but he wanted to send the king of Byblos to Jaffa in exile, which Rib-Hadda refused to agree to, most likely so that he could remain as close as possible to his city to the very end.

After the death of Rib-Hadda, two letters were addressed to the pharaoh by Ili-Rapih, his successor on the throne of Byblos, possibly his brother who had ousted and exiled him. In any event, he also complained about the crimes committed by Aziru, denouncing him to the pharaoh as a rebel, and asked him to intervene to protect Byblos. Aziru met Suppiluliuma, the king of the Hittites in around 1340 and probably negotiated the terms of his submission. Yet, he continued to put on a display of loyalty towards the pharaoh: he again promised that he would rebuild Simyra and announced that he would pay him a tribute of eight ships laden with timber and oil. The pharaoh ended up understanding his grave error and threatened them, both him and his family, with death. The threat came too late, because Aziru consolidated his alliance with the Hittites and allied with Niqmadu II of Ugarit, a city already annexed by the Hittites. Akhenaten finally decided to prepare a military expedition to Syria, but it was too late and his death put an end to the plan. All later Egyptian attempts to retake the lost Asiatic provinces were to fail. Ugarit and Amurru remained in the hands of the Hittites, as indicated by three successive treaties. Aziru's long reign ended around

1315. His descendants strengthened the links with Ugarit and the Hittites through several royal marriages.

The contrasting policy of the kings of Beirut Yapah-Hadda and Ammunira

Beirut does not appear to have been as powerful as Byblos in the fourteenth century and its links with Egypt were not as ancient or as close either. Nevertheless, both of these cities were also caught up in the storm and the upheavals caused by the confrontation of the major powers. The Amarna correspondence reveals two kings of Beirut, Yapah-Hadda and Ammunira, who conducted very contrasting policies.

King Yapah-Hadda was probably on the throne of Beirut at the time of Abdi-Ashirta, king of Amurru up to around 1345, and at the start of the reign of Aziru. The pharaoh ordered him to join forces with Rib-Hadda of Byblos to welcome the Egyptian auxiliary troops who were to help in the fight against Abdi-Ashirta. But the promised troops failed to arrive and Yapah-Hadda, the opportunist, opted to conclude an alliance with Abdi-Ashirta in order to preserve Beirut.

Aziru succeeded Abdi-Ashirta and threatened to take Simyra. Rib-Hadda of Byblos, always a loyal vassal of Egypt, tried to rescue the city, but Yapah-Hadda of Beirut refused to help him despite the pharaoh's order to do so. He chose to side with Aziru and to take part in his war of conquest. He led his ships into the naval base of Wahliya, which was in the hands of Aziru, and went to war against Rib-Hadda of Byblos. He tried to starve him by blocking his source of cereal supply in Yarimuta, and to ruin him by taking possession of two of his ships and their substantial cargo. The king of Byblos drew up the list of these acts and asked the pharaoh to rule on their dispute. It was a complicated business. Even though Rib-Hadda later scaled down his demands, it was most likely because he had to shoulder his own share of responsibility as well. In addition, in the quantity of goods stolen by Yapah-Hadda there was a servant girl with her dowry who was destined for the pharaoh's harem. In the letters of Rib-Hadda of Byblos, Yapah-Hadda of Beirut was presented as a traitor and a conspirator who had his knife into him, whereas, in his own letters, Yapah-Hadda used a sober and direct style, giving the impression of being a realistic and cautious man. Admittedly, he did not approve the conquests of Abdi-Ashirta of Amurru, but that he was forced to side with him was entirely the fault of the pharaoh, who did nothing to protect him.

King Ammunira, who succeeded him on the throne of Beirut, was completely different from both a human and a political perspective. In sharp contrast with the style adopted by his predecessor, in his letters he used a highly emphatic courtier style of language. He presented himself to the pharaoh as the "dust of his feet" and as a "footstool." He said he was a loyal servant "who listened very very attentively" to his orders and who was ready to satisfy even the smallest of his demands. He executed the preparations as instructed for the arrival of the Egyptian archers and he guarded Beirut, which was not his city but the "city of the pharaoh." He wasted no time in settling the problem left by his predecessor and sent the servant detained in Beirut to Egypt without delay.

He implemented a radical change in policy, breaking Yapah-Hadda's alliance with Aziru and putting all his trust in Egypt. He concluded an alliance with his northern neighbor, Rib-Hadda of Byblos, who had paid him a visit and who remained one of the last to remain loyal to Egypt. He welcomed him generously in his fortified city when he was exiled from Byblos, at the same time as one of his sons. He offered him asylum for at least a year, unbothered by the fact that, old and very ill, he was abandoned by all. He accepted the consequences of accommodating this burdensome guest, whose presence must have increased Aziru's hostility towards him as well putting a strain on his relations with Egypt. Yet, he took care to explain to the pharaoh that the brother of Rib-Hadda had shamefully chased him out of Byblos and had handed his sons over to the rebels of Amurru. He pointed out that he would keep him with him until Egypt provided assistance. But four months later the pharaoh had still not received the son of Rib-Hadda, sent by his father, and had dispatched no Egyptian messenger to Ammunira. The king of Beirut, the last pro-Egyptian bastion in the north of Canaan, must have felt extremely isolated. In his last letter, Rib-Hadda imagined the worst-case scenario: "If Aziru and his brothers capture Beirut, then my lord the king shall no longer have a country."

A coup d'état in Tyre

By around 1350 Tyre had become a city with a large and prosperous territory. At that time, it was comparable with the city of Ugarit, considered by its contemporaries to be the most opulent of the coastal cities in the Near East. From the Amarna Letters, the king of Tyre, Baal-Shiptu I, appears to have been a loyal vassal of Egypt. He even prepared a caravan to go and visit the pharaoh and to ask him to provide a garrison to guard Tyre during his absence.

The prosperity of his city sparked the envy of his close neighbor, the king of Sidon, a certain Yabni-..., whose full name has not been preserved, who coveted his riches as well as his territory and started to fight him. Tyre was well established on its island base and possessed part of the facing coast, particularly the town of Ushu and its abundant spring water from Ras el-Ain. Sidon was hemmed in on its territory, wedged between that of Beirut to the north and Tyre to the south, and dreamed of expansion.

King Rib-Hadda of Byblos, meanwhile, decided to strengthen his ties with the king of Tyre. Both were loyal vassals of Egypt and Tyre possibly provided Byblos with food supplies, as it had substantially more agricultural land. So the king of Tyre married the sister of Rib-Hadda to cement their alliance. Their union lasted several years, during which they had several sons and daughters. But the city of Tyre housed an opposition group, probably in connivance with Abdi-Ashirta, king of Amurru. The brother of Rib-Hadda of Byblos, while staying in Tyre, wrote to the pharaoh on several occasions to alert him to the threat posed by these anti-Egyptian opponents, but in vain. A coup d'état took place: the Tyrian opponents massacred their king, his wife, their sons, their daughters, and even the brother of the king of Byblos. Following this, they pretended to be loyal to the pharaoh and hypocritically asked him to intervene, especially as the Tyrian royal family no longer had an heir. In the wake of this coup d'état, Rib-Hadda of Byblos informed the pharaoh that Abdi-Ashirta had taken control of the sea around the island of Tyre and that he was progressively grabbing all the Egyptian possessions, with the support of the Egyptian commissioner of Simyra, the traitor Pahamnata. He urged the pharaoh to open an enquiry into the coup d'état in Tyre and to make a wise decision regarding the Tyrian royal succession.

The king of Byblos lost a lot in this sad affair: his sister and all her family, and his brother who should have been his legitimate heir. For him, it was important that the pharaoh should punish the guilty parties and guarantee the continuation of a pro-Egyptian dynasty in Tyre. The successor chosen by the pharaoh was, in all likelihood, Abimilku. As his letters clearly point to an Egyptian education, he must have been a member of Tyre's legitimate dynasty who had been brought up in Egypt. Indeed, it was customary for the pharaoh to bring young foreign princes to his court where he would ensure their education while gaining their loyalty, so that he could place them on the throne of their hometown should the need arise.

The confrontation between the kings Abimilku of Tyre and Zimredda of Sidon

The rivalry between Tyre and Sidon persisted, particularly active on the Sidon side. Zimredda succeeded King Yabni-... on the throne of Sidon and in turn coveted the territory and riches of Tyre. He concluded an alliance with Abdi-Ashirta, king of Amurru, at the same time as he concluded on with Yapah-Hadda, king of Beirut. When the pharaoh ordered him to help the king of Byblos to rescue Simyra, he did not obey. When Aziru replaced Abdi-Ashirta on the throne of Amurru, Zimredda of Sidon officially became his spy, writing to him every day with all the information he had been able to glean about Egypt. The kings of Byblos and Tyre accused him of being a traitor. The peasants of Byblos, fleeing because of famine, took refuge in Sidon where they found food and shelter from Aziru, as the city was in his camp. Zimredda of Sidon played a double game however: he wrote to the pharaoh saying that he had remained loyal, but that all his towns had joined the Apiru and he was in need of help. The pharaoh replied, asking him in turn to be his spy to report everything he found out about Amurru. That is how Zimredda became a double agent. Abimilku of Tyre was not fooled by this double game and denounced him to the pharaoh: "Aziru has captured Simyra thanks to the instructions of Zimredda, who reports to him what the pharaoh says." He himself was in turn ordered by the pharaoh to report what he had learned. He wrote to him, for example, to tell him that a fire had destroyed half the palace in Ugarit, that the king of Danuna had died, and that his brother had replaced him, or again that there were no Hittite troops in the vicinity.

Zimredda of Sidon continued his predecessor's war against Abimilku of Tyre who, as a loyal vassal of the pharaoh, asked him for assistance. Zimredda's harassment had become insupportable: the king of Tyre accused him of capturing a palace servant every day and of carrying out predatory raids within his territory. His situation became critical when Zimredda captured the town of Ushu, located opposite the island of Tyre. He explained to the pharaoh that his island city could not do without its mainland territory, and developed convincing arguments to support this. First, it had no source of freshwater. Then, as it was rocky and entirely built over, there were no trees, no grass, and no soil. As a result, there was no wood for heating, no straw or clay to make pottery. Sand was also needed for the production of glass: the pharaoh had actually ordered glass from Abimilku, who dispatched the hundred last remaining units to him. Lastly, the island of Tyre did not have sufficient space to bury its dead and the pharaoh was only too aware that funeral rites had to be respected to the letter, as was the practice in Egypt.

Abimilku begged the pharaoh to come to his assistance by allowing him to recover, above all, the town of Ushu with its source of spring water at Ras el-Ain. Every day he tried to go in search of drinking water, but he was prevented from doing so by Zimredda. He also asked the pharaoh to help him regain his mainland possessions, which provided access to his forests. Meanwhile, he was obliged to organize the distribution of wood for the island's most needy inhabitants. As the pharaoh was slow to react, Abimilku decided to go to Egypt himself in order to convince him directly. He had a caravan prepared and he set off. But Zimredda was informed about this journey and forced the caravan to backtrack. He met up with Aziru and the people of Arwad; they exchanged oaths and started preparing a large-scale offensive to capture Tyre, assembling their ships, their chariots, and their infantry.

Was Zimredda of Sidon intending to organize a genuine blockade of the island of Tyre? He possessed a fleet just like Abimilku, and in addition had the use of that of Arwad. He probably had the capability to block Tyre's harbor, which would explain why Abimilku wanted to depart with his caravan for Egypt. However, this apparently did not come about, as Abimilku succeeded in dispatching the glass order to the pharaoh and in sending him gifts and messengers on several occasions, obviously using ships as the means of transport. If ever there was a blockade, was not total, or perhaps was not in place throughout Sidon's year-long war against Tyre. In reality, Zimredda of Sidon knew that the island was very hard to take and it was the Tyrian mainland territory that he was targeting by occupying Ushu and its water source. This occupation was profitable to him because, at the same time, it jeopardized the island's inhabitants and contributed in weakening his rival, King Abimilku.

In his last letter, the king of Tyre cleverly wrote that he was the servant of the pharaoh and of Mayati, and that Tyre was Mayati's city. This was a reference to Meritaten, the eldest influential daughter of Akhenaten. His reign was a troubled period because Egypt was given over to persecutions against the Amun worshippers. Meritaten replaced Nefertiti at the pharaoh's side, and then married his enigmatic successor Smenkhare.

We do not know how the conflict between Tyre and Sidon ended. In any event, in the thirteenth century, Tyre had reclaimed the town of Ushu, as we can read in a document dating to the reign of Ramesses II, probably a good geography test for school children: "What does Ushu look like? There is said to be another town in the sea, called Tyre-the-Port. Water is brought there by boat and it is richer in fish than in sand."

The alliance of Arwad with Aziru of Amurru

The island of Arwad, with its double harbor, was one of the major stop-over points on the route between Ugarit and Egypt. Its distance from the coast, 2.5 kilometers, made it even more impregnable than the island of Tyre, a mere half kilometer off the coast. Rocky and densely populated, the island encountered the same problems as Tyre for its livelihood: no wood, no straw, no clay, no room to bury its dead, it was totally dependent on the mainland area. On the other hand, according to Pliny the Elder, it did have a subsea source of freshwater, which the inhabitants could tap into using a pipe. However, it is unclear whether this source was already known about and exploited in the second millennium. In any event, the documentation of the period makes no mention of it, nor of Arwad having possessions on the Syrian coast. Yet, it had to draw its livelihood from somewhere.

Arwad was a northern city, with ties with Alalakh and Ugarit rather than with the southern Canaanite cities. Even though it is not mentioned in the annals of Thutmose III and it had not been captured by the pharaoh, it was, like Ugarit, part of the coastal area of Canaan and Syria where Egyptian control was established. At the time of Amarna, it must have been included in the Egyptian province of Amurru. The Egyptian conquest changed the geopolitical balance of the region. The towns of Ullasa and Simyra had become Egyptian fortresses, used as points of support for exploiting and controlling the lines of communication. Simyra especially gained in importance from this as a transit point between seaborne and overland traffic, and as the crossroad for the coastal route and the Homs Gap towards the Orontes and Euphrates Valleys. It became the capital of the Egyptian province of Amurru and overshadowed Arwad, which, while secure but isolated on its island, remained on the sidelines of the Egyptian system and probably declined somewhat. This could explain the clear-cut stance taken by Arwad against both Simyra and Egypt. No letter from Arwad figures in the Amarna correspondence, which is significant: it does not position itself as a vassal of the pharaoh and did not appeal to him when difficulties arose. Yet, contacts with Egypt were not totally nonexistent since the city sent ships there in around 1345.

Details about Arwad in the Amarna correspondence appeared in four letters from Rib-Hadda of Byblos and Abimilku of Tyre, both of whom tended to disparage its actions. Arwad was still in the camp of the kings of Amurru. It started to intervene militarily at the end of Abdi-Ashirta's reign because, in Rib-Hadda's letter announcing the death of the king of Amurru, he recalled that Byblos had been attacked by Arwad's ships. The operation was therefore prepared under Abdi-Ashirta. In fact, in his progressive conquest of the coastal towns of Amurru and Canaan, he used land forces. Neither the tribes from the mountains nor the Apiru who supported him were familiar with the sea nor did they possess any ships. They were accustomed to forays conducted by armed bands, sometimes using chariots. But in capturing the coastal towns, Abdi-Ashirta gradually came to understand the benefit he could derive from maritime forces and started to use Arwad's ships. They attacked Byblos and, thanks to their involvement, Abdi-Ashirta even became the master of the seas facing Tyre.

It was particularly in the reign of Aziru that naval operations increased and that the kingdom of Amurru also became a maritime power, essentially thanks to Arwad's fleet. It was this fleet that carried out a blockade of the harbor of Simyra while the troops of Aziru laid a land-based siege. It captured Ullasa and controlled the harbors of Shigata and Ampi to block the shipments of cereals destined for Simyra. It impeded Byblos's maritime communications, preventing it from coming to Simyra's assistance, in particular intercepting three of its ships. Lastly, it took part in the attack conducted by Zimredda of Sidon against the town of Ushu, and partially blocked the island of Tyre or at least prevented the Tyrians from collecting provisions on the mainland. They were always targeted and effective actions that must have been planned in advance.

Arwad's political system in this period is an enigma. Arwad perhaps had kings in the third millennium and again in the first millennium, but there is no mention of kings in the Amarna correspondence nor in the Ugaritic texts of the second millennium. Nor is there evidence of a Council of Elders as in the neighboring city of Irqata, but only of the people of Arwad. Hence, the civic body replaced the royal institution, but none of the sources gives any further insight into this phenomenon.

The people of Arwad were tied to Aziru of Amurru by oath. This alliance with the kings of Amurru, implemented by Abdi-Ashirta, was not a vassalage relationship but an agreement between two partner states, probably based on issues of mutual interest. The kings of Amurru needed a powerful and experienced fleet to support their conquests. Arwad needed to have access to the mainland's resources to guarantee its livelihood. When they had control over the coastal cities, the kings of Amurru must have allowed the people of Arwad to come and exploit the Syrian coast opposite their island. They also left them free to develop their trading activities. The presence of some people from Arwad in Ugarit, but not people from Simyra, meant that Arwad had succeeded in eliminating competition from its pro-Egyptian rival by allying with the kings of Amurru.

Nevertheless, in this particularly troubled period where alliances were constantly being made and broken, armed bands such as the Apiru and the Suteans often laid down the law. Raids and looting were frequent. Piracy also existed, as evidenced by the cargo thefts from two ships from Byblos by Yapah-Hadda of Beirut. Ships from Arwad that arrested enemy ships probably also engaged in acts of piracy now and again. There is no doubt that the alliance with the kings of Amurru contributed considerably to Arwad's prosperity at the expense of that of Simyra.

The division of the small states between the major powers

At the end of the Bronze Age, in the twelfth and the thirteenth centuries alike, the major powers still had control over the small states in the Near East. That did not prevent them from having independent relations, be they fraternal or hostile, between them. A lot of documents attest to the alliances concluded between the small states, expressed in this way for example: "The house of the country of Beirut and the house of the country of Ugarit have, for a long time, formed one single house: now their alliance truly is sealed."

The Hittite Empire took advantage of the Egyptian torpor to extend its southern borders from Ugarit to Byblos, and from Kadesh to the Bekaa. The Canaanite towns were split into two areas. However, Egypt could not totally lose its source of timber supplies from the Lebanese mountains, which were vital for it, and so gradually started to react. Horemheb, commander-in-chief of Tutankhamun's army, provisionally retook control of the Bekaa plain. The Hittite king Suppiluliuma in turn recovered the plain, taking back prisoners of war from the area, without suspecting that they were infected with plague. An epidemic broke out and ravaged the Hittite Empire, where the scourge was interpreted as divine punishment. On the death of the pharaoh Tutankhamun, his widow endeavored to unite the two enemy powers by proposing to the Hittite king to marry one of his sons; he accepted and sent prince Zannanza who, unfortunately, was killed before reaching his destination in Egypt. To eradicate the plague epidemic, his son and successor Mursili II repaired the wrong done to the gods by handing back the Bekaa to the

Egyptians. When he became pharaoh in around 1319, Horemheb above all made every effort to restore order in the Near East. An inscription on a bowl made out of granite commemorated his victorious campaign against Carchemish, which he conducted from Byblos.

He handed power over to another military man, Ramesses I, founder of the Nineteenth Dynasty. Ramesses's successor Seti I had to contend with revolts in Canaan, and carried out four expeditions to pacify Canaan and Amurru as far as south of Kadesh. His exploits are related on a bas-relief in the temple of Amun in Karnak, where he is represented cutting down trees in Lebanon. He restored Egypt's status in the Near East and concluded a temporary peace agreement with the Hittite king Muwatalli II, which however enabled his adversaries to rebuild their forces.

Ramesses II, the best known of the pharaohs, succeeded his father in 1279 for a long reign. He covered the Nile Valley with monuments and was renowned as a warrior king. His first campaign took him to Byblos, where he received the submission of Amurru. In the following year, year 5 of his reign in 1274, a major confrontation took place with the Hittite king Muwatalli II, who amassed a huge coalition of his Anatolian and Syrian vassals against Egypt. The famous Battle of Kadesh (modern Tell Nebi Mend 25 kilometers from Homs) is represented to the glory of the pharaoh in the bas-reliefs of the temples of Karnak, Luxor, and Abu Simbel. However, there was no real victor and the ensuing truce was hardly a success for Egypt, as Ramesses II lost Amurru again and had to continue pacifying Canaan with several successive campaigns. He left traces of his various incursions on three stele at the mouth of the Nahr al-Kalb, between Byblos and Beirut, in years 4, 8, and 10 of his reign. He recaptured Kadesh and Amurru, taking advantage of the growing difficulties of the Hittites, threatened internally by a dynastic crisis on the death of Muwatalli II, and externally by the increasing power of the Assyrians. Shalmaneser I established himself on the throne of Assur and captured the state of Hanibalgat, in Upper Mesopotamia, from the Hittites.

The two adversaries, Ramesses II and Hattusili III (brother of Muwatalli II), eventually decided, in 1258, year 21 of the pharaoh's reign, to put an end to sixteen years of conflict with the first inter-state treaty in history, whose versions in Egyptian and Akkadian have survived. This treaty established sustainable peace between the two kings who reinforced their agreement through royal marriages. The dividing line for the Near East went from north of Byblos down to Damascus. Amurru and Kadesh remained in the area under Hittite influence.

A vast quantity of sculptured fragments and vases discovered in Byblos bore the name of Ramesses II, and reflected the resumption of ongoing relations between Byblos and Egypt. Vases bearing the name of Ramesses II were also unearthed in Beirut and Tell Abu Hawam, to the south of Tyre. One stele in his name, dating to around 1275, was found in Tyre; it represents a symbolic offering scene of Egypt's prisoners; the pharaoh brandishes his white club while grabbing hold of a bunch of stricken enemies by their hair.

The border drawn between Egypt and the Hittite Empire did not prevent contact on both sides. Relations between the small states, regardless of the status of rivalry of the empires to which they belonged, were cordial and confident. Travelers appeared to move from one area of control to another without displaying the slightest fear. The roads formed a dense network and people moved around a lot. A vast trading market brought together, from south to north, Egypt and Anatolia and, from west to east, the Mediterranean and the Euphrates. Sidon, Tyre, Byblos, and Beirut therefore played a very active role in Near East trade. These cities established close ties, to a greater or lesser extent, with Ugarit. Sidon is mentioned in fifteen Ugarit texts, Tyre in thirteen, Byblos with its town of Batroun in seven, Beirut in five, and Arwad in just one. These references reflect the links of each of these cities with Ugarit and their respective importance. The kings of Sidon and Beirut are the only ones specifically named, in order of protocol, before the king of Ugarit, which could indicate their preeminence.

King Addu-Yashma of Sidon accused an inhabitant of Ugarit of having committed the ultimate sin against the Sidonian storm god. He narrowly avoided being stoned by his fellow citizens and asked the king of Ugarit for speedy redress to solve the internal crisis his city was going through. Other kings of Sidon are known through the Ugarit letters and through two seals inscribed with the names Addumu, his son Anniya who perhaps reigned; Yapa-Addu; and Addu-..., whose name has only partially been preserved. In the diplomatic correspondence between Ramesses II and the Hittite king Hattusili III, Sidon is presented as being an important stronghold where the pharaoh settled for a time. Tablets discovered in the Middle Euphrates mention the commercial and diplomatic activities of the Sidonians, one of which represents the pharaoh alongside a local Assyrian official. (Assyrians specializing in the clothing trade had settled in Sidon.)

Tyre during this same period was a rich and active port city, which did however suffer from a plague epidemic. The king of Tyre, Baal-Shiptu II, complained to the king of Ugarit about his harbor entry duties imposed by customs officials on his tradesmen. Another king of Tyre informed the king of Ugarit that his ships, loaded with cereals from Egypt, were surprised by a storm and forced to take refuge in the harbors of Tyre and Akko. A messenger from the king of Tyre, Baal-Targumu, is recorded on a list of crossings at the Egyptian border under the pharaoh Merneptah.

Byblos became a powerful city after regaining its towns, for example, Batroun. A Ugaritic text stipulates the conditions governing an important deal concluded between the kings of Ugarit and Byblos. The king of Byblos undertook to rent ships to the king of Ugarit in return for a payment of 540 shekels of silver, with an add-on of 60 shekels to fit them out. Hence, in this period, Byblos possessed a more important fleet than that of the king of Ugarit as it supplied Ugarit with ships. Were they war ships? In this period no specific war fleet existed, and merchant ships could be used as instruments of war. The king of Beirut therefore maintained friendly relations with the king of Ugarit. He agreed with him that they would treat their respective messengers correctly and to meet their demands. Arwad only figures in one list of foreigners living in Ugarit, two of whom came from Beirut. This is surprising as it was the closest city and belonged to the same territory under Hittite domination as Ugarit.

At the end of the Bronze Age, these proto-Phoenician cities were characterized by a number of common features, but there were also many features that separated them. They had been divided into two groups since their split between the Egyptians and the Hittites, and were in contact with two radically opposing cultures. They had a Semitic language base, of which there were several variants in terms of dialect and script. Their scribes mainly used Sumero-Akkadian, at least in international correspondence. In a port city like Byblos, traditionally linked to Egypt, Egyptian had been known and used for a long time, which, around the eighteenth century, gave birth to an original script, pseudo-hieroglyphic, which has still not been deciphered. The distribution between Assyrian and Babylonian varied from one city to another. Sidon only used Assyrian. Beirut's language was only partly Assyrianized and Canaanite influence was significant. Elsewhere, it was Middle Assyrian or peripheral Babylonian that was in use. In Tyre, a tradesmen's vernacular or slang was attested, which guaranteed them discretion in their discussions and consistency in their organization: it was a language with a limited vocabulary and a simplified syntax. In reality, the languages, dialects, and scripts that have come down to us only reflect a part of the ancient complex mosaic. The numerous archives provided by Ugarit give an idea of this complexity in just one city: eight languages (Ugaritic, Akkadian, Sumerian, Hittite, Hurrian, Luwian, Egyptian, and Cypriot) and five writing systems (syllabic cuneiform, alphabetic cuneiform, Egyptian and Hittite hieroglyphs, and Cypro-Minoan).

The political institutions of the proto-Phoenician cities also differed considerably from one another, even though they shared common basic elements, and foreshadowed those of the Phoenician cities. Byblos, Beirut, Sidon, and Tyre were governed by kings who identified themselves as officials of the pharaoh. Each of their cities possessed its own territory, which was, at the same time, an Egyptian administrative district. Dynastic succession normally operated through the son or, possibly, through the brother, knowing that the pharaoh could sometimes impose the successor of his choice. To govern, the king of Byblos had to take into consideration the opinion of his fellow citizens. The king of Sidon referred to the great and the small Sidonians, perhaps the Elders and the people. Arwad functioned differently, without a king and based on a broad civic body.

Although the major powers kept the small states firmly under their control at the end of the Bronze Age, they never succeeded in completely eliminating the armed bands and liminal groups, the troublemakers. The Apiru were still perceived as outlaws. Sometimes they threatened the established order, sometimes they allied with a political power, while at other times they were employed as workmen, for example in Egyptian quarries under Ramesses II. The pharaoh had to drive back the Shasu, troublesome Bedouins from the east and, thanks to his fleet, thwarted the attempts of the Sherden, formidable pirates.

The pharaoh Merneptah, thirteenth son of Ramesses II, chosen during his father's lifetime, reigned until 1203. He still benefited from the effects of the Egypto-Hittite treaty of his father, and even supplied wheat to the Hittites during a famine. The border between the two empires was maintained on the Byblos-Damascus line and Egypt kept its garrisons in Syria-Palestine. Nevertheless, the events of Merneptah's reign show that Egypt's military power and external security had significantly diminished: in around 1210, local revolts forced him to lead an expedition against Ashkelon, Gezer, and Israel, the latter's first mention in the report of an Egyptian expedition. The Hebrew exodus from Egypt as described in the Bible more likely occurred in the reign of Ramesses II than under that of Merneptah, but it was the latter who would confront the first attack by a new threat.

Part Two

THE PERIOD OF
PHOENICIA'S INDEPENDENCE
(1200–883)

1

The Emergence of Phoenicia
(around 1200)

The invasion of the Sea Peoples

The transition from the Bronze Age to the Iron Age around 1200 corresponds to a period of great upheaval in the eastern Mediterranean. Despite the nomenclature, the shift from one era to the next is more historical than technological, as iron weapons and tools were already being made in the Bronze Age and bronze continued to be used during the Iron Age. However, the use of iron developed during the eleventh century and became widespread in the tenth. Moreover, the date of this shift is approximate, as the chronology varies somewhat depending on the regions under consideration. One of the first chronological landmarks was the destruction of the proto-Phoenician city of Ugarit around 1185. The change of period is essentially determined by the large-scale movements of populations, the main one being the invasion by the so-called Sea Peoples. These waves of marauders, began as groups of people comprised families fleeing their native regions, especially for sociopolitical reasons.

The invaders were referred to by the Egyptians as the "foreign peoples of the sea," among which several groups are identified. The texts of Merneptah and Ramesses II mentioned the Sherden, Lukka, Ekwesh, Tursha, and Shekelesh. In addition, the texts of Ramesses III name the Peleset (Philistines) and the Weshesh, and those of his successors the Tjeker (or the Sikalayu) and the Denyen. Several of these peoples also figured in the Amarna Letters, and in the Ugaritic, Hittite, and Mycenaean texts. They came from diverse regions, particularly from Anatolia and the Aegean: Lycia for the Lukka, Cilicia for the Denyen, possibly Iasos of Caria for the Weshesh, the Adriatic for the Tjeker, and Lydia for the Teresh, who later migrated to Italy and became known as the Etruscans. The Ekwesh could be the Achaeans and the Peleset who we know as

Philistines may well have come from Crete (Caphtor) according to a biblical tradition (Deuteronomy 2:23; Jeremiah 47:4).

In reality, the whole eastern Mediterranean basin had been in turmoil for more than a century. The invasions of the Sea Peoples were something of a backlash from the Doric invasions in Mycenaean Greece, which would have driven the ancient Aegean populations before them. These population movements sometimes lasted for several generations. After an initial wave of destructions around 1250, the Mycenaean world collapsed around 1200 after a second wave of destructions, due perhaps, among other causes, to invasions by Sea Peoples. These groups that beset Egypt and the Near East had a long seafaring tradition, based on their representation on Egyptian bas-reliefs. Their angular and symmetrical-hulled ships were Cretan-style sailing ships. They were easy to handle, ideal for the high seas, capable of carrying more than twenty crew members, and could be deployed rapidly. They were the forerunners of the ninth-century Phoenician ships known as "hippos." The invaders were armed with spears, round shields, and short swords (about 50 centimeters in length) of European style in origin; they did not use bows and arrows.

Some Sea Peoples already make their appearance in the fourteenth century Amarna Letters. The king of Alashiya (Cyprus) complained to the pharaoh about the maritime raids carried out against him by the Lukka. Abimilku, king of Tyre, informed the pharaoh of a dynastic change within the Denyen. As for the Sherden, they were referred to on several occasions by King Rib-Hadda of Byblos: they were mercenaries in the service of whomever engaged them. He fought a Sherden who tried to assassinate him by striking him nine times with a bronze sword. He drew particular attention to this sword as it did not exist in the weaponry of the soldiers of Byblos. This Sherden was a mercenary he knew and who had been bribed by Abdi-Ashirta of Amurru. Wearing horned helmets surmounted by a disc, the Sherden therefore appeared to be formidable pirates who sold their services as and when required. They had a long history of infiltration in the eastern Mediterranean. Since the reign of Amenhotep III, they had carried out raids on the coasts of the Nile Delta. Ramesses II succeeded in defeating them and taking them prisoner in year 2 of his reign, around 1278. He integrated them into his army and used them as assault troops in the Battle of Kadesh, in 1274. In the thirteenth century, Ugarit built a fleet of at least 150 ships to protect its commercial interests, and engaged Sherden who played the nebulous role of mercenaries and privateers.

In year 5 of Merneptah, around 1208, a coalition of Libyans and Sea Peoples attempted a raid against Egypt. After a month, the pharaoh managed to repel them, killing six thousand soldiers and taking nine thousand prisoners. A new wave broke out in Egypt twenty years later. Other invaders succeeded in upsetting and devastating the Hittite Empire and the southern vassal countries, from Carchemish to Cyprus. In their path, they ravaged Ugarit, Amurru, and Arwad, which figured in the list of cities destroyed during the reign of Ramesses III. In Simyra, the palatial buildings were violently destroyed early in the twelfth century and the site was momentarily abandoned. Then invaders attacked Egypt again, taking with them their families and their belongings in zebu-drawn carts. Their fleet and their army succeeded in entering the Nile Delta. Ramesses III managed to repel them in year 8 of his reign, around 1179. A further wave surged into Egypt in year 11, around 1176, whose flow he again succeeded in stemming.

These victories were exaggerated by pharaonic propaganda. Egyptian domination in Canaan was actually seriously compromised, as some groups of invaders came to rest along the Levantine coasts between Akko and Ashkelon. The Tjeker settled in Dor from the beginning of the twelfth century to the middle of the eleventh, when they were replaced by the Phoenicians. With the Sherden and possibly the Denyen, they took the cities in the plain of Akko, specifically Tell Keisan and perhaps Tell Abu Hawam. They also occupied the hinterland cities such as Beth Shean and Megiddo; a Sherden fortress has in fact been discovered at El-Ahwat. The Philistines settled on the southern coast of Canaan, before and after the defeats inflicted by Ramesses III. It was the group among sea people that best maintained its identity and its political independence, and ultimately gave its name to the region: Palestine. After a settling-in period, the Philistines founded what is referred to as the "pentapolis," a group of five cities, Ashdod, Ashkelon, Ekron, Gath (Tel Zafit), and Gaza in the plain of Philistia.

The heart of Phoenicia—Tyre, Sidon, Beirut, Byblos, and Tripoli—seems to have been spared from the Sea Peoples' invasions, although this impression could be a result of the deficiency of documentation. In Byblos, the Late Bronze Age city, perhaps carried away by sea-cliff landslides, has not been found, and the Early Iron Age levels have yet to be discovered. But the presence of a few ceramic shards resembling Philistine ceramics (Mycenaean IIIC), raises the question of a Sea Peoples presence. However, this ceramic style is also found at Tyre, Sarepta, Tell Sukas, and Ras Ibn Hani in very small quantities, and its origin cannot be unequivocally guaranteed. At Ras Ibn Hani, the modest facilities built after the ruin of the palaces are evidence of the temporary installation of a few groups of Sea Peoples. New impressive fortifications were constructed in Beirut, but their dating between the end of the Bronze Age and the tenth century is too imprecise to be able to establish a definite link with an attack by Sea Peoples. Justin related how Tyre was founded by the Sidonians when they were defeated by Ashkelon, the city of the Philistines, but this account is not solid enough to deduce a Philistine raid on Sidon. From what we know at present, the cities of central Phoenicia do not appear to have suffered a lot as a result of the invasion of the Sea Peoples, and should therefore have preserved the heritage of the Canaanite civilization.

The difficult transition from the Bronze Age to the Iron Age

The various population migrations that occurred around 1200, the most important being the invasion of the Sea Peoples, constitute the key external causes for the major upheavals of this period. However, this phenomenon is not enough by itself to explain the profound changes that occurred, not just terms of the human element, but also in the socio-political and cultural spheres. There were also internal causes, specific to the Late Bronze Age, that contributed to this period of acute and widespread crisis.

The end of the Hittite Empire was sudden and unexpected. Even though the whole of western Anatolia was united against it in the reign of Suppiluliuma II, nothing proves that it was destroyed by Sea Peoples. Instead, perhaps those mainly responsible were invaders who had come from Europe, such as the Mushki, Phrygians who had left Thrace and settled on the Anatolian plateau, or even the Kaska, tribal populations from the forested mountains of the Pontus whom the Hittites never really succeeded in bringing into submission. To these can be added the military defeats suffered, the secession of the territory of Tarhuntassa, pressure from the Assyrians, and internal dynastic problems. Since the reign of Hattusili III, in fact, the royal authority and the confidence of the vassals had been dwindling. The empire's center of gravity shifted towards northern Syria and Carchemish. A famine ravaged Anatolia at this time and prompted the peasant farmers to flee their homes, raiding and pillaging, which could have triggered even greater population movements.

The fall of Ugarit, the Hittite vassal city in the south, is attributable to external causes: the last preserved documents announce the imminent arrival of enemies by sea and lament the absence of troops and ships, which had been sent to defend the Hittite Empire. The whole site was then ravaged by a violent fire. This prosperous city would never rise from its ruins, unlike other destroyed cities. Beyond the material destruction, internal factors must also be borne in mind, such as the decline of the royal system, the demographic imbalance between social groups, and the difficulties facing the peasant farming community, as well as the destabilizing role played by liminal groups who were not integrated into society. All of these factors could have led to the disintegration of Ugaritic society, which was not able to rebuild or renew.

Outside Ugarit, little is known about Syria's situation in this period, but it was also having to endure upheavals. There was significant unrest among Aramaic tribes as a consequence of the collapse of the major powers that stabilized the region in the Late Bronze Age. These tribes repeated the Amorite movement initiated a millennium earlier. A massive exodus drove them towards Mesopotamia, as far as the shores of the Persian Gulf. Aramaic expansion also extended to western Syria, inland areas, where some Neo-Hittite enclaves, such as the kingdom of Hamath, survived. Lastly, Aramaic populations succeeded in settling almost anywhere heading southwards, roughly following the Orontes, the Bekaa, and the Jordan, at dates and in circumstances that are impossible to pin down.

The decadence of the New Kingdom of Egypt began in the reign of Ramesses III. This pharaoh had to confront internal difficulties of a political nature with a harem conspiracy, and of an economic nature in that he had to confront the first recorded strike in history—that of workmen at Deir el-Medina whose wages were paid up to three months late. The last years of the Ramesside Twentieth Dynasty, from Ramesses IV to Ramesses XI, were very confused. The disappearance of the crown princes, conflicts between royal relations, and usurpations became more and more frequent. Egyptian possessions in the Near East diminished, first becoming limited to the areas north of Canaan and south of Gaza, then they disappeared completely. At the end of the New Kingdom, Egyptian power was yet again to find itself divided between Upper and Lower Egypt: in the north, Smendes founded the Twenty-First Dynasty while, in the south, the high priests of Amun, greatly enriched by the Ramesside Dynasty, reverted to a theocracy.

The Israelites, or Hebrews, seminomads in the process of sedentarization, settled in the hinterland of a Canaan that was now free from Egyptian domination. They settled before the campaign of the pharaoh Merneptah, who boasted fallaciously having annihilated Israel in around 1208. The biblical accounts of these events, all written later, have differing traditions about the appearance on the scene of the Israelites: infiltration of isolated tribes or sudden and bloody arrival. Much has been written about their possible relationship with the Apiru or Habiru, given the resemblance with their name, but the debate is not closed yet. What is referred to as the Israelite confederation was in the beginning a cluster of groups and tribes that developed geographically and demographically on the fringes of the Canaanite society of the cities under the Egyptian protectorate.

Biblical traditions mention four main groups connected with the patriarchs Abraham and Isaac, source of the "house of Judah," and Jacob and Israel, source of the "house of Israel." The first groups must have penetrated the sparsely populated hills of central Cisjordan. The Israelites were not a homogeneous group and entered Canaan in different places and at different times. But the country of Canaan itself was heterogeneous; it was composed of a mosaic of small states whose division and weakness had been carefully maintained by the Egyptian occupants. After the end of Egyptian domination, their dispersal only increased. The destructions of several fortified Canaanite cities towards the end of the Late Bronze Age do not all date to the time and could have been caused in ways other than by an Israelite "conquest."

The consequences of all these upheavals, although they differed in nature and intensity from one region to another, give us a better understanding of the emergence of Phoenicia. The first outcome was the recomposition of the human landscape. The influx of people was sometimes substantial but, in general, the nature of the population had varied little since the Late Bronze Age. The changes were more sociopolitical than ethnic, and affected social structures and ways of thinking. Processes of urban concentration and sedentarization also occurred, giving birth to small isolated village sites.

The second outcome of the upheavals that took place around 1200 was the return to political, cultural, and economic independence. After the end of the domination of the major powers of the second millennium, no local political entity was powerful enough to impose its control over others. Yet, each small state benefited in its own way from this overall process.

The third outcome of the upheavals was regionalization. The large central sites of the Late Bronze Age were replaced by a territorial reorganization, through a new distribution of sites, which differed in their size and nature depending on the region. Some regions were weakened whereas others developed, and each one evolved at its own speed. The move from the Bronze Age to the Iron Age was not only a period of transition, it was also a period of transformation, with the emergence of new elements.

In the context of this reconfiguration, the Phoenician cities were among the small states of the Near East that preserved the greatest continuity with the proto-Phoenician cities of the Bronze Age. As noted above, they do not appear to have suffered as much from the invasions of the Sea Peoples as Ugarit did. Only Tell Sukas and Arwad suffered extensive damage. It is difficult to know whether the destruction of a building in Sidon by fire and some walls in Tyre (after which the site possibly was partially abandoned) were related to an invasion. In any event, the composition of the population of the Phoenician cities did not alter much. The main change was their liberation from Hittite domination for the northern cities, such as Arwad, and from Egyptian domination for the other cities. The pressure created by the arrival of Arameans and Hebrews in the hinterland, and by that of Philistines and other peoples who settled to the north and south of the coastal region must have pushed the proto-Phoenician populations towards the central coastal area. What singled out the Phoenician cities was their limited involvement in the various invasions that occurred, and their concentration in this coastal region. As a result, closer bonds were formed between them and they influenced one another's development. As the possibility of territorial extension and commercial expansion in the Near East had disappeared, they opened up new routes towards the western Mediterranean, thereby preparing the way for the major phenomenon of colonization, which initially took the form of sporadic commercial visits.

Phoenicia, between continuity and innovation

If Phoenicia came into its true identity around 1200, this was due as much to its continuity with the previous period as to its capacity for innovation. Phoenician history followed naturally from proto-Phoenician history, well known especially from Ugarit and Byblos. The connection with the sea had already been solidly established with the proto-Phoenicians, with the development of harbors and shipbuilding. But the Phoenicians continually improved their harbors and their ships using the trireme, the quinquereme, and the rudder, and their commercial expansion in the Mediterranean was unparalleled in light of the new phenomenon of colonization. They still employed the same urbanization techniques, but invented the orthogonal street plan incorporating a sewer system. They perfected building techniques that were likely to provide better resistance to the region's frequent earthquakes. The purple dye and weaving industries were still active. The inhabitants of Arwad were probably the inventors of the so-called "Roman" scales.

Working glass was not new, but it took on specific Phoenician characteristics. The Phoenicians continued to produce metal, ivory, ceramics, and sculpture artworks, but innovated in the sculpting of sarcophagi and large coroplastic works. There was continuity in religious life, but new divinities such as Milqart and Tanit emerged within Phoenician cults.

The alphabet, transmitted by the Greeks, was one of Phoenicia's most important innovations. Herodotus stated: "From those Phoenicians who had accompanied Cadmus, the Greeks learned a lot, and especially the alphabetic writing, which they had no knowledge of until then." It was a crucial invention that forms the basis of most writing forms in the Western world.

From the middle of the second millennium, several attempts were made in the Near East to create local writing systems different from the hieroglyphic and cuneiform writing of the major powers. These proto-Canaanite, then ancient Canaanite writings, are attested by a very small number of documents that are scattered and difficult to interpret. The signs created were based on the acrophonic principle, that is, their value was derived from the object they represented, for example *Bet*, "house," stood for the letter *B*. Ugarit's cuneiform alphabet developed on the model of ancient Canaanite writing, with a long form of thirty signs and a rarer short form of twenty-one signs.

Following this development, during the twelfth century, an alphabetic writing was invented in Phoenicia, more precisely in Byblos, according to the oldest surviving documents. The Phoenician alphabet differed from previous syllabic writings where each sign represented in principle one syllable, that is, a combination of sounds. It consisted of twenty-two signs, all consonants, vowels not being noted originally. Initially, the letters were written in any direction before they acquired a stable position. The writing was read from right to left as in modern Arabic. Word separators, dots or dashes, were only used in the most ancient inscriptions. The Phoenician alphabet had one crucial advantage: a limited number of signs, which facilitated learning and usage. Writing was no longer limited to professional scribes, theoretically it became accessible to all. However, literacy is a lengthy process and illiteracy never disappeared completely, even by the end of Phoenicia's history.

The Phoenician alphabet began to spread in the East and in the West. It was not adopted everywhere at the same time, but rather in several places and at different stages of its formal development. The Hebrews and Arameans adapted the script from at least the tenth century to write their respective languages, and it spread northwards as far as Asia Minor. The island of Cyprus, very close to Phoenicia, adopted the Phoenician alphabet from at least the ninth century. The Greeks borrowed it probably around the year 800, because the first-known Greek texts are dated between 775 and 750. The diversity of archaic Greek alphabets can be explained either by a single borrowing out of which later versions were born, or by a simultaneous borrowing in several places. The route followed by the Phoenician alphabet to reach the Greeks was probably the maritime one, following in the wake of Phoenician and Greek merchants. Possible points of transmission include Asia Minor; Al-Mina, Ras al-Bassit, or Tell Sukas on the northern Levantine coast; Lefkandi in Euboea; or Ischia in Italy. The new features added to the alphabet by the Greeks were the systematic notation of vowels and the direction of the writing, from left to right.

The political institutions of the Phoenician cities were rooted in the proto-Phoenician cities of the Bronze Age, but they developed specific features after 1200, conditioned by the new political, economic, and cultural realities. They were city-states in relatively small territories, generally bordered by natural boundaries: the sea, the coastal range of mountains, and the rivers running down from them. Their territory consisted of three parts: the urban area with a central agglomeration, the coastal agricultural area, and the mountainous inland area. Phoenician cities were small states totally separated from one another, except when the hegemony exercised by one of them resulted in temporary regroupings. When they fell under the control of the major powers, the latter were able to modify the local geopolitical layout. Phoenician political systems were complex, with numerous variants depending on the city in question, that constantly evolved throughout their history. It is a pity that there are no political texts available to us similar to the Constitution of Carthage, described by the Greek philosopher Aristotle.

Kingship was the distinguishing feature of Phoenician cities from the beginning of their history. It was unique, lifelong, and hereditary. To strengthen it and to guard against dynastic crises, the Phoenicians sometimes resorted to consanguineous marriages, to succession through a collateral branch, and to co-regency between a mother and her son who was too young to govern, or between the aging king and the crown prince. The first responsibility of the king was religious. He upheld the cult of the dynastic divinity, had temples built and restored, and acted as the intermediary between his people and the gods. The king also used religion to legitimize his political power and show that he was placed under divine protection. Equally, his military role was very important: he was commander of the army and war fleet. This role was not theoretical; in times of war, he took part in person in military operations.

The king had diplomatic duties and played a role in international relations with the other Phoenician cities and with non-Phoenician states. He also had a judicial function about which little is known. Lastly, he could organize and conduct commercial expeditions in distant countries, and played a role in colonization. These undertakings came within the framework of the palatial economic system, which did not prevent the existence of private endeavours. When the palatial system disappeared, it was replaced by a civic economic system.

Despite his numerous prerogatives, the Phoenician king does not appear to have had absolute power. Representative structures of the various social bodies limited it more or less. Participation of each city's citizens in political and administrative management was assumed by assemblies, though not always clearly identified. The existence of a Council of Elders is certain. Another assembly could have been the Council of One Hundred, run by a leader of the Hundred. Lastly, the political will of all citizens was expressed in a People's Assembly whose prerogatives we have no knowledge of. In any event, Phoenician cities appear to have been states where citizens had the right to express themselves in various ways: through political representation, opposition groups, specific delegations, and various factions. The Phoenician institutions were characterized by mixed proclivities, including aristocratic, oligarchic, and democratic, as in the Constitution of Carthage.

The question of the "invention" of democracy has been posed: could the Phoenician city-states have contributed to the development of the Greek city model? Incidentally, what is referred to as Greek democracy in reality only concerned a minority of the social body, from which foreigners, women, and slaves, more numerous than fully fledged citizens, were excluded. This was the traditional pattern in ancient states. The Phoenician cities had political institutions, which, in some respects, were similar to those of Greek cities, but it would be premature to say which model influenced the other.

2

Egypt's Loss of Influence in Phoenicia (1200–1000)

Phoenicia developed without Egypt

The period following the Sea Peoples' invasion is an obscure period for the Near East as a whole, as it is sparsely documented. The wealth of information provided by Egyptian texts is no longer available as Egypt withdrew into itself during the Third Intermediate period, around 1076–723, and was no longer directly involved in the Near East.

Phoenicia does not appear to have gone through a particularly difficult period, but it developed without Egypt—even though links were not totally severed. The site of Tell Sukas, despite some destruction, was not abandoned and bounced back very quickly under Phoenician impetus. In Beirut, there was no detectable break between the end of the Bronze Age and the beginning of the Iron Age, although the Iron Age town occupied a smaller area. A tomb in Beirut produced an amulet in the name of Ramesses IV. Sidon appears to have been a prosperous city. In a late Bronze Age building in Sidon, mixed in with some Mycenaean IIIB-period ceramics, an earthenware bowl was discovered bearing the name of Queen Twosret. Despite her short reign as pharaoh, around 1192–1191, she manifested Egypt's interest in the Sinai and Palestine. No apparent change is visible in Sarepta either, where an important pottery industry developed from the Late Bronze Age onwards; typically Phoenician architecture appears there from the middle of the eleventh century. Tyre also seems to be a prosperous site based on a sounding that was carried out there and which brought to light a bead factory established in the Late Bronze Age and still functioning. The levels dating between 1200 and 1000 have uncovered a few Egyptian scarabs.

The situation experienced by the city of Dor was unique. Having been occupied by the Tjeker since the beginning of the twelfth century, it was destroyed by a violent fire in the middle of the eleventh and reoccupied by the Phoenicians. It was probably Phoenicians from Sidon or Tyre, who had taken advantage of the now-open southward route to expand in that direction. Maybe they wanted to destroy this rival city, which was in the hands of the Tjeker, who had a reputation for piracy. In any case, they lost no time in settling in the town and rebuilding it. The presence of some Egyptian jars provide evidence that commercial ties with Egypt continued.

The period 1200–1000 appears to have been one of prosperity for the Phoenicians. The alphabet was widely disseminated, as was the red en-gobe technique on ceramics. After the disappearance of the Mycenaean world and its supremacy in the Mediterranean, Phoenician ships gradually took over the maritime routes and established practical stopover harbors. Phoenician settlements in numerous sites, such as Dor, Sarepta, and Tell Sukas, were not always established peacefully. The Phoenicians knew the art of warfare. The use of archers in particular is evidenced by dozens of inscribed arrowheads. These arrows had been used, as is obvious from their sometimes bent head, and they are a testament to confrontations that occurred during the early phase of Phoenician history.

These objects, dating between the end of the twelfth century and the beginning of the tenth, bear the first-known inscriptions in the Phoenician alphabet. Some of the arrows came from Lebanon. A find from al-Khader near Bethlehem probably represents the contents of a quiver: three inscribed arrows and twenty-three uninscribed, like the vast majority of arrows. The inscriptions give the name of the owner of the arrow, often followed by the name of his father. Sometimes they indicate his origin (Sidon, Tyre, Kition, and Amurru), the name of his patron, and his function (king, chief, leader of the Hundred, head of the traders).

Two mysterious arrows bearing the name of Zakerbaal, king of Amurru, one of comes from Lebanon, refer to the kingdom of Amurru in the early Iron Age, after the invasion of the Sea Peoples. This would mean that the kingdom had survived for some time, with a king bearing a Phoenician name and using Phoenician writing, unlike the previous kings. Another interpretation could point to Zakerbaal, king of Byblos, mentioned in the voyage of Wenamun, also bearing the title of king of Amurru. In any event, the purpose of these inscriptions escapes us.

The misadventures of the Egyptian Wenamun visiting Zakerbaal of Byblos

The Egyptian story about the misadventures of Wenamun, as he carried out an assignment in Byblos, sheds light on the relations between Byblos and Egypt, and paints a picture of the internal situation in Phoenicia. It is the oldest account of sailors and pirates, and a sort of historical novel whose aim was to instruct while entertaining. It is all the more valuable in that it is the only document from this period to have survived. It is dated to year 5 of the "Renaissance," an era beginning under Ramesses XI, that is, around 1090. But the manuscript itself appears to be later. Wenamun was sent as a messenger to Byblos by Herihor, the powerful high priest of Amun who may have descended from a Libyan family. Ramesses XI had serious problems at that time: insecurity and famine were taking hold in Upper Egypt and bitter struggles were stirring up the priests who assumed virtually royal prerogatives. The "Renaissance" era consecrated a sort of triumvirate: the first man was the pharaoh Ramesses XI, the second was the administrator Smendes, based in Tanis to manage Lower Egypt, the third was the high priest Herihor, based in Thebes (Luxor) and responsible for Upper Egypt.

Wenamun was sent to Byblos to acquire the timber required to build a boat for the god Amun. Leaving Thebes, he was bearer of a letter of accreditation as messenger and of a second letter describing the purpose of his assignment. Travelling via Tanis, he negligently showed his letters to Smendes and to his wife who kept them, probably to compromise the mission of Herihor's messenger. Despite this, Wenamun continued his journey, stopping off at Dor, the Tjeker town, where prince Beder offered him hospitality. But one of the sailors left his ship, taking with him the gifts destined for the king of Byblos and the kings of the towns where stops were planned, namely, Weret and Mekmer, perhaps kings of Tyre and Sidon. He went on to demand compensation from the prince of Dor, who refused because the theft had not been committed by one of his subjects.

So, Wenamun continued his journey and stopped off in Tyre. He embarked on a Tjeker ship, which took him to Byblos. Before disembarking, he confiscated some 3 kilos of silver, pending the return of the gifts that had been stolen from him during his halt in Dor. He settled in the harbor of Byblos where he pitched his tent, together with the statue of Amun, which accompanied him on his journey. King Zakerbaal refused to receive him and gave orders every day for twenty-nine days that he had to leave the city, evidence of the lack of consideration granted to the Egyptian messenger.

By chance, an ecstatic prophet from Byblos advised the king to grant him an audience: it is hardly surprising that the local clergy should support the envoy of the high priest of Amun. Leaving the statue of Amun in his tent, Wenamun was escorted to the hill close to the harbor where the royal palace was situated. The first image he had of the king was very suggestive: "I found him sitting in his reception room, back to the window, while the waves of the great sea of Syria battered the base of the building behind him." Zakerbaal addressed him reprovingly, maybe in Egyptian: he criticized him for coming without letters of reference, without an escort, and on a Tjeker ship, which was suspicious. Why had he not used the usual sea links between Byblos, or Sidon, and Egypt? In fact, the king of Byblos was on good terms with Lower Egypt and distrusted this messenger coming from Upper Egypt. In addition, Wenamun arrived empty-handed, without offering him the gifts he had lost in Dor. At no time was it a question of the price of the timber because his approach was not a commercial negotiation, but fell within the scope of a system of exchanges involving gift exchange. Zakerbaal had the accounting register of his ancestors brought in, wherein all the gifts received in exchange for timber were recorded. His view was that, if he gave timber to Wenamun without receiving anything in exchange, he would be acting like a vassal obliged to obey his suzerain. He therefore insisted that he was independent and master of his forests in the Lebanon: "Am I your servant? Am I the servant of he who has sent you? When I cry out towards Lebanon, barely has the sky opened when the trees are here, felled by the seashore."

Wenamun was crafty and put forward other arguments. In fact, Lebanon did not belong to Byblos or to Egypt, but to the god Amun. It was not the Egyptian messenger that Zakerbaal had kept waiting for twenty-nine days in the harbor, but the statue of the god, which was substantially more serious. If he supplied the wood to him, Amun would enable him to live a long life, and in good health. He asked him to send a messenger to Smendes in Lower Egypt to bring him a set of gifts, the list of which he noted down. Consequently, the king of Byblos was persuaded and sent some pieces of timber to Egypt as a sign of goodwill. He dispatched a messenger to Smendes who sent back to him all the gifts requested.

In the end, Zakerbaal was satisfied and mobilized three hundred men and three hundred oxen to fell the trees and drag them down to the seashore. He asked Wenamun to take the timber away as quickly as possible, pointing out to him that he had been treated better than other Egyptian messengers who had preceded him and who had remained in Byblos for seventeen years before dying. It is not known what incident he was referring to, but in any case the context was one of a weakened Egypt and a city liberated from pharaonic control. Wenamun read the threat in the king's words and attempted to divert his attention through flattery. He proposed to erect a stele in Byblos in honor of the king for having generously sent timber for the holy boat, and in exchange to ask Amun to grant him fifty additional years of life. All future messengers from Egypt, capable of reading the stele's inscription, would make offerings to him. This passage could attest to the use of the new writing in Byblos, using the Phoenician alphabet. Wenamun added that his master Herihor would also show his generosity towards the king.

That was not the end of Wenamun's misadventures, because he then saw eleven ships arrive, ships of the Tjeker who prevented him from loading the timber and wanted to capture him. They had probably not forgotten the 3 kilograms of silver that he had taken from them as compensation. He collapsed in tears and complained bitterly to the king's secretary. Zakerbaal was touched and offered him some wine, a sheep, and a female Egyptian singer to cheer him up. The very next day, he convened his assembly to receive the Tjeker who wanted Wenamun to be handed over. His response was that he did not have the right to arrest him on his territory, probably on the basis of a law protecting foreigners. He added, however, they would be able to capture him later, on the high seas. Without telling him about the outcome of the meeting, he had him board one of his ships. In this account, Zakerbaal comes over as being highly gifted, able to use irony, cunning, and suspicious, and simultaneously tough and compassionate.

A providential storm allowed Wenamun to escape from the Tjeker and sail the ship as far as Cyprus. On the verge of being lynched by the population, he managed to get himself escorted to see the queen. Once again, he knew how to be persuasive: if he, Amun's envoy, was killed, the Egyptians would not let that crime go unpunished. And if his Byblian crew was massacred, the king of Byblos would take revenge by massacring the crews of ten Cypriot ships. The queen was persuaded and offered him hospitality. The end of the Wenamun story is lost and we do not know whether he managed to get back to Egypt with his cargo of timber from Byblos.

The story presents a picture of an Egypt whose power was in steep decline, politically and economically, but its relations with the Phoenician cities were not entirely cut off. Regular links existed between Byblos, Sidon, and Lower Egypt. Trade between Phoenicia and Egypt continued. In the reign of Ramesses IX, Egypt imported wine from Kharu (Phoenicia) and Amurru (Syria). Byblos carried on supplying Egypt with raw timber and worked wood and imported papyrus for writing; ropes for ship rigging; linen; leather; precious metals; ivory; jewelry; and foodstuffs: vegetables and salted meats from Egypt. So, Byblos appeared to be a trading hub for the eastern Mediterranean, at the crossroads of the main commercial routes, hence its stability and its economic importance. The system of gift exchange practiced during the Bronze Age continued to function between the pharaoh and the Phoenician kings. Diplomatic practices governing the dispatching and welcoming of messengers had not changed since the time of Amarna, in the fourteenth century. A foreigner's right to hospitality and compensation in the event of theft were evidence of international regulations, which carried on those that existed in the Bronze Age. Hence, despite the upheavals prompted by the invasion of the Sea Peoples, the period between 1200 and 1000 maintained in Phoenicia a certain continuity with the earlier period. However, Zakerbaal of Byblos, while respecting traditions, asserted his independence and henceforth dealt with the Egyptian pharaoh, the su- zerain of his ancestors, on an equal footing.

3

Early Assyrian Exploration
towards the West
(1100–1000)

The expedition of Tiglath-pileser I in Phoenicia

The Aramean invasion of Mesopotamia prompted in Assyria a military reaction with far-reaching consequences and the rise of new politica powers in Babylonia. The conflict between Assyria and Babylonia persisted because neither of the two states was capable of achieving a decisive advantage. They came up against pressure from the Mushki and especially the Elamites, who were formidable adversaries. King Nebuchadnezzar I of Babylon succeeded in restoring the power of his state to the extent that it became a dangerous rival for Assyria.

The Assyrian king Tiglath-pileser I ascended to the throne of Assur in 1114 and launched himself energetically into a large-scale military venture. Initially he probably wanted to avert the latent threat posed to Assyria by the Mushki. But defensive interests were rapidly to reveal the more ambitious aims of an expansionist policy. First, he routed the Mushki and cleared the upper reaches of the Tigris. A second series of operations enabled him to expand his grip from the Upper Euphrates to the Zagros mountains. A third series of operations took him as far as Lake Van in Turkey. Following a chain of conquests, he then veered westwards against the Arameans and carried out a raid up as far as Carchemish, bringing back prisoners, herds of animals, and goods. However, the initial Assyrian raids did not constitute a real conquest, they were merely one-off rapid incursions.

After having dispersed the Aramean nomads who offered little resistance, Tiglath-pileser I headed directly towards the Mediterranean, which he had never seen and which he called the "great sea." Yet, even though the Assyrian state was entirely landlocked, he must have heard about this sea, as his ancestors had reached it. In the eighteenth century,

Shamsi-Adad I had gone to Lebanon and erected a stele on the shore of the great sea, and, in the thirteenth century, Shalmaneser I had also erected a stele on its shore. At the end of his race to the sea, Tiglath-pileser I arrived in Phoenicia. He may have gotten there on several occasions, as he crossed the Euphrates twenty-eight times in the course of his reign, on average twice a year, always in pursuit of the elusive Arameans.

In Phoenicia, he carried out three activities, whose chronology we cannot reconstruct: felling cedars, receiving tribute, and fishing in the sea. He cut down cedars on Mount Lebanon and took them back to Assyria to rebuild the temple of Anu and Adad in Assur. He boasted of acclimatizing in Assyria foreign species such as cedar, oak, and walnut trees. He received tributes from Byblos, Sidon, and Arwad, perhaps in Arwad as there is no indication that he actually went to Byblos and Sidon. In any case, the kings of the Phoenician cities had heard about Assyria, the new major emerging power. As they were not big enough to confront, they wanted to appease it by paying a punctual tribute. Byblos was the first in the order of cities named, since at that time it was more powerful than Sidon and Arwad. The king of Byblos who spontaneously decided to pay tribute to Assyria could have been Zakerbaal who had received Wenamun, the Egyptian messenger.

The king of Assyria retained, above all, an unforgettable memory of a sea-fishing outing off Arwad, which he described at length in his annals. The authorities of Arwad, whose king is not mentioned, had him board their ships in a harbor in the mainland area of Arwad's territory, opposite the island. Sailing down the coast for six hours, they took him to Simyra in Amurru country, 28 kilometers to the south. Tiglath-pileser I himself killed a "sea horse" in the water with a harpoon. The identification of this animal has been debated, but it was probably a hippopotamus, whose current name of Greek origin means "river horse." Simyra, perhaps Tell Kazel, was located on the Nahr al-Abrash whose estuary possibly served as a harbor. The hippopotamus in question must have lived in this river, and must have been killed where the river opened out to the sea. The inhabitants of Arwad endeavored to conciliate the king of Assyria. They knew he was a famous hunter and an enthusiast for all big-game animals, so they flattered him by offering him some exceptional hunting opportunities and also diverted his attention by taking him to Simyra instead of leading him to their island, which they wanted to keep jealously independent.

The aim was achieved: the king was so enthused by the fishing, which was more like hunting in fact, that he had a basalt statue representing a hippopotamus erected at the entrance to his palace in Assur. This exotic trophy also served perhaps to ward off evil, as this episode could have had religious significance. In this period in Egypt, there existed a "harpooning the hippopotamus" festival, celebrating Horus's victory over Seth, the usurper transformed into a red hippopotamus. The rite practiced in Edfu involved throwing ten harpoons into a cake in the shape of a hippopotamus, a symbolic incarnation of evil. In the Bible, the hippopotamus was considered to be the monster par excellence, whose appearance, both terrestrial and marine, impressed the ancients.

From his expedition to Phoenicia, Tiglath-pileser I understood that the Phoenician cities were capable of paying him a ample tribute, that their forests were as abundant as those of the Amanus where he usually got his timber supplies from, and that the "Amurru land's great sea," meaning the Mediterranean, constituted a western limit towards which the state of Assyria ought to extend. He appears to have restored the empire established in the thirteenth century by his ancestor Tukulti-Ninurta I, but his victories were illusory as he had to confront a threat that was significantly more serious than the conflict between Assyria and Babylonia. The Arameans invaded Mesopotamia, blocking the roads and seizing the villages, which had been deserted by their inhabitants. The country was threatened by pillaging and a degree of famine so dire that it even led to acts of cannibalism. Tiglath-pileser I was forced to flee and hide in the mountains. The struggle for survival began, for Assyria and Babylonia alike, and the common danger brought the two states closer together.

New raids by Ashur-bel-kala and Adad-nirari II into Phoenicia

After the flight of Tiglath-pileser I, Assyria foundered under the weight of invasions by the Arameans and the Suteans, and began its decline. Babylonia collapsed. However, Ashur-bel-kala ascended the throne of Assyria in 1073. According to the Babylonian Chronicles, he conducted military operations in Babylonia and installed a usurper, perhaps of Aramean origin, on the throne of Babylon. Ashur-bel-kala married the Babylonian king's daughter and Assyro-Babylonian friendship emerged temporarily strengthened from this episode.

Ashur-bel-kala was a very energetic king who was to resume the stubborn resistance and lightning raids of Tiglath-pileser I. Several of his expeditions, particularly the ones he undertook westwards, mirrored those of his ancestor. Did his scribes simply recopy earlier passages from the Assyrian annals? The change of certain details does seem to indicate that most of the events related had been experienced. The similarity is actually due to the fact that, broadly speaking, he had the same adversaries, located in the same regions, used the same military strategy, with the same belligerent intent, and that he too was a reputed hunter and a great builder.

He also reached the Mediterranean, the "land of Amurru's great sea," which he considered as the limit of the countries conquered by Assyria going westwards. This was propagandistic rhetoric as all his forays towards the Mediterranean were one-off and led to nothing permanent. He campaigned up to the foot of Mount Lebanon, without specifying whether he actually climbed it and felled trees; in any case, cedarwood was used in the reconstruction of his palace in Assur. He did not receive any tribute from the Phoenician cities either. His annals also recount a hippopotamus hunting excursion on Arwad's ships. But the scene is not as detailed and enthusiastic as in the annals of Tiglath-pileser I. In addition, it is included in the hunting trips made at the foot of Mount Lebanon, where he killed some magnificent wild bulls, cows, and elephants. He captured some of them and took them back to Assyria alive. He had statues of these animals sculpted in basalt to decorate the doors of his palace, among which were two hippopotami, not just a single one as with his predecessor.

The eight kings who subsequently acceded to the throne of Assyria between 1050 and 935 left few written traces, which could suggest a chaotic situation. However, dynastic continuity was assured and their reigns were quite long, which indicates a degree of stability. The serious crises that occurred during this period consequently managed to be overcome, at least partially. When King Ashur-dan II ascended to the throne of Assyria in 934, he found a country exhausted, and abandoned by a portion of its inhabitants. He made every effort to put an end to the exodus, to protect the population, and to strengthen the army with a powerful chariotry. His successor, Adad-nirari II, continued his efforts and reignited Assyria's military ambitions. During each of the twenty-one years of his reign he undertook campaigns. His message was new. He claimed that he outperformed his brave ancestors and used an abundance of adjectives to describe himself: imposing, magnificent, invaluable, proud, radiant, heroic, powerful warrior, virile lion, exalted, terrifying. Thanks to him, the Assyrian army changed tactics. It abandoned the lightning one-off raids that gave the nomads, once dispersed, the opportunity to regroup on their rearguard. He adopted their methods of continual harassment, taking places by surprise. He learned how to get around obstacles and to store supplies close by and then carry out operations later.

He practiced siege warfare, constructing small forts and walls around the towns he was besieging. Lastly, in passing, he levied taxes on the populations he subjugated, the result being that the Assyrian army started to look like a never-ending caravan, dragging along prisoners, chariots, livestock, and precious goods.

In his annals, Adad-nirari II no longer referred to the Mediterranean as a limit, because he pushed his pretension as far as asserting that Assyria now dominated the four parts of the world. He rebuilt his palace in Assur using cedar and other species of wood, without indicating where the timber came from. Curiously, he did not mention the tribute from the Phoenician cities, surprising for one who imposed taxation wherever he went. But he briefly described a hippopotamus hunt on the ships of Arwad, before going on an expedition hunting powerful wild bulls at the foot of Mount Lebanon. He courageously killed elephants with his bow and a hundred and twenty lions with his spear, some while in his chariot, some while on foot. His account partly echoes that of Ashur-bel-kala. He too decorated the doors of his palace with two statues of hippopotami, but they were in alabaster, no more in basalt. He received a crocodile and a buffalo for his menagerie of exotic animals as a gift from Egypt, probably from the Twenty-Second Dynasty pharaoh, Osorkon I. The courts of the major powers continued to exchange gifts.

The incessant guerilla warfare conducted by Ashur-bel-kala and his successors, like Adad-nirari II, had some decisive consequences. It transformed Assyria into a country of remarkably well-trained warriors. It gradually led to the creation of a formidable military machine that was to shake up the Near East just a few decades later. Despite the start of the Assyrian offensive towards the west, the Phoenician cities were not really concerned yet and retained their full independence. The two major Near Eastern powers at this time, Egypt and Assyria, were incapable of posing a threat to them, the first still weak and the second not yet strong enough.

4

Dynastic Crises in Byblos
(1000–900)

Ahiram's dynasty

Ahiram, king of Byblos, is known because of his famous sarcophagus, on display in the National Museum of Beirut. The sarcophagus was discovered in tomb V of the royal necropolis of Byblos, with two huge Middle Bronze Age sarcophagi and a few objects bearing the name of Ramesses II, the thirteenth-century pharaoh. The tomb appears to have been reused and thoroughly cleaned out, given the presence of objects relating to earlier occupants. The inscription engraved on the lid of the sarcophagus indicates that Ithobaal had it sculpted for his father Ahiram, king of Byblos.

Father and son are shown face to face on the lid, separated by two lions. The father is holding a wilted lotus flower and the son an erect lotus flower, symbols indicating that one is dead and the other alive. The body of the sarcophagus "sits" on four crouching lions. The scenes sculpted down the long sides represented the late king holding a wilted lotus flower, seated on his throne guarded by two Phoenician-style winged sphinxes. He is bearded, his hair dressed in Egyptian fashion, and is wearing a finely pleated tunic. In front of him is placed a table laden with huge quantities of food for the funeral banquet. A ritual procession is advancing towards him to pay homage and bring him offerings, led possibly by his son. Along the shorter sides of the sarcophagus, professional mourners are tearing their clothes and hair as a sign of grief, following the custom of the time. This magnificent sarcophagus, made of local limestone, is the first Phoenician sculpture where Phoenician art successfully combines Syrian, Hittite, and Egyptian influences. The funeral banquet scene follosd Ugarit religious tradition.

As the sarcophagus is a unique item with no known parallel, its dating is controversial, somewhere between the thirteenth and the ninth

Sarcophagus of King Ahiram in the National Museum of Beirut. By O. Mustafin [public domain], from Wikimedia Commons.

century. Some even believe that the inscription is a later addition to what was an older sarcophagus. It is probably best to believe the inscription, which tells us, "This sarcophagus has been made by Ithobaal, son of Ahiram king of Byblos, for Ahiram his father, as an eternal dwelling place." In accordance with the inscription, both father and son are represented on the sarcophagus, one dead and the other alive: this is more logical than interpreting the figures as representations of earlier kings. Ahiram's sarcophagus was sculpted inside the actual tomb and could be a complete off-cut from a massive Late Bronze Age sarcophagus, like the two others discovered next to it. The inscription and the sarcophagus were most likely completed at the same time, around the year 1000.

King Ahiram was a usurper, given that, contrary to Phoenician custom, the name of his father is not mentioned in the inscription. He therefore founded a new dynasty. The last known king of Byblos before him was Zakerbaal who featured in the Egyptian story about Wenamun. Zakerbaal was on the throne of Byblos around 1082. So it was not him whom Ahiram drove from the throne, but one of his successors some half a century later, perhaps of the same dynasty. When Ithobaal had the sarcophagus sculpted for his father, he was not yet king because the inscription does not mention his royal title. He must have had it prepared in his status as crown prince when his father started to decline. After the death of Ahiram, he succeeded him as king of Byblos, ensuring continuity of the new dynasty until around 970, but we know nothing about his reign and his tomb has not been found.

The second part of the inscription contains a powerful curse should the tomb of Ahiram be desecrated. Ithobaal imagined Byblos being captured by a king, governor, or warlord foreign to his dynasty. He cursed him so that his power would be broken and his conquest lost. He feared a military invasion, no longer by the Hittites whose empire had collapsed, nor by the Egyptians whose power had weakened, but rather by the Assyrians in the wake of Ashur-bel-kala's expeditions in Phoenicia. He also feared a palace coup, a new king of Byblos who would usurp power from the illegitimate dynasty founded by his father and which was still fragile.

Nor did Ithobaal forget to curse any likely profaner who might be attracted by the lure of profit: his name would be wiped out and he would be deprived of funerary honors. Deletion of the name was extremely serious because it equated to condemning the deceased to oblivion. If he was forgotten, nobody would perform the funeral rituals necessary for his passage into life beyond the grave. This religious belief was borrowed from Egypt. Ithobaal was so obsessed by the risk of profanation, as were all Phoenicians, that he took every precaution. The sarcophagus was sculpted underground, out of sight. The tomb was at the bottom of a deep, walled pit. A protective roof covered the pit at half-height and the entry was sealed with slabs. In addition to the curse inscribed on the sarcophagus, he had a small inscription engraved on the pit wall: "Beware! If you go down deeper, you will be in danger!" The two warning inscriptions suggested that any likely profaner would be capable of reading them, and hence that writing had become widespread in Byblos.

All the precautions taken by Ithobaal to preserve Ahiram's body were in vain. When the tomb was discovered in 1923, it had been totally looted. The thieves did not gain entry using the expected route, namely, the pit, but by digging a tunnel through the layer of clay underneath the tomb and emptying it of all its items of value.

Yehimilk's dynasty and the statues affair

The illegitimate dynasty of Ahiram did not last very long as it was dislodged by a new usurper, Yehimilk. He does not mention the name of his father, which means the latter had not been king. Yehimilk's inscription was engraved on a stone to commemorate the restoration of a temple the name of which is not specified. Yehimilk also restored the other temples of Byblos, which were in ruins. Were these temples been damaged by a military offensive, or did they become progressively dilapidated through religious neglect or a lack of resources to have them repaired? Whatever the case, Yehimilk had the necessary funds to carry out the restoration of the temples so as to legitimize his new dynasty. He declared himself to be a legitimate and upright king. He invoked all the city's gods to protect his reign: Baal Shamim ("master of the heavens"), Baal Gubal ("master of Byblos"), and the assembly of the holy gods. The goddess Baalat was not invoked explicitly. She was replaced by Baal, a very important god for Yehimilk as indicated by the fact that he gave his children and grandchildren names ending in *-baal*: Abibaal, Elibaal, and Shipitbaal.

If Ithobaal reigned around 1000–970, King Yehimilk would have reigned around 970–950. In this period—particularly in the reign of the pharaoh Siamon, whose scarab was discovered at the site of Tell el-Farah—Egypt developed a more dynamic foreign policy in its old Near Eastern provinces. Siamon undertook an expedition against the Philistines who were threatening Egyptian trade with Phoenicia. He seized Gezer before David, king of Israel and Judah, crushed the Philistines and imposed his conditions on Egyptian merchants. Then the pharaoh allied with Solomon, an alliance consecrated by giving Solomon one of his daughters in marriage. We do not know whether relations between Byblos and Egypt already resumed in the reign of Yehimilk, but they certainly did in the reign of his successor.

Abibaal succeeded Yehimilk, who was probably his father. He is known from an inscription on the seat of a broken gray-granite statue of the pharaoh Sheshonq I. It appears that Abibaal had this statue sculpted in Egypt to offer to Baalat so that she would protect his reign. He was an innovator compared to his father as he updated the worship of Baalat, who consequently became the principle deity and patron of the dynasty of the kings of Byblos. He also innovated by having his inscription engraved on an Egyptian statue already inscribed in the name of a pharaoh. His initiative was to be copied by his successor Elibaal. Much has been written about the affair of the statue and it has not been fully clarified. During the Middle Kingdom of Egypt, pharaohs sometimes dedicated their statues in the sacred sites of subjugated regions, including the temple of Baalat in Byblos. Pharaohs of the New Kingdom, perhaps to copy their predecessors, also offered statues in Egyptian and Levantine temples. The enthronement of a new pharaoh was the opportunity to sculpt many statues and to offer them to the divinities of Egypt and the ancient provinces. The case of the Byblos statue is different however,

113

Bust of Pharaoh Osorkon I, containing a Phoenician inscription. Department of Near Eastern Antiquities of the Louvre [CC BY-SA 2.0 fr, CC BY-SA 3.0 fr] from Wikimedia Commons.

as it was Abibaal who ordered it from Egypt, as a king of Ugarit had also done. The originality is especially due to the fact that the king of Byblos offered the statue to Baalat in his name. In any event, he obviously wanted to gain Egypt's favor through this elaborate gesture and to reestablish relations through Baalat, their common divinity.

Faced with the threat of the rising power of Assyria, Sheshonq I, the powerful pharaoh who reunified Egypt, also had an interest in asserting his presence in the Near East by reestablishing links with Phoenician cities such as Byblos. His victorious military campaign in Palestine around 925 perhaps had something of the nature of the new Egyptian policy initiated by Siamon, to try and regain control of the old Asiatic provinces. The Egyptian advance was halted at Megiddo where the pharaoh had a commemorative stele erected. The date of Abidaal's reign inevitably coincided with that of Sheshonq I. If the statue arrived in Byblos at the time of the pharaoh's enthronement, Abibaal was on the throne in 943.

Elibaal was pro-Egyptian, just like his brother Abibaal. Elibaal succeeded him on the throne of Byblos as Abibaal probably did not have a son, or in any case no son of an age to succeed him. To maintain the dynasty, another son of Yehimilk was called upon. The new king also had a statue of the pharaoh sculpted, a reddish sandstone bust of Osorkon I, successor of Sheshonq I. He had his inscription engraved around the pharaoh's name and offered the statue to Baalat so that she would protect his reign. Elibaal's reign was therefore connected to that of Osorkon I. If the statue arrived in Byblos in 922 on the accession of the new pharaoh, he was on the throne at that time. Egypt pursued its policy of diplomatic and commercial relations with the cities of the Near East. Egyptian texts mention the gifts that these cities sent to Osorkon I. Byblos's cedar trade with Egypt appears to have picked up again from the beginning of his reign.

Shipitbaal I was the last known king of the Yehimilk dynasty. He was the son of Elibaal, and Yehimilk's grandson. He had an inscription engraved on a stone of a retaining wall in the temple of Baalat. He had restored this wall for Baalat, his protective divinity, whom he asked to grant him a long reign. The date of his reign is deduced from that of the reign of this father Elibaal, so around 900. The pharaoh Osorkon I was still in power, and relations between Byblos and Egypt continued. However, around 897, the unfortunate expedition of an Egyptian general against the kingdom of Judah was to put an end to Egypt's foreign policy in the region.

5

The Development and Expansion
of the Phoenician Cities
(1000–883)

The development of Sidon

Sidon and Tyre were two large Phoenician cities barely 35 kilometers apart, a fact that contributed to their rivalry, open or latent, throughout the whole of their history. They developed alternately: when one was prosperous and powerful, the other was weak and in decline. Sidon developed substantially during the second half of the second millennium. Already in the fourteenth century, in the Amarna period, the city was more powerful than Tyre, which was constrained on its island and at war with its rival. Sidon was then the ally of Amurru and the Hittites, whereas Tyre had turned towards Egypt. At the beginning of the eleventh century, at the time of Tiglath-pileser I's expedition in Phoenicia, he received tributes from Byblos, Sidon, and Arwad, but not from Tyre, as it was probably a second-tier city at the time. The Egyptian story of Wenamun's journey reveals that Sidon was a prosperous city, as its harbor sheltered fifty merchant ships, which were involved in business relations with Werekter, a Semite based in Tanis, the Egyptian capital, where he was both a ship owner and merchant. Besides that, King Zakerbaal of Byblos boasted of owning twenty merchant ships used in relations with Smendes, the future pharaoh. Nothing is said about the activities of the harbor of Tyre, where Wenamun stopped over.

It is to these important commercial activities of the harbor of Sidon that the role of the Sidonians in Aegean trade must be attributed. It was so essential that in the epic poetry ascribed to Homer, the Phoenicians are referred to as "Sidonians." Perhaps Sidon was the major Phoenician city at the time Homeric poetry was developed. This poetry was the fruit of mythical collective thinking, born in oral form and for a long while transmitted by the equivalent of our medieval troubadours. It possessed

116

a living past almost a millennium long before being crystallized in writing in several stages between the eighth and the fifth centuries. When did the term "Sidonians" find its way into Greek cultural heritage? Possibly it was during Sidon's period of prominence, during the second half of the second millennium.

The same process appears in the Bible where on several occasions the Phoenicians are referred to as "Sidonians." In Genesis, Sidon was the firstborn of Canaan. In the list of countries to be conquered by Israelite tribes in the book of Joshua, Phoenicia is represented by the cities of Byblos and Sidon, which corresponds to their importance in this period. Sidon appears as a powerful city called the "Great Sidon," in possession of an extensive territory. Some scholars have thought that Sidon and Tyre constituted a single political entity at this time, whose habitants were known as Sidonians. Subsequently Tyre would have developed to the point of regaining its independence. This is an assumption that is unconfirmed by the sources.

Among the reasons behind Sidon's prominence in the twelfth and eleventh centuries, are the extent and wealth of its rich agricultural area, and the access via Jezzine to the fertile southern Bekka Plain and the major north–south trading route from Syria to the Jordan Valley. Unlike Byblos, and Tyre to a lesser extent, Sidon was not impacted by the decline of Egypt, as it was more involved with its northern trading partners.

The alliance of Hiram I, king of Tyre, with David, king of Israel and Judah

The only source for the history of this period is the Bible. The disparate nature of this collection and the history and date of the texts need to be taken into account, as well as the ideological aims that governed its writing, which occurred a long while after the events related.

The Israelite groups were organized, very early on, into twelve tribes, according to the Bible, but their organization seems vague, adversarial, and fluid prior to David's time. The northern tribes settled in a traditionally Phoenician area. On the one hand, the Israelite and Phoenician populations amalgamated as a result of mixed marriages. On the other hand, the Israelite tribes' search for territories led to inevitable clashes with the Phoenicians. As we do not know the extent of the territory belonging to the Phoenician cities in this period, it is difficult to verify the biblical account. The tribe of Dan may have captured Laish (Leshem, Dan) from the Sidonians and the tribe of Asher must have

117

encroached on Tyre's territory. The Israelite conquest appears to have been conducted more in the hinterland than in the coastal area, which was occupied by the Phoenicians in the north and the Philistines in the south. Israelites from the tribes of Asher, Dan, and Zebulun apparently served on Phoenician ships, but it is not known in what context.

Philistine expansionism led to a confrontation, near the springs of the Yarqon, with the Israelite confederation, which was defeated. Saul, of the tribe of Benjamin, conducted a long and bloody war of liberation against the Philistine occupation. He was proclaimed king, but he only relied on his own family and came up against Samuel and David; he perished in a battle against the Philistines. His reign marked an important change, taking Israel from a fairly lax confederation to a military kingship reliant on a professional army. Several traditions surround David's accession to the throne. In short, after having been anointed by the prophet Samuel, he placed himself at the service of Saul as a lyre player, then as commander of the army. Having come into conflict with him, he had to flee the royal court and took to the wilderness at the head of an armed band. On the death of Saul, he had himself proclaimed as king in Hebron by the leaders of the Judean clans. After seven years of reign, he established his capital in Jerusalem, on the border of the kingdoms of Israel and Judah, as a token of his political will to unify them. He succeeded in halting the military expansion of the Philistines and confined them to the south of the Levant. He beat the Aramean coalition army from central Syria, led by Hadadezer. The kingdom of David became the dominant power in the region, benefiting from the weakening of Egypt and Assyria.

Towards the north, David's kingdom extended as far as the Sharon Plain and Galilee, and possibly encompassed part of the Phoenician coast as well. The biblical list of its borders must not be taken literally as it is partly theoretical and idealistic, embracing the conquests programmed by the new expanding state. Nevertheless, David controlled the land routes leading to Tyre. Abibaal was on the throne of Tyre at the time, before leaving it to his son Hiram I around 970. According to the Bible, Hiram I sent an embassy to David when he settled in Jerusalem, with cedarwood, carpenters, and stone cutters to build the royal palace. The two kings became friends. Both of them had long reigns: David would have reigned around 1010–970 and Hiram I around 970–936. These dates pose a chronological problem, but they are approximate. In fact, the first contacts between Tyre and David were almost certainly made by Abibaal, Hiram I's father. However, Tyre must have waited until David had secured his throne, freed his country from the Philistine yoke, and enlarged his kingdom northwards, until he became his immediate neighbor. Establishing contact followed a well-attested tradition in the second millennium. There were probably diplomatic contacts between two independent states, to which were added a commercial dimension and technological support. They were two fast-developing neighboring states, one maritime and the other essentially land locked, who had an interest in forming an alliance together instead of conducting border warfare, which would have been detrimental to their respective prosperity.

The relations between Hiram I and Solomon

More is known about Hiram I's relationship with Solomon than with David through numerous Bible passages, however difficult they are to interpret. They also figure in the account of Flavius Josephus, which is precious because it goes back indirectly to Tyrian annals that are lost. "The Tyrians," he wrote, "have had, over a period of very many years, public chronicles, written and kept by the state with the utmost care, about events worth remembering which occurred in their city, and about their dealings with foreign countries." But this first century CE testimony was, nevertheless, made a very long while after the events it relates.

David did not have as much success with his domestic policy as he did with his foreign policy. He had difficulties controlling the disputes between Israel and Judah and the internecene rivalries. On his death, the young Solomon took power after the liquidation of the opposition leaders, partisans of David's other sons. He reigned from 970 to 931 approximately. He was a skillful politician and a good administrator, who devoted himself especially to the management of the large centralized state bequeathed to him by his father, more in the spirit of continuity than of innovation. He developed the Israelite cult and culture by building the first temple, the religious center of the kingdom of Jerusalem up until 587. He created a royal school to train the king's sons and future senior officials. He had major public works carried out to celebrate the glory of his reign. In defensive matters, he developed chariotry, a new weapon for him, and had a fair number of fortified towns constructed. However, unlike David, Solomon does not appear to have waged war, preferring to settle possible conflicts through diplomacy. As the royal treasury's revenues from spoils and vassal tributes waned, he fueled them through long-distance caravan and maritime trading operations. He established diplomatic and commercial relations with the kingdom of Saba, whose caravans controlled the spice trade. He allied with Egypt by marrying one of the pharaoh Siamon's daughters. Siamon wanted to control the young king who positioned himself in Egypt's area of influence, within the framework of a peaceful foreign policy. Solomon developed trade with Phoenicia, particularly by strengthening his father's relations with Tyre, having understood that their two states had economies that, in part, were complementary.

On the accession of Solomon, Hiram I of Tyre sent him an embassy bearing gifts, as was common practice in the Near East, so as to carry on the rapport established with his father David. Following an exchange of correspondence, the two kings concluded a solemn agreement. It must have been a "good neighborliness" agreement like the peace treaties in Near Eastern diplomacy. Trade clauses may have been specified too, without the agreement being a commercial treaty.

Hiram I offered to carry out Solomon's wishes while inviting him to carry out his own. This wording calls to mind the system of gift exchange in use in the palace economies of the second millennium. However, except for gold, it did not involve prestige goods like those that Solomon may have exchanged with the queen of Saba, but everyday consumer goods, quantifiable and marketable, which both states needed. Hiram I undertook to supply timber each year while Solomon had to send food supplies. Archaeological finds have shown that in this period, Tyre also exported handmade goods to Solomon's kingdom, specifically, ivories, fabrics, and ceramics such as transportation jars. From Israel Tyre imported cereals, oil, and possibly honey, balms, and various spices.

Solomon needed technical help from the Phoenicians for his prestigious constructions, particularly his palace and the temple in Jerusalem. He called on the craftsmen and technicians of Tyre, Sidon, and Byblos: quarrymen, masons, carpenters, joiners, and bronze smiths. The Bible describes at length the luxurious constructions of his palace, labelled the "house of the forest of Lebanon," and of the temple or "house of Yahweh." The precious decorations and interior furnishings were also described. The temple of Jerusalem has never been found, and yet it is perfectly known thanks to these detailed descriptions. Hiram I carried out similar construction in his own city. Flavius Josephus describes the impressive works undertaken in Tyre, including a gold column erected in the temple of Baal (Zeus), several temples dedicated to Ashtart and Milqart, and the extension of the inhabitable area on the island of Tyre using embankments.

After about twenty years of good relations, Solomon ceded the district of Cabul in the Akko hinterland to Hiram I, including twenty towns, which the king of Tyre does not appear to have appreciated. This transfer of territorial sovereignty is curious because it was quite uncommon in the Near East. If this cession of territory was a transaction, it would have served to pay Solomon's debt towards Hiram I, who had not been paid enough for supplying agricultural products. If it was a matter of the peaceful regulation of the border between the two states, this transfer could represent one of the regions occupied by David and handed back to Hiram I by Solomon. The Bible's description of the territory of Cabul corresponds roughly with that of the Asher tribe. In the reign of Solomon, his kingdom was reduced in the north whereas Tyre's territory was rapidly expanding.

Solomon allowed Sidonian women, probably meaning Phoenician women, to enter his harem in order to strengthen his relations with his northern neighbors. The biblical reference to his marriage with Hiram I's daughter is erroneous, as it was a subsequent addition to the text. According to the Bible, Solomon's harem comprised no fewer than seven hundred princesses and three hundred concubines. At that time, royal marriages were a sign of sovereignty, and an act of diplomacy. The different foreign wives represent the annexed territories and allied states. The Phoenicians in contrast do not appear to have indulged in polygamy.

Hiram I and Solomon jointly organized maritime trade expeditions. Solomon needed the Phoenicians, who had solid maritime trading experience. He probably participated in King Hiram I's expedition, which is mentioned in the Bible, going as far as Tarshish, identified with the region of Huelva in the south of Spain. They must also have organized together some expeditions to Ophir, probably located in East Africa, to the south of Egypt, to bring back gold. Solomon's marriage with an Egyptian princess facilitated direct commercial relations with this region. The fleet's departure point was Ezion-Geber on the Red Sea, because the canal between the Nile and the Persian Gulf, started by Necho II and completed by Darius I, did not exist at this time and the Phoenicians did not yet know that Africa could be circumnavigated. Ezion-Geber is identified nowadays with the island of Jezirat Faraun in the Gulf of Aqaba, which had an artificial harbor. To have a fleet at that time in the Red Sea, it had to be built in position by bringing in all the necessary material, or it had to be transported by caravan in separate parts. In either case, it would have been a difficult task, yet possible. Only Hiram I had the technical ability to build a fleet, but Solomon must have authorized him to cross his territory, and he probably helped finance the project. The wealth amassed by Solomon would suggest that these joint expeditions with Hiram I really did take place. Nevertheless, they were experimental and risky expeditions, which at this stage gave no sign of being organized or regular.

Solomon was confronted by severe setbacks in foreign policy. The pharaoh Sheshonq I supported his political opponents, Jeroboam for example, who fled to Egypt. Hence, he clearly endeavored to affirm his power over the old Egyptian province of Canaan. Solomon did not react to prevent his adversary Hadad from proclaiming the independence of the kingdom of Damascus. Hadad was probably also supported by the pharaoh, who was quite happy to weaken Solomon. The unified kingdom of David and Solomon developed at the same time as the neighboring state of Tyre under Hiram I, without really being prejudicial one to the other and especially by mutually supporting each other. But the next stage of their history was to go down different paths. The end of Solomon's reign got bogged down in the schism between Israel and Judah, which was to continue until 722. For a while, the city of Tyre had broken its dynastic ties with its neighbors and did not take part in Sheshonq I's Egyptian expedition to Megiddo. We know the names of Hiram I's successors, translated into Greek in a list in six different versions, thanks to Flavius Josephus. He specifies the length of their reigns, from which approximate dates have been derived: Baleazoros (935–918), Abdastratos (918–909), Methusastratos (909–897), Astharymos (897–889), and Phelles (889–888). During this period, Tyre was prey to serious dynastic problems. King Abdastratos was assassinated by the four sons of his nursemaid. The surviving kings were three brothers who successively usurped power. Astharymos was assassinated by Phelles who in turn was to be assassinated by Ithobaal I. This unrest could have prompted the exodus of Tyrians fleeing the regime and could have indirectly encouraged Tyrian colonization.

Phoenician expansion in the Mediterranean

Trading activity played a key role from the very beginning of Phoenicia's history. Phoenician merchants used the overland routes towards most of the regions of the Near East. According to the Greek geographer Stephanus of Byzantium, they even founded the colony of Eddana (Eden) on the Euphrates. But Phoenician expansion mainly developed in the Mediterranean Sea. The maritime routes followed by Phoenicians had already been used during the Late Bronze Age by their precursors, the proto-Phoenicians, and the Mycenaeans who dominated sea-borne trade at that time. Long-distance trade focused on the search for metals, such as copper, silver, and tin, as far as Sardinia, Spain, and Portugal.

Mining at Rio Tinto and in the Sierra Morena, for example, started as early as the fourth or third millennium. Details about the profits made from east–west travels across the Mediterranean must have been circulated and passed down through the generations among sailors and merchants alike.

Phoenician expansion in the Mediterranean was a highly complex phenomenon, characterized by three successive phases. The first phase is the appearance of Phoenician objects in Mediterranean sites, the second a strong cultural influence in the staging areas of Phoenician expansion, and the third the colonization or foundation of permanent Phoenician settlements. Ancient sources only provides information about the foundation of colonies, which do not always concur with archaeological discoveries. On the other hand, the traces of precolonization are difficult to detect.

In the Aegean world, luxury objects imported from the East are, to begin with, quite rare. They become progressively more numerous in wealthy tombs and sanctuaries such as the Heraion of Samos. Later, the first oriental workshops of ivory workers, silversmiths, and ceramicists appear in Greek cities such as Eretria, Knossos, and Athens. Phoenician merchants and craftsmen who settled in Kommos on Crete had their own sanctuary. These contacts are what led to the birth, in the eighth century, of the orientalizing cultural phenomenon distinguished by the imitation of Near Eastern models.

In the central Mediterranean, precolonial commercial ties were established between the regions rich in metal ores and the cities of the Levant. The central position of Sardinia and its rich ore resources made it a necessary stopover for the Phoenicians very early on. Between the twelfth and the ninth centuries, Aegean–Oriental and Cypriot groups of merchants were also encountered there. The Phoenicians had no direct access to the sources of supply; access was obtained via a preferential relationship with the local leaders who maintained control over the means of production. They were also interested in northern Etruria, rich in ore deposits, especially silver. Merchants and craftsmen later settled on the island of Pithekousai (Ischia), at the entrance to the Gulf of Naples, which belonged to the Euboeans. However, the orientalizing influence in Italy could have been initiated by the Greeks as a secondary phase of Phoenician expansion.

The south of Spain played a major role in Phoenician expansion, due to its rich mineral deposits. At the turn of the first millennium, the Phoenicians discovered Tarshish in the region of Huelva, close to the main mining region in the south of Spain. They settled in the bay of Gades (Cadiz). The Peña Negra mining deposits in the Rio Segura Valley, south of Alicante, were frequented from the ninth century by the Phoenicians who, at the beginning of the eighth century, constructed the fortified site of La Fonteta, at the mouth of the river. They were also interested in the metal ores in the Pyrenees.

During the precolonization phase, these pioneering Phoenician merchants met differing reactions from the local populations in the various regions where they traded. It was partly on the basis of these reactions that they conceived the following phase. Phoenician colonization was not a clearly defined process that started simultaneously in the whole Mediterranean, nor can it be pinned down as a specific historical event. It was more of a multifaceted structural change that spanned several centuries. The colonies founded by the Phoenicians replaced settlements within local communities and small commercial establishments, be they temporary or more stable. They set up permanent establishments, characterized by their long-term dependency on their mother city. The place chosen for the founding of colonies generally satisfied a number of precise criteria: a naturally defined and not very large area; easily defendable, like an island or a peninsula; a good harbor location; coastal landmarks to aid navigation; and easy access inland.

The date of the foundation of the most ancient colonies is difficult to establish. According to Stephanus of Byzantium, Byblos founded a colony on the island of Milos at the end of the second millennium. Byblos does not appear to have taken part in Phoenician colonization, but it could have participated in the precolonization process when it was still powerful and prosperous. If our information is accurate, the settlement on Milos was not a colony, but a small trading establishment, where merchants and possibly craftsmen settled amidst the local population. Kition, present-day Larnaca on Cyprus, appears to have been the most ancient permanent Phoenician settlement. The site had been occupied since the thirteenth century. A large sacral complex was built in the ninth century in the Kathari district, on top of a Late Bronze sanctuary. According to Flavius Josephus, Hiram I of Tyre undertook an expedition against a town that refused to pay him tribute and placed it under his control. The name of the town is not clear; some have opted for the name of Utica, but the Cypriot town of Kition, close to Tyre, is more plausible. So, the Tyrian colony of Kition could have been founded by Abibaal, father of Hiram I, who reigned until around 970. According to literary tradition, the most ancient Phoenician colonies were Gades, Carthage, Utica, and Lixus. Gades (Cadiz), in the south of Spain, would have been founded around 1104 based on classical sources, but archaeological

evidence goes back no further than the beginning of the eighth century. Utica, northwest of Tunis, would have been founded, according to the classical sources, 287 years before the founding of Carthage, hence around 1101, but excavations have revealed no material dating earlier than the eighth century. Lixus, 5 kilometers from Larache in Morocco, would have been founded around 1100, but archaeology only points as far back as the eighth or seventh century.

Even though all the Phoenicians traded in the Mediterranean, not all seem to have taken part in the colonization phenomenon. Nothing is known of any possible role played by Arwad and that of Byblos appears to have been very limited. Sidon, in contrast, did participate in the precolonization phase, at a time when it was a prosperous and powerful city. According to the Story of Wenamun, Sidon possessed fifty ships doing business with Werekter of Tanis, and, according to Homer, Sidonian merchants were very active in the Aegean Sea. If the dates of the foundation of colonies at the end of the twelfth century are accurate, they would not concern Tyre, which was not very powerful then, but rather Sidon, the major Phoenician city at that period. However, in the long process of Phoenician expansion, the founding of colonies is difficult to conceive during the precolonization phase. After the decline of Sidon, the city of Tyre led precolonization: this was in the time of Hiram I in the tenth century when it became a prominent Phoenician city. Once it had resolved its dynastic issues, it was to lead the colonization movement from the end of the ninth century. Later, Sidon was also to go through a phase of expansion towards the northern and southern shores of the Near East, and was to establish some trading communities in Athens and Delos.

The distances covered by Phoenician ships were sometimes substantial, which implies a high level of technology. The first Phoenician voyages towards the West benefited from cooperation, for example, between the Phoenicians and the Mycenaeans, and between the Tyrians and the Israelites. Hence, large-scale maritime trade was conducted at two levels: ventures organized by the state such as those of Hiram I and Solomon, and private enterprises like those of Byblos and Sidon in business relations with Egyptian merchants and ship owners.

PART THREE

PHOENICIA UNDER ASSYRIAN DOMINATION (883–610)

1

The Beginnings of Assyrian Expansion
(883–745)

The ferocious expeditions of Ashurnasirpal II

The three century-long period of real independence came to an end for
Phoenicia, even if it still experienced brief periods of autonomy from
time to time, particularly during the first phase of Assyrian expansion
before their domination was established. One of the tangible signs of
subjugation was the payment of tribute. When subjugation was only
fleeting, tribute was a one-off levy on the spoils taken by the victor,
without the violence of pillaging. However, it could result in long-term
vassalage, in which case the tribute was intended as a welcome gift
given in homage by the vassal to his suzerain when he passed through
his territory and as payment for the protection that the suzerain granted
him. On top of the initial welcome tribute came more and more regular
and annual payments, which reflected the vassal's solid loyalty to the
king of Assyria. Any discontinuance in the regular payment of the tribute by the vassal was interpreted as an act of rebellion and opened the
door to retaliatory measures—an increase in the tribute, for example.
In the ninth and eighth centuries, the Assyrian kings often carried out
peaceful campaigns, making the journey to come and collect tribute directly from their vassals.

Ashurnasirpal II's coming to power in 883 marked a profound
change. The new Assyrian king was a megalomaniac who attributed
fifty or so eulogistic titles to himself in his annals. He was also a bloodthirsty and sadistic king who complacently described the atrocities he
committed: pyramids of severed heads and cut-off limbs, circles of people impaled in front of the gates of the conquered towns, inhabitants
burned alive in their houses, and defeated leaders skinned alive with
their skin draping the walls. Through this reign of terror he pursued
the task of restoration and reconquest undertaken by his grandfather

129

Adad-nirari II and his father Tukulti-Ninurta II. However, this "frightfulness" was also calculated, as he alternated between intimidation and friendly persuasion depending on his target.

Ashurnasirpal II broadened the scope of Assyrian incursions, both eastwards and westwards. In 878, he seized Bit-Adini, a region stretching out on both sides of the large loop of the Euphrates. The success of the Assyrian army and the terror it inspired motivated the western states not to put up any opposition as he passed through, especially as the Assyrians did not establish a permanent occupation. Ashurnasirpal II was seduced by the riches of the Syrian states that delivered tribute to him. Between 876 and 868, he reached Mount Lebanon and the Mediterranean, which he too called the "great sea." He immersed his weapons in it and made sacrifices to the gods. He listed the Phoenician cities that rushed to send him their tributes as a sign of submission in his annals. From south to north they were Tyre, Sidon, Byblos, Mahallata, Mayza, Kayza (possibly in the region of Tripoli), Amurru and Arwad, "which is an island." It was probably in the vicinity of Arwad that he reached the Mediterranean, and he then went up as far as the Amanus to cut down trees and erect a commemorative stele. The Phoenician cities' tributes are described in great detail: silver, gold, tin, bronze, a bronze basin, linen fabrics with multicolored ornaments, large and small female monkeys, ebony, boxwood, and hippopotamus ivory—in other words, local products as well as goods brought back by the Phoenicians from their distant expeditions.

This very successful campaign highlighted both the wealth and the weakness of the Syrian and Phoenician states. The idea of a fixed and regular tribute emerged, even though the logic of annual campaigns remained essentially that of pillaging. Ashurnasirpal II put in place an embryonic provincial administration by multiplying the number of permanent supply depots, which were positioned on the strategic routes. Some of these depots were fortified centers, entrusted to governors for protection. Yet, contrary to what he averred, he had not really conquered the region between the Tigris and Mount Lebanon and up to the Mediterranean.

This Assyrian king was also a great builder. Having resided in Nineveh for the initial years of his reign, he had the fabulous capital Kalhu (Nimrud) built. The city was encircled by a massive wall and comprised several sanctuaries, a ziggurat, and a canal that irrigated gardens and a zoological and botanical park. For the inauguration ceremony, the king of Assyria boasted of having offered a banquet to 69,754 guests. For all the constructions of this megalomaniacal king in Nimrud and in all the other cities of the Assyrian Empire, the forests of the Amanus and of Mont Lebanon made abundant contributions. He invited to the inauguration ceremony for his new capital representatives from Tyre and Sidon, probably major cities at that time, with which relations must not have been bad. The Phoenician Elimilk was a high-ranking Assyrian official, an eponym (meaning that he gave his name to the year) in 886, perhaps in recognition of the help he gave Ashurnasirpal II in his expedition to Phoenicia.

Thus, Assyria became a major power again, but it was not the only one. Indirectly, its resurgence had stemmed the flow of nomads in Babylonia, enabling the latter to begin a renewal. The Assyrian military campaigns had passed by the kingdom of Damascus, governed by Bar-Hadad I, who exploited the dissensions between Israel and Judah to enlarge its territory and impose its regional hegemony. In particular, Bar-Hadad I took advantage of the upheavals experienced by the kingdom of Israel, involving conspiracies, coups d'état, and civil war over a four-year period, after which Omri seized power and established his new capital in Samaria. In Egypt, the Twenty-Second Dynasty sparkled with its final lustre under Osorkon II. This pharaoh undertook some major construction works and pursued the foreign policy of his predecessors. He maintained his alliance with Byblos where his statue has been discovered. But Egypt paled in comparison with the rising power of Assyria.

Ithobaal I of Tyre and his dual kingdom

In the city of Tyre, the assassination of King Phelles around 888 put an end to a long period of dynastic crises. According to Flavius Josephus, the coup d'état was fomented by the clergy because it was a priest of Ashtart, Ithobaal I (Ithobalos), who seized power. He would have reigned around 888–856: it was he, therefore, who paid tribute to Ashurnasirpal II. During his reign, Tyre apparently experienced a year of severe drought. The new king of Tyre carried the title "king of the Tyrians and of the Sidonians," probably because he had annexed the city of Sidon to Tyre, which was then the most powerful of the Phoenician cities. Sidon was not really integrated into the kingdom of Tyre and retained a degree of autonomy, although it remained subject to the same king in the form of a dual kingship. Ithobaal I was probably king of Tyre and Sidon, just as David and Solomon after him were kings of Israel and Judah, unifying in their person two distinct political entities. This would therefore explain the mention of Tyre and Sidon in the Assyrian annals, but only of the king of Tyre, sole representative of both cities. The dual kingdom of Tyre and Sidon might have lasted until 701, based on the few allusions gleaned from biblical and Assyrian sources.

Ithobaal I of Tyre and Omri of Israel were both usurpers who took power at the same time, the first around 888 and the second around 885. Each had the opportunity to establish his legitimacy by concluding an official agreement with the neighboring king. They were probably guided by the alliance concluded between their illustrious predecessors, Hiram I and Solomon. Ithobaal's daughter, Jezebel, married Ahab, the son of Omri. This diplomatic marriage was definitely not a private event, but one that sealed a political alliance between the two kings and their kingdoms, also including their commercial relations. The precise date of the marriage is not known; at the earliest it took place around 885 under Omri's reign, but it could also date to the first years of Ahab's reign, which began in around 874. This marriage introduced into Samaria a taste for Phoenician luxury and the kingdom of Israel benefited from its privileged relations with the wealthy city of Tyre. Also in this context, the cult of the Phoenician god Baal (probably Milqart of Tyre) was introduced into Samaria for the queen and her court, as well as for the Tyrian merchants and craftsmen who had settled in the city due to the very active trade. A Phoenician temple was constructed in the capital of the kingdom of Israel, a building that might have been planned as part of the alliance. The success of the Phoenician religion was a threat to the Israelite religion, all the more so because it had been practiced in earlier times by the Canaanite populations. Various prophetic factions of the Bible stress the fact that Jezebel bore the responsibility for King Ahab's apostasy, and only touch on the negative consequences of the rapprochement between Tyre and Israel.

Among the consequences of this rapprochement, Phoenician influence spread as far as Judah in the reign of Jehoshaphat. The king of Judah attempted to relaunch maritime trading activities on the Red Sea, but failed to master the necessary naval technology. Israel and Judah then allied for the first time since the start of the schism. This alliance was sealed by the marriage between Jehoram, son of Jehoshaphat, and Athaliah, an Israelite princess, daughter of Ahab and perhaps of Jezebel. In any event, Athaliah lived at the court of Samaria and shared the same Jezebel's interest in the Phoenician cult. She too was therefore much criticized in biblical texts. We know about the tragic fate of the two queens accused of flouting the Israelite religion: Jezebel was put to death with the other members of the Omride dynasty on the accession of King Jehu around 841. As for Athaliah, queen of Judah from 841 to

835, she introduced the cult of Baal into Jerusalem, under the priest-hood of Mattan, certainly a Tyrian. She was assassinated and her temple destroyed by the priest Jehoiada who had Jehoash proclaimed king of Judah in around 835. One of the consequences of these events was probably the break-up of the Tyre–Israel alliance.

In the reign of Ithobaal I, the expansion of the Phoenician city of Tyre continued. According to Flavius Josephus, Ithobaal founded the city of Batroun to the north of Byblos. In fact, it was a refounding, since a city called Batruna already existed in the Amarna period in the fourteenth century. The king of Tyre was also alleged to have founded the colony of Auza in Libya. This founding possibly marked the start of colonization in the Mediterranean, in which Tyre took the leading role towards the end of the ninth century.

Shalmaneser III or the fascination for the West

The new king of Assyria, Shalmaneser III, who came to the throne in 858, was fascinated by what, for him, was the West, meaning the Mediterranean Levant. Throughout the whole of his reign he stubbornly pursued the same goal: the conquest of the coastal states of the Mediterranean, of which the Phoenician cities were part. The wealth revealed by the western campaign of his father, the facility with which he conducted it, and the possibility of wiping out the Aramaean threat definitively reinforced his commitment to this plan. Assyria had become quite wealthy, with its accumulation of spoils of war, and was sufficiently seasoned after so many military campaigns. Full of zeal, Shalmaneser III set off for the Mediterranean in the very first year of his reign.

Up until then, the Assyrian kings did not have any clear geographical awareness: for them, the Mediterranean was a huge sea populated with strange animals, located a long way away "upwards," in the region "where the sun sets." They distinguished the inhabitants living "in the middle of the sea," like those of Arwad, the only ones they had known, and the inhabitants "of the shoreline." Divided between these two categories, the Phoenicians did not appear to them as belonging to a political entity separate from the other western maritime states. Shalmaneser III's reign represents a further step in Assyrian expansion and knowledge of the Mediterranean coast, which had been reached at several points, namely, Alexandretta (Iskenderun in Turkey) close to the Amanus, Arwad, and Tyre. But strangely, no link was made between the different parts of the sea, which were encountered as if being different seas. Their vision remained fragmented: the "great sea of the setting sun in the land of Hatti," the "great sea in the land of Amurru of the setting sun" and the "sea which is close to the land of Tyre." In his annals, there are as many as thirteen different names attributed to the Mediterranean.

His first western campaign in 858 led him to the northern end of this sea, close to the Amanus. He thus repeated his father's achievement of reaching the Mediterranean, receiving tribute from the maritime towns, and felling trees in the Amanus. However, the power of surprise and calculated frightfulness no longer worked; the Phoenician kings were in no way impressed as on this occasion they did not send him any tribute. Like his father, he loved displays of power and piled up pyramids of heads in front of the towns he had devastated. Curiously, these demonstrations of atrocities produced the opposite effect: instead of terrifying the states and inciting them to surrender, it encouraged them to unite against him. His strategy for expansion involved annexing a territory after a lengthy process of harassing the enemy, which, when it could no longer resist the strong and unrelenting pressure exerted against it, had to submit. After three years of increasingly severe harassment, he succeeded in destroying the kingdom of Bit Adini, whose capital Til Barsip became Port Shalmaneser.

In 853, he undertook his second large expedition towards the west and marched on Aleppo. Those who had lost out in the first coalition, together with their immediate neighbors, submitted and paid tribute. However, the rest of the Syro-Palestinian world decided to put up a united front against the invader rallying around the figure of Irhuleni, king of Hamath. The coalition was formed by twelve kings of Hatti and the coastal region who prepared for the confrontation. The three main contingents were supplied by Irhuleni of Hamath (700 chariots, 700 cavalry and 10,000 infantry), Adad-idri of Damascus (1,200 chariots, 700 cavalry and 10,000 infantry), and Ahab of Israel (2,000 chariots and 10,000 infantry). Among the other kings making up the coalition, Mattanbaal I (Matinubaal) of Arwad is the only clearly identified Phoenician king. Identification of other names of Phoenician cities in the list of coalition partners, such as Byblos, Arqa, Siyanu, and Ushnu, obtained only by correcting the text, cannot be validated. The Phoenician cities did not feel very concerned by this coalition as they were not so directly threatened by Assyrian expansion as were the Aramaean states. Only Arwad, which was linked to northern Syria, participated. However, Mattanbaal I only provided two hundred infantry, a disproportionately small number relative to the power of his city and the contingents provided by the other coalition partners: his participation was more symbolic. Shalmaneser III claimed victory at the battle of Qarqar and boasted about having built a dam on the Orontes with the bodies of the enemies killed, a sort of bridge. Yet, this battle was an Assyrian failure, because he was unable to advance further and he brought back with him neither booty nor tribute. Probably to mask this failure, the annals related how, at the end of this campaign, he went for a boat ride, possibly at Arwad.

After having reorganized the army, the king of Assyria returned to the offensive in 849 to achieve his plan of expansion towards the Mediterranean, but again he came up against fierce resistance. There was another attempt in 848 and another failure. In 845, he wanted to finish things off and launched 120,000 men against the allied forces, the biggest army ever raised; but it was totally in vain. In 841, however, he almost succeeded owing to the mistakes made by his adversaries, who had not learned their lesson from past events and rekindled their quarrels and intrigues, both in Damascus and in Israel and Judah. Shalmaneser III decided to attack Hazael, the new king of Damascus, while he was alone. Advancing up the Orontes corridor, he emerged in the north of the Bekaa Plain, where Hazael was waiting for him with his army to prevent him gaining access. He followed him up to Damascus, which he did not manage to take. So, he wreaked havoc everywhere across Hazael's territory, before going through the Wadi Brissa Valley and crossing Lebanon's mountain chain via the Baalirasi range (present-day Reshbaal) where he had his statue erected. Then he descended to the coast and received the tributes from Tyre and Sidon and from Jehu, the king of Israel, as a symbol of submission to Assyria. The king of Tyre in 841 was Balimanzer, probably the same as Balezoros, son of Ithobaal I, who had reigned around 848–830, in the list of Tyrian kings drawn up by Flavius Josephus. Shalmaneser III continued with the ascent of Mount Lebanon before returning to Assyria via the Orontes corridor, with considerable plunder, but without having crushed the kingdom of Damascus.

In 838, he made one final attempt against Damascus, which ended in another failure. On this occasion, he again received the tributes of Tyre, Sidon, and Byblos. The handing over of the tribute from Tyre and Sidon is represented on the bronze gates of Balawat (Imgur-Enlil near Mosul). The king of Tyre then was Mattan I, son of Balezoros, who reigned around 830–821 according to Flavius Josephus. The tribute from the two cities, which still formed a single kingdom, comprised gold, silver, pewter, bronze, wool, lapis lazuli, and carnelian. It was shipped from the island of Tyre to the coastal plain where Shalmaneser III was waiting with his army. The soldiers, mounted on their chariots, indicated that the army was merely passing through and had not established an encampment there. After this final failure against Damascus, the king of Assyria gave up personally leading new operations to the north and west of his empire, and entrusted them to one of his generals. It was the twilight of a reign filled with excesses, and which ended with an admission of failure. He had crossed over the Euphrates more than twenty-five times, but had not succeeded in conquering the West. After his reign, winds of revolt blew through the cities of Assyria.

Adad-nirari III's attempted conquest of the West

Shamshi-Adad V succeeded Shalmaneser III in 823, during the last year of the nobles' revolt in the former provinces, supported by the new postconquest provinces. The king of Assyria was forced to abandon the territories situated to the west of the Euphrates to focus his troops on the heart of his threatened empire. All the western states, including the Phoenician cities, abstained from pledging allegiance to the new king. He put an end to Babylonia's independence and pillaged its towns. Although no campaign towards the west is mentioned in his annals, an amulet found in Byblos guaranteed the protection of a certain Ili-ittiya, governor of Assur and head of Shamshi-Adad V's guard. The presence of the amulet of an Assyrian official in Byblos remains unexplained.

The next king, Adad-nirari III, was greatly influenced by the queen mother Shammuramat, called Semiramis by Herodotus. Taking advantage of Assyria's weakness, Hazael of Damascus, king of Aram, extended his domination, direct or indirect, over Transeuphratene, from the south of Palestine up to the Euphrates, which he might well have crossed. From at least 810, this domination included the Phoenician cities of Tyre, Sidon, Byblos, and Arwad. Nevertheless, they had become allies rather than vassals of the king of Damascus, who took an interest in their territories because they constituted his natural outlet towards the sea. They recognized the hegemony of Hazael within a coalition of thirty-two kings that was not really structured or centralized. This relationship with Damascus is particularly apparent from the offering of diplomatic gifts.

Between 805 and 796, King Adad-nirari III of Assyria undertook a series of campaigns towards the west to bring the western states back under his yoke; they had taken advantage of the Assyrian difficulties to suspend the sending of tribute. In 804, he went to Baali, possibly Baalirasi to the north of the Lebanese chain. In 803, he reached the sea. He subjugated the whole of the territory of Hatti (northern Syria) and Amurru (middle Syria), and received tribute from Tyre and Sidon. All the subjugated kings had to deliver tribute and undertake to renew this act of allegiance in the future. He had his statue erected on the island of Arwad, but makes no mention of tribute. It would have been surprising if Arwad, jealously guarding its independence, allowed the Assyrian king to disembark on their island. The annals refer to what was probably a desired but unrealized feat. On the return journey, Adad-nirari III climbed Mount Lebanon and felled one hundred cedar trees, which he took back to Assyria to use in the building work for his palace and the temples of Nineveh, Nimrud, and Assur. During another campaign, he received the submission and tribute of Mari, king of Damascus, apparently in his palace. It is not known whether Mari is the name of a new Aramaean king or a title of King Bar-Hadad II who succeeded Hazael, as the word means "my master" in Aramaic and could have been misunderstood by the Assyrian scribes. On leaving Damascus, Adad-nirari III returned to the Mediterranean coast, perhaps near Beirut, where the king of Tyre had his tribute brought to him. King Jehoash of Israel brought his tribute himself to the Assyrian king, but not at the same time as the delivery of the tribute from Tyre. The lack of synchronization between the two tributes has been interpreted as the absence of a concerted policy between the kings of Tyre and Israel, but that is only speculation.

Pumiyaton (Pygmalion) occupied the throne of Tyre in the wake of Mattan I, around 821–774 according to Flavius Josephus. This period seemed to favor the reestablishment of Phenico-Israelite relations. At the beginning of the eighth century, Tyre was still the preeminent Phoenician city, reigning over the dual kingdom of Tyre and Sidon, whereas Israel had become an important kingdom in the hinterland of Tyre.

King Jehoash of Israel defeated Amaziah of Judah, plundered Jerusalem, and destroyed part of its fortifications. Judah became the vassal of Israel until almost the end of Jeroboam II's reign. Israel dominated trade in the Red Sea, which eminated from the Philistine Plain and Gaza. It was the new trade route that linked Israel and Tyre with Arabia and the Red Sea. The extent of the reconquest of Transjordan by Jehoash and his successor Jeroboam II is not known with any accuracy, but the kings of Israel controlled at least the southern outlet of the Gulf of Aqaba. Israelite trading interests in the Red Sea appear to have led to a new political and economic alliance between the king of Tyre and Jeroboam II of Israel, sometime during the period 776 to 750.

One event during the reign of Pumiyaton took place at the original founding of Carthage. According to Flavius Josephus, it apparently occurred during the seventh year of his reign, when he was eighteen years old. Although there are no Phoenician sources covering the event, we do have many classical sources, especially the account by Justin who recounts this episode in lavish detail. But it is difficult to distinguish what is legend and what is historical fact. Pumiyaton became king very young, through the will of the people, and his sister Elissa, who was stunningly beautiful, married her maternal uncle Zakerbaal (Acerbas), a priest of Milqart (Heracles), who, for this reason, was the city's second-ranked official. Zakerbaal possessed an abundance of treasures, which he hid through fear of Pumiyaton's greed. But the king of Tyre got wind of the existence of the treasures and had the priest's throat cut—the priest being his uncle and brother-in-law—in order to get his hands on the riches. What can be taken as authentic is the clash between the ruling dynasty and the powerful Milqart clergy, owner of the riches of the temple, and the rivalries between members of the royal family, which were frequent in the Near East.

Elissa, full of hatred towards her brother, secretly prepared to flee, involving top-ranking personalities, enemies of Pumiyaton, in her plan. She allayed her brother's distrust by making him believe that she was going to live with him, bringing with her the treasures of her dead husband. Under cover of night, she managed to get all the Tyrian aristocrats who were hostile to the king to board several ships, along with the treasures and relics of Milqart, the city's protective god. This whole episode has to do with the voluntary political exile of highly placed figures and not with the departure of ordinary Tyrians.

The founding of Carthage

Still according to Justin, the exiles from Tyre first stopped over on the island of Cyprus, very close by. They were warmly welcomed there by the high priest of Jupiter and his family, who decided to join the convoy. Nothing could have been more natural than for the Cypriot clergy (probably from Kition, a colony of Tyre) to support Elissa, the wife of the assassinated priest of Milqart. Elissa also got eighty young women to board her ships, women who had come down to the seashore to indulge in sacred prostitution, according to a Phoenician custom of the cult of Ashtart attested in Kition. Her intention was that they would become the wives of the young exiled Tyrians and populate the town she intended to found. When Pumiyaton discovered the flight of his sister and his Tyrian opponents, he prepared to chase after them, which, given his control of the sea, would have been an easy task. However, he had to abandon his plan under pressure of his mother's prayers and the divine oracles, which threatened him if he intervened against his sister's expedition, as the gods were on her side. While it seems natural that the clergy of Tyre protected the flight of Elissa, the wife of a priest, the oracle reference is less certain as it could have been borrowed from Greek accounts about the founding of colonies.

Having reached the coast of Africa, Elissa sought the friendship of the inhabitants, who saw the arrival of these foreigners as a potential commercial opportunity. Pretending to allow her travel-weary companions time to rest before moving on again, she accepted as much land as could be encompassed by an oxhide. Using a famous piece of trickery, she had the hide cut into fine strips so as to encircle as large an area as possible on the hill of Byrsa, and then rented this space to the inhabitants. Attracted by the hope of gain, people from the neighboring area came to settle there. The elected representatives of the Tunisian town of Utica (which means "ancient" in Semitic) were happy to come and meet up with their Tyrian brothers, offering gifts to Elissa and urging her to found a city. The Africans accepted Elissa's plan and gave her the name of Dido, made famous by the Latin poet Virgil. While digging the foundations of the new city, the Tyrians unearthed an ox's head which, to them, appeared to be a bad omen. They established the city on another site where they discovered a horse's head, more auspicious in their view. The involvement of inhabitants from Utica is plausible as their town was probably Tyre's oldest colony. It would also appear that several attempts were made to find the best location for the city. But the foundation rites, embellished with plays on words, were taken from Greek tradition. The oxhide became the city wall, containing the city in the same way that it had contained the animal.

Attracted by the fame of Carthage, whose name meant "new city" in Phoenician, a lot of Africans came to populate it and help it expand. Iarbas, a Libyan price and neighbor of Carthage, wanted to marry Elissa, threatening to make war otherwise. She would have accepted to save her city, but allegedly threw herself into the flames to remain faithful to the memory of her husband, who had been assassinated in Tyre. She then became the object of a local cult, which is plausible. The marriage proposal is also attested by the Greek historian Timaeus in the fourth century, but the name of the Libyan prince is absent from sources prior to Virgil. The death of Elissa alludes to human sacrifices, a Carthaginian custom according to Greco-Roman tradition, but a very controversial point nowadays. In sum, it is very difficult to unravel the historicity of the story from its legendary aspects.

The date of the foundation of Carthage is still debated, as the textual sources do not totally concur with the archaeological finds on site.

According to ancient authors such as Timaeus, Carthage was founded at the end of the ninth century, around 814, but, the oldest tomb excavated on the site dates from the end of the eighth century. The archaic habitat, comprising houses with hard clay floors, only goes back to the eighth century, with a small quantity of ceramics imported from 760. However, the results of carbon-14 dating point to the period 835–800, which would be in line with the traditional date, but they are yet to be confirmed.

Among the possible explanations for the foundation of Carthage and the phenomenon of Tyrian colonization, dynastic problems in the reign of Pumiyaton probably played a role. The significant rise in Tyre's population and, consequently, the shortage of territorial resources would also have been a reason. In contrast, the growing pressure exerted by Assyrian domination could not have been a determining factor for Tyre before the reigns of Sargon II and Sennacherib, that is, well after the start of Tyrian colonization. At most, we could say that the foundation of colonies helped the Tyrians to better meet the demands of the Assyrian kings with respect to tribute, and thereby to obtain a privileged place within the Assyrian Empire. However, what emerges most clearly from Tyrian colonization is that it was part of a long-term process and the logical continuation of the precolonization phase. Furthermore, it was an enterprise that was part of a carefully planned and organized commercial strategy.

The foundation of Carthage, to which a great deal of importance is attached because of its substantial impact, actually followed other, more ancient, foundations, which are difficult to date. The Phoenician stele of Nora in Sardinia dates from the end of the ninth century. Based on the archaeological finds made in the colonies in the south of Spain, Morro de Mezquitilla would have been founded at the end of the ninth century; Toscanos, Almuñecar (Sexi), and La Fonteta at the beginning of the eighth. Phoenician colonization started in a climate of cooperation and cultural exchange with the Greeks. Then, Phoenician expansion was in competition with the Greek colonization movement. Towards the end of the eighth century, a wave of Phoenician colonization focused on the west coast of Sicily (Motya, Solunto, Palermo), followed by a wave of Greek colonization on its east and south coasts (Syracuse, Agrigento, Gela). Once Carthage was to start founding its own colonies in the western Mediterranean, it can often be difficult to distinguish between Phoenician and Punic colonization.

The Phoenician colonies maintained relations with their mother country, at least at the outset of their foundation. Hence, Kition had to pay a tribute to Tyre. Carthage also paid a tithe to Tyre according to Diodorus and Justin. This tithe could have been conceived as a portion of the profits of Milqart's temple on commercial activities, but probably it was essentially destined for the Tyrian political authority, represented above all by the king. Paid regularly to begin with, this tithe contributed further to the enrichment of the city of Tyre. But, from the middle of the sixth century, with the progressive assertion of Carthage on the political scene of the western Mediterranean, the tithe was to become intermittent and was reduced. Religious relations were also established between the colony and the mother city, with envoys being sent to take part in the major religious festivals. These customs were to last right up until the end of Phoenicia's history.

Troubles in Assyria, respite in Phoenicia

Little is known about the period between 782 and 745 because documentation is scanty. Shalmaneser IV succeeded his father Adad-nirari III on the throne of Assyria. In the first year of his reign, he led an expedition against Urartu, followed by five others. Despite all, he failed to prevent the kingdom of Urartu, initially centered on Lake Van, from becoming the first power in the Near East until 744, and from extending its influence as far as northern Syria. Assyria, in the reign of Shalmaneser IV, still found sufficient energy to hold its enemies at bay. However, this relative success was not due to the king but to his general Shamshi-ilu—most likely to be identified with Bar-Gayah, king of Kittika (Til Barsip). It was in the interest of the Assyrian kings to entrust important functions to local kings who were their dependencies. The drawback was the erosion of royal authority in favor of these prominent figures. In 775, an Assyrian expedition was organized to the "mountain of cedars," but it is not specified whether the destination was Mount Lebanon or the Amanus. In 773, General Shamshi-ilu organized a campaign against Damascus and collected the tribute. Phoenicia and the other western states probably suspended sending tribute as they were no longer in fear of this weakened Assyria.

On the death of Shalmaneser IV, his brother Ashur-dan III succeeded him. The number of expeditions dwindled: three campaigns were organized to the west in 772, 765, and 755 against Hatarika, probably Tell Afis in northern Syria. The Phoenician cities did not feel threatened. Assyria was a country on the defensive, ravaged by outbreaks of plague and internal rebellion. Ashur-nirari V succeeded his brother in these disastrous circumstances. An expedition was conducted westwards against Arpad to try and stem Urartu's advances into northern Syria, but without much success. General Shamshi-ilu probably contributed in limiting Assyria's setbacks, but at the expense of royal authority.

For the Phoenician cities, this initiated a long period of respite as they were not threatened by either Assyria, Egypt, or Urartu, whose westward expansion did not reach as far as their territory. They interacted with the kingdoms of Israel and Judah. But there is a dirth of information about this period, as Flavius Josephus stops his list of kings of Tyre at Pumiyaton. The name of Milkiram, inscribed on a few objects dated around 750, could have been that of a king of Tyre. The Bible does not mention the Phoenicians directly during this period, except for the oracle of Amos, spoken against Tyre two years before a memorable earthquake. Its dating is hard to establish, but the prophet Amos probably witnessed Israel's prosperity under the long reign of Jeroboam II, who denounced the luxury and social injustice of Samaria's ruling classes. At that time, the Tyrians were the principal providers of luxury for Samaria, particularly in cut-stone architecture and ivory decor.

According to the sibylline words of the oracle, the walls and palaces of Tyre were threatened with destruction by fire because the Tyrians had not "retained the memory of the alliance between brothers" and had "delivered deportees en masse to Edom." The alliance in question was probably the one that should have been reestablished between the king of Tyre, Pumiyaton or Milkiram, and Jeroboam II of Israel, on the basis of economic interests between two very prosperous states. The continuation of commercial expeditions from Tyre and Israel towards the Red Sea is attested by the Phoenician and Hebrew inscriptions of Kuntillet Ajrud. The existence of Israelite bazaars in Damascus imply that Israel played an economic role there. However, the fact that King Azaryahu had control of over nineteen districts in the region of Hamath, as well as the neighboring towns on the Mediterranean coast, must have been a concern for the king of Samal, more than for his counterpart the king of Judah, who is unlikely to have had influence in northern Syria. Arwad probably escaped this control as its insular position enabled it to retain its independence, especially as Samal had no naval forces. The oracle against Tyre could date to the end of Amos's ministry, after the disappearance of Jeroboam II, when Assyria resumed its western conquests. Tyre probably dropped its alliance with Israel after the assassination of King Zechariah around 750, which opened up a period of internal and external upheaval. Tyre dissociated itself from Israel while submitting to Assyria and helping it to carry out the deportation of conquered populations towards Edom, which would explain the words of the oracle.

The period of respite between 782 and 745 enabled the Phoenician cities to prosper. Tyre took advantage of this to pursue its colonization enterprises in the western Mediterranean.

2

The Conquest of the West by the Assyrians (745–721)

Tiglath-pileser III's policy of conquest

One might assume that the revolt that broke out in Kalhu in 746 was just another in a country beset by difficulty. However, Tiglath-pileser III took advantage of it to ascend to the throne of Assyria where he was to reign for eighteen years. Did he take office through a coup d'état? He never asserted his origins, except on a brick in Assur, where he called himself the son of Adad-nirari III, and in a royal list, which referred to him as a son of Ashur-nirari V. Whether he was a usurper or not, he was nonetheless an energetic, adventurous, methodical, and reformist king who was to redress Assyria's situation in a most masterful manner. He was no stranger to cruelty, as his bas-reliefs always represent a row of opponents impaled near the conquered towns with severed heads being brought to a eunuch to be counted. But this was the ordinary cruelty of a conqueror keen to impress his enemies and not the style of sadism exhibited by Ashurnasirpal II.

The precise chronology of his military campaigns cannot be guaranteed because there are serious gaps in his annals, but the major phases of his conquests can be identified. His adversary, the king of Urartu, had just won the Syrian states over to his cause and, logically, he should have led his first campaign against him in 745. However, instead, he opted to start with Babylonia, where agitation was endemic. He succeeded in pacifying it, thereby strengthening the position of King Nabu-nasir, who had been threatened by the Aramaean and Chaldean tribes. He deported the defeated populations to Assyria in their thousands. He began to restore Assyrian authority over the adjacent Zagros regions, such as Parsua, the future country of the Persians, and the region of the Medes. In 744, the pacification of these regions was sufficient to allow him to deal with other Assyrian borders.

He devoted the following years to heading off the Urartu threat on his northern border. The power of this kingdom had grown substantially over the previous decades, its influence spreading to the small states of the Taurus region and northern Syria. The Aramaic king Mati-ilu of Arpad broke the oath he had sworn to the earlier Assyrian kings and organized a vast coalition including Urartu and the Aramaic states of northern Syria. The Phoenician cities do not appear to have taken part in this coalition, except perhaps Arwad, which could have been within the sphere of Urartu's influence. In any event, in 743, Tiglath-pileser III won a victory over the king of Urartu, Sarduri II, which helped him to regain the initiative to the west of the Euphrates. In 740, he captured the city of Arpad after a three year-long siege. The news of this capture had significant impact, as the kings of several Near Eastern states immediately pledged their allegiance to the king of Assyria. They sent him their tribute while he was still in the town of Arpad. Those who submitted were the kings of Kummuh, Que (Cilicia), Carchemish, Gurgum, and the king of Tyre, Ithobaal II (Tubail). In fact, the pressing threat from Urartu on the borders of Assyria led Tiglath-pileser III to structure his domination better, moving from the vassal and network system to that of a directly controlled empire.

Making allowances for royal propaganda, three types of measures can be distinguished in the Assyrian annals: conquests resulting from a military campaign, submissions obtained by the physical presence of the Assyrian army but without combat, and acts of allegiance with tribute being sent by states that were not invaded but were under threat. The Phoenician cities fitted into this last category at the start of Tiglath-pileser III's reign. Those in the north, closer to Arpad, such as Arwad and Byblos, had not responded, unlike the distant city of Tyre. This is surprising for Arwad, an important northern Phoenician city, especially if it had taken part in the anti-Assyrian coalition. Byblos did not respond either, but this is more understandable for a city that was gradually disappearing from the region's political scene. As for Sidon, it is completely absent from the Assyrian annals of this period as it was still integrated in the dual kingdom of Tyre and Sidon, then governed by the king of Tyre, Ithobaal II.

Did the Phoenician cities figure among Tiglath-pileser III's objectives in his conquest of the West? The position of Phoenicia at a major crossroads, controlling the Homs Gap to the north—the main route for communication heading inland—and the Akko depression towards the Jordan Valley in the south, fostered its commercial activities while at the same time making it a strategically attractive region. In the event of a confrontation between Assyria and Egypt for control of the Near East, Assyria would need the Phoenician fleets. In addition, a landlocked empire like the Assyrian Empire needed outlets towards the sea. Yet, the political line adopted by Tiglath-pileser III did not exactly follow these considerations, which to us seem logical. He preferred to start by focusing on the interior states such as Arpad, Hamath, and Damascus, in order to break Assyria's isolation, and to control the caravan trade routes and access to the metallic mineral and forest wealth from the Amanus to the Taurus. As regards the Mediterranean coast, he was only really interested in the southern part, where the Philistine cities provided access to Egypt.

Domination over the north of Phoenicia

The capture of Arpad in 740 did not pacify the Aramaic states, which persisted with their revolt. In 738, Tiglath-pileser III gained a further victory in northern Syria. He annexed the kingdom of Unqi and captured several towns in the kingdom of Hamath, some of which were on the coast: Gabala (Jeble), Ushnu (Tell Daruk), and Siyanu to the east of Jeble; Simyra, Arqa, and Kashpuna (Kusba) to the south of Tripoli. However, the trading post of Al-Mina, at the mouth of the Orontes, which developed from the eighth century onwards, was not one of the conquered towns, no more than Tell Sukas, to the south of Jeble, which was focused on maritime trade. The king of Assyria also captured some coastal towns close to Hamath, which had been taken by Azaryahu of Samal. He installed six Assyrian officials in the coastal towns who were responsible for military, political, tax, and customs control.

Part of the Syrian coast, from Jebel al-Aqra up to the piedmont of Mount Lebanon and to its hinterland, was therefore incorporated into the Assyrian Empire. It was the first time that Phoenician towns came directly under Assyrian domination. Yet, the submission of the coastal towns from Gabala to Kashpuna was not Tiglath-pileser III's objective, but an indirect consequence of the submission of the hinterland. The limited space given over to Phoenicia in his annals is a clear indication of the minimal importance he attached to it.

The campaign of 738 marked a major turning point for northern Syria with the creation of a large Assyrian province following a harsh suppression. The Phoenician city of Simyra disappeared definitively as an independent city and became the capital of the new province. Tiglath-pileser III named one of his eunuchs governor of the province. The change in Simyra's status left no visible traces in the site's archaeology.

Compared to the Late Bronze Age when it was a wealthy and powerful fortified city, in the first millennium it kept the same architectural and artisanal traditions. The transformation into an Assyrian provincial capital did not prevent its commercial activities from carrying on without any significant change. Only luxury goods had virtually disappeared. Tiglath-pileser III banked on the province of Simyra's strategic importance to control the Phoenician cities of Byblos, Sidon, and Tyre, as well as eastern Mediterranean trade around the hub of Cyprus.

He deported the populations of northern Syria in their thousands to other regions of Assyria, settling in their place in the new province populations conquered during his earlier campaigns. The enforced displacement of defeated populations was general practice in the Near East, as much so in Egypt, the Hittite Empire, and Urartu. Tiglath-pileser III initiated cross-deportations: in other words, one region partially emptied of its population was repopulated with deportees from a far-off region. In these massive deportation exercises, whole families were displaced, sometimes with their livestock and even their furniture. The travelling conditions were very harsh with the rate of mortality between 5 and 20 percent among the groups of deportees. Once they reached their destination they were reinstalled, as the aim of these operations was not simply to break down any impulse to revolt, but also to obtain a labor force to enhance the value of land so far unexploited, and to participate in the massive royal construction works. Deportees who had specialized skills, such as scribes, stonemasons, and craftsmen, were in demand and sometimes attained high status in their new place of residence. The huge intermixing of populations accelerated the dissemination of Aramaic as the common language. Based on the figures obtained from Assyrian texts, 32,000 people were deported in the reign of Shamshi-Adad V, and at least 593,958 in that of Tiglath-pileser III. The ambition of the latter was to integrate the conquered peoples by allowing the displaced communities to retain their identity.

The deportees took part in his major construction works. He had the temples of Assur and Arslan-Tash built and restored. In Kalhu he had three palaces built for himself in the Syrian style, but more resplendent than any foreign palace, calling them the "palace of happiness," the "palace of abundance and blessing," and the "palace of eternity." His bedroom sparkled with precious stones. For all these works, he called on the know-how of craftsmen from northern Syria, particularly the Phoenicians. He used all sorts of species of wood: cypress, juniper, and especially cedar and pine, which were attractive to the eye and fragrant. These woods came from the Amanus and from Mount Lebanon, which bordered on the new Assyrian province. He also exploited the Anti-Lebanon, which he referred to as the "boxwood mountain." Unlike other Assyrian kings, Tiglath-pileser III did not boast about having felled trees himself on Mount Lebanon or of having brought them back to Assyria. He used the trees that the kings of subjugated states sent him as tribute. Without neglecting his royal propaganda, he was pragmatic and preferred to continue to consolidate his conquests rather than waste time climbing Mount Lebanon, which would not have produced any concrete benefit.

The first revolts of Arwad and Tyre

There is some uncertainty about Arwad's revolt against Tiglath-pileser III because the inscription describing his repression is broken where the names of the city and its king would have appeared. Yet, the context does seem to indicate that Arwad and Mattanbaal II, mentioned a few lines further on, were involved. The king of Assyria first attacked one of Mattanbaal II's mainland towns, possibly Amrit (Marathos). He massacred its inhabitants, then ravaged and destroyed the town. He did similarly in the city of Arwad, which was located in the "middle of the sea." Consequently, the king of Arwad was terror stricken. He carried a bag, a symbol of mourning and penitence, a traditional custom for Phoenicians and Assyrians alike. His life was spared, but he submitted to the king of Assyria and offered him a rich tribute that included ivory, ebony, precious stones, top-quality oil, a variety of spices, and some Egyptian horses. Following this, Tiglath-pileser III placed the whole of the coast, from Arwad to Kashpuna, under the control of his eunuch, the governor of Simyra. Even though the mainland territory of Arwad was now subjugated and its king in submission, it is difficult to believe that the king of Assyria had managed to assemble a war fleet capable of defeating Arwad's own powerful fleet and that he had landed on the island. He would have bragged about this naval victory if it had happened. In this campaign, Mattanbaal II of Arwad probably did lose his mainland territory, which was annexed to the Assyrian province, and he lost no time in submitting to the king of Assyria in order to retain the autonomy of his island. From this point, he was dependent on the provincial authorities to provide subsistence for the population of Arwad living on the island. This was the price he paid to remain free on his island to carry on with his maritime commercial activities as he saw fit.

This episode did not occur in 738, at the time of northern Phoenicia's annexation to the Assyrian Empire, as it was not mentioned in the account of that campaign. Mattanbaal II of Arwad had initially stood up to the Assyrian conqueror as he had not sent tribute, unlike his counterpart the king of Tyre. He was therefore considered to be in revolt against Assyrian authority. The whole coastal area between Gabala and Kashpuna was subjugated, except for the territory of Arwad. Tiglath-pileser III did not want to give up in failure and his campaign against the king of Arwad probably took place around 734. His annals mention a tribute paid by Mattanbaal II of Arwad, possibly around 732, at the same time as that of King Hiram II of Tyre and King Shipitbaal II of Byblos.

Shipitbaal II started paying tribute around 737, then again around 732. Gubal was annexed to the Assyrian province of Simyra in 738. Although Byblos and Gabala are written Gubla in Akkadian, these two cities cannot be mixed up due to the context of events. It was Gabala that was annexed, while Byblos does not appear to have been troubled at any time by Tiglath-pileser III's army. Nor does anything indicate that the city fell under the influence of the dual kingdom of Tyre and Sidon. In this period, it appears to have been a small, calm city, meekly subject to the king of Assyria and paying its tribute without argument. Prudently, it stayed well away from the anti-Assyrian revolts of Arwad, Tyre, and other Near Eastern states.

The suppression of the Tyre revolt did not occur at the same time as that of Arwad; it happened during the second phase of the Assyrian conquest, further south, around 733 or 732. Having dealt with the Medes and Urartu, which he failed to subjugate, Tiglath-pileser III started his second phase of conquests, which were directed against Damascus and Palestine where there was a succession of revolts. The king of Israel, Pekah, set up a new anti-Assyrian coalition with the king of Damascus, Rahianu (Rezin in the Bible). The king of Judah, Jotham, then his successor Ahaz, refused to join in. The conspirators, supported by the Philistine towns and the Edomites, decided to lay siege to Jerusalem in order to replace Ahaz by an anti-Assyrian king. Ahaz called on the king of Assyria for help, proclaiming himself his vassal. Tiglath-pileser III interpreted this call for help as pretext to intervene, his main objective being to beat the coalition and to start cashing in on tributes again. In Tyre, King Hiram II, who reigned around 739–730, was the successor of Ithobaal II, who paid tribute in 740. Hiram II paid tribute around 737, and again around 732. He joined the anti-Assyrian coalition alongside King Rezin of Damascus. He possibly broke his alliance with Pekah of Israel from 734, for which the prophet Amos reproached him. In any event, the era of close relations between the kings of Tyre and Israel was over.

Before confronting Damascus, which had always been the center of anti-Assyrian coalitions, Tiglath-pileser III wanted to cut King Rezin off from any possible sources of help from the rear. First he attacked his coastal allies and captured Gaza whose king, Hanun, fled to Egypt before returning and submitting to Assyria. It was in the reign of Hanun that the Phoenician trading post of Tell er-Reqeish, located 15 kilometers southwest of Gaza, was founded. The king of Assyria then made a show of force on the Egyptian border to dissuade the pharaoh from getting involved. In reality, Osorkon IV, based in the eastern Delta, was powerless in the face of the rise of Sais and its chief, Tefnakht. Egypt was plagued by so much internal discord between rival powers that it was incapable of putting up any opposition to Assyrian expansion. Going via the coast, en route the king of Assyria suppressed the revolt of Hiram II of Tyre. He captured several towns in his mainland territory, particularly his stronghold of Mahallib (Khirbet el-Mahallib), 6 kilometers northeast of Tyre. He "blanketed the plain with a carpet of warriors' corpses, like grass," and took possession of property and cattle.

Hiram II came to make his submission to the king of Assyria on the coast, kissing his feet and paying him a rich tribute of 20 talents of gold (equal to some 720 kilograms), multicolor trimmed linen clothes, Egyptian horses, eunuchs, and male and female singers. Tiglath-pileser III accepted his apologies, pardoned him for his revolt, and spared his territory, but nevertheless took Tyrians back to Assyria as prisoners or hostages. In fact, he did not take the island of Tyre because he was unable to withstand its powerful fleet. Nor did he want to destroy a prosperous city that traded with the whole of the Mediterranean and received tithes from its many colonies, as he could benefit from this situation in the form of booty and tribute. The existence of a Tyrian colony on Cyprus, the crossroad of Tyrian trade in the Mediterranean, in the reign of Hiram II, is attested by two votive inscriptions on copper bowls discovered in the region of Limassol. They were dedicated to Baal of Lebanon by the governor of Qarthadasht (the "new town"), minister of Hiram, king of the Sidonians. Hiram II still reigned over the dual kingdom of Tyre and Sidon, and the Cypriot "new town" could have been Kition or Limassol.

In 733 or 732, Damascus was taken by the Assyrian army, its kingdom annexed, and its inhabitants deported. King Pekah of Israel was less cautious than Hiram II of Tyre, as he refused to submit. The kingdom of Israel lost its territories in the north (Megiddo), the east (Gilead), and the west (Dor), all of which became Assyrian provinces. Pekah's failure prompted internal opposition: he was assassinated and replaced by Hoshea. The kings of the conquered states were subjected to heavy tributes. Hiram II of Tyre was replaced by Mattan II who, in around 729, paid an even heavier tribute than his predecessor: 150 talents of gold instead of 20 (approximately 5.4 tons), and in addition, 2,000 talents of silver (approximately 74 tons). An incident occurred when Mattan II succeeded Hiram II, possibly a coup d'état, which was punished with a huge increase in tribute owed. The Assyrian chief eunuch came to Tyre in person in order to collect the payment.

Hence, Arwad and Tyre paid a heavy price for their first revolts against Assyria. Their mainland territory was occupied and they had to pay a substantial tribute to be able to retain access to resources provided by the coastal region for feeding their island-based populations. They did however benefit from the self-serving liberalism of Tiglath-pileser III, who refrained from destroying their commercial enterprises, which he took advantage of.

Control over the Phoenician timber trade

The letters written by the senior official to the king of Assyria provided edifying insight into the relations between Phoenicia and Assyria. Qurdi-Assur-lamur may have been governor of the province of Simyra, but was certainly responsible for giving precise and ongoing information to the king of Assyria about everything that was going on in the Phoenician cities, from Kashpuna to Tyre. He appears to have been based in Ushu, a mainland town of Tyre opposite the island, when he wrote "in the palace of Tyre, that of the town of Ushu, all is well." He did not intervene in what happened in the main palace, located on the island of Tyre, which retained its autonomy, but the king was under very close surveillance nonetheless.

Tiglath-pileser III was keen to develop private commercial activities in the Assyrian "trading posts" that he had created by levying a tax on goods passing through by means of his own tax collectors established locally. Qurdi-Assur-lamur had to set up and control any new organization. He gives a very lively glimpse of activities in the harbor of Tyre: "All the quays are occupied by Tyrians. They enter and exit the warehouses, they hand over and receive goods. They freely come and go to Mount Lebanon, which is just behind Tyre, and they have the timber brought down to here. I levy a tax on those who bring down the wood." The timber was probably forwarded by floating it down the often torrential rivers that descended from the mountains. The Nahr Litani to the north of Tyre, which was permanent, was the most practical. For Sidon, two rivers were permanent, the Nahr Zaharani and the Nahr al-Awali. Other rivers that dried up in the summer, such as the Nahr Abou Assouad and the Nahr Sainik, could be used during the spring high waters. In any event, the exploitation of the forests of Tyre and Sidon had been a well-honed operation since the second millennium and the Assyrian governor did not get involved in the technical operations. On the other hand, he sent tax collectors to the Assyrian trading posts on Mount Lebanon, probably at the tree trunk departure point. The Tyrians balked at having to pay taxes on forestry activity in their own territory, and consequently attacked and killed the tax collectors. To settle the situation, the Assyrian governor sent the Sidon warehouse tax collector, but he too was attacked. However, this likely outcome had been planned for: to be able to intervene rapidly and restore order, the governor had a contingent of Itueans—a sort of foreign legion—at his disposal. When they showed up, the rebels fled and the Sidon tax collector returned to tax the Sidonians.

After having restored the situation, Qurdi-Assur-lamur harangued the Tyrians and the Sidonians: "Get that wood down here and do it however you like, but selling it to Egyptians and Philistines is forbidden. Otherwise, I shall deprive you of your freedom and you will no longer be able to climb up the mountain." In this way, the Assyrians' intention was to benefit from a preferential trading relationship by banning Tyrian and Sidonian trade with Egypt, which could, as always, continue to source its requirements from Byblos, and with Philistia, which was not yet one of the conquered territories. This prohibition clause imposed by Tiglath-pileser III was to be lifted by his successors.

The Assyrian governor was charged with various missions, collecting the tribute on the Sidonians, for example. He had to deal with a flight of slaves and an irrigation dispute between Tyre and Sidon concerning a canal aimed to serve the temples of Sidon, which seemed to have been diverted towards Tyre. He prevented King Hiram II from transporting to Tyre a cult object taken from a temple on the Sidon mountain. He also had the Kashpuna fortress cleaned and its ramparts repaired. He organized a contingent of soldiers to ensure the defense of this stronghold, located to the south of Tripoli, as well as the domestic staff, and he was responsible for installing the supply of drinking water.

The new organization of the Assyrian Empire

To understand the new organization of the Assyrian Empire, the change in perception of the Mediterranean in Tiglath-pileser III's annals is instructive. His expeditions to the west and the annexation of western states enabled real progress to be made in terms of knowledge of the Mediterranean: during this reign the Assyrians acquired a comprehensive concept of this sea. The real establishment of the Assyrian Empire's western border on the Mediterranean coast represented one of the most important outcomes of the new annexation policy: the Assyrian Empire, up to this point being wholly mainland, also became a maritime empire. Tiglath-pileser III was aware of this fundamental change because he added to his title a new expression that defined his empire as stretching from the "sea of the setting sun" to the "sea of the rising sun," implying having a dual maritime façade on the Mediterranean and the Persian Gulf.

From the Phoenician point of view, the reign of Tiglath-pileser III represented a genuine historical "break." It marked the end of the period of respite between the sporadic Assyrian raids and the transition to a status of relative autonomy for the majority of the cities, with some of them having to endure total subjugation. From the Assyrian standpoint as well, all the foundations for the new imperial tributary system had been laid: ideological justification of the system, creation of a highly structured state with mainland and maritime ambitions, a permanent policy of conquest, generalization of the tributary system, implementation of administrative coverage throughout the whole empire, and development of communications. The payment of tribute to the Assyrian kings by the western states, although sometimes characterized as "annual" obligations in the texts, appears to have been irregular. However, the amount of the tribute increased substantially from the end of the ninth century.

In 729, Babylonia also came under the control of Tiglath-pileser III. However, he did not make the mistake of reducing the region, the root of all religious traditions, to the simple status of an Assyrian province. In 728, he cleverly had himself crowned king in Babylonia under the name of Pulu. When he disappeared in 727, all the regions of the "Fertile Crescent" were unified under the unprecedented label of a dual Assyro-Babylonian kingship. Admittedly, a lot still had to be done to overcome pockets of local resistance and to consolidate and optimize the system. This fundamental task was to be left to the Assyrian Sargonid dynasty.

The obscure reign of Shalmaneser V

Tiglath-pileser III ensured the stability of his government despite his multiple military campaigns. He introduced the regency of his son, crown prince Shalmaneser V, a custom that would be maintained by his successors. Shalmaneser V ascended to the throne in 724 for a short reign of four years, about which we have scarce information because he left practically no inscriptions. He probably died before his scribes had had time to write up his annals. As we know virtually nothing about this king, there is a tendency to attribute events to him without proof, such as an alleged siege of Tyre. In the powerful and vast empire that Tiglath-pileser III left him, not all moves towards independence were discouraged, and he had to undertake several military expeditions about which we know nothing. According to one letter, he sent emissaries to collect tribute in the western regions conquered by his father, from northern Syria to Ashdod and Moab. There is no mention of the Phoenician cities, but they probably continued to pay tribute.

In 725, 724, and 723, he campaigned against Samaria, which he devastated. Hoshea, king of Israel, was in fact pursuing a policy hostile to Assyria by refusing to pay tribute, which provided the main reason for the Assyrian intervention. In addition, he made contact with the pharaoh So, according to the Bible. As Egypt was still divided between several rival powers, it is hard to identify this pharaoh, who could have been Osorkon IV, king of Tanis. Under Shalmaneser V, Bit-Adini was ravaged, the kingdom of Samal was destroyed and reduced to the status of an Assyrian province. In 722, Shalmaneser V restored the temple of Nabu. Like his father, he had himself crowned king of Babylon under the name of Ululaiu. So, he appeared to continue the work of Tiglath-pileser III, namely, consolidating the empire through military campaigns, the collecting of tribute, and building works.

3

Domination of Phoenicia by the Sargonids (721–610)

The western policy of Sargon II

The designation "Sargonids" refers to the dynasty of Sargon II and his successors. However, there might not have been a change of dynasty, as Sargon II could have been a son of Tiglath-pileser III. Be that as it may, after the death of Shalmaneser V, at the end of winter 722, he seized power illegitimately, as he was probably not his natural successor. He had to overcome strong internal opposition which he stamped out by deporting 6,300 Assyrians, described as criminals, to Hamath. It took him more than a year to consolidate his authority on the throne of Assur. As Sargon II was a proud warrior, it was hard for him to admit that he had not conducted a military expedition during his first year on the throne. He therefore rigged the dating system of his annals slightly, making the first year of his reign start in 720 instead of 721.

The account of his annals started with the capture of Samaria, which refused to submit and pay tribute. He brought back 27,280 inhabitants of the town in captivity and recovered 200 chariots. He settled other prisoners of war in Samaria, appointed a governor in the capital of this new Assyrian province, and imposed tribute and tax. The conquest of Samaria, which Sargon II took credit for, was instead perhaps the work of his predecessor Shalmaneser V, who had laid siege to the town for three years. Either way, it was definitely he who dealt with the organization of the new province. The fall of Samaria marked the end of the kingdom of Israel.

The difficulties encountered by Sargon II at the beginning of his reign represented, for all the subjugated peoples, an opportunity to free themselves from Assyrian rule. King Yaubidi of Hamath was the instigator of a massive rebellion of the western regions of the Assyrian Empire, from Syria to Palestine. In Babylonia, the Chaldean Merodach-Baladan II seized the throne, thanks to the support of the king of Elam Humban-Nikash I. In 720, Sargon II led his first campaign against the fortified Babylonian town of Der, which was defended by the Elamites. He claimed he had secured a victory but actually suffered a bitter failure. He was forced to conclude a treaty with the king of Babylon, which was to be observed for ten years or so. After having temporarily resolved his problem with Babylonia, in the same year he turned against the Syro-Palestinian coalition. This coalition, led by Hamath, included the towns of Arpad, Simyra, Damascus, and Samaria in particular. Although transformed into Assyrian provinces, Simyra and Samaria still rebelled. Sargon II crushed the coalition at Qarqar in northern Syria, just as his ancestor Shalmaneser III had done. He exploited his advantage further and went down as far as Philistia. A reversal of alliances had taken place: the Egyptians paired up with the Philistines, their ancient ene-mies, again in order to confront jointly the Assyrian threat, which was getting close to Egypt. King Hanun of Gaza rose up against Assyria with the help of an Egyptian expeditionary force. However, Gaza and Raphia were devastated, their inhabitants deported to Assyria and Hanun was taken prisoner.

Once the western front had provisionally been stabilized, Sargon II devoted most of his campaigns to the other fronts of the Assyrian Empire. During his absences, he entrusted the government to his son Sennacherib. Assyria's main rivals in the north and northeast were the king of Urartu and Midas, the king of Phrygia, who occasionally allied. In 714, Sargon II succeeded in overcoming Urartu definitively, and in re-establishing his authority over the land of the Medes and Parsua. Midas became a tributary of Assyria only in 709. In the west, in 717, the king-dom of Carchemish was turned into an Assyrian province. In 716, the king of Assyria subjugated several Arab tribes and forced Egypt to trade with him: the pharaoh brought him twelve exceptional Egyptian horses as a gift. In 715, for the first time, he confronted Ionians who had come from Cyprus, and transformed Que (Cilicia) into an Assyrian province. In 712, he suppressed the revolt of Iamani of Ashdod who refused to pay tribute. Iamani fled to Egypt, thinking it was his ally. However, the pharaoh, probably Shabaka, extradited the king of Ashdod because he did not want to risk a clash with Sargon II. He may even have gone as far as concluding an agreement with Assyria, which was to give him some fifteen years of respite.

With the exception of Simyra, the Phoenician cities were not men-tioned in the Assyrian texts before 706, probably because they posed no particular problem. The Phoenician kings had to be included among the "kings of the seashore," tributaries of Sargon II, who made no distinction between the Phoenicians and the other coastal peoples.

Sargon II's expedition to Cyprus

Apart from Arwad and Tyre, close to the coast, the Assyrian kings were not acquainted with the inhabitants of the islands. Cyprus (Iadnana), the island rich in copper, was divided into ten or so kingdoms, some of which were Phoenician, like Kition and Lapethos. The Assyrian annals mentioned seven kings living in Ia, a district of Cyprus, "which is seven days' distant in the middle of the sea of the setting sun," and which none of Sargon II's ancestors had ever heard of. The king of Assyria had always been stimulated by the desire to do better than his predecessors. Despite being isolated in the middle of the sea, the Cypriot kings had caught wind of the exploits accomplished by Sargon II in Babylonia and Syria-Palestine. They had also heard about the defeat of their compatriots, the Ionians from Cyprus, who had settled in Cilicia. Terrified, they decided to pledge their allegiance. They boarded their ships and took their tributes to the king of Assyria in Babylon themselves: gold, silver, objects made of maple wood and boxwood, "their natural riches," not forgetting to kiss his feet. This journey took place when Sargon II was in Babylon, hence in 710 or 709. In response to a call from the clergy of the god Marduk, he triggered an offensive against Babylonia. He prevented the Elamite allies of King Merodach-Baladan II from coming to his aid and forced him to flee. So, at the beginning of year 709, he was crowned king in Babylon and celebrated the new year religious festival lasting twelve days. It could have been at this juncture that the Cypriot kings came to make their allegiance to him.

Despite some gaps in the annals, an Assyrian expedition to Cyprus appears to have been organized after the submission of the Cypriot kings. Sargon II possibly led the expedition himself after he left Babylon at the end of 709 or in 708. He was very tempted, in fact, to campaign that far westwards, to go into the middle of the sea and extend the western border of his empire as far as Cyprus. For the first time, the fleets of subjugated countries were used, either a Phoenician fleet, or a fleet from recently conquered Cilicia.

The expedition is confirmed by the discovery of a stele of Sargon II, made out of local basalt, in a sanctuary in Kition, the colony of Tyre. The stele had initially been placed on a hill, as indicated in the text, before being taken to Kition. It was customary for Assyrian kings to have steles erected during their campaigns, in the major countries they subjugated.

They usually chose locations that were clearly visible to all, and thus symbolic locations. Sargon II was represented on the stele in his official costume, with the royal scepter in his left hand and, in his right hand, a libation cup facing towards images of the Assyrian and Babylonian gods. The inscription was engraved underneath the images of the gods. The stele had an advertising function, delivering an ideological message by describing the submission of the Cypriot kings and Sargon II's other notable conquests. Even though the Akkadian script was unknown on Cyprus, the royal image was there to assert Assyrian presence clearly. The Assyrian kings already knew how to communicate through images, by unrolling a whole sequence of cartoon-style pictures to narrate their exploits in the bas-reliefs decorating their palaces. Steles had symbolic value as "ownership charters" and the one on Cyprus marked the western border of the empire. One wonders who sculpted this stele, which was in pure Assyrian style. The Assyrian kings probably took their own sculptors with them on their military campaigns.

If Sargon II had won a battle on Cyprus, this victory would have been mentioned on the stele, but this is not the case. According to the annals, the Cyprus expedition was organized because a king or a Cypriot city, possibly Kition, refused to pay tribute and deserved to be punished. The Cyprus expedition was therefore justified because of the economic stakes. Sargon II's policy in relation to the Phoenician cities was primarily aimed at using their networks of trade relations in the eastern Mediterranean to his own advantage, hence at controlling them as much as possible. The Phoenician and Cypriot cities were specifically at the center of the timber trade: precious woods for constructing palaces and temples, and softwood lumber for shipbuilding.

Beginning in 717, Sargon II had a new capital built for himself in Khorsabad, which he inaugurated in 706. The bas-reliefs of his new palace depicted, in simplified form, the complex process of the timber trade in a prominent location because he considered it to be one of his most glorious successes. The overland transportation of tree trunks from the forests on Mount Lebanon or from the mountains of Cyprus was represented, then their shipment by sea all the way to Assyria. It was the subjugated peoples, experts in timber exploitation and transportation, who were mobilized, meaning the Phoenicians and the Cypriots. First, the timber arrived from the mountain at a fortified city on a rocky island, which could have been Tyre. Then it was transported to a second fortified city on a flat island, which must have been Arwad because it bears the symbol of its fishtail, bearded god. The timber was then taken to a third city at the mouth of the Orontes, possibly Al-Mina.

Khorsabad relief depicting Phoenician ships transporting trees. From the palace of Sargon II at Khorsabad, north facade, Court of Honor. Musée du Louvre, inv. AO 19889. Image and original data provided by Erich Lessing Culture and Fine Arts Archives/ART RESOURCE, N.Y.

It was then forwarded on the Orontes, then on the Euphrates, finally reaching Assyria. The harbor of Kition was also another possible shipping point for timber destined for Assyria, then transiting via Tyre. After Tiglath-pileser III had placed Tyre and logging operations on Mount Lebanon under strict surveillance by installing Qurdi-Assur-lamur in Ushu, Sargon II also wanted to control the disobedient Tyrian colony of Kition, and to subject it to tribute. However, he had no adequate means of controlling this far-off island, nor the possibility of collecting tribute on a regular basis.

The policy of Sargon II towards the Phoenician cities and the Cypriot cities shows that his hold was progressive and gradual, because he was capable of being both opportunistic and pragmatic. The Assyrian Empire was strengthened by the annexation of territories and the imposition of tributes, but also by the political propaganda transmitted via the symbolism of monumental inscriptions, and by keeping a grip on trade benefits through control of the sea routes.

The blockade of Tyre by Sargon II

The annals of Sargon II, recounting the latter years of his reign, have not come down to us. However, a late text in four copies, dated 706, briefly mentioned his subjugation of Tyre. As the king of Assyria was, contrary to his usual practice, so discreet in referring to this victory, its credibility can be questioned. He probably did clash with the Tyrians, but he certainly did not emerge victorious: it was a victory he wanted, but one he failed to obtain. A text written by Flavius Josephus throws some light on the event. He says his account is based on the work of the early second-century Greek author Menander of Ephesus, who in turn could have gone back indirectly to the Tyrian annals of the eighth century. Errors have slipped into the account through these successive transmissions and have led specialists to attribute this siege to different Assyrian kings. The first piece of information ties in with other sources: the king of Tyre at that time was Luli (Elulaios), who reigned for thirty-six years, more likely thirty-three in reality, between 728 and 695 roughly. He probably succeeded Mattan II who paid a very heavy tribute to Tiglath-pileser III in 729. The reading of the name of a new king of Tyre, named Shilta, in an incomplete text about Sargon II's expedition to Cyprus is not plausible.

According to Flavius Josephus, King Luli of Tyre went to suppress the revolt of his colony of Kition. The king of Assyria subjugated all the Phoenician cities, signed a peace treaty with them and returned to Assyria. Several towns, including Sidon, Ushu, and perhaps Akko, revolted against Tyre and pledged allegiance to the king of Assyria. The Tyrians refused to follow suit and the king of Assyria came back to attack Tyre, with sixty ships manned by eight hundred oarsmen, which had been provided to him by the other Phoenicians. The Tyrians confronted them with a mere twelve ships, dispersed them and took five hundred prisoners. Tyre had won the battle, but the king of Assyria, before leaving, placed guards on the river and on the aqueducts to prevent the Tyrians from having access to drinking water. The siege, or rather the blockade, of Tyre, lasted five years, during which the Tyrians resisted. The name of the Assyrian king involved is written in several different ways: Selampsas, Salmanasses, Elampsas. Even if there is a slight resemblance with Shalmaneser, this means nothing, because the Akkadian name of the king had first been translated into Phoenician, then into Greek by several successive authors.

The revolt of the Tyrian colony of Kition was understandable after the expedition of Sargon II, who quelled it. The intention was undoubtedly to free itself of Tyre's tutelage and of the tithe it had to pay, on top of the Assyrian tribute. The prime victim of Sargon II's Cypriot expedition was Tyre because it could not do without its colony of Kition, which was the center of its maritime trading activities and its essential stopover point for journeys towards its colonies in the western Mediterranean. King Luli had no choice but to retake Kition, but Sargon II could not accept that. The other towns integrated in the dual kingdom of Tyre and Sidon took advantage of Luli's difficulties to revolt, in turn, against him, starting with Sidon, which wanted to regain its autonomy. If they gave their allegiance to the king of Assyria, it was also because they did not want to endure the same difficulties as the rebel city of Tyre.

After his expedition to Cyprus, Sargon II had a fleet at his disposal again. If the figures given by Flavius Josephus are accurate, the ships provided by the other Phoenicians must have been supplemented by Cypriot or Cilician ships to be able to reach the total of sixty, whereas Tyre only had twelve. Tyre's naval victory is surprising given its numerical inferiority. As we cannot vouch for the reality of the figures, we can merely note that Sargon II did not succeed in beating Luli's fleet or in capturing the island town of Tyre. He therefore organized his blockade to cut off the water supply, just as king Zimredda of Sidon had done much earlier, in the fourteenth century. If, as Flavius Josephus writes, the blockade of Tyre really did last five years, it could have been taken place between 709 and 705.

The Tyrians managed to cope by digging wells in order to reach the water table and by using tanks. Nevertheless, the accumulation of difficulties probably began to undermine the power and prosperity of Tyre. During the period of the blockade, the dual kingdom of Tyre and Sidon no longer existed in its entirety. As luck would have it for Luli, the brutal disappearance of Sargon II freed him from the blockade and allowed him to recover at least some of his dissenting towns, Sidon, for example. Yet, the Assyrian administration did not disappear from Ushu and the timber trade continued to be controlled and taxed.

The subjugation of Tyre by Sennacherib

While he was not the eldest son, Sennacherib held the office of crown prince from the accession of his father Sargon II, so for sixteen years. It is therefore not surprising that he knew all the dossiers well. He ascended to the throne in 704. He was of a vindictive character, was easily influenced, and was subject to the intrigues of his harem, particularly from Zakutu, one of his wives, who was to have a profound impact on Assyrian politics. In 704, Merodach-Baladan II retook the throne of Babylonia with the support of the Elamites. He tried to set up a broad coalition, sending an ambassador to King Hezekiah of Judah, who was also keen to rid himself of Assyrian tutelage. Sennacherib's first two campaigns, in 703 and 702, were devoted to restoring order in Babylonia. He forced Merodach-Baladan II to flee, replacing him with Bel-ibni, a Babylonian prince brought up in the court of Assyria.

In 701, Sennacherib conducted his third campaign, this time going westwards. It took place in three phases: against Tyre to begin with, then against Philistia and Egypt, and lastly against Judah. The texts do not give the reasons for the expedition against Tyre, whereas they do reveal those behind the intervention against all the other adversaries. The other Phoenician cities were not targeted, as their kings had been paying their annual tribute to the king of Assyria since 704: Abdileti of Arwad, Urimilk I of Byblos, and Menahem of Samsimuruna, who came to kiss his feet. Samsimuruna ("setting sun") was a Phoenician town, possibly Baalbek as the Greeks called it Heliopolis, "city of the sun." A sounding carried out underneath the large courtyard of the Roman sanctuary of Jupiter revealed houses and tombs dating back to the end of the third millennium. Sennacherib's attack against Tyre was immediate, direct, and devastating: "Luli, king of Sidon, when the terrifying splendor of my sovereignty hit him, fled." (His title "king of Sidon" indicates that the dual kingdom had briefly been reestablished after the lifting of Sargon II's blockade of Tyre.)

Luli may have taken part in the anti-Assyrian coalition led by Hezekiah of Judah, both of them steered by shared interests, namely, freeing themselves from Assyrian tutelage and no longer having to pay tribute. However, Sennacherib's attitude was mainly governed by personal reasons. His father's failure against Luli had not been erased, even though the blockade of the island had been lifted at the beginning of his reign. The first intervention by the king of Assyria, after two campaigns aimed at settling immediate problems, was therefore directed against Luli. The high priority he attached to this issue in his interventions in

162

the west can be explained by the fact that his father had not succeeded in resolving it. On top of his wish to do better than his predecessors, he did not accept that a Phoenician king could escape his control at the start of his reign and taunt him, especially the powerful Luli.

Frightened by the Assyrian offensive, Luli "fled to the land of Iadnana (Cyprus), which is in the open sea, and found refuge there." Fear of a confrontation with the king of Assyria was not the reason he fled. He was courageous, in fact, because he did not leave Tyre when Sargon II had attacked him, nor had he hesitated confronting him in a naval battle, a battle he had won, moreover. He was resistant, as he had endured the five-year blockade of the island. He had showed his inventiveness in organizing the day-to-day life of the island's inhabitants during that difficult period. He was convinced that the island of Tyre was impregnable and he had remained in residence there, because it was the safest and the most prestigious place in his kingdom. Nevertheless, during the blockade he had learned that being cut off from his mainland territory, which was essential for supplies, particularly of drinking water, was not easy to bear. Such a situation was even more critical for a city that had to manage its international trade and relations with its numerous colonies if it wanted to remain rich and powerful. He was starting to get old, as can be deduced from his nearly thirty-three-year-long reign. The best solution, in his eyes, was to retreat to his Cypriot colony of Kition, which he had recaptured from the Assyrians a few years earlier. From there, without being disturbed, he could continue to control Tyrian affairs on the island as well as manage the commercial activities and the distant colonies. The biblical oracle of Isaiah about the destruction of Tyre also alludes to the flight to Cyprus.

There is no further mention of the island of Tyre in the texts of Sennacherib, who preferred to ignore its existence given that he had been unable to take control of it. In his eyes, the victory over Luli and his forced flight constituted a remarkable exploit of his reign, so much so that he had it depicted on a large bas-relief in his palace in Nineveh. Part of the fortified island town is represented, with crenellated towers, shields suspended on the battlements, and a fine edifice showing several floors inside, possibly the royal palace. A small brick doorway leads out onto the quay. A man bends over to pass a child down to a lady below, on board a merchant ship that is docked. The scene is surrounded by a substantial fleet of twelve ships, half of them warships, the other half merchant or transport vessels, all very different in appearance at that time. The representation of Tyre's fleet reminded Sennacherib of the one that had defeated his father, and the message in this bas-relief is that he

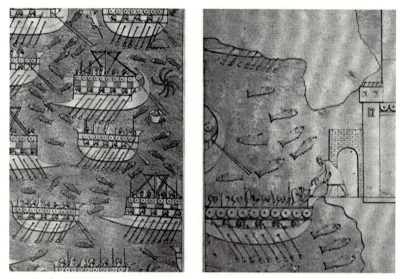

Drawing by Sir Austin Henry Layard of a relief depicting the flight of Luli. From the SW Palace of Sennacherib at Nineveh, Room I, Slab 20 in 2 parts (a and b); BM, WAA, Or. Dr., IV, 7-8.

had finally avenged that failure. Even though he had not succeeded in taking the island of Tyre, at least he had its king and his family ousted.

What became of Luli after his flight to Cyprus in 701? He found a safe refuge in Kition, where he lived for several years, possibly until 695, the date of the text that announces his death. It is impossible to know whether the kings of Cyprus continued paying tribute as they are never mentioned in the annals of Sennacherib. In any event, they were not troubled by the king of Assyria who had a multitude of more urgent problems to deal with. Consequently, Luli remained undisturbed during his long stay on an island that had become virtually independent. When he died in 695, a new king certainly belonging to the dynasty of Luli was inducted, either on the island of Tyre or on Cyprus. However, we do not know what his relationship was with King Baal I, who was to be on the throne of Tyre in 677.

Decline of Tyre, revival of Sidon

The dual kingdom of Tyre and Sidon disappeared definitively during Sennacherib's third campaign against Luli. The king of Assyria took hold of all of Luli's possessions: "Sidon the Great," "little Sidon" (Tell el-Burak), Bit-Zitti (Zaita), Sarepta (Sarafand), Mahallib, Ushu, Achzib, and Akko, its

164

fortified towns well supplied with rations and water sources. They submitted, "bowing down at his feet." This territory, Sennacherib decided to offer to Ithobaal, the new king he installed on the throne of Sidon. Ithobaal probably belonged to the ancient Sidonian ruling family that had been dispossessed by the Tyrian royal family. Sennacherib gave Luli's old possessions to Ithobaal of Sidon in order to ensure a wholly devoted king.

The policy of the king of Assyria was obvious and was to be systematically applied by his successors: to take advantage of the rivalries between two neighboring cities to weaken the rebel city and favor the other. This governing principle was to be formalized by Esarhaddon: "to humble the powerful and rise up the weak." It was a highly effective policy in the case of the rival cities of Tyre and Sidon. The tribute imposed by Assyria on subjugated states then became annual, starting with that of Ithobaal of Sidon: "every year and for an indefinite period I imposed on him the taxes and tribute due to my sovereignty."

Even though the tendentious texts of Sennacherib ignore the existence of the island of Tyre, the expedition against Luli led to the juxtaposition of two Phoenician territories of very different size. On the one hand, the city of Sidon, governed by a pro-Assyrian king, possessed a vast territory stretching at least from Sidon to Akko. The city of Tyre, on the other hand, remained independent, but its territory had become tiny, practically reduced to just its island. Sidon benefited from Tyre's misfortunes: after having received its territory and its wealth, Sidon benefited from Assyria's protection, which encouraged its development, thereby ruining Tyre. In fact, we know nothing about the two cities before the reign of Esarhaddon: Baal I, a weakened king, was to reign in Tyre, while Sidon was to be governed by the powerful Abdimilkot. In 701, Tyre received a blow from which it would never really recover. Deprived of its mainland territory opposite the island, it held on to a few territories to the south of Mount Carmel and retained its colonies, but these possessions were a long way away. Without any mainland territory nearby to cater to its immediate needs, the island of Tyre was in a stranglehold and inevitably began to suffer. The process was a slow one, however, given the massive resources it was still able to draw on from its colonies.

Archaeology has confirmed how Tyre, reduced to its island territory, became choked. A pottery-manufacturing workshop dating from this period has been discovered on this rocky island. From 701 onwards, Tyre was forced to live totally closed in on itself to such an extent that it even had to bring earth onto the island to be able to make its vases. It was unable to get this earth from the neighboring mainland territory that now belonged to Sidon, with whom relations were strained to say the least. It had to go in search for it on another part of the coast, either to the north of Sidon or south of Akko, that is to say at least 40 or so kilometers away. Perhaps the deterioration in the quality of the red glazed pottery and the suspension of pottery importation in this period were also linked to these difficulties.

Sennacherib's third campaign had been a total success. After having settled the Tyrian problem, he unraveled the Philistine and Egyptian ones at the same time by settling strong pro-Assyrian states along the borders of Egypt. As regards Judah, although Jerusalem had not been taken, its king Hezekiah submitted by paying a heavy tribute, while most of his towns were destroyed. The pharaoh Shebitku had tried to help the coalition partners, but in vain. In the Bible he was ironically called the "broken reed that penetrates and pierces the hand of whoever relies on him." According to the Bible and to Herodotus, the king of Assyria conducted a second campaign westwards, particularly against Judah, which was not mentioned in the Assyrian texts. But this campaign would have been unjustified due to the success of Assyrian policy in the Levant, the best proof being the long period of peace that followed his intervention in 701.

In his confrontation with the Chaldeans and their allies in 694, Sennacherib made use of Tyrian, Sidonian, and Cypriot craftsmen and sailors to equip a fleet in southern Mesopotamia. After the capture of his son Ashur-nadin-shumi, king of Babylon, in 693, Sennacherib constantly sought to take revenge on the Babylonians. In 690, he laid siege to the town, captured it in 689 and completely flooded it under the waters of the Euphrates. This sacrilege seriously undermined future Assyro-Babylonian relations and Sennacherib was never to be recognized as a legitimate king by the Babylonians. In 683, he appointed his youngest son, Esarhaddon, crown prince, compelled by the latter's mother Zakutu. This decision was taken very badly by his other sons who conspired against him. In 681, he was assassinated and the letters in his archives were destroyed.

The revolt of Abdimilkot of Sidon against Esarhaddon

In the reign of Esarhaddon, Assyrian domination over the Phoenician cities was heightened further but still fell short of complete incorporation into the empire. The assassination of Sennacherib was followed by a short civil war from which Esarhaddon emerged victorious, and he had himself crowned king in Assur in 680. He was apparently suffering from an inflammatory disease, which from time to time made him depressed, and he relied a lot on astrologers. However, his morbid character did not prevent him from procreating and having a flock of children. Every change of reign in Assyria prompted sporadic or widespread uprisings. At the start of Esarhaddon's reign, Chaldea was in a state of turmoil, the Scythians and the Cimmerians were restless in Asia Minor, and the pharaoh Taharqa was stirring up hostility in the Phoenician cities, which were frustrated with the Assyrian authorities' control over their trading opportunities with Egypt.

Abdimilkot, the new king of Sidon, revolted against Esarhaddon in 677. We know nothing of what happened in the quarter of a century that elapsed since 701 when Sidon received the Tyrian possessions, but he hoped to free himself from the yoke of Assyria and regain his independence. The reasons behind his revolt were probably the opportunity provided by a difficult change of reign, the pressure of taxation, the excessive control of commercial activities, and the sensation of power he felt he had over his vast territory. To achieve his aims, he first had to break out of his isolation and find allies. He knew he could not count on the king of Tyre, his vanquished rival, and Byblos did not want to create trouble for itself. For Arwad, the example of its neighbor Simyra, reduced to the status of Assyrian province, dictated caution. He therefore concluded an alliance with Sanduarri, king of Kundu and Sizu in Cilicia, with whom he probably had commercial links.

After Esarhaddon dealt with the succession crisis and stabilized the situation in Babylon, he set off to campaign in the west in order to put down the rebellions of Abdimilkot and Sanduarri. However, he seemed to be more interested in Sidon than in Cilicia. His heightened interest on the Phoenician coast was partially due to its strategic location on the route to Egypt. His prime objective in the west was not the total and permanent domination of the coastal states, which were still inadequately subjugated, but rather the conquest of Egypt. His second aim was to develop Assyria's maritime power. The change in the vocabulary used in his annals to describe the sea shows that he had finally mastered a proper understanding of the Mediterranean. Esarhaddon reproached Abdimilkot for not having feared his authority, for not having obeyed him, of "putting his trust in the terrifying sea," and of rejecting the yoke of Assur.

The Sidon revolt was crushed so violently that it made a lasting impression on people's minds, as it is the only event of Esarhaddon's reign that occurred in the west that is recounted in the Babylonian Chronicles. The defeated King Abdimilkot figures on the colossal stele of Esarhaddon in Zinjirli, where he is represented as very small, kneeling down, and leashed to a ring that pierces his lips. He is represented in the same position, with his name written beneath his feet, on another Esarhaddon stele erected in Til Barsip. The Assyrian annals recount the repression of Sidon at great length and in considerable detail. The king of Assyria flattened the town into the sea, just like a deluge would have done. He demolished the ramparts and houses of Sidon, throwing them into the sea, and reduced the town to ruins, meaning the main fortified urban area situated on the coast. Abdimilkot took refuge on one of Sidon's two small islands, either the one that today houses the sea castle, or Zire Island where an outer harbor was sited. Esarhaddon captured him in the open sea, like a fish, hence with the help of ships, possibly those of Tyre, Sidon's rival. He cut off his head, then made his way to the Sidonian royal palace, where he seized substantial plunder, including gold, silver, precious stones, multicolored trimmed clothes and linen, elephant hide, ivory, ebony, boxwood and numerous other riches. A huge caravan set off for Assyria, including the king's wife, his sons, his daughters and palace staff, along with oxen, small livestock, and a large number of donkeys. He convened all the kings of the Hatti-land and of the coast, including the Phoenician kings, and ordered them to build a new town called Kar-Esarhaddon, probably next to the Sidonian ports, which had to continue operating. He had it populated with deportees transferred from the mountains in the east. He wanted the Sidonians, on seeing the new Assyrian town built on the ruins of Sidon, to be dissuaded from any future revolt.

Then Esarhaddon took possession of all the towns in its territory, reorganized them into an Assyrian province headed by an Assyrian governor, and subjected them to tax and tribute even heavier than before. The list of the Sidonian towns gives an idea of the size of the territory ruled over by Abdimilkot. It comprised a first set formed by the towns situated between Sidon and Beirut, and a second set with the towns situated between Batroun and Tripoli. Between these two sets, the small territory of Byblos was preserved, from Nahr al-Kalb north of Beirut up to the area south of Batroun. The king of Assyria only gave to King Baal I of Tyre the two towns of Marubbu and Sarepta, situated south of Sidon. Simultaneously, he imposed an additional tax on him, on top of the annual tribute. In other words, he made a small gesture to reconcile with him and to rebalance his territory slightly while avoiding making him too powerful. At the same time, he wanted to exploit Tyre's wealth as a tributary to the maximum.

The revolt of the Cilician king Sanduarri was suppressed during the same campaign. Esarhaddon reproached him for not having respected his sovereignty, for having relied on the refuge offered by his rugged mountains, and for having allied with Abdimilkot of Sidon. He trapped him "like a bird" and cut off his head. He brought the two heads, that of Abdimilkot and that of Sanduarri back to Assyria to exhibit them, in 676, in the triumphal procession that passed through the streets of Nineveh accompanied by singers and musicians. He had them hung from the shoulders of two prisoners, both nobles—a Sidonian and a Cilician. Esarhaddon's cruelty was not gratuitous, it served as an example to prevent the western tributary states from rebelling against Assyria. Up until the end of the Assyrian Empire, there was to be no further king in Sidon. Sidon was wiped off the map as an autonomous city, as the northern part of its territory had become an Assyrian province and the southern part was recovered by Baal I of Tyre.

The maritime treaty between Baal I of Tyre and Esarhaddon

It was probably in the wake of this geopolitical reorganization of Phoenicia that Esarhaddon concluded a vassalage treaty with King Baal I of Tyre. Although it was a period of detente between Tyre and Assyria, Esarhaddon was suspicious of this Phoenician city, which had always had ambitions of revolt, by virtue of its insular position, which had kept it impregnable. He therefore imposed on the king of Tyre a treaty that rigorously defined his rights and his obligations, and that established a strict control over his activities. At the same time, as the Assyrian Empire had become a maritime power, the king of Assyria felt the need, for the first time, to regulate the maritime trade of the Levantine coast, and it was one of the key points of the treaty. Owing to the textual gaps, however, part of this important treaty remains unknown to us.

It was concluded between Esarhaddon on the one hand, and Baal I of Tyre, his descendants, and all Tyrians on the other. It referred first to the very recent crushing of the Sidon revolt. An Assyrian representative was positioned in Tyre, probably meaning in Ushu. His role was to control any messenger received at the palace and any letter sent to the king and to the Council of Elders. In his absence, the Tyrian authorities could receive no messenger nor open any letter. The treaty provided for first rights to plunder in favor of Esarhaddon in the event of the shipwreck of a vessel belonging to the king of Tyre or to the Tyrians, who belonged to two different categories of commercial enterprises. The cargo would be recovered, but each member of the crew would be authorized to return to his country of origin.

The treaty then went on to list the harbors and trading routes that Esarhaddon granted to Baal I, his servant: the harbors of Akko and Dor; the whole Philistine coast; Byblos; the land of Lebanon; and the mountain towns; and the coastal territory of Assyria, meaning the provinces of Simyra and Sidon. At that time, Byblos appears to have been a small autonomous territory encompassing its mountainous hinterland and its towns. Baal I and the Tyrians were authorized to travel with their ships to all these regions, which belonged to Assyria, on condition that they paid customs duties as in the past. The gods of Assyria and Tyre were invoked at the end of the treaty in order to guarantee it. From the Tyrian standpoint, this vassalage treaty was partially favorable. Tyre had become the foremost Phoenician city after the crushing of Sidon. It was able once again to conduct its maritime trading activities and to reestablish relations with its colonies. Yet, for king Baal I, the constant surveillance and tight control imposed on him by the treaty must have been hard to bear.

After settling the problem of Sidon once and for all by reducing it to an Assyrian province, and placing Tyre under strict surveillance, Esarhaddon could focus on his main aim: the conquest of Egypt. In 674, he undertook an initial campaign that ended in failure. This event is only reported in the Babylonian Chronicles; the Assyrian texts remain silent on the subject. The Tyrians must have been pressed into service to prepare this campaign, financially and militarily because Tyre still represented for the Assyrians, as later for the Persians, an ideal strategic base for preparing the conquest of Egypt. This campaign constituted an additional constraint for Baal I and he probably started moving closer towards allying with Egypt once the pharaoh had succeeded in warding off the attempted Assyrian attack.

The revolt of Baal I of Tyre against Esarhaddon

After the failure of the first Egypt campaign, the following year in 673, Esarhaddon conquered Shubria, near Lake Van, which at last enabled him to chastise the assassins of his father who had taken refuge there. He found that his palace in Nineveh had become too small for him, and so had a new palace built. He placed demands on twenty-two western kings to supply the materials needed for this construction: twelve kings of the land of Hatti on the coast and ten Cypriot kings. The Phoenician kings figured in the first group, even though they were

not specified as such: Baal I of Tyre, Milkyasap of Byblos, Mattanbaal III of Arwad, and Abibaal of Samsimuruna. Sidon's absence is normal because this city had been reduced to an Assyrian province in 677. At that time, four autonomous Phoenician cities remained and Baal I headed the list, which indicates the importance he had acquired in this period. The number of tributary kings of Cyprus had also increased from seven to ten since the expedition of Sargon II. We can recognize the names of the cities of Idalion, Chythroi, Paphos, Soli, Kourion, Tamassos, and Ledra; Nuria corresponds perhaps with Marion, Sillua with Salamis, and Karthadasht with Kition. Most of their kings had Greek names; only those of Kition and Salamis bore Phoenician names. Esarhaddon consulted the oracle of Shamash to know whether he should conclude a maritime trade agreement with two Phoenicians from Cyprus. To underline the universality of his power in the west, he claimed: "All the kings of the middle of the sea, from Cyprus to Ionia as far as Tarshish, laid prostrate at my feet." It was probably through Tyre that he was aware of Tarshish, a harbor in southern Spain in regular contact with the Phoenician city.

King Baal I of Tyre allied with the pharaoh Taharqa, probably from 674. Like him, he refused to be a tributary of Assyria and consequently was de facto in revolt. Esarhaddon criticized the king of Tyre for having allied with the pharaoh, for having shaken off the Assyrian yoke, and for having sent him insolent messages, probably a reference to his refusal to pledge allegiance and pay tribute. In 671, the king of Assyria undertook his second expedition against Egypt. In the Assyrian texts, the crushing of the revolt of Tyre and the conquest of Egypt are mentioned together in his second campaign. In reality, he first dealt with the problem of Tyre in passing. Knowing his earlier policy, he obviously would not have launched his Egypt expedition without taking adequate rearguard precautions. This was all the more necessary if he used Tyrian territory as a logistical base for his campaign to Egypt, unless he set out from Ashkelon on this occasion.

He took Memphis, capturing the Egyptian crown prince and several members of the royal family. Taharqa retreated into southern of Egypt, where he still apparently maintained control, while the Assyrians favored his rivals in the north, starting with those of Sais. A stele of Esarhaddon erected in Qaqun 6 kilometers from Tul Karm in Israel, relates the tenth campaign from the moment it set out from the city of Assur: the attack against Baal I of Tyre, the crossing of the south of Palestine up to the Sinai Desert, and finally the attack against Egypt, which figures in the broken section of the stele. He commemorated his victorious campaign in Egypt, of which he was very proud, on another stele that he had sculpted on a rocky cliff of the Nahr al-Kalb, north of Beirut. It describes the campaign in Egypt where he had collected a fabulous plunder, and mentions Tyre and Ashkelon, but in a part of the inscription that is too damaged to be legible.

Esarhaddon's campaign against Tyre was not one of the most glorious for the king of Assyria because, yet again, he failed to capture the island. Though he dared to write in a text of the annals, "I conquered the city of Tyre in the middle of the sea," it was an exploit he coveted but failed to achieve, as another text indicates that he simply blockaded the island, cutting off its water and food supplies, which were vital for King Baal I. Esarhaddon confiscated from him "his mainland towns," a passage that could not be clearer in that the island is not included. What did he do with the mainland territory captured from Baal I? At this point the text is fragmentary. Maybe he created a new Assyrian province similar to that of Sidon. But he probably did not want to weaken the king of Tyre completely so that he could continue to make use of his wealth.

Understanding that it was also in his own interests, Baal I surrendered very quickly and kissed Esarhaddon's feet in order to limit Assyrian reprisals and to retain his throne. Esarhaddon siezed his belongings and his daughters, endowed with their substantial dowries. In the way this action was formulated, it appears more like a marital agreement than hostage-taking. Baal I was subjected to a heavy tax in addition to the annual tribute.

The conquest of Egypt is mentioned in the Babylonian Chronicles, but Esarhaddon's partial victory in Tyre must have gone unnoticed. In reality, it was in the interest neither of the king of Assyria nor of the king of Tyre to publicize the event too much, it being no honor to either of them. In any event, the Phoenician kings who were tributaries of Assyria were very careful at the end of Esarhaddon's reign not to omit payment of their heavy tributes and taxes each year. Byblos, for example, paid these and supplied various types of textiles.

The Assyrian victory over Egypt in 671 was a short-lived conquest. The Assyrians could not ensure direct administration of the Delta and were obliged to rely on local help. Hardly had they turned their backs when Taharqa fomented unrest in the north, forcing Esarhaddon to prepare a third campaign against Egypt. In 670, he first had to quell a conspiracy directed against him harshly, after which he was struck down by an acute health issue linked to the worsening of his illness. Still, he set off for Egypt in 669, but died suddenly en route. The throne of Nineveh fell to his son Ashurbanipal and that of Babylon to his son Shamash-shum-ukin. The appointment of these two crown princes had taken place in 672, accompanied by a succession treaty, possibly advised by Zakutu, the queen mother.

The revolt of Yakinlu of Arwad against Ashurbanipal

When Ashurbanipal acceded to the throne in 668 after the death of his father, his grandmother Zakutu organized some *"adê,"* or oaths by which the royal family, the dignitaries and all the Assyrians swore allegiance to the new king, who was still very young to reign alone. Ashurbanipal had received an education in which he had studied both scribal arts and learned disciplines; this led him to develop the libraries of Nineveh. In addition, he had been initiated into the art of governing by his father, by attending royal audiences. As the order of his texts was not chronological, it is very difficult to situate the events one with another and to put a date on them.

Overall, he pursued the main elements of Esarhaddon's policy. To begin with, he undertook the reconquest of Egypt, which had rebelled on the death of his father. He sent an expeditionary force as far as Memphis and defeated Taharqa, who fled to Thebes. In 665, he decided to chase after him. To his army he added Phoenician, Cypriot, and Syrian auxiliaries, and contingents that had come from the Delta to cooperate with him. The Assyrians pushed further south, forcing the submission of Upper Egypt, but did not succeed in getting their hands on the elusive Taharqa. Directly after their departure, the northern chiefs returned to join forces with Taharqa. The response from Ashurbanipal was immediate: he had the key actors among them executed or deported, except for Necho I, king of Sais. Tantamani succeeded Taharqa, attempted to retake Egypt, and subjugated the chiefs of the Delta. Ashurbanipal again sent his army against Egypt in 664. He retook Memphis, then Thebes, which he ravaged, burned, and plundered. The situation remained undecided and the country was disorganized.

In 667, Yakinlu was on the throne of Arwad and paid tribute to Ashurbanipal in the company of twenty-two western kings, tributaries of Assyria. Since its revolt against Tiglath-pileser III around 734, the city of Arwad maintained a cautiously reserved stance towards Assyrian domination, paying the tribute demanded now and again so as not to live in total isolation on its island and to continue to conduct its maritime trade. But since the reign of Esarhaddon, King Yakinlu had not taken kindly to being in submission to Assyria, perhaps because conditions had become more difficult. He therefore felt insecure on his fortified island. Even though he was not as powerful as the king of Tyre, he possessed some additional advantages because his island was further from the coast and, in the event of a blockade, in addition to wells and tanks, he could use a source of fresh water on the seabed, collected with the help of a leather pipe. His revolt took place in three phases: first his conduct was denounced because he did not comply with the rules imposed, then his revolt was crushed, and last his succession was organized by the king of Assyria.

Yakinlu's rebelliousness went back to the reign of Esarhaddon. When he was crown prince, Ashurbanipal already distrusted him and consulted the oracle of Shamash with regard to him: "Will Yakinlu listen and will he accept his message if it is handed to him personally by the messenger Nabu-sharru-usur?" In his annals, he presented him as a long-standing rebel: "Yakinlu, king of Arwad who lives in the middle of the sea and who has not submitted to the kings, my fathers." What he meant was that the island had still not been conquered.

In three letters written to Ashurbanipal, Itti-Shamash-balatu criticized the actions of Yakinlu and the corruption of certain Assyrian officials. He himself was an Assyrian official in the province of Simyra or the city of Arwad, installed opposite the island. He recalled that the situation had been going on since the reign of the previous king, but that he had not dared denounce it due to the reputation of the Assyrians involved. He wanted to convince Ashurbanipal that he had not got involved with them, apologized for his inaction and described the wrongdoings, calling for the king of Assyria's intervention. He accused Yakinlu of managing the maritime trade of his region counter to Assyrian interests: "He is blocking ships, so that they cannot dock in the king's harbor, my lord. He is pocketing the harbor's revenues himself. If someone moors in his harbor first, he allows him to leave, but if he moors at the Assyrian trading post, he kills him and confiscates his ship, on the pretext that he has committed abuses." Yakinlu's harbor was the harbor of the island of Arwad. The Assyrian trading post must have been in one of the coastal harbors neighboring the island: Carne (Tell Qarnun), Tabbet al-Hammam, an artificial harbor created in the ninth century, or Simyra. The city of Arwad had to collaborate closely in the proper functioning of Assyrian maritime trade if it wanted to retain a certain degree of autonomy in its own trading activities. But Yakinlu took advantage of his maritime power and of the slack Assyrian control to exploit the situation in his favor and increase his profits.

Ashurbanipal intervened in Arwad between 665 and 649, possibly during his third campaign of 662 against Tabal and Tyre. His annals give very vague indications as to the reasons for his intervention: Yakinlu committed the error of "putting his trust in the terrifying sea, refusing to submit to my yoke and imploring my royal pardon." They make no allusion to the accusations brought by Itti-Shamash-balatu in his letters, probably to stifle the accusations of corruption against the Assyrian officials. The texts give two quite differing versions of Yakinlu's submission, perhaps because it took place in two phases. First, he pledged allegiance as a vassal and was subjected to an annual tribute. Then, he personally conveyed his daughter to Nineveh, endowed with a substantial dowry, so that she could enter the harem of Ashurbanipal, whose feet he kissed. Maybe he took this initiative on hearing about the failure of the revolt of Baal I, his counterpart, and through fear of being targeted in turn.

The account of Yakinlu's succession followed that of his submission, but it is impossible to say what the length of time was between these two events, which in any case occurred before 649. The circumstances of his death are not clear, but the expression used does not suggest a natural death. He may have been assassinated by a pro-Assyrian party or by his own sons. Whatever the case, after his death, his ten sons left the island of Arwad together, taking rich gifts with them, and went to Nineveh to see Ashurbanipal, whose feet they kissed. Either they asked the king of Assyria to arbitrate, as they failed to agree over the succession, or they concluded a preliminary agreement with the Assyrians. In any event, their action showed that they recognized Assyrian authority over Arwad. Ashurbanipal chose Ozbaal I (Azzibaal), who must have been the most pro-Assyrian son, to take the throne of Arwad. He held the other nine sons hostage with him at the court of Nineveh, so that they would not be tempted to plot against their brother. Nonetheless, he arranged a luxurious exile for them, by bestowing honors on them, and offering them splendid clothes and gold rings, as he was anxious to treat loyal tributary peoples tactfully. He agreed to keep the island of Arwad autonomous, provided that it was governed by a king in his pay, because for the kings of Assyria it had always represented a privileged point of contact with the sea, and it was a source of maritime trade with great wealth.

The revolts of Baal I of Tyre and of Ushu and Akko against Ashurbanipal

The revolt of Baal I of Tyre and the revolts of Ushu and Akko against Ashurbanipal were not grouped together in the Assyrian texts because they were spread out over time. Nevertheless, all three concerned the region of Tyre and raised the same issues. Baal I had been on the throne of Tyre for a long time, at least since 677, when he had received the towns of Marubbu and Sarepta from Esarhaddon, after the repression of the revolt in Sidon. He first rebelled against him in 671. He rebelled for the second time against his son Ashurbanipal in 662. His annals made several mentions of the repression of this revolt, which reflects the importance attached to it by the king of Assyria. The king of Tyre's participation in the first Assyrian campaign against Egypt proves that his relations with him had normalized at the beginning of his reign. Esarhaddon's partial success against Tyre had therefore been forgotten, undoubtedly thanks to the submission of Baal I and the payment of a substantial tribute. The reasons for the king of Tyre's revolt against Ashurbanipal in 662 are not very clear from the texts: "In my third campaign, I marched against Baal, king of Tyre, who lives in the middle of the sea, when he did not comply with my royal order and did not obey my words." Baal I may have violated the trade treaty concluded with Esarhaddon. He found Assyrian economic control in the eastern Mediterranean hard to tolerate, especially as it had become even stricter since the reign of Sargon II. He was heartened by the wealth of his city, the advantages provided by its insular position, and his long reign.

The Assyrian king described his siege operations of Tyre: "I encircled it with siege walls, and I blocked its sea and land routes." These siege walls were constructed on Tyre's mainland territory in order to block the land access routes. To block the sea routes, Ashurbanipal organized the blockade of the whole island, or only its access to the coast. The overpopulated island of Tyre was totally dependent on its mainland territory for its water supply, agricultural products, and wood. Baal I knew this from experience, already having lived through Esarhaddon's blockade. These extreme conditions explained why he rapidly surrendered, knowing that he would gain from doing so regardless of the price he would have to pay. To obtain pardon, he surrendered of his own accord to Ashurbanipal. He brought him a substantial tribute; his daughter and his nieces, endowed with sizeable dowries to enter the royal harem; and his young son Yehimilk, perhaps the crown prince, "who has never yet crossed the sea." The king of Assyria sent his son back to him, a gesture dictated by generosity according to the Assyrian scribes. That explanation is possible, but in so doing Ashurbanipal especially wanted to gain recognition from the king of Tyre. Their reconciliation was almost as much in his own interest because the island of Tyre remained impregnable, and the prosperity of this city, along with its fleet, benefited the Assyrian Empire. He therefore had all its routes unblocked and the siege walls destroyed: clearly Baal I had maneuvered well and had recovered part of his mainland territory.

The extent of the territory given back to him is not known. In any event, part of the old Tyrian territory was transformed into an Assyrian province because, in 639 or 637, Bel-shadua was governor of the province of Tyre. Already in 650 he was probably governor of the province of Sidon, and based in Kar-Esarhaddon. The towns of Ushu, opposite the island of Tyre, and Akko, to the south of Tyre, were definitely part of the province of Tyre. It had been created, either after Baal I's first revolt in 671, or after his second revolt in 662.

The towns of Ushu and Akko in turn rebelled against Ashurbanipal quite a while after the repression of Baal I's second revolt, perhaps in 644 or 643, at the end of his ninth campaign against the Arab tribes, on his return journey to Assyria. Baal I of Tyre, or his successor, had nothing to do with their rebellion or the Assyrian annals would have mentioned it. Nor did any text say whether the two rebel towns had the support of the new pharaoh Psamtik I. At any rate, Ushu and Akko were part of an Assyrian province of Tyre with a governor at its head and they were subjected to an annual tribute. Their rebellion was rooted in their refusal to obey the Assyrian governor and to pay tribute and taxes every year. Ashurbanipal's repression was extremely severe: the rebel inhabitants of Ushu were beaten, killed, or deported to Assyria with their gods. The rebels from Akko were massacred and their bodies impaled around the town, the survivors were deported and enlisted as soldiers in the Assyrian army. The practice of dissuasive cruelty for the subjugated people did not change right up to the last Assyrian king. "Which is the one that your cruelty has not affected?" wrote the biblical prophet Nahum.

Phoenicia's change in status in the reign of Ashurbanipal

In the reign of Ashurbanipal, the Phoenician cities were subjected to several types of constraints. They had military obligations: the twenty-two western tributary kings, of which they were part, had to join their armed forces to the Assyrian expedition against Egypt. The Phoenician fleets were requisitioned when the Assyrian king needed them, for example, to implement the blockade of the island of Tyre during the second revolt of Baal I. The Phoenician cities had to supply timber to Assyria and to participate in the construction works each time they received the order to do so, by sending materials and making their specialists—carpenters, joiners, and cabinetmakers—available. When Ashurbanipal wanted to rebuild the temple of Sin in Harran in the early part of his reign, he used cedar and cypress wood from Mount Lebanon and Mount Sirara, and possibly Mount Hermon. For the restoration of the Esagila temple in Babylon, he had cedar and cypress wood dispatched from Mount Lebanon and the Amanus. It was the "kings of the coast" who had to take care of the difficult transport operations: "They dragged it laboriously from their mountains, where access was quite difficult, all the way to Harran." As a matter of fact, other than the lower Orontes, there was no other waterway route providing access to Harran. The Sargonids therefore preferred to take timber from the Amanus, being closer to Assyria, but the cedars of Mount Lebanon were more appreciated for their gigantic size.

Another obligation imposed on the Phoenician kings was that of supplying young women from the royal family—their daughters or nieces—for the Assyrian king's harem. They were provided with substantial dowries, which gives this obligation the appearance of a matrimonial contract. The Assyrian kings, like those of Mari and Ebla and the Egyptian pharaohs, all had harems and contracted multiple marriages to seal political alliances between major powers or to strengthen its ties with the leaders of subjected states.

Under the Sargonids we see the emergence of another obligation: the Phoenician kings had to send their sons, who might have been in line to succeed them, to the court of the king of Assyria. There, they were received with the honors due to their standing and were trained so as to serve Assyrian policy. In this way, the king of Assyria could choose whomever he saw fit when a succession opened, like Ozbaal, appointed to replace Yakinlu on the throne of Arwad. To avoid the possibility of dynastic conflicts, his brothers were kept under house arrest at the Assyrian court.

The Phoenician kings were subjected to tribute and various other taxes. Hence, they were taxed for exploiting the timber from their own forests; they paid customs duties when they went via the Assyrian trading posts installed on the coast. The tribute was generally collected locally by Assyrians officials. It could also be handed over when the king of Assyria was passing through during his military campaigns: the Phoenician kings had it sent to him or handed it to him themselves when carrying out the ritual of allegiance that involved kissing his feet. If they really wanted to placate the king of Assyria or to seek forgiveness for a wrongdoing, they came themselves, bringing it to him in his palace. The wealth of the tribute paid by the Phoenician cities give an idea of their prosperity, despite the hardships caused by Assyrian domination. The nature of the tribute indicates the specific products of these cities and their trade imports. Under Ashurbanipal, for example, Phoenician tribute consisted of gold; ivory; dark red, violet, and purple wool; fish; and birds. His texts do not describe them at such length as those of the early Assyrian kings who set out to conquer the west and who were amazed by all the goods received, most of them exotic in their eyes. Under the Sargonids, tributes were part of the routine. Their values increased considerably, to such an extent that they started to have a serious impact on the wealth of the tributaries. Under Ashurbanipal, the Phoenician cities were subjected to two types of tribute: episodic tribute as with Arwad and Tyre before their submission, and Byblos; and annual tribute as with Arwad and Tyre after their submission, or Ushu and Akko.

At the end of the Assyrian Empire, the individual cities of Phoenicia enjoyed a differentiated political status. The history of that status also varied: it could have been established in ancient times, or at the very end of the empire; or it could have evolved over time, or gone through several successive stages. One kind of status concerned the cities that were transformed into Assyrian provinces, which had lost their autonomy, their local powers, and their institutions, and which were managed entirely by Assyrian governors. This was the status heald by Simyra since the reign of Tiglath-pileser III in 738, which was never to regain its autonomy. This was also the case of Sidon in the reign of Esarhaddon in 677, and of part of the mainland territory of Tyre in the reign of Esarhaddon in 671 or that of Ashurbanipal in 662. However, the creation of these two Assyrian provinces was not definitive.

A second kind of status applied to the tributary cities, left autonomous out of necessity, but placed under strict surveillance: Tyre since 662 in the reign of Ashurbanipal, and Arwad, perhaps since 662 also. These two cities, made up of their impregnable island and a small mainland territory, were authorized to keep their king and their political institutions. The third kind of status covered the cities that retained their autonomy together with substantial flexibility because they never posed a problem: that was the case of Byblos.

The political line taken by the Assyrian conquerors is as follows: the Phoenician cities possessed key attributes, which meant they had to be handled tactfully. Their fleets represented the basis of the naval power needed by an empire that had also become maritime. The Phoenician coastal sites were critically strategic positions en route to Egypt and for controlling Cyprus; and their economic prosperity constituted an abundant source of profit that was essential to the proper functioning of the imperial tributary system. The policy of the Assyrian kings did not imply appropriating all these assets, but rather letting the Phoenician cities manage them in their own best interests, knowing that in this way they would draw the greatest benefit. The war fleets were constructed by Phoenician craftsmen in the Phoenician arsenals. They were manned by Phoenician crews and commanded by the local kings. Each city had its own army and system of fortifications. It exploited its agricultural resources to suit its own method of production. It organized its trading activities as it saw fit, especially the important maritime trade, provided that it did not impede the trade of the Assyrians and that a substantial proportion of its profits was handed over to them. The other aspects of city life—institutional, social, religious, and cultural, for example—were of no use for the Assyrian occupiers, who showed no interest in them. All they had to do, under normal circumstances, was to monitor the local authorities, to check that they were docile and did not endanger the interests of the empire. But this political line had to be corrected on a number of occasions due to setbacks, with various political consequences for the Phoenician cities, and especially increasingly mounting pressure, which was hard to bear at the end of the Assyrian Empire.

Another consequence of the conquest of the Phoenician cities by the Assyrian kings was a tremendous mixing of populations. After the repression of each Phoenician revolt, part of the population was deported to Assyria, while other conquered populations were settled in the Phoenician cities. The deportations of Phoenicians throughout the entire empire have left traces in Assyrian texts. Under Tiglath-pileser III, inhabitants of Simyra, Siyanu, Kashpuna, and Dor found themselves in Ulluba and Unqi. Under Sennacherib, inhabitants of Sidon, Tyre, and Jaffa were deported to Assur. Esarhaddon also deported inhabitants of Sidon to Assur, and Ashurbanipal deported inhabitants of Ushu and Akko there too. In addition, the Assyrian conquests drove Phoenicians, Syrians, and Jews into exile, which explains the origin, for example, of an important community in Elephantine in Egypt. Some Phoenicians, displaced throughout the Assyrian Empire, succeeded in occupying important positions, such as Mattan, eponym in 700, and Gersaphon, a high-level dignitary at the court of Nineveh and eponym in the year 660, at the start of Ashurbanipal's reign.

The end of the Assyrian Empire: respite for the Phoenician cities

The abrupt disappearance of the powerful Assyrian Empire remains an enigma. How was it that the seasoned and victorious Assyrian troops gave way, in less than twenty years, to the Medes and Nabopolassar's Babylonians? Yet, Ashurbanipal, threatened by the Elamites, crushed them in 653. He also came under threat from the dangerous Cimmerians who had penetrated into Asia Minor, driven by the Scythians, and who coveted the kingdom of Lydia. The king of Assyria had difficulty defending the Lydians and was no longer able to maintain control over the most western provinces of his empire. In Egypt, the pharaoh Psamtik I had been recognized by the Assyrians who had entrusted the administration of the country to him. Without abandoning traditional values, he opened Egypt up to the outside world: he welcomed Greek and Carian traders to thank their mercenaries who had helped him consolidate his power. In 653, he took advantage of the confrontation between Assyria and Elam to free himself from the rule of Ashurbanipal and chase the Assyrian garrisons out of Egypt, as far as Ashdod. The Assyrians lost Egypt, and Cyprus was beyond their control.

The Assyrian Empire began to waver when civil war broke out between Ashurbanipal and his brother Shamash-shum-ukin, king of Babylonia. The town of Babylon fell in 648 after a terrible siege. Kandalanu was installed on the throne and a period of ruthless purge followed. In 646, an expedition against the Elamites ended with the sack of Suza. Very little is known about the end of Ashurbanipal's reign, between 639 and 627, because the Assyrian archives stopped in 640 and the Babylonian Chronicles contain little information about Assyria. He abandoned his capital Nineveh, going first to Arbela, then to Harran near the Syro-Turkish border. In 630, his son Ashur-etil-ilani acceded to the throne of Assyria. It was perhaps he who had ousted his father and sent him to Harran. It is also possible that Ashurbanipal, wearied by his forty-two-year reign, the longest in Assyrian history, simply decided to step down from power in favor of his son.

The death of Ashurbanipal in 627 triggered the process of the collapse of the Assyrian Empire, as all his sons were fiercely to contest power until 612. There was an uninterrupted succession of civil and foreign wars. In 626, Nabopolassar had himself acknowledged as king of Babylon. Initially allied with Sin-shar-ishkun, who had seized the throne of Assyria in 623, he went to war against him, and undertook offensive operations as far as the middle Euphrates. In the meantime, in the years 629–627, the Scythians invaded Assyria; going down as far as southern Palestine, they pillaged Ashkelon and threatened Egypt. It was probably not a full invasion, more the action of a few avant garde groups. The Phoenician cities were not necessarily affected by the route taken by the Scythians who, coming from Assyria, must have followed the Orontes–Jordan corridor rather than the coastal route, which would have been hardgoing. Psamtik I apparently dissuaded them from going further south with "gifts and prayers" according to Herodotus. The Egyptians appeared to have captured the Philistine town of Ashdod in 611, after a twenty-nine-year-long siege. In fact, the pharaoh then became aware that the Assyrian Empire was in great difficulty, threatened by both Babylonians and Medes, and realized the danger that its total collapse would represent for Egypt. He therefore decided to intervene, first in 616, by supporting the Assyrians against Nabopolassar, which was a complete waste, as he did not succeed in preventing their defeat. In 614, Cyaxares, at the head of Median and Scythian tribes, captured the town of Assur. In 612, he allied with Nabopolassar to take Nineveh. Ashur-uballit II held on to the Assyrian throne until 610 in Harran, where the Egyptian troops brought him support, but it was too late.

Now and again, the Phoenician cities experienced short periods of independence during the transition from one empire to another. It took quite a while for the new empire to overthrow the previous one. A period of reorganization, longer in the peripheral regions like Phoenicia, was needed before the tributary system could be properly reestablished. During the last part of Ashurbanipal's reign, after the Ushu and Akko rebellions in 644 or 643, until his death in 627, Assyrian control in Phoenicia weakened more and more. It totally vanished during the period between 627 and 611. The Phoenician cities benefited from the situation by regaining their independence, a status they would retain until the end of Nabopolassar's reign in 605. They recovered their confiscated territories at least partially. Only Simyra failed to restore its independence. Arwad took back its mainland territory and possibly annexed the ancient Assyrian province of Simyra. The Assyrian province of Sidon restored its royal institutions and its former territory. The city of Tyre also recovered all of its mainland territory, including the Assyrian province of Tyre, with the towns of Ushu and Akko. For Byblos, nothing apparently changed, but it took advantage of the fact that it was no longer subject to tribute or obligations to develop even further. No more is heard of the city of Samsimuruna, the fate of which is a complete mystery.

PART FOUR

PHOENICIA UNDER BABYLONIAN DOMINATION (610–539)

1

Phoenicia between Egypt and Babylonia
(610–605)

Nabopolassar facing the Egyptian expeditions

The history of the (Neo)Babylonian Empire is known through the Babylonian Chronicles. They only give a summary of the battles, a chronology, and the reign changes, which is good in itself, but there are many gaps. Practically all twenty years of Nabopolassar's reign are devoted to the struggle against Assyria. His tactics were quite surprising: his army exercised the utmost restraint and he was helped by the Medes in capturing Nineveh. The Babylonian army must have been as worn out as the Assyrian army after all those years of endless strife. Yet, maybe Nabopolassar's display of caution was calculated, skillfully combining force and cunning to break down the Assyrian Empire. He concluded an alliance with Cyaxares after their joint victory, in order to share the influential areas. The Medes took western Iran and Anatolia, while Nabopolassar recovered all the southern part of the Assyrian Empire. He was the founder of the Babylonian Empire. However, his task did not end with the taking of the last Assyrian bastion in Harran in 610, as he then faced the Egyptians who were attempting to control Syria-Palestine up to Carchemish. Egypt had regained its prosperity under Psamtik I and it represented a still-powerful state that had to be reckoned with. However, it mainly owed this prosperity and power to the decline of Assyria. The Egyptians took advantage of this to assert themselves again in the Near East, at least until the Babylonians were capable of brushing aside their refound ambitions.

In 610, Psamtik I disappeared and left it up to his son Necho II to continue his work. In 609, the Egyptians managed to cross the Euphrates again, but did not succeed in retaking Harran from the Medes. Necho II took advantage of the vacuum left by the disappearance of the Assyrian Empire to occupy Palestine. The Phoenician cities were not really troubled by Egyptian domination for several reasons. It was a much lighter burden than that imposed by the Assyrians as it relied on only a few garrisons and on pro-Egyptian leaders in the Near East. The pharaoh had certainly not become involved in the internal reorganization of the Phoenician cities after their liberation from the Assyrian yoke: He had subjected them, at most, to an episodic tribute. Relations between Phoenicia and Egypt seemed to be as cordial with Necho II as they had been with his father. This is borne out by a statue in the name of Psamtik I discovered in Arwad, a statue dedicated by Necho II to Horus, the god of Byblos, and a libation table dating from the same period found in Tyre. The long three-year voyage around Africa, from the Red Sea to the Strait of Gibraltar, was probably made in the reign of Necho II by Phoenician sailors. Did the Phoenicians help the Egyptians in their military expeditions in Syria? If they arrived by sea, they would not have needed Phoenician fleets because they had at their disposal the fleet constructed by the pharaoh Psamtik I. Nevertheless, they would have had to use Phoenician harbors, such as Tyre, to be able to penetrate inland.

The conciliatory attitude of the Phoenician cities towards Egypt contrasts with the resistance of the Judeans. Josiah, who became king of Judah at the age of eight, in 640, was to regain his independence and extend his kingdom both northwards and towards the Mediterranean with the help of Greek mercenaries. Even though he was in contact with the Tyrians in his trading activities, he does not appear to have established any political ties with the king of Tyre. In 609, he confronted the Egyptian army, trying to obstruct its advance near Megiddo: he was defeated and was killed in the battle. Necho II got involved in the kingdom of Judah, dethroning Jehohaz, the youngest son of Josiah, and replacing him with his eldest son Jehoiakim. He became a vassal of Egypt and had to pay a heavy tribute. The destruction of the site of Mesad Hashavyahu, in the north of Philistia, indicates that the Egyptians also dominated all the coastal region.

Necho II pursued a policy of expansion in Western Asia more energetically than his father. For a number of years, the Euphrates became the border between Egypt and Babylonia. The pharaoh established his residence in Riblah, in the region of Hamath in northern Syria. It was from there that he organized the new Egyptian province of Asia. On the coast, he extended his influence as far as Sidon.

An Egyptian royal estate in Lebanon

At Herakleopolis in Middle Egypt, a black granite statue bearing an Egyptian inscription was found. It was an offering by Hor, the commander of the town, and mentions the works carried out in the temple of Herishef (Harasphes). This god was to be identified with Herakles by the Greeks. Hor describes the beneficial actions he had carried out in Herakleopolis, particularly the restoration and construction of religious buildings. For example, he had adorned the large forecourt of the temple of Herishef with a pink-granite colonnade, covered the pink granite lintels with gold and the main doorway with electrum, and carved the temple doors out of "precious cedar from the royal estate." He had all the works carried out with a joyful heart, hoping that the god would grant him a long life of prosperity, good health and happiness, the favor of the pharaoh, and recognition of the town of Herakleopolis for eternity.

This inscription dates to the reign of Psamtik I or, more likely, that of Necho II. The cedar in question probably came from the forests on Mount Lebanon, whence Nebuchadnezzar II was also to get his supplies. According to the inscription, at that time the pharaoh owned a royal estate in these forests. Either this was a return to a thousand-year-old tradition established between Byblos and Egypt, to the time when relations between the two states were excellent, when the forest of Byblos was there to serve Egyptian needs for timber. Alternatively, the closer ties between Egypt and Tyre especially under Necho II led to an agreement reserving a royal forest estate in the hinterland of Tyre for the pharaoh. Egypt had always been a major consumer of cedar and other species of trees from Phoenician forests for its construction works, and also of their byproducts for mummifying its deceased. In the context of this new Egyptian domination of the Near East, the fact that the pharaoh possessed a forest estate in the hinterland of Byblos or Tyre was totally natural.

The establishment of the Babylonian Empire

Necho II now dominated Palestine, the Phoenician cities, and the ancient Aramean provinces of Assyria up to the Euphrates, whereas the Jezireh belonged to Nabopolassar, who was known as "king of Akkad." During the final years of his reign, he began to halt Egyptian expansion and to recover the ancient possessions of the Assyrian Empire. He undertook initial reconstruction work in Babylon to restore the ziggurat. He used cedar, probably from the Amanus, as he did not have access to Mount Lebanon, which was still under Egyptian domination at that time. In 608 and 607, the Babylonian army conducted two expeditions in the mountainous regions, along the borders of the ancient kingdom of Urartu. Each year, Nabopolassar went campaigning and returned home when it was over. In 607, for the first time, he involved his eldest son Nebuchadnezzar, the crown prince, as military chief. With him, he reached the Urartu mountains and came back to Babylon alone, leaving him to conquer and pillage the mountain villages to train him in warfare. He then marched on the town of Kimuhu on the Euphrates, to the south of Carchemish, captured it and set up a Babylonian garrison there. In 606, the Egyptian army laid siege to the Kimuhu garrison and took the town four months later. Nabopolassar, without his son, pitched camp in Quramatu on the bank of the Euphrates, then crossed the river, captured three Syrian towns, plundered them, and returned to Babylon. After he left, the Egyptian army attacked the camp of Quramatu and forced the Babylonians out.

The following year, 605, Nabopolassar remained in Babylon, "because he himself could not endure the fatigues" of the expedition, according to Flavius Josephus, and instead sent his son Nebuchadnezzar, at the head of his army, to attack the Egyptians. They had settled in the town of Carchemish, whence they launched raids along the banks of the Euphrates. Nebuchadnezzar crossed the river and attacked Carchemish, which he captured rapidly, forcing the Egyptians to flee. He then marched on the region of Hamath and wiped out the rest of the routed Egyptian army, "so that no Egyptian would be able to go home." King Necho II was not part of this Egyptian army, which was more of a garrison, mainly comprising Ethiopian, Libyan, and Lydian mercenaries, according to the Bible. Nebuchadnezzar captured the whole region of Hamath. His victory meant the end of Egyptian domination in Syria and in a substantial part of the Near East. Logically he ought to have driven home his advantage and finished chasing the Egyptians out of the Near East. But he learned that his father Nabopolassar had just died, on the eighth day of the month of August. He left the Babylonian garrisons in position and returned to Babylon to succeed his father.

On the first day of September, Nebuchadnezzar II ascended to the throne of Babylon. For the Phoenician cities, it was the end of the period of independence and vague Egyptian domination. According to Flavius Josephus, quoting Berossus, a Babylonian priest from the end of the fourth century, the new Babylonian king took prisoners after his victories in northern Syria—Jews, Phoenicians, Syrians, and Egyptians. They were taken back to Babylon by his army, which was loaded down with plunder. He himself is said to have returned with a small escort across the Syrian desert, possibly hurried by the fear of a rival seizing power in his absence. However, as the Babylonian Chronicles does not speak of these prisoners, this taking of captives may not have occurred in 605:

Flavius Josephus may have mistaken it with other events that took place in the following years.

2

The Peak of the Babylonian Empire
(605–562)

The conquest of the Phoenician cities by Nebuchadnezzar II

The year 605 was a decisive one for the Phoenician cities because Nebuchadnezzar II was victorious over the Egyptians, was master over northern Syria, and was installed on the throne of Babylon. That did not mean, however, that the whole of Syria, Palestine, and the Phoenician cities, which he called the Hatti region, submitted straightaway. The conquest and pacification of these regions were to be a lengthy undertaking. Nebuchadnezzar II, the most prestigious of the Babylonian kings, is difficult to figure out. He was a conqueror, even though reservations can be had about his military capabilities. There was no lack of statesmanlike qualities, given his success in building the Babylonian Empire. He was a great builder, who restored a country that for a long time had been devastated by war. That is roughly all we know about him because the Babylonian Chronicles and other texts say little about his personality.

His first concern, after having been enthroned in September 605, was to set off straight away for the Hatti region to pursue its conquest. The Babylonian Chronicles do not indicate the start date for his first campaign, only the date of his return to Babylon, in February 604, laden with a huge amount of plunder. However, he had not yet gotten as far as the Phoenician cities and had provoked no fear, because no western state owed him allegiance or paid him tribute. He came back to Babylon after his campaign, as he was to do after all his campaigns. In April, for twelve days he celebrated the New Year festival in honor of the god Marduk. In June of the same year, he set off for the land of Hatti again, where he won victory after victory through December. This time, the western states understood that the Babylonian threat was a serious one and all the kings of Hatti, including the Phoenician kings, came to meet him, bringing a sizeable tax payment in sign of submission. In so doing, they mirrored the instinctive reactions of their ancestors in the period when they were in dread of the powerful Assyrian kings. After receiving them, Nebuchadnezzar II continued his conquests as far as Ashkelon, which refused to submit and requested, in vain, the pharaoh's support. He took the town, plundered it, ravaged it, and captured its king. He returned to Babylon in February 603. In 602 and 601, he pursued his conquests in Hatti, each time bringing back a large quantity of spoils to Babylon. The text of the chronicles for these two years contained too many gaps for us to know exactly which western states he subjugated. However, it is clear that he struggled to subjugate the whole of Hatti and the conquest advanced step by step. His campaigns were aimed not only at conquering new territories, but also at crushing the recurring revolts, at discouraging thoughts of independence, and at collecting tribute. No text indicates that he confronted the Phoenician cities, which had only pledged allegiance to him so as to avoid trouble.

King Adon's call for help

In an Aramaic letter on papyrus found at Saqqara in Egypt, King Adon asked the pharaoh, probably Necho II, for help against the king of Babylon, Nebuchadnezzar II. Aramaic was a language of communication in the Near East at that time. The name of Adon's city is illegible as the papyrus is damaged in several places, but this king bore a Phoenician name and he invoked the Phoenician god Baal Shamim. According to Adon's explanations, the Babylonian king had reached the town of Afqa or Aphek (both toponyms are written the same), he had captured it and was therefore close to his city which was under threat.

On the reverse of the papyrus one line is written in demotic, but this is also partially erased: the specialists are not sure whether this can be read as the name of Ekron or not. If yes, Adon would have been the king of this city and Nebuchadnezzar II would have conquered the Palestinian town of Aphek, in the south of the Sharon Plain. However, the presence of a Phoenician king in Palestine would be surprising. A second interpretation is more plausible: the Babylonian king captured Afqa, the high place for worship in Byblos at the end of the Nahr Ibrahim Valley, and threatened Adon, king of Byblos. Given the continued unique relations that the kings of Byblos maintained with Egypt, Adon's call to the pharaoh for help was only natural. The route to Afqa from the Beqaa Valley was difficult, but Nebuchadnezzar II was not put off by having to cross the coastal chain of Lebanon, for example, in the northern part, north of the Qurnat as-Sawda, at a very high altitude.

Whether Byblos or Ekron, the letter points to the existence of a treaty between King Adon and the pharaoh, meaning that there were ongoing ties between Egypt and the Near East. It must date to 603/602, because for this year the Babylonian Chronicles mentioned the taking of a town whose name has not been preserved. To take this town, Nebuchadnezzar II employed siege equipment, which he had transported across the mountains. This would correspond with a location at Afqa and not Aphek. We do not know whether the pharaoh heard Adon's call for help or whether he did come to his aid, nor whether Adon's city was taken by Nebuchadnezzar II.

In fact, it is very unlikely that Necho II came to Adon's assistance because, in 601, Nebuchadnezzar II continued his victorious advance in Hatti and marched towards Egypt. When he became aware of this, the pharaoh assembled his troops and confronted the king of Babylon's army, probably close to its eastern border. He managed to retake Gaza, but, according to the Babylonian Chronicles, the battle between the two great powers resulted in very heavy losses on both sides. For that reason, Nebuchadnezzar II returned to Babylon and remained there the following year, in 600, to rebuild his forces, especially the cavalry and war chariots. As for Necho II, he exhibited pragmatism: he gave up his ambitions in the Near East, no longer venturing beyond his eastern border to the south of Palestine until the end of his reign in 595. According to the Bible's book of Kings, "the king of Egypt did not leave his country again, because the king of Babylon had taken from him everything that had belonged to him, from the torrent of Egypt to the river Euphrates." On the other hand, he pursued his policy of openness towards the Greek world, encouraging Greeks to settle in Egypt. He also worked to further strengthen the powerful Egyptian fleet, with the aim of being able to compete with the other fleets of the eastern Mediterranean. He undertook the construction of the canal linking the Mediterranean with the Red Sea, via a branch of the Nile, the Wadi Tumilat, and the Amer lakes, in order to create a new trade route. He employed 120,000 workmen on the project and, while waiting for it to be be finished, set up a transit center for caravans at Tell el-Maskhuta, some 20 kilometers west of Ismailia. However, he failed to complete the project, and as a result appears to have been something like the man of lost opportunities.

The pharaoh Psamtik II and Phoenicia

The partial failure of the Babylonians against Egypt in 601 had raised hopes of liberation in the western states, especially as they had experienced a two-year respite. This was because, in 600, there had been no Babylonian military expedition and, in 599, only one expedition was organized against the Arab desert tribes. However, the Phoenician cities preferred to adopt a cautious stance and remained in a state of uncertainty. But Jehoiakim, the king of Judah, decided otherwise and refused to continue paying tribute to Nebuchadnezzar II. According to the Bible's book of Kings, Judah was the target of several raids by Arameans, Moabites, and Ammonites, who were probably subservient to the Babylonian king. Jehoiakim counted on aid from Egypt, but none came. His young son Jehoiachin succeeded him in 598, but only for three months.

During the seventh year of his reign, Nebuchadnezzar II undertook a new campaign against Hatti, with the aim of quelling the revolt of Judah. He set up his camp near Jerusalem, capturing it in March 597. He pillaged the town and its temple, seized a substantial amount of booty and deported King Jehoiachin to Babylon. He replaced him on the throne of Jerusalem with Josiah's third son, Zedekiah, who had apparently submitted to him. Two factions emerged, sustaining agitation in Jerusalem and among the Judean deportees in Babylon. One, possibly fueled secretly by Egypt, was waiting for the return of King Jehoiachin and advocated resisting the Babylonians. The other faction was in favor of temporary submission to the oppressor as an act of political common sense as well as in acceptance that it was the will of Yahweh to chastise his people. This view was supported by the prophet Jeremiah, who roamed the streets of Jerusalem wearing a symbolic yoke on his neck.

In 596, Nebuchadnezzar II launched a campaign against Carchemish. In 595, he went on an expedition on the banks of the Tigris and put the king of Elam to flight. In 594, he suppressed a rebellion in Babylonia.

Psamtik II succeeded his father Necho II on the throne of Egypt in 595. His reign was brief, but he displayed the same energy as his grandfather Psamtik I. He focused his attention on foreign policy to try and offset the negative effects of that of his father, particularly in the Near East. As soon as he came to power, he drove Zedekiah, king of Judah, to rebel. He was probably the instigator of the anti-Babylonian conference that was held in Jerusalem in 594. According to the Bible, this conference brought together the ambassadors of the kings of Edom, Moab, Ammon, Tyre, and Sidon. Its aim clearly was to prepare a new revolt against Babylonian domination. The prophet Jeremiah incited the participants to accept the yoke, but to no avail. King Zedekiah was presented as a weak and indecisive king, incapable of standing up to the warmongering of his advisors. He persecuted the prophet Jeremiah, even though he was in awe of him. After the conference, he was obliged to take Judah's tribute to Babylon himself, because in so doing Nebuchadnezzar II wanted to remind him that he had chosen him as king and there was no question of contesting him. At the end of year 594 and in 593, the king of Babylon set off again to campaign against Hatti, whence he returned with a large quantity of spoils. That is the date that unfortunately marks the end of the Babylonian Chronicles.

In 593 and 592 the pharaoh Psamtik II suppressed a revolt of the Kushites, and followed that with the degradation of monuments of the Ethiopian kings of the Twenty-Fifth Dynasty, the ancient opponents of the Saite lineage. In this campaign, he used Greek and Phoenician mercenaries, who left graffiti in their respective languages at Abu Simbel. He also attacked the memory of his father Necho II, whom he reproached mainly for his military failures against the Babylonians. In reality, he knew he did not have sufficient resources to defeat Nebuchadnezzar II either, so he employed devious means with the aim of achieving victory long term, without realizing that he would not have enough time. In order to show that Egypt was still watching over the Near East, in 591 he went there himself, into the heart of the territory conquered by the Babylonians.

The account of his journey appears on a demotic papyrus dating to the ninth year of the reign of Darius I, king of the Persians, that is, in 512, which relates the story of the priestly Petisis family. The pharaoh Psamtik II went for a "walk in the land of Khor," probably referring to Byblos. He undertook, in all innocence it would appear, a peaceful journey to this Phoenician city. What could be more natural for a pharaoh than paying a visit to the temple of Baalat and the king of Byblos, by virtue of the religious and friendly relations established between the two states over thousands of years? He requested that the main temples of Egypt send him priests to carry bouquets for the major gods, which he would take to Byblos with him. These bouquets were brought to him as a mark of favor to the gods during certain festivals, at the beginning of the year, when leaving on campaign and when returning victorious. The priests of Amun agreed to appoint Petisis as the worthiest to escort the bouquet of their god on this journey, accompanied by a servant and a guard. The pharaoh took bouquets of gods on his pilgrimage and probably offered them to Baalat, a venerated divinity of long standing in Byblos and in Egypt. The journey took place during the fourth year of Psamtik II's reign, hence in 591. On setting out, the pharaoh was irreproachable in the eyes of Nebuchadnezzar II, and on returning he celebrated it as a triumphant expedition. Symbolically, he wanted to show that Egypt still took an interest in the Near East and that it was ready to help the western states rebel against the Babylonians, Zedekiah of Judah, and the Phoenicians in particular. It may have been the result of Psamtik II's encouragements that, in 589, Zedekiah of Judah refused to pay tribute to the king of Babylon, followed, soon afterwards, by the king of Tyre.

The pharaoh Apries and Phoenicia

Psamtik II passed away before his shrewd Near Eastern policy paid off. His son Apries, whom the prophet Jeremiah called Hophra, ascended to the throne of Egypt in 589 and had to manage the consequences of his father's policy. He had to contend with the situation prompted by the revolt of Zedekiah, in which Egypt was involved. Hearing of this revolt, Nebuchadnezzar II's reaction was not long in coming; he set off on campaign in 589 and came to set siege to Jerusalem, using all his siege equipment and starving the town.

The situation of the Phoenician cities during this incident is unclear. According to Herodotus, the pharaoh Apries led an army against Sidon and fought the Tyrians at sea. The account of Diodorus is even harder to interpret: Apries conducted a campaign against Cyprus and Phoenicia with his land and maritime forces, and he took Sidon, thereby terrifying the other Phoenician cities, which submitted. He also won a large naval battle against joint Phoenician and Cypriot forces, and returned to Egypt with an abundance of plunder. Questions have sometimes been raised as to whether the Tyrians and the Sidonians may actually have sided with the pharaoh against the Babylonians, even though the texts say the opposite.

What really happened? In 589, the Phoenician cities were vassals of Nebuchadnezzar II and paid him tribute. But Apries dreamed of establishing himself in the Near East again. Even though the Phoenician cities found it hard to accept Babylonian domination and although they sometimes called on the pharaoh for help as a last resort, this did not necessarily mean that they wanted to submit to Egypt again. Byblos was a special case because its relations with Egypt were still strong, and at this point it no longer had any military power. Consequently, it had no role to play on the international scene. Given these conditions, it was possible that Apries, taking advantage of the fact that Nebuchadnezzar II was occupied by the siege of Jerusalem, tried to reconquer the Phoenician cities of Tyre and Sidon to regain a foothold in the Near East. However, it is hard to believe that the Egyptian fleet had become powerful enough to beat the combined Phoenician and Cypriot fleets, as Diodorus writes. Nor is it clear what role Cyprus played in this affair. The island had become independent again at the end of the Assyrian Empire and there was nothing to indicate that the Babylonian kings either succeeded, or even sought, to conquer it. Anyway, if the Phoenician cities did submit to Apries, their submission was merely temporary and they must have rapidly been reintegrated into the Babylonian Empire. The establishment of the "Tyrian Camp," a Phoenician colony in Memphis, dates to his reign. So perhaps the Tyrians supplanted the Giblites as the Phoenician trading partners of the Egyptians.

The pharaoh tried to assist King Zedekiah, who was besieged in Jerusalem, but he had to retreat before the Babylonian forces. The Phoenician cities did not attempt to help him. Jerusalem resisted by itself, heroically, for two years before succumbing in July 587. This event is described at length in several books of the Bible and by Flavius Josephus, as it sealed the disappearance of the kingdom of Judah. Zedekiah fled, but he was caught and captured in Jericho. Nebuchadnezzar II wanted to make a terrible example of him because the king of Judah was no ordinary vassal, as it was Nebuchadnezzar II himself who had inducted him. He was taken to the Babylonian headquarters at Riblah in northern Syria, where he attended the execution of his sons before having his eyes gouged out. He was then fettered and sent in captivity to Babylon. Jerusalem was destroyed, its walls dismantled, and 3,023 Judeans deported. The new province of Judea was entrusted to the Babylonian governor Gedaliah. However, partisans of resistance against the Babylonians assassinated Gedaliah and fled to Egypt. It took a further deportation in 582 to dissuade any residual Judean inclinations to resist. According to the Bible, the three waves of deportations in 597, 587, and 582 took the total to 4,600 Judeans.

The failure of Apries to help Zedekiah in 589 was perceived by the Egyptians as a defeat in the face of Nebuchadnezzar II. If it is true that the pharaoh captured Tyre and Sidon, this conquest must have been short lived, as it was not recorded as an achievement by the Egyptians. The Elephantine garrison rebelled against Apries, who gave the general Neshor the task of suppressing the mutiny. However, it was the early-warning sign of the unrest that was to mark the end of his reign.

Ezekiel's oracles against Tyre

The biblical oracles of Ezekiel paint an impressive picture of the strength of Tyre. The prophet describes Tyrian commercial activities in such detail that he must have spent some time in this Phoenician city during its period of great opulence to be so well informed. Questions have been raised as to whether the situation in Tyre as he describes it was that of the early sixth century, just before Nebuchadnezzar II's siege, or that which it experienced a few decades earlier, prior to being weakened by the last Assyrian kings. However, since the decline of the Assyrian Empire, Tyre had had plenty of time regain its prosperity. Chapter 26 of the book of Ezekiel, which describes the siege of Tyre by Nebuchadnezzar II, its destruction, and the consequences thereof, dates to the eleventh year of Zedekiah's reign, hence to 587. Chapter 27, which is a lament over the disappearance of the powerful city and its economic empire, is not dated, nor is chapter 28, which contains two oracles against Tyre. However, in the oracle against Egypt, a correction was made regarding the siege of Tyre, indicating the twenty-seventh year of Zedekiah's reign, in 571.

The description of the siege of Tyre by Nebuchadnezzar II resembles the other sieges already undergone by the city under the last Assyrian kings. However, it does not apply to the island of Tyre, but to one of its fortified towns on the mainland, probably Ushu, which was located just opposite. This is because the description of the Babylonian army only refers to land forces, specifically, chariots, cavalrymen, and a vast number of foot soldiers. The Babylonian king used the customary siege techniques: earthworks, an embankment, anti-arrow shields to protect the Babylonians against the fearsome Tyrian archers, battering rams to shatter the fortifications, and picks to demolish the towers. The consequences of the siege, according to Ezekiel, were to be the massacre of women in the Tyrian countryside, the opening of a breach in the walls, the extermination of the whole population, a colossal amount of plunder being taken, and the demolition of the town. His mistake was to say that this concerned the island of Tyre, instead of a mainland Tyrian town such as Ushu.

Ezekiel imagined Tyre as a ship of pure beauty, doomed to sink in the sea with crew and cargo. We cannot help but think of a disturbing discovery made by archaeologists: they have observed that, since antiquity, the island of Tyre has been sinking deeper into the sea. Through the ship image, the prophet provided details about the city's relations with the other Phoenician cities. He described the crew of the ship Tyre thus: "As oarsmen, you have the inhabitants of Sidon and Arwad. You have taken wise men aboard, O Tyre: they were your sailors. The Elders of Byblos and its wise men were with you as caulkers. The sons of Arwad with your army around you on your battlements. They hung their shields on your city walls." At that time, Tyre was the richest and most powerful of the Phoenician cities, exercising both political and economic supremacy. Citizens of Sidon, Byblos, and Arwad were employed in the fleet and in the army of Tyre, with the Tyrians occupying the commanding ranks. The three cities did not all receive the same treatment. The citizens of Arwad were the most in demand as they were oarsmen in the fleet and soldiers positioned on the top of Tyre's fortifications, with a dual role, both offensive and defensive. The Sidonians were also employed as oarsmen in the fleet, with an offensive role. The citizens of Byblos consisted of two different political groups used by Tyre: the Council of Elders, well attested in the Phoenician cities, and the Council of Wise Men, unknown elsewhere. These two groups enjoyed preferential treatment from Tyre: they were caulkers, so symbolically responsible for ensuring that everything on the ship was in good working order and for caulking it thoroughly to make it completely watertight. They had no military role because they had no fleet or land forces at that time. Rather than impose on it the hegemony it wielded over Sidon and Arwad, Tyre must have concluded some form of alliance with Byblos.

The description of Tyre's economic empire given by Ezekiel is remarkable. He presents it as having existed for several centuries already. Tyre had a strategic position and a key role in international trade: "You who live in the avenues of the sea, you who trade with the peoples, with the countless islands, you whose territory is at the heart of the seas." The prophet gives a long list of Tyre's trading partners, not all of which have been identified: Tarshish in the south of Spain, Ionia, Cilicia, Phrygia, Cappadocia, Rhodes, Edom, Judah, Israel, Damas, Dedan, Arabia, Kedar, Saba, Harran, and Assyria. He also quotes a vast number of products exchanged with each of the partners, among them precious goods such as gold, silver, ivory, turquoise, coral, agate, and ebony. The large Tyrian routes evoked in these oracles, from Anatolia to the Arabian Peninsula, and from the north of the Aegean Sea to the western Mediterranean, ended up in regions rich in metal ores. As this showed, the main motivations of Tyrian trade were to meet the demands of metal supply.

The correction made by Ezekiel to his prophecies in 571 was essential because it had become obvious to him that the siege of Tyre had dragged on for many years and had finally failed. The besiegers were in a pitiful state: their heads had become bald and their shoulders chafed by having to carry the heavy loads required in setting siege to the town: "Nebuchadnezzar, king of Babylon, subjected his army to a huge effort against Tyre, but in Tyre he found no wages for himself or his army in reward for the effort he had provided against the town." Ezekiel predicted that Yahweh would give him Egypt and all its riches in compensation. He could not have known at that time that Nebuchadnezzar II's attempt to invade Egypt in 568 would end in failure.

The siege of Tyre by Nebuchadnezzar II

This siege of Tyre is known through the oracles of Ezekiel and through Flavius Josephus: "Nebuchadnezzar besieged Tyre for thirteen years at the time of king Ithobaal." The Greek author gave a new list of kings of Tyre, with the number of years of reign for each one, making a total of fifty-four years and three months. He added that the Babylonian king started the siege of Tyre in the seventh year and that Cyrus II took power in Persia in the fourteenth year of the reign of Hiram III of Tyre. Complex calculations have been made to date the reigns of the kings of Tyre: hence, Ithobaal would have reigned for nineteen years, around 591–573. However, these dates are approximative as Flavius Josephus wrote several centuries after these events and depended on the sources available to him, namely, Menander of Ephesus and Philostratus.

The precise dates of the siege of Tyre and of the reign of Ithobaal III are difficult to establish. If it was the seventh year of Nebuchadnezzar II's reign, it would be 598; if it was the seventh year of Ithobaal III's reign, it would be around 585. Some authors have proposed an earlier date for the siege of Tyre—around 603–590—arguing that the Babylonians would have hesitated attacking Egypt without having settled the Tyre problem first. However, it is hard to imagine Nebuchadnezzar II starting his conquest of Hatti with the siege of Tyre. Most authors think that Flavius Josephus made a mistake and meant to write "the seventeenth year" of Nebuchadnezzar II's reign, that is to say 588. They propose a later date for the siege of Tyre of around 586–573. If we interpret it as the seventh year of Ithobaal's reign, the siege would have taken place around 585–573. The later period is the most likely as it agrees with Ezekiel's oracles in 587 and 571, and with the dating of the reign of Ithobaal III by Flavius Josephus.

Nebuchadnezzar II, after taking Jerusalem and dealing with the issue involving the kingdom of Judah in 587, naturally wanted to settle the Tyre problem before attacking Egypt again. That is probably the situation described by Flavius Josephus when he writes: "accounts consistent with those of Berossus appear in the Phoenician annals: they recount how the king of the Babylonians conquered Syria and the whole of Phoenicia." The primary and constant objective of Nebuchadnezzar II's conquests to the west was the domination of the Near East, and in particular the strategic base of Tyre, in order to attack Egypt. The Babylonian Empire also needed naval forces to defeat Egypt's war fleet, so it could hardly do without the powerful Tyrian fleet. Like several of his ancestors, King Ithobaal of Tyre felt secure on his island, and thought himself rich and powerful enough to resist another siege. It is possible that the pharaoh Apries, keen to hamper the Babylonians, supported Tyre's revolt by helping to supply provisions to the island, as he had already tried to support the revolt of Zedekiah.

How did the siege of Tyre end? In failure for Nebuchadnezzar II as the island town was probably not taken, but the reality is more complicated. All the mainland territory of Tyre, including its fortified towns, such as Ushu and Akko, was conquered by the Babylonians; it was plundered and devastated, its populations deported. Just as the Assyrian kings had done previously, Nebuchadnezzar II must have blocked the supplies of drinking water, food, and other resources from reaching the island of Tyre from its mainland territory, without succeeding completely because Tyre's fleet was too powerful. It was subjected to a partial blockade for thirteen years, sometimes supervised by the Babylonian king in person. At the end of that period, Ithobaal III of Tyre must have been eager to finish it because his city had been so exhausted by the endless siege. It was also the time when it lost its colonies in the western Mediterranean, but it still held on to some Cypriot colonies, such as Kition. Carthage had become an independent state, occupying the ancient Tyrian colonies and founding colonies of its own. Tarshish was colonized during this period by the Phocaeans, as attested by Greek ceramics discovered in Huelva, imported in vast quantities during the first half of the sixth century. As for Nebuchadnezzar II, he no longer wanted to continue with the siege of Tyre because he saw no way out, especially as he had the possibility of presenting Ithobaal III's submission as a victory, even if the island of Tyre was not captured. A treaty was probably concluded: the king of Tyre stepped down, in exchange for which Tyrian kingship was preserved and Tyre recovered at least part of its mainland territory. It is possible that Ithobaal III was deported to the court of Babylon.

His replacement, installed on the throne by Nebuchadnezzar II, was Baal II, whose path of ascent is unknown. He reigned for ten years, according to Flavius Josephus, around 572–563. We know nothing about him, except that he was certainly pro-Babylonian. The administration that had been put in place under the Sargonids, with provinces controlled by governors and autonomous cities under strict surveillance, had more or less disappeared during the return to independence of

the western states and during the brief period of Egyptian domination. Nebuchadnezzar II therefore applied to them his own system of domination: he counted on the loyalty of local hand-picked kings, without being obliged to appoint Babylonian high commissioners to oversee them. For ten years, Baal II of Tyre appear to have posed no problem as a vassal subjected to the Babylonians and paying his annual tribute. He took advantage of his mainland territory that he had recovered and of the independence of his island town to try and repair the damage of the previous siege and to regain a little of his prosperity and power, while at the same time respecting Babylonian interests.

Nebuchadnezzar II was as obsessed as the last Assyrian kings with the conquest of Egypt, and for this reason needed the economic resources and fleets of the Phoenician cities. However, he adopted a different policy towards them: he relied on the local pro-Babylonian kings and, when they rebelled, he mercilessly destroyed their cities, plundered them, and destroyed all their resources. He did not know how to formulate a compromise in order to preserve his economic advantages in the way the Sargonids did. He acted in a perfunctory manner, rather like the early Assyrian kings, pillaging the subjugated countries, amassing as much booty as possible and collecting tributes himself, without worrying about whether in so doing he was draining his vassals of their resources. Although the siege of Tyre ended around 573, he did not undertake an expedition against Egypt before 568, probably because not all the Near East had been pacified yet. It was only after having finished this process of pacification that he attacked Egypt. He also took advantage of the country's internal disturbances, where a civil war broke out between nationalist forces and Greek and Carian mercenaries. Amasis succeeded in defeating the pharaoh Apries in 570 and taking the throne of Egypt. This former general managed to halt the Babylonian army in 568 and to save Egypt. Faced with the unrest of the Greek settlers, he found a solution in year 16 of his reign, by concentrating them in the town of Naucratis, to the southwest of the future Alexandria. He granted them economic and social privileges and recognized Naucratis's status as an autonomous trading post, with its own places of worship. He also maintained relations with the Phoenician cities, as evidenced by the discovery of two objects in his name in Sidon: a sistrum handle and a hammered copper vase.

The steles of Nebuchadnezzar II in Phoenicia

Nebuchadnezzar II had six steles erected in Phoenicia, and perhaps others that have not been discovered. He therefore followed the tradition of the Assyrian kings, choosing very visible or symbolic locations. His pretentions were limitless because, thanks to his god Marduk, he extended his domination, not only from "the upper sea to the lower sea," but "over all territories, the whole of the inhabited world." He reigned over an empire that stretched from the Persian Gulf to Cilicia and to the "country of the Ionians." The first stele was erected on the rocky bank of the Nahr al-Kalb, north of Beirut, among other steles sculpted by the successive conquerors who had passed by this site. It bears a very damaged inscription in Akkadian on four columns. In the legible part, Nebuchadnezzar II described his construction and restoration works in Babylonia. In addition to this stele, which is positioned in a conventional place, he had five other steles installed in unexpected places, in the north of Lebanon's coastal range. Two steles were sculpted at the Wadi Brissa, on rocks on the edge of the current road. Actually, the neighboring village is named Brissa; the river, which runs west to east, is the Wadi Charbine. The two bas-reliefs bear inscriptions and representations of the king of Babylon, one where he is upright in front of a tree, and the other where he is fighting a standing lion. Two other steles are situated forty meters one from the other, near the Wadi es-Saba, running north–south, on the eastern slope of the Jebel Akroum mountain. One shows the same combat scene of the king against a lion, the other the king in front of astral symbols, with illegible traces of an inscription. The stele of Shir as-Sanam, which in Arabic means the "outcrop of the idol," is also located near the Jebel Akroum and the Wadi Oustane, on a rocky outcrop 7 meters above ground level. It also represents the Babylonian king in front of astral symbols, and bears a long inscription that has not yet been deciphered due to the difficulty of access.

The siting of the five northern Lebanon steles is easier to understand knowing that, during his campaigns in Hatti, Nebuchadnezzar set up his headquarters at Riblah, in the Orontes Valley, between Hermel and Homs. From Riblah, he could very easily get to the coast via the region with the steles. The Wadi Brissa rises on a gentle slope towards a wide mountain pass, which gives access to the valleys leading to Tripoli. In antiquity, Akroum, some 10 kilometers north, seems to have been the starting point for a quick path across the Mount Lebanon chain, discovered by the Babylonians, then used by the Romans, the Arabs, and the Crusaders. As the crow flies, Akroum was barely 34 kilometers from the coast. Going via the Wadi es-Saba, one could circumvent the Jebel Qamua ridge as far as Qoubaiyat, without exceeding an altitude of 1,300 meters, meaning that it was a path that could be used almost year-round. The Shir as-Sanam stele is located at an altitude of some

1,600 meters, where three paths cross: one that descends towards Akkar Atika and reaches the coast, a second that leads towards Qoubaiyat, and a third that goes to Qantara and Arqa. This stele commemorates the crossing of the Lebanon ridge by the Babylonian army, to the north of the Qamua plateau, before dropping down to the coast. The location of these steles shows that Nebuchadnezzar II controlled the main northern routes of the Lebanese chain, leading to both the forests and the Mediterranean coast.

The inscriptions on the Wadi Brissa and Nahr al-Kalb steles highlight another key objective of the Babylonian king: the restoration and reconstruction works in Babylonia. He continued the work initiated by his father Nabopolassar. At the end of ten years of civil war, Babylonia was utterly devastated, the towns lay in ruins, crops were destroyed and irrigation canals abandoned. Its agricultural economy had to be reorganized, its shrines restored, and the destruction repaired. Nebuchadnezzar II devoted a considerable amount of effort in several towns like Borsippa and Kutha, and especially in Babylon. He reorganized the cult, provided the temples with regular donations for the offerings and the maintenance of statues, and established cult regulations. He turned Babylon into a vast quadrilateral, surrounded by a double wall comprising eight gates and a canal. The town had more than fifty shrines at that time, the most famous being the Esagila, a temple of Marduk, and the Etemenanki, a 100 meter-or-so-tall ziggurat. The famouse hanging gardens of Babylon were considered in antiquity to be one of the seven wonders of the world.

This remarkable work was realized by Nebuchadnezzar II thanks to incessant expeditions into distant Hatti, on the steep, strenuous, and difficult mountain tracks of Phoenicia. He collected, stacked up, and brought back each year to his capital the plentiful tribute of the mountains, the sea, and the land: gold, silver, precious stones, magnificent objects, and huge cedars. Unlike the Assyrian kings who also went into the Amanus, he preferred getting his supplies from the forests of Lebanon and took a special interest in cedars, felling the most beautiful specimens himself. He chose "the most solid, the thickest and tallest, of splendid beauty and sublime appearance." According to him, the forest of Lebanon was a "forest which belonged to the god Marduk." He used cedar wood in all his constructions: joists, roof beams, planks, supports, and doors. Other species, including pine and oak, which probably came from the forests of Lebanon as well, were less frequently used.

Nebuchadnezzar II's exceptional interest for the forest resources of Phoenicia led him to undertake what no other king had done before him, but which a number would subsequently imitate, namely, the opening up of routes in these inextricable and impenetrable forests. "I have cut through the high mountains, he wrote, I have shattered the mountains' rocks, I have made way for passes, I have made a route to be able to transport the cedars for King Marduk." Five steles that he set up on the way confirm that the Babylonian king opened up of forest routes. The clearly stated purpose of this initiative was to facilitate the exploitation of Lebanon's forests. The other objective was territorial control, which was no less important in an empire built by military conquest and under permanent threat of revolt. Thanks to these routes, the Babylonian army could advance more rapidly in this mountainous territory, which was difficult to access. It could get to the Phoenician coast in the region of Arqa or Tripoli, in order to control the city of Arwad northwards, Byblos and especially Sidon and Tyre southwards.

The opening up of routes inevitably brought with it the pacification of the region. Nebuchadnezzar II embarked on subjugating and con-ciliating the turbulent mountain people. The account of these events is somewhat lacunary on one of the two Wadi Brissa steles, but the essentials can be understood. Lebanon's mountain people had been op-pressed, chased out, and dispersed by their enemy, who took possession of Mount Lebanon in order to exploit the cedars for his palaces and tem-ples. The Babylonian king regularly sent his army into the mountains of Lebanon in order to expel the enemy and to prevent him coming back to attack the mountain folk. He got them all together and had them taken back to their homes. He guaranteed them security in high grazing lands, above the forests. He had steles placed in the high mountain passes, so that his eternal, near-divine image as a protector king would keep the enemy at bay. Nebuchadnezzar II insisted on the dissuasive role of his steles: the message of the inscriptions was clear for all who could read Akkadian, and the message contained in the images was just as clear for the others.

So who was the Lebanese mountain folk's enemy, who chased them out in order to exploit their rich forest resources? We might think it was the Egyptians who traditionally exploited the forests of Lebanon, but they were more used to getting their supplies in the forest of Byblos, a little further south. Furthermore, the Wadi Brissa and Nahr al-Kalb ste-les date to the last part of Nebuchadnezzar II's reign, possibly between 570 and 562, whereas he chased the Egyptians from the Near East at the beginning of his reign. Maybe the enemy of the mountain folk was one of the coastal vassal cities, between Tripoli and Arwad, which also exploited the forest resources in the hinterland, as indicated by the cedar wood used in the buildings of Arqa.

At the end of this account, the Babylonian king actually explained what the behavior of a model vassal should be. He should not ignore the king's decrees nor change his regulations; if, rather, he was docile, his throne would remain intact and he would be able to prosper under the king's protection.

The Phoenicians in Babylonia

Phoenicians were present in Babylonia in the reign of Nebuchadnezzar II for various reasons. First, he requisitioned the kings of Hatti, including the Phoenician kings, to transport the huge cedars from Mount Lebanon to Babylon. It was a heavy task, especially as the construction works were titanic and carried on right through his reign. Some Phoenicians had already been living in Babylonia for a long while. For example, a text dating from 603, the second year of Nebuchadnezzar II's reign, mentions wool supplied by a certain Taqish-Gula, the son of an inhabitant of Byblos, whose Babylonian name suggests he was perfectly assimilated. The Phoenician Hanun pursued a very successful career in Babylonia around 570, as chief of the Babylonian king's commercial agents. This is no accident because the Phoenicians played a leading role in the imports of goods coming from far-off countries, which they shipped to Babylon. However, they did not have a monopoly on this trade because Babylonian merchants, often financed by the temple, also imported western merchandise.

Texts dating from 592 make mention of Phoenicians working in the royal palace of Babylon: 190 sailors from Tyre and 126 Tyrians, with no specialty indicated. Other texts mention Phoenician craftsmen: three carpenters from Arwad and eight from Byblos, who were paid in rations of oil. The carpenters from Byblos were more appreciated than those from Arwad, as they received a double ration. They were probably assigned to building reconstruction and restoration work. These craftsmen were not prisoners of war, as the texts do not specify that they were, and they were well paid. In addition, there could not have been any prisoners from Byblos, which at that time was a small, subjugated, and pacified city. They had probably been engaged by the Babylonian king, like a lot of other specialists in his empire, for the reconstruction of Babylon's royal palace. The palace employed personnel from the four corners of the empire, including a lot of westerners.

Deportation was a common practice under Nebuchadnezzar II and a lot of Phoenicians figured among the deportees in Babylonia. They are recognizable from their West Semitic names, frequent, for example, in the region of Nippur, and sometimes from the name they gave their new Babylonian village. Hence, the Tyrians had been grouped together in a locality that they called "Tyre," as a commemoration of their city of origin. Eight texts from the archives of Uruk, dated between 574 and 563, refer to this Babylonian Tyre. It was on the edge of the domains of the temples of Uruk and Sippar. Tyre of Babylonia was a center of production and a market for trading agricultural products, also used for recruiting shepherds and farmers. These Tyrians must have been deported mainly after the end of the siege of Tyre and settled in this war-torn region in order to reestablish its agricultural potential.

The exiled Phoenicians were sometimes illustrious. The king of Babylon was accustomed to deporting to his court his rebellious vassals, once ousted and replaced, such as King Jehoiachin of Judah and his five sons. Administrative documents specify the food rations they were granted, particularly the oil. A list of Babylonian court officials, dated around 570, mention sixty or so members of his "official suite," comprising his Babylonian dignitaries and his representatives in the empire. The final names are those of the kings of Tyre, Gaza, Sidon, Arwad, and Ashdod. The king of Byblos is missing, but this may be due to the text being cut off towards the end. The text is ambiguous, because it seems to present officials who were present at the court of Babylon. Even if the Phoenicians had gone to Babylon, either because they were invited, or to bring their tribute in person, they did not live there like the political deportees, of which the king of Judah was one. Nevertheless, King Ithobaal III of Tyre must have been deported to Babylon at the end of the siege of Tyre, as King Baal II of Tyre was to be ten years later.

Tyre's difficulties at the end of Nebuchadnezzar II's reign

After the thirteen-year-long siege of Tyre, Baal II, the new king installed on the throne by Nebuchadnezzar II, reigned for ten years between approximately 572 and 563, apparently without any major problem. At the end of that time, a serious event occurred in Tyre that had a dramatic impact on the city. We know from Flavius Josephus that the Tyrian royal dynasty was interrupted around 563 by the establishment of judges, five in total. He did not say for what reason nor who changed the Tyrian institutions, but it was inevitably Nebuchadnezzar II. These judges were to remain in power in Tyre for seven years and three months. The first of them was Eknibal, son of Baslech, replaced after two months by Chelbes, son of Abdaeus, who held office for ten months. The following judge, Abbar the high priest, only held power for three months. Then,

for six years, around 561–556, two judges governed Tyre, probably at the same time: Myttynos (Mattan) and Gerastratos (Gerashtart), son of Abdelim. During this period, King Baal II and the Tyrian royal family were retained in exile at the court of Babylon.

The extremely severe treatment inflicted on Tyre by Nebuchadnezzar II was inevitably motivated by a very serious offense committed by Baal II. He must have rebelled against the king of Babylon, who came to besiege Tyre for a second time, as suggested in texts from the Uruk and Sippar archives. These administrative texts listed the supplies granted to the soldiers who had to accompany the Babylonian king on his expedition against Tyre—the Phoenician city, not the Babylonian locality of the same name. They were allocated food rations, breastplates, shoes, clothing, coats, and blankets for sleeping in their tents. Thus, this was not a permanent Babylonian garrison based in Tyre's mainland territory, but a temporary Babylonian army camp, installed in tents and facing winter conditions. It was essentially a second siege of Tyre, involving a blockade of the island town to prevent access to its mainland territory. The texts are dated, giving the exact length of the siege, fourteen months from July 564 to September 563. With a winter spent in position, coats and blankets in the tents would have been necessary. King Baal II of Tyre did not resist for as long as his predecessor Ithobaal III. Despite the ten-year respite that Tyre had enjoyed, the city remained weakened. Baal II must have given allegiance to Nebuchadnezzar II, but still without handing over his island. As was customary, the Babylonian king wanted to set a strong example, especially as the episode involved a vassal whom he had installed on the throne himself and who had broken his oaths. He deported him to Babylon, together with the whole Tyrian royal family, and abolished the kingship in Tyre around 563.

The kings of Tyre were replaced by judges or "shophets." This Semitic title was used both for a magistrate administering justice and for a ruler. In Ugarit, the term was also used in reference to the king. In Israel, before the monarchy, the judge was the highest civil authority in the federation of tribes. In the Phoenician cities, it was the first time that the office of judge was attested as a ruler. In a city governed by a king, the office of judge was simply a municipal magistracy, which was to be attested in Kition in the fourth century. This municipal magistracy was found in all the Punic or Punicized cities of North Africa up until the Roman period. However, from the fifth or perhaps even the sixth century, Carthage was governed by two shophets. They were elected simultaneously for one year. Greek and Latin authors attributed to the two Carthaginian shophets the right to convene the Senate and the People's

Assembly, and to submit issues to them for debate. They administered justice, assisted by ordinary judges, and also assumed military and religious functions. We do not know how the institution of judges in Tyre functioned exactly during this period of seven years and three months. The institution as such was not an innovation as it had already existed earlier in the Near East. In Tyre, it was put in place in a disorganized manner, as though they were testing it to see in which way it would work best. In fact, the origin of the judges was diverse (one was a high priest), the exercise of power was granted sometimes to one judge and sometimes to two at the same time, and the term of their mandate varied between two months and six years. It would appear that after several tests, they arrived at the formula of two judges holding office at the same time, which must have worked well as it was used for six years, from 562. Even though the Tyrians may have had a say about this new power structure, it was closely controlled by the Babylonian king.

According to Flavius Josephus, Nebuchadnezzar II fell ill after beginning the building of the city walls. This was probably the "Wall of Media," aimed at protecting the region of Babylon against the flooding of the Tigris and the Euphrates, and at isolating the town with the help of a flood-prone area in the event of an enemy attack. On the death of Nebuchadnezzar II, the Babylonian Empire was at its height. During his reign, he had brought about a genuine economic renaissance in Babylonia. The damage caused by the bloodstained anti-Assyrian struggles had been repaired, Babylon had been magnificently rebuilt and had again become a prestigious capital siphoning off rich tributes from the whole of the empire. The bourgeoisie of the large Babylonian towns benefited from this prosperity. Thanks to the profits of the temples, the exploitation of the rural population, and sound management of inherited assets, it acquired wealth that was transmitted from generation to generation and was the source of substantial fortunes. However, the amazing splendor of Nebuchadnezzar II's reign masked latent problems. On several occasions, there were hints of profound instability in Babylonia's domestic situation. In 595, for example, a revolt was harshly repressed by arms. An eminent Babylonian, Baba-aha-iddina, accused of having violated oaths (*adê*) to the king, was condemned to death for high treason and his property confiscated. This sentence shows that the method of government had barely changed: just as with the Assyrian Empire, the Babylonian Empire was based on a system of loyalty to the king sealed by oaths.

3

The Decline of the Babylonian Empire
(562–539)

Restoration of the kingship in Tyre

Nebuchadnezzar II's successor in 562 was his son Amel-Marduk, known in the Bible as Evil-Merodach, who only reigned for two years. A series of conspiracies bathed the Babylonian throne in bloodshed between 562 and 556, provoked by personal ambitions or power struggles between rival factions, particularly between various Babylonian clergy. Very little is known about the reign of Amel-Marduk, likewise about his personality. Flavius Josephus says he was arbitrary and violent, whereas the Bible praises his clemency. On acceding to the throne, he pardoned Jehoiachin, king of Judah, who was still in prison in Babylon. He released him, had him given suitable clothes, took care of all his needs and regularly invited him to dine with him. He viewed him as a friend and granted him top ranking among the deported kings, which also included the king of Tyre. The reign of Amel-Marduk corresponded, in Tyre, with the three-month governing term of the judge Abbar, followed by the joint government of the two judges Mattan and Gerashtart.

In 560, Amel-Marduk's brother-in-law, Neriglissar (Nergal-sar-usur) assassinated him to seize power. Neriglissar was a general, a veteran of Nebuchadnezzar II's campaigns, who controlled the army and owned huge estates in northern Babylonia. He is referred to in the Bible under the name of Nergal-sar-usur, commander-in-chief. He pursued restoration work on the ziggurat and on the royal palace in Babylon. He was an energetic military officer who conducted additional westward campaigns, particularly an expedition to Cilicia, in 557 and 556. He started by leading his army towards the Adana Plain, in western Cilicia, conquered under Nebuchadnezzar II. Appuashu, king of Pirindu in Cilicia Tracheia, was forever plundering and ransacking Syria. To confront him, the Babylonian king headed towards the town of Hume. Before his arrival, Appuashu deployed his troops to carry out an ambush and his cavalry in a mountain pass. But Neriglissar defeated him, decimated his army and chased him into the rugged mountains as far as Ura, near the modern-day town of Silifke. He captured Ura and pursued him to Kirshu (Meydancikkale), his capital, which he burned. Thanks to a war fleet, he disembarked on the rocky island of Pitussu, the current Dana Adasi, close to the coast of Cilicia Tracheia. He succeeded in capturing the island and took the six thousand soldiers stationed there prisoner. He put the whole region to fire and sword, from Selinus on the coast as far as the Lydian border, without being able to get his hands on the elusive Appuashu. He returned to Babylon in March 556.

To conquer the important island garrison of Pitussu, Neriglissar used a substantial fleet, which could well have been the fleet of Tyre. This decisive help from the Tyrians would explain why, as a reward, he allowed the Phoenician city to reinstate the kingship. According to Flavius Josephus, King Balator (Balazor) reigned for one year in Tyre, around 556. He did not specify whether this king of Tyre belonged to the same dynasty as the last king Baal II nor whether he had been released from captivity at the court of Babylon, as Jehoiachin of Judah had been by Amel-Marduk. The treatment reserved for Judeans by the Babylonian kings was probably nothing special compared to that of the Tyrians, but it is better documented thanks to the Bible.

Amel-Marduk and Neriglissar cared little about Egypt during their brief reigns. According to Herodotus, the pharaoh Amasis took advantage of their lack of interest and that of their successors to claim military victories in a number of Cypriot towns, bringing their fleets into his service and collecting tributes. Kition seems however to have remained under the dependence of Tyre. Neriglissar, who was getting on in age when he came to power, only reigned for four years. He left the throne of Babylon to his young son Labashi-Marduk, who was assassinated after four months of reign.

The expeditions of Nabonidus towards the west

Nabonidus, the last Babylonian king, came to power in 556, for a long reign of seventeen years. He was an enigmatic character, both in his personality, in the conditions surrounding his accession to and fall from power. He came to the throne following the conspiracy that had eliminated Labashi-Marduk. The conspiracy seemed mainly inspired by the son of Nabonidus, Bel-shar-usur, known as Belshazzar in the Bible. Out of self-interest, with a view to arranging his political future, he put forward

his father. Of Aramean origin through his mother, Nabonidus had spent his career in the service of Nebuchadnezzar II. He was getting quite old and appeared inoffensive in the eyes of his son. Yet, against all expectations, he displayed a lot of energy and took initiatives, thwarting all the ulterior motives of the conspirators who had brought him to power.

He continued the program of renovation and reconstruction in the main towns of Babylonia, initiated by his predecessors, and he brought to fruition urban planning works in the capital. In the first year of his reign he visited the south of Babylonia. In order to revive religious tradition, he reorganized the administration of the temples and worship practices, providing them with labor resources from among the prisoners of war. Hence, Egyptian prisoners worked in the temple of Shamash in Sippar, but we do not know where they came from because the surviving texts make no mention of clashes between Babylonian and Egyptian troops. Concurrent with the urban projects, Nabonidus undertook military campaigns in the west. According to the Babylonian Chronicles, which are lacunary but at least survive, in the second year of his reign, in January 554, he went to Hamath where he found the climate very cold, understandably for someone who had come from the Iraqi desert. The third year, he took precautions and set off in July towards the Amanus, whence he brought back various forest products to Babylon. On his return he fell ill, but rapidly recovered. He embarked on a new campaign in the land of Hatti, possibly in December.

During the first three years of his reign, Nabonidus kept the Hatti region, which included the Phoenician cities, firmly under control, even though they were not explicitly mentioned. He probably took advantage of his western campaigns to collect tribute as he needed money for the ambitious building works launched in year two of his reign. For this purpose, he mobilized all the craftsmen "from Gaza to the Egyptian border, from the upper sea beyond the Euphrates to the lower sea." He had huge quantities of timber felled in the forests of Lebanon and the Amanus. Consequently, he boasted of having brought back 1,050 cedar trunks to build the Ebabbar temple in Sippar in the course of one single campaign in Lebanon. Substantial input was called for from the Phoenician cities to supply wood and carpenters, and possibly even to transport the timber to Babylon, as was the case in the reign of Nebuchadnezzar II. The vast program of restoration and reconstruction continued right up until the end of Nabonidus's reign, under his direction or following his instructions, using the Phoenician cities to exploit the timber up to the very end. A list of goods imported to Babylon in 550 also mentions iron coming from Lebanon.

Tyre and Sidon at the time of Nabonidus

After one year of reign, around 556, King Balazor of Tyre died of unknown causes according to Flavius Josephus. The Tyrians sent to Babylon, where the Tyrian royal family was living under house arrest, for another king. It was Maharbaal, who reigned for four years, around 555–552. The Babylonian king Nabonidus knew the Tyrians well because one of his steles bears the sign of Tanit, a Tyrian symbol par excellence, and he willingly agreed to the return of Maharbaal. In principle, this king must have belonged to the same dynasty as his predecessor Balazor. The Babylonian king also gave his agreement when, after the end of Maharbaal's reign in 552, the Tyrians sent to Babylon for his brother Hiram III, who reigned for twenty years, around 551–532. This long reign straddled the Babylonian and Persian empires.

There are several indications that at this time, Tyre was no longer the powerful and prosperous city as described in the oracles of Ezekiel. Its endemic insubordination, its obstinate refusal to give up the island, all the sieges it had been subjected to at the hands of successive conquerors attempting to capture it, the loss of almost all its colonies—everything pointed to a weakening and a decline of this Phoenician city at the end of the Babylonian Empire. To crown it all, Tyre apparently fell victim to an earthquake around the year 550. Excavations of its mainland necropolis at Tyre-Al Bass, bordering on the Palestinian encampment, have revealed a thick layer of sterile sand in the levels corresponding to this date, which was also found spread over the island agglomeration. The town must have been partially abandoned following this earthquake.

As had repeatedly been the pattern throughout Phoenicia's history, neighboring Sidon took advantage of the situation to grow. This development is visible on the site of Bostan esh-Sheikh, 2 kilometers northeast of Sidon, on the steep left bank of the Nahr el-Awali, referred to as the Bostrenus or the river Asclepius by ancient authors. The primitive sacred place must have been dedicated to worship out in the open country. The oldest votive offerings found at this site, limestone and terracotta statues, date to the first half of the sixth century. The oldest construction of the Eshmun sanctuary consists of a four-sided sloping podium, which must have supported a temple. This first podium was never completed because it very quickly collapsed, except for one of its corners. As the date of construction was around 550, it is very tempting to link its collapse during construction with the earthquake that shook the neighboring town of Tyre at this time.

A new dynasty came to power in Sidon during the first half of the sixth century. It was founded by King Eshmunazar I, priest of Ashtart, who was a usurper since he does not name his father. The sarcophagi of his son, his grandson, and perhaps his daughter have been found. During a Babylonian campaign in Egypt, which he took part in, he must have brought back four anthropoid sarcophagi made of stone, including his own, which has not yet been discovered. The other three came from the same workshop and belonged to a type that was made in Egypt between 663 and 525, possibly during the reign of Amasis (570–526). One of them bears the hieroglyphic inscription of the first occupant, general Ptah, and the other, unfinished, a hieroglyphic inscription that is illegible, as it had been scraped.

The Egypt campaign in which Eshmunazar I participated could have taken place during the reign of Nebuchadnezzar II, for example, in 568, or during that of Nabonidus who went as far as the Egyptian border and who used Egyptian prisoners in his construction works. The Babylonian Chronicles are too fragmentary to be able to pinpoint which campaign it was. The sarcophagi of Tabnit, Eshmunazar II, and a woman who was perhaps Queen Amashtart, were exhumed in necropoleis in Sidon. Amashtart was the sister of King Tabnit and at the same time his concubine, both being children of Eshmunazar I. Consanguineous royal marriages are a well-attested practice at Ugarit and in the Phoenician myths reported by Philo of Byblos. They were aimed at strengthening dynasties, especially when they were illegitimate and very recent, as was that of Eshmunazar I.

As his successor Tabnit had died before the birth of his son Eshmunazar II, his reign was brief. In the inscription of his sarcophagus, he is referred to as priest of Ashtart, just like his father. Fearing the profanation of his tomb, he gives two dissuasive arguments. There was no point opening it through greed as it contained no silver, no gold, no precious objects, and whoever might actually dare to open it would be damned, would never find a resting place after death, and would have no offspring. Indeed, it was essential for the kings of Sidon to ensure the succession through their progeny. Queen Amashtart was to attempt everything possible to maintain the dynasty. The chronology of the dynasty of Eshmunazar I straddled the Babylonian Empire and the Persian Empire and can be established approximately. Eshmunazar I reigned around 575–550, Tabnit around 550–540, Amashtart's interregnum took place around 539 and the co-regency of Amashtart and Eshmunazar II around 539–525. It was a dynasty that marked the return of Sidon to prominence among the Phoenician cities.

Continuation and end of the reign of Nabonidus and of the Babylonian Empire

In 552, the fourth year of his reign, Nabonidus undertook a long expedition towards the west, to the south of Palestine. However, the economic situation in Babylonia was bad: disturbances broke out in Babylon, Borsippa, Nippur, Ur, Uruk, and Larsa. The external situation was explosive as Cyrus was growing increasingly powerful. Nabonidus did not take the Persian threat into consideration and entrusted the government of Babylonia, in his absence, to his son Bel-shar-usur. He started by heading towards the kingdom of Edom, leaving a stele at Sela in Jordan, to commemorate his journey in the same way as Nebuchadnezzar II had done. The image of the king of Babylon is distinguishable, but the inscription is illegible. Nabonidus then marched towards northern Arabia where he took control of the oasis of Tayma and the towns of Dedan, Fadak, Haybar, Iadia, and Iatribu (the current Medina). He probably integrated the ancient kingdom of Edom into the large province of Arabia, with its capital at Tayma and introduced the use of Aramaic. He settled in Tayma where he was to stay for ten years, from 552 to 542. Some of the North Arabian graffiti discovered in Tayma, dating to the sixth century, were written by Nabonidus's servants.

The exact reasons for this long retreat in the desert still remain very mysterious. Many theories have been put forward, but it is impossible to know which is the right one. Even if no disagreement has been detected between Nabonidus and his son, the latter may have wanted to sideline his elderly father given that he had been dreaming of wielding power for years. The Bible cites Nabonidus's madness, presenting his life in the desert as a near-wild condition. The "Prayer of Nabonidus," discovered in Qumran, describes a malignant inflammation that apparently made him impure. His retreat in Tayma could also have been prompted by economic factors, facilitating control the trade routes to Mesopotamia from there. He also followed the tradition of Assyrian kings who launched several expeditions against northern Arabia. Prevented from extending his empire northwards by Cyrus's military expansion, he extended it southwards and Tayma became a more central capital of the Babylonian Empire than Babylon.

Above all, it is his religious beliefs that are invoked. The period spent in Arabia could have triggered his latent mysticism. His mother, Adad-guppi, a centenarian, played a major role in her son's religiousness. She was a devotee of Sin, the moon god, in Harran where she was from. She appears to have been taken to the court of Babylon in the wake of the capture of Harran by Nabopolassar's army. Attached to the royal palace, she promoted her son's career. Nabonidus neglected the Babylonian gods, such as Marduk, and turned almost exclusively to the god Sin. In fact, Tayma was a site of traditional worship of the god Sin. Because of his absence from Babylon, the king prevented the religious festivals from being celebrated each year. However we cannot put Nabonidus's retreat down to a quarrel between theologians—the partisans of Sin and those of Marduk—in a context of emerging monotheism.

Regardless, the traditional clergy were highly incensed at Nabonidus who had promoted the god Sin to the head of the Babylonian pantheon, and presented him as the prototype of the bad king. During his absence from Babylonia, his son Bel-shar-usur dealt with day-to-day affairs, carried on construction works and continued to collect tributes to finance them, including in Phoenicia, but he took no military initiative.

The international situation evolved rapidly during these ten years. The Babylonian Chronicles relate several campaigns conducted by Cyrus, that went unanswered by the Babylonian army. After 559, Cyrus II, who had become king of Anshan, unified the Iranian tribes under Persian hegemony and transferred his capital to Pasargadae. He progressively extended his domination over western Iran and, in 550, after a series of hard-fought battles, succeeded in defeating Astyages, king of the Medes according to Herodotus, and in capturing Ecbatana. He then continued his policy of expansion towards the west. He took Sardis, capital of Lydia, in 546. Its king, Croesus, had nonetheless concluded an alliance with the Babylonian king Nabonidus and with the pharaoh Amasis, but he received no help from either of them. Cyrus II temporarily suspended his expansion towards the west to make conquests in the east, Hyrcania, Parthia, and the territories beyond the river Oxus. The Persian danger became pressing again when Gobryas (Ugbaru), the Babylonian governor of Gutium, rallied to Cyrus II. Xenophon even recorded that the king of the Persians led a campaign in Arabia when Nabonidus was still there.

The Babylonian king finally decided to come back to his capital in the thirteenth year of his reign, in 542, when he was more than seventy years old. Among the possible reasons for his return, he may have been in disagreement with his son Bel-shar-usur and at last realized the danger that the power of the Persians represented, especially if Cyrus II had gone to Arabia. He inaugurated the new temple of Sin in Harran and allowed religious ceremonies to be held in Babylon again, after a ten-year interruption. He must also have started making military preparations to try and counter Cyrus II's offensive against Babylon. He had

statues of the gods brought to the capital from the most threatened regions of the empire to keep them safe, since leaving the statue of a god
in the hands of the enemy was the equivalent of losing its protection.
Nabonidus confronted the Persian army during the winter of 540–539 in
the region of Uruk and was defeated. Events accelerated in the autumn
of 539. Cyrus II won a victory at Opis on the Tigris. Then he took Sippar
without a fight and forced Nabonidus to flee. An initial detachment led
by the Babylonian Gobryas (Ugbaru), having switched sides to join the
Persians, entered Babylon by surprise. Bel-shar-usur was killed inside
the royal palace, Nabonidus was taken prisoner and exiled to Carmania
as governor, according to Berossus. In October 539, Cyrus II entered
Babylon in triumph, spelling the end of the Babylonian Empire.

The Phoenician cities felt less pressure overall from Babylonian
domination than from that of Assyrian domination under the Sargonids.
The reign of Nebuchadnezzar II was especially burdensome for them.
Tyre was particularly affected due to the two sieges of which it had
been victim, one lasting thirteen years and the other fourteen months.
It also suffered from the control placed over its mainland territory, from
the grip on its institutions and the mass deportations of Tyrians, especially of the royal family. According to the fragmentary sources available
to us, Sidon and Arwad appear to have suffered little from Babylonian
domination. As Tyre lost its supremacy during the period of Babylonian
domination, Sidon took advantage of the situation to develop and regain
its position of leadership. Byblos remained completely on the side lines,
benefiting from a sort of moral authority, both in relation to the other
Phoenician cities and to the Babylonian kings. Neither the kings, nor the
inhabitants of Byblos appear to have been deported to Babylon. Yet, its
status between the two major confronting powers, Babylonia and Egypt,
was not an easy one to hold on to. It probably maintained excellent relations with Egypt while still managing not to offend the Babylonians, but
preserving neutrality and reserve. It therefore benefited from this relative
tranquility to recover. Nonetheless, all the Phoenician cities were required to contribute to the never-ending Babylonian construction works
and they were burdened by the annual tributes and various other taxes,
which strained their resources. In fact, the reign of Nabonidus, apart
from the early years of campaigning towards the west, constituted a
period of respite for the Phoenician cities, a respite that was to be pro-
longed while the Persian Empire established itself.

The Babylonian conquerors, following in the footsteps of the
Assyrian conquerors, must have come to the same conclusion: No
matter what they did, they never succeeded in totally integrating the

peoples of Phoenicia, Syria, and Palestine into the Mesopotamian empires. Was it through rebelliousness, a spirit of independence, a refusal to be exploited economically? Or perhaps all three reasons together? In any event, Egypt still played an nebulous game with the Phoenician cities, somewhere between protector and predator. Egypt was attached to them for traditional reasons, but at the same time still dreamed of reconquering the Near East. As for the Assyrians and the Babylonians, their permanent dream was to conquer Egypt, the achievement of which necessarily involved the Phoenician cities.

peoples of Phoenicia, Syria, and Palestine into the Mesopotamian empires. Was it through rebelliousness, a spirit of independence, a refusal to be exploited economically? Or perhaps all three reasons together? In any event, Egypt still played an nebulous game with the Phoenician cities, somewhere between protector and predator. Egypt was attached to them for traditional reasons, but at the same time still dreamed of reconquering the Near East. As for the Assyrians and the Babylonians, their permanent dream was to conquer Egypt, the achievement of which necessarily involved the Phoenician cities.

PART FIVE

PHOENICIA UNDER PERSIAN DOMINATION (539–332)

1

The Establishment of the Persian Empire
(539–479)

The conquest of the Phoenician cities by Cyrus II

Cyrus II became king of Persia in 549, but the fall of Babylon in 539 truly marks the end of the Babylonian Empire and the beginning of the Persian Empire. In the absence of impartial sources, the founding of the Persian Empire remains mysterious. Cyrus II's conquests may have been part of a well-designed and preestablished overall plan. However, another scenario is possible: the various stages of the conquest may have followed one from another based on their outcomes and on decisions made by the adversaries. The first king of the Persians was held in great esteem, both in Persian propaganda and in biblical and classical sources. He spoke glowingly of himself: "I am Cyrus, king of the world, great king, powerful king, king of Babylon, king of the land of Sumer and of Akkad, king of the four extremities of the world." For Diodorus, Cyrus II surpassed all the men of his time in terms of his bravery, his wisdom, and his virtue. For Herodotus, he was a benevolent father who provided his subjects with all good things possible. The Bible refers to him as an elected one, led by Yahweh, the god of Israel, for the good of his people. Through this unbridled propaganda, he appears as a conqueror breaking with the barbaric and cruel practices of his Assyrian and Babylonian predecessors, possibly even as the inventor of human rights. Only the Babylonian Chronicles present him as a conqueror no different from any other: after the victory at the Battle of Opis, he massacred all those who attempted to resist him and amassed considerable plunder. But perhaps a source written by the vanquished can equally be suspected of partiality? In short, the sources are too biased and fragmentary to tell us exactly who Cyrus II, the Great, was.

He proclaimed his legitimacy and affirmed his commitment to take possession of all the territories in the defeated empire, taking on the traditional title of the Assyrian and Babylonian kings. In 545, the Phoenician cities were not yet subject to Cyrus II when he emerged victorious over Croesus, king of Lydia. They were probably integrated into the new Persian Empire in 539 without any military action. Their kings spontaneously pledged their allegiance and paid tribute to the new ruler, as indicated in the Cyrus Cylinder: "All the kings, enthroned on ceremonial seats, from the upper sea down to the lower sea, all the kings of Amurru living in tents, they all brought me a substantial tribute and kissed my feet in Babylon." Whereas his predecessors distinguished between the kings of the interior, those of the coast, and those of the islands, Cyrus II made a distinction between the kings enthroned in palaces, like those of the Phoenicians, and those living in tents, like the kings of nomadic tribes. He created the vast province of Babylonia and Transeuphratene, which the first satrap Gobryas (Gubaru) governed from 535 to 529. The Greek historian Xenophon wanted to increase his prestige, seeing him as the creator of an immense empire, attributing to him conquests—of Arabia and Egypt, for example—that he certainly did not make.

Persian domination over Transeuphratene, of which the Phoenician cities were part, is attested through the Bible, which only covers relations between Cyrus II and Jerusalem. In 538, he took measures in favor of Judean exiles, who had partially integrated into Babylonian society to allow them to return to Jerusalem if they wished, to repatriate their religious objects, and to rebuild their temple. Even though the Persian edict was not reproduced in its exact form in the biblical book of Esdras, in substance it was. The decision to send the Judean exiles back home assumes that Transeuphratene was already under Persian control. On their return from exile, the Judeans called for help from the Sidonians and the Tyrians to reconstruct the temple of Jerusalem, in accordance with the authorization granted by Cyrus II. They needed Sidon and Tyre to send cedar timber from Lebanon by sea to Jaffa, in exchange for payment in food, drink, and oil.

The Bible presents the Persian measures as favors granted to an ethnoreligious community. In fact, it was not that at all, because the phenomena of deporting a population with its gods and of repatriation of populations already existed in the Assyrian and Babylonian Empires. It was not only the Judeans who were deported. Tyrians, Sidonians, and Aradians had also been deported, either in groups or *en masse*, sometimes with their reigning families. Cyrus II probably also authorized Phoenician exiles, if they wanted, to return to their respective cities. However, the Phoenician sources mentioning these repatriations are not preserved, unlike the biblical sources. In any event, the Tyrians must have gone back home as the town of Tyre in Babylonia appears no longer to have hosted a Tyrian population during the Persian period. The Phoenician exiles who were repatriated were probably just as grateful to Cyrus II as the Judeans were. He did not restore the ancient monarchical structures in Judea, but chose the governor of the province, Sheshbazzar, from among the Judeans. The kingship was preserved in the Phoenician cities, and there is nothing to indicate that Cyrus II intervened in the choice of kings, except as regards the repatriation of the entire Tyrian royal family, but king Hiram III was authorized to retain the throne of Tyre. Persian policy in the Near East followed the line taken by Assyrian and Babylonian predecessors, aiming above all to open up opportunities on the Mediterranean front and to benefit from maritime trade.

As little is known about the end of Cyrus II's reign in 530 as his rise to power and his reign itself. By Herodotus's own admission, the circumstances surrounding his death prompted varied accounts. He opts for the one that chronicles the death of the king of the Persians during an expedition against the Massagetae of Central Asia, in a memorable combat against Queen Tomyris. Before setting off on the expedition, he apparently made arrangements to ensure his succession by appointing his eldest son Cambyses crown prince. In Xenophon's fictional account, he died in Persia, designating Cambyses as his successor and offering to his other son, Bardiya (Smerdis), a very important government in Central Asia, with authorization to keep the tributes collected. According to the account of Ctesias, he died in Central Asia, Cambyses II succeeded him without any difficulty, and is said to have repatriated the remains of his father to Pasargadae.

The Phoenician cities' refusal to help Cambyses II to conquer Carthage

The reign of Cambyses II only lasted eight years. The picture painted by the sources of his reign are as negative as Cyrus II's are positive. According to his Persian informants, Herodotus characterized the first three kings in this manner: "The Persians say of Darius that he was a trafficker, whereas Cambyses was a despot and Cyrus a father." For Xenophon, after the death of Cyrus II, what he called the Persian decadence began: the children revolted, the cities and the people defected, and everything deteriorated.

The island of Cyprus, which paid tribute to the pharaoh Amasis in 539, was subjugated by the Persians in the reign of Cyrus II or of

Cambyses II. In any event, the Phoenician and Cypriot fleets helped Cambyses II in his expedition against Egypt in 525. The plan of conquering Egypt was probably already made by his father Cyrus II. The Persian conquerors wanted to build an empire even more powerful than those of the Assyrians and the Babylonians. To achieve this, they had to conquer Egypt. The most reliable allies of the pharaoh Amasis appear to have been the Greek cities in Europe and Asia Minor whose friendships he cultivated. In 526, Amasis was replaced by Psamtik III. This pharaoh was counting mainly on the forty-galley-strong war fleet belonging to Polycrates of Samos, but he rallied to the side of the Persians. Udjahorresnet, a priest in Sais and doctor and officer in the Egyptian war fleet, in turn defected. Cambyses II annihilated Psamtik III's army at Peluse, which opened up access for his fleet to the route to Memphis. This town, the last bastion of Egyptian resistance, was taken and the pharaoh captured, put in chains and taken to Susa. Egypt became a province of the Persian Empire, governed by the Persian Twenty-Seventh Dynasty from 525 to 404. Cambyses II was welcomed warmly by some members of the Egyptian aristocracy and by minorities such as the Jewish community in Elephantine. He entrusted command over the satrapy of Egypt to the Persian Aryandes. He reigned over Egypt as pharaoh, adopting the local title and continuing the work of the previous pharaohs.

However, he was the target of violent nationalistic anti-Persian propaganda, also reported in the Greek sources, where he was presented as unholy, barbaric, and mad. He is said to have displayed the ultimate gesture of savagery, namely, killing the sacred Apis bull in Memphis, having the priests whipped, and executing the Egyptians worshipping its cult. He supposedly plundered and set fire to the temples of Thebes, carrying off 2,500 statues and sacred items. He is alleged to have desecrated tombs and mocked holy statues. For the Elders, ridiculing holy things embedded in tradition was a clear sign of madness. However, excavations of the Memphis Serapeum where the Apis bulls were buried show that Cambyses II had been calumniated: far from killing an Apis bull, he conformed devotedly to the rituals of its cult. Persian soldiers may have committed abuses and provoked disturbances, but that would fall within the customary right of the vanquished in a conquered land. There is no way of interpreting this as an anti-Egyptian policy deliberately applied by Cambyses II. In contrast, the administrators of the Egyptian temples did not forgive him for having drastically cut back the income in kind that they received in the time of Amasis. The issue of relations between the temples and the political authorities was always a complicated one in Egypt because the pharaohs had, at one and the same time, to recognize the temples' rights but also to limit their financial power.

After the conquest of Egypt, Cambyses II assumed the pharaohs' ambitions towards the south and west. According to Herodotus, he planned for three expeditions: against the Ethiopians, against the oasis of Amon, and against the Carthaginians. He apparently failed in the first two, through lack of adequate preparation. In this period, Carthage had exited the colonial phase, even though it continued to pay tithes to Tyre and to take part in the Tyrian Milqart celebrations. The Magonid dynasty held power in Tyre's ancient colony and conducted an imperialistic policy, leading to the first Sicilian wars, under the leadership of general Malchus. His son, the priest Carthalon, is said to have offered to Milqart, the god of Tyre, the tithe of the plunder taken by his father.

Cambyses II was probably informed of the rising power of Carthage and considered himself invincible after his conquest of Egypt. However, the western Mediterranean was much too far from the Persian Empire for an expansionary move of this nature to have any likelihood of success. Anyway, if Cambyses II really had conceived this plan, he definitely needed the Phoenician fleets to conquer the far-off Punic city. According to Herodotus, he ordered his war fleet to set sail against Carthage. His fleet primarily comprised Phoenician fleets from Sidon, Tyre, and Arwad. The Phoenicians refused to obey orders, arguing that they were bound to the Carthaginians by major oaths. If they broke them, they would be acting impiously towards "their children" as Carthage had been founded by the Tyrians. Without the support of the Phoenician fleets, the Persian naval army was no longer powerful enough to conquer Carthage. Cambyses II showed understanding, not wishing to go against the Phoenicians as they had spontaneously submitted to the Persians. Consequently, the plan to conquer Carthage was apparently abandoned and the Carthaginians therefore escaped subservience to the Persians. For once, Herodotus's source of information was favorable to the king of the Persians, unlike his other informants.

Cambyses II is considered to be the founder of the Persian royal war fleet, based on the Phoenician and Cypriot fleets together with the Greek fleets of Ionia and Aeolis. According to another informant who comes out very much in favor of this king of the Persians, he was far more meritorious than Cyrus II because, not only did he possess all that his father had possessed, but he had added control of the Mediterranean as well as Egypt to the Persian Empire's assets. In spring 522, Cambyses II hastily left Egypt, hearing of a rebellion in Persia against his power.

While crossing Syria, he accidentally wounded himself with his sword: his wound turned gangrenous and he died in early summer 522.

The status of the Phoenician cities in the new imperial system

Much obscurity surrounds the accession to power of Darius I. When Cyrus II transmitted his succession to Cambyses, his younger son Bardiya (Smerdis) was unable to accept the paternal decision and aspired to the kingship. He ostensibly rose up against Cambyses II in March 522 and ascended to the throne in July, after the mysterious death of his brother Cambyses in Syria en route back from his campaigns in Egypt to Persia to confront him. Bardiya succeeded in rallying the important Persian families to him proclaiming a three-year exemption from military service and tribute payments. Cambyses II died without an heir, as it was said that he killed his sister-wife who was pregnant, together with his closest relatives.

It is here that the various accounts differ, each one more fictionalized than the other. By one account, Cambyses's brother Bardiya had also apparently been secretly killed on his order; Cambyses admitted as much on his deathbed. As Bardiya's death was unknown, Gaumata, a Magian priest and Bardiya's lookalike, is said to have impersonated him and placed himself on the Persian throne. However, the imposter was found out and a plot involving seven conspirators, led by Otanes, in which Darius had a low-profile role, was devised to eliminate the false Bardiya. Darius killed the usurper with his sword. The seven then agreed to elect as king the one whose horse would be the first to neigh at sunrise. With the help of his groom, Darius prepared a ploy to make his horse neigh: making it smell the odor of a mare.

In any event, when he became king, Darius's primary concern was to proclaim his legitimacy in the trilingual Behistun Inscription. He presented himself as defender of the truth, who had eliminated those he called the "liar kings" in nineteen battles. He claimed to be the legitimate king, the descendant of Achaemenes, founder of the Achaemenid dynasty. After Cambyses II had killed his brother Bardiya, he eliminated the false Bardiya and restored the legitimate dynasty thanks to the protection of the god Ahura Mazda. Hence, Darius I was not really a usurper insofar as the legitimate dynasty had been totally extinguished with the death of Bardiya. However, the eponymous ancestor, Achaemenes, was pure invention on his part, to justify his ancient family rights. He pushed the deception as far as having false inscriptions of Cyrus II made mentioning Achaemenes. In addition, to tie himself directly to the legitimate strain, he married two daughters and one grand-daughter of Cyrus II.

In other words, instead of holding power through his dynastic lineage, it was through the power he claimed for himself that he fabricated his dynastic rights.

Darius I was energetic and decisive, but he was a manipulator, willing to do anything to achieve his goals. He was also pretentious: "Those who were king before me," he declared, "have not done as much during their life as was done by me during one single year." He was an extremely ambitious conqueror, who spared no efforts in extending the imperial territory, by continuing the action of his predecessors Cyrus II and Cambyses II. In reality, the dream of universal domination had barely changed since the Assyrian Tiglath-pileser III up until the last Achaemenid Persian king, and the Phoenician cities were always taken hostage by this persistent dream.

The long thirty-six-year reign of Darius I allowed him to complete numerous conquests successfully, as a great warlord. He was also a builder king, keen to extol his power and to transmit to posterity a vivid testimony of it. He established new royal residences in Susa and Persepolis, without overlooking the ancient capitals Pasargadae, Babylon, and Ecbatana. The town of Susa was completely remodeled and he undertook the initial works in Persepolis: the treasury, the palace, and the audience hall (Apadana), where foundation deposits were unearthed comprising coins and inscribed gold and silver plaques. It was also in his reign that Necho II's canal was finally completed linking the Nile to the Red Sea.

Darius I is especially renowned as the organizer of the Persian Empire, even if he and his advisors based their approach on preexisting structures. However, he did contribute a certain number of improvements to the system implemented in the Phoenician cities by his predecessors. Territorial control was a key problem for an empire built on the back of military conquests and continually threatened by secessions. The Sargonids had understood this, as did, at a later date, the Babylonians who had opened up mountain routes to the north of Mount Lebanon. However, it was the Persians, particularly, who developed the road network, targeting security by setting up garrisons and guard posts, and logistical capacities for troop movements from one region to another thanks to food stocks, water storage, and weapon supplies. Territorial control implied having an efficient communications system and a network of strongholds. The Persians made a particular effort to develop the defense of the Mediterranean front of their empire, which had become more critical than under their predecessors, given the further expansion westwards.

The improvement in territorial control enabled better political control and greater exploitation of the sources of wealth. Tribute was again levied on an irregular basis at the start of Persian domination: "In the reign of Cyrus and later under that of Cambyses," wrote Herodotus, "nothing was established as regards tribute: it was gifts that were taken to the king." Tribute became regular at the end of Darius I's reign. The regular collection of tribute over more than a century and a half had affected the economic life of the Phoenician cities. On top of the tribute, they were subjected to other taxes, which had existed already but which became a greater burden, covering, for example, land and craftsmen's premises. Timber exploitation increased as a result of the extension of royal estates, essentially woodlands; the development of the road network, which made them more accessible; and increasing demand. Even though the supply of timber had changed little for palace construction and restoration works compared to the earlier empires, it increased considerably for dockyards. The development of sea-based warfare under the Persian Empire forced the Phoenicians to build large and powerful fleets for Persian needs and to reconstitute them in the wake of defeats. The requisitioning of Phoenician craftsmen, already practiced under the Assyrians and the Babylonians, progressively intensified in order to meet increasing Persian demands.

Despite a certain evolution, the aims and policy of the occupier towards the Phoenician cities had not fundamentally changed during these four centuries of intense foreign domination, since the historic turning point marked by the reign of Tiglath-pileser III. The cities of Tyre, Sidon, and Arwad still possessed the essential assets that led their conquerors to handle them tactfully. Their fleets formed the basis of the Persian naval power needed to maintain the empire, their coastal sites were critically strategic positions, offensively and defensively, and their economic prosperity constituted a source of abundant profit. The political skill displayed by the Persian conquerors, like that of their predecessors, consisted not in making these assets their own, but in leaving the Phoenician cities autonomous while monitoring them, to be able to take maximum advantage of the situation.

Byblos and Tyre in the reign of Darius I

According to an Akkadian tablet, in the reign of Darius I, Rikish-kalamu-bel was governor of the Phoenician town of Gubla, whose name may refer to Byblos or Gabala (Jeble) to the north of Arwad. Regardless, this text raises the question of the control of the Phoenician cities by the central Persian authority. Even though Persian politico-administrative coverage was present, Darius I did not install any military settlements there. In the capital of the satrapy of Transeuphratene, possibly Sidon, the Persian satrap lived with his family, his court, and his subordinates, bureaucrats, and soldiers. Governors were installed in other towns of the satrapy that represented strategic points. The presence of a governor in Gabala would have been justified for the defense of the Mediterranean front as it was situated some 20 kilometers from the fortress of Baniyas. His presence in Byblos would have been equally justified, it being a fortified and politically stable town. The mission of this governor was to control the strategic site that both towns represented. The change in the situation for the Phoenician cities in the geography of the Persian Empire had serious implications. Already in the reign of Sargon II, and especially in that of Darius I, they no longer constituted the western limit of the empire, but were access points to the western world, be it already conquered or yet to be conquered. Consequently, for the Persians, several of them represented strategic positions for controlling the coastal route and the sea, like the fortresses of Byblos and Baniyas, or operating bases on the route towards Egypt or the Greek cities, like Sidon and Akko. The governor's presence was less demanding than that of the satrap. In both cases, satrapy and province, the satrap and the governor did not prevent local institutions from continuing to function. Nevertheless, servicing Persian residents and garrison troops, supplemented by auxiliary troops, represented a particularly heavy burden for the cities.

The reigning king of Byblos around 500 was Shipitbaal III. He is known through the funerary stele of his son, whose inscription is poorly preserved. It contains the traditional warning not to open the tomb, followed by the curse aimed at any potential tomb defilers. Shipitbaal III is also mentioned in a somewhat uncertain inscription incised on a strip of silver, rolled up and placed in a bronze case to be used as an amulet. His relations with the Persian governor, if there was one, must have been cordial because Byblos was a problem-free Phoenician city.

Tyre was still governed by Hiram III, brother of Maharbaal, who reigned for twenty years according to Flavius Josephus. This king of Tyre spent his youth at the court of Babylon to which his entire family had been deported by Nebuchadnezzar II, and he was fully steeped in Babylonian culture. However, since roughly 552, he had been recalled to Tyre to succeed his brother. When Cyrus II founded the Persian Empire in around 539, the entire Tyrian royal family had been repatriated to Tyre, and the reign of Hiram III was able to proceed under normal conditions. He reigned until around 532, according to the chronology of

Flavius Josephus. His son Ithobaal IV appears to have succeeded him according to the inscription on a small votive ship made out of malachite, but it is difficult to see why the Sidonians are mentioned on it as well, as the cities of Tyre and Sidon were totally separate entities in this period. Hence, the legitimate Tyrian dynasty continued to rule since King Balazor who reigned for one year in around 556. This continuity brought Tyre the stability it needed to rebuild itself after the difficulties accumulated under the Babylonian Empire. Despite the loss of almost all its colonies, implying its main sources of wealth, it endeavored to emerge from this period of decline. It was to succeed, gradually, because in 480 it would become the second Phoenician city, after Sidon.

King Eshmunazar II of Sidon and his successors

The dynasty of Eshmunazar I of Sidon continued under the Persian Empire. After the death of Tabnit and before the birth of his son, his sister and wife Amoashtart ensured the interregnum around 539, during her pregnancy. She was an extremely energetic woman, who held the highest state function of maintaining the continuity of the dynasty, and held a prominent religious role as priestess of Ashtart, just as the two previous kings, who were priests of Ashtart. On the birth of her son, her task was far from over because she became co-regent. She carried out royal functions, at least during the minority of her son Eshmunazar II, who reigned slightly fewer than fourteen years, around 539–525. He was buried in a beautiful Egyptian black amphibolite sarcophagus, preserved in the Louvre museum. Its first occupant was apparently the Egyptian general Penptah, whose hieroglyphic inscription is no longer visible today. The engraver started the Phoenician inscription at the head of the basin, but after seven lines, he noticed that he did not have enough room to finish it. So he engraved the twenty-two line inscription on the lid of the sarcophagus, taking care to correct the spelling errors of his first attempt.

The inscription begins with the king lamenting that he had been an orphan and "son of only a few days," in other words, that he died young. So, it was not he who prepared this inscription while alive, as was sometimes the case. Then came the usual warning not to open the tomb, and the curse aimed at any likely defilers, who were threatened with a lack of progeny and a restless afterlife. Next, the construction of six temples are listed at length as occurring during the fourteen years of Eshmunazar II, but probably are attributable mainly to the queen mother. In Sidon-land-of-the-sea, they constructed three temples for Baal of Sidon, for Ashtart, and for Ashtart-name-of-Baal. At High Heavens, probably in

Inscribed sarcophagus of Eshmunazar II. Louvre Museum [CC BY 2.0], via Wikimedia Commons.

the mountainous hinterland of Sidon, they built two temples for Ashtart and for Eshmun. Lastly, at the Ydlal Spring in the mountains, meaning on the mountainous slope of the valley of Bostan esh-Sheikh, they built the temple of Eshmun. It is the only one of the six temples whose remains have been found. The construction of these temples between the death of Tabnit and the end of Eshmunazar II's reign serve as evidence that Sidon had regained its prosperity.

The king and his mother received a donation of lands from the "Lord of the kings," who could have been Cambyses II. These lands were the towns of Dor and Jaffa, and the mighty wheat lands of the Sharon Plain, referred to as "mighty" because their value was not only economic, but also political. Such a donation was not unusual: it was used to win the loyalty of those who had been subjugated when they behaved with docility. In this case it was recompense for actions taken by Eshmunazar II, probably military ones, as his mother was not part of them. Even though the king of Sidon was only fourteen years old, he was capable of commanding the army or the Sidonian fleet. A famous example was that of Alexander the Great who, from a very young age, was entrusted with the leadership of his kingdom by his absent father Philip II. In a fragile system of co-regency, it would have been in the interest of Sidon's political power for the young king to start assuming his functions, the first one being military, as soon as possible. He might have commanded the Sidonian fleet in Cambyses II's campaign against Egypt in 525. It is possible he was killed there and received this recompense posthumously.

After the premature death of Eshmunazar II without an heir, the continuation of the dynasty was assured by a member of a collateral branch, Bodashtart, grandson of Eshmunazar I and hence son of a brother or sister of Tabnit. He ousted Amoashtart, his aunt, from power. The fact that the dynasty had been preserved did not mean that Sidon did not have a number of internal issues to settle. Knowledge about Bodashtart's reign comes from thirty or so inscriptions engraved on blocks of stone, from various points in his reign, which give us an approximate chronology.

The first inscription dates from year one of his reign, around 524. The gaps in it have fueled debate over its interpretation. Engraved one year after Eshmunazar II's inscription, it mentions the land of the Sharon, which had just been given to the king of Sidon for his military exploits. Bodashtart must have taken charge of managing it and dedicated it to the Sidonian goddess Ashtart. As Sidon was still prosperous, during the following six years he continued the construction and restoration work of his predecessor. He had works carried out in various districts such as Sidon-of-the-sea, High Heavens, Land of the Reshephs, and Sidon-of-the-Plain. In the seventh year of his reign, around 518, he carried out hydraulic works on the Nahr Al-Awali, described in an inscription that has since disappeared, possibly when an electric power station was being built. However, it has been partially deciphered, thanks to some old photographs. Those works involved, among others, the construction of a canal to take the river waters 3 kilometers downstream, as far as the sanctuary of Eshmun, the healer god, at Bostan esh-Sheikh. Water was a key element in the therapeutic cult of this sanctuary. The flow rate from the Ydlal Spring, where the water came from previously, had become insufficient due to the development of the large religious complex there in this period.

After having established a good water supply for the temple of Eshmun, Bodashtart continued his building work in Sidon-the-domineering. After a while, he restored the second podium of the hillside temple of Eshmun. In the first phase of work, he inserted into the façade of the podium two rows of inscribed blocks, initially intended to be visible to be read. They all bore the same inscription, duplicated, in which he celebrated the construction or restoration works of the temples in the various districts of Sidon, and of the temple of Eshmun, which he had carried out since the beginning of his reign. The custom of placing

Throne of Ashtart, in the temple of Eshmun. Via Wikimedia Commons.

View of the Achaemenid and Eshmunazar II podiums in the temple of Eshmun. Courtesy of BiblePlaces.com pictorial library.

duplicate inscriptions in temple foundations existed in Mesopotamia. Bodashtart probably accomplished a ritual act in honor of the god Eshmun. After a period of time, consolidation work on the first façade of the podium became necessary. Three additional rows of inscribed blocks had to be added, but this time in such a way as to hide the inscribed sides. They all carried the same inscriptions, mentioning the legitimacy of his son Yatonmilk and the restoration of the temple of Eshmun. This time, Bodashtart carried out a secret ritual act, a personal dialogue with the god Eshmun, whom he took as witness of his merits as a pious king and a builder. He associated his son with this new restoration of the temple of Eshmun so that the god, protector of his dynasty, would ensure him legitimacy. Bodashtart reigned until at least 515. In principle, Yatonmilk succeeded him, but nothing is known about his reign.

The Phoenician fleets in the wars of Darius I against the Greeks

Since the conquest of Egypt, the Persians had wanted to extend their domination towards the Aegean Sea. After the conquest of Thrace, according to Herodotus, Darius I's plan was to conquer Greece. In this he was encouraged by his wife Atossa, daughter of Cyrus II. A reconnaissance mission set out from the harbor of Sidon to map the Greek coasts. "Darius is powerful thanks to the Phoenician fleet," wrote Thucydides, the Greek historian. This fleet was considered to be unique, although made up of the fleets of Sidon, Tyre, and Arwad. It seems to have carried out the operations, in addition to repressing the Cypriot insurrection and the revolt of Ionia, and conquering Aegean islands.

The priority for Darius I was the defection of the Cypriot cities— with the exception of Amathus—which was serious for the Persians because it threatened their Syro-Phoenician bases. He dispatched the Phoenician fleet against the Cypriot insurgents. The naval battle turned in favor of the Cypriots who were supported by the Ionian fleet, that of Samos in particular. However, the Persians won the land battle in a few months, crushing the armies of the Cypriot kings, who fell back into subservience in 497. The defeat suffered by the Phoenician fleet in Cyprus can perhaps be attributed to a lack of motivation. Some of the Cypriot cities were actually ancient Phoenician colonies, and we recall how the Phoenicians had refused to help Cambyses II attack their ancient colony of Carthage. According to Herodotus, Darius I had planned to deport Phoenicians to Ionia and Ionians to Phoenicia, perhaps to punish those Phoenicians who were responsible for the naval defeat of 497. This information does not seem very credible.

After having reconquered Cyprus, the king of the Persians undertook to crush the revolt of Ionia. These events were complex and have continued to be debated by historians. In brief, the Ionian city of Miletus, governed by the tyrant Aristagoras, was at the heart of the insurrection. The Persians decided to converge on Miletus, both by land and by sea. The Persian fleet, consisting essentially of the Phoenician fleet, confronted that of the Ionians at the Battle of Lade in 495. The Phoenicians were the most determined fighters against the Ionians as they wanted revenge and this time they were not fighting against their ancient Cypriot colonies. The Ionian fleet was weakened and disorganized by the fact that some of them rallied to the side of the Persians. The naval Battle of Lade was a total success for the Persians, Miletus was stormed in 494, partially razed to the ground, and part of its population deported.

The behavior of the Phoenicians towards the Persians changed as a result of these events. At the outset, they merely obeyed orders. After the victory of Lade, they made an effort to create a good impression in the eyes of the Persians. They took the initiative in capturing Miltiades, the Athenian general, and in handing him over to Darius I. Greco-Phoenician commercial competition did not enter into the equation in this new attitude because the Persians only favored the Phoenicians or the Greeks based on what they could get out of it. However, the Phoenicians understood that, thanks to their victories, they were the primary beneficiaries of the maritime supremacy that they had regained for the Persians. They held a privileged position in the Persian fleet. The final phase of the Ionian revolt marked a strengthening of Phoenico-Persian relations. Henceforth, Phoenician ships controlled this area of the Mediterranean the strategic and economic importance of which was quite special: the coasts of Ionia, the Hellespont, the Propontis and the Chersonesus.

Greek propaganda wanted to make it appear that Darius I was obsessed with vengeance for the Athenian raid against Sardis, and that in retaliation, in 480, he went to plunder and burn the temples of the acropolis of Athens, which had been evacuated by its inhabitants. In fact, the objective of the king of the Persians was to secure his supremacy over the sea by conquering the islands and coastline of the Aegean Sea. The two complementary components of his strategy were the patronage granted to the temples of the docile cities and the ruthless repression of the recalcitrant cities. Knowing the Greeks were very divided, he counted on the support of some of them. He programmed a landing in Attica, probably to install a leader in Athens who would be committed to Persian interests. In 490, the Persian fleet—or rather a small part of it, as the rest of it must already have been en route to Athens—offloaded the Persian combatants at Marathon. There was no naval battle. In the plain, the Athenians, joined by the Plataeans, defeated the Persians and forced them to re-embark hastily. In a painting of the Greek victory at Marathon, the painter represented the Greeks chasing after and massacring the Persian "Barbarians" on the Phoenician galleys at their moorings. The Athenians transformed the victory at Marathon, the First Persian War, into a memorable triumph for democracy. For the Persians, their failure at Marathon was a minor event that had no impact on their conquest strategy in the Aegean Sea. According to Herodotus, Darius I planned a new expedition against Greece and prepared it for three years. However, in 486 an insurrection erupted in Egypt, which the king of the Persians got ready to suppress because, in his eyes, this was more important than the Greek problem. This was not to happen, as he died of an illness in November, at about 65 years of age.

The Phoenician kings at the Battle of Salamis

Darius I's succession is known from several conflicting accounts. It was not easy to resolve as it involved choosing between several of his sons: three from his first wife, the eldest being Artobarzanes, and four from Atossa, of whom the eldest was Xerxes. The highly influential Atossa had been able to convince Darius I, while still alive, to choose Xerxes, who ascended to the throne in 486. The declarations of the new king attested to his concern to link himself with the work and the person of his father, but without excessive pretension. Greek anti-Persian propaganda was, nevertheless, ferocious towards him, presenting him as a megalomaniacal, despotic, intolerant, cruel, indecisive, puerile, cowardly, and licentious conqueror. Plato even singles him out as the initiator of Persian decadence: "It can be said that starting with him, there was no king among the Persians who merited, other than in name, being called the Great King."

On coming to power, Xerxes I was confronted with two problems inherited from his father: the failure at Marathon and the Egyptian rebellion. He used the troops and equipment assembled by Darius I with the help of the Phoenicians over the previous three years, for the expedition to Egypt, which he deemed to be the priority. He succeeded in crushing the Egyptian revolt and, in around 481, had to suppress another revolt in Babylonia. Then he resumed his father's plan to march against Greece. This expedition would, in addition, allow him to cross a large number of subject countries and, in passing, to renew the bonds of domination, which he would normally have done during the Persian court's periodic wanderings. He organized the new military preparations for his expedition against Greece, the Second Persian War. The Greek accounts distort their scale to enhance the value of the Greek victory. The Greek author Aeschylus compared the Persian army to a "monstrous human flock" and to the "invincible swell of the seas." The Persians are said to have assembled more than five million men, without counting those accompanying them, and the Persian fleet comprised 1,207 galleys. In reality, the Persian numbers were not that much higher than those of the Greeks, who would total 60,000 men at the Battle of Plataea, for example. The number of galleys was at least two times less. According to Herodotus, the Phoenicians provided three hundred galleys, a plausible figure. They sported helmets similar to Greek helmets, wore linen breastplates, and carried shields with no edging and spears.

The Sidonian fleet was in the forefront of operations because Xerxes I recognized its value after testing it out during a nautical race organized at Abydos. He established preferential relations with the Sidonians, always choosing to travel in one of Sidon's galleys. At the council of war over which he presided before the Battle of Salamis on September 480, in order of prominence he allocated first place to the king of Sidon, commander of the fleet, second to the king of Tyre, and third to the kings of Arwad and the other cities. The king of Byblos was absent, as he did not possess a fleet at this time. Xerxes I favored the fleet of Sidon for its valor, but perhaps also because the city was very powerful at that time and he had a particular rapport with its Persophile king. The ranking of the three Phoenician cities in order of precedence could have corresponded to their respective importance in this period: Sidon, Tyre, and Arwad.

The Phoenician kings each commanded their fleets, which implies strong commitment on the part of the Phoenician cities in the naval battles. Tetramnestus, son of Anysus, was king of Sidon in 480, but their Phoenician names are unknown. We do not know whether his father Anysus had reigned after Bodashtart and whether he still belonged to the dynasty of Eshmunazar I. Mattan III was the king of Tyre, perhaps succeeding Hiram IV. Maharbaal (Merbalos) was king of Arwad, perhaps replacing his father Ozbaal II (Agbalos). According to Greek sources, Xerxes I sent a Persian and Phoenician embassy to Carthage to negotiate an alliance in order to exercise a powerful grip over the whole of the Greek world. The account of the embassy is probably an invention of the Greeks, as is the alleged coincidence of the timing (on the same day) of the Greek victories at Salamis in Greece and Himera in Sicily.

The accounts of the naval battle at Salamis, which was a failure for the Persians and therefore for the Phoenicians, were particularly unfavorable towards the Sidonians. According to Herodotus, the Phoenicians blamed the Ionians for the loss of their galleys. However, having witnessed an Ionian exploit first hand, Xerxes I hit back at their accusers and had them beheaded because "he makes everyone responsible for his defeat." This account comes from anti-Phoenician informers; the king of the Persians probably did not change his policy towards the Phoenicians after the battle, especially as he still needed their fleets. Moreover, it was Phoenician ships that formed the pontoon he constructed to cross the strait of Salamis. It was also on a Phoenician ship, most likely Sidonian as was usually the case, that he then returned to Persia. For their part, it was in the interest of the Phoenician fleets to remain loyal so as to be able to continue to constitute the core of Persian naval power.

In the near-simultaneous Persian defeats of Plataea and Mycale in Ionia in September 479, the classical sources all highlighted the absence of the Phoenician fleets in the Persian fleet. However, this absence was not a sign of disgrace as Xerxes I had temporarily sent them away. He actually thought that his forces were not sufficiently strong to engage in another naval battle and so he carefully tried to avoid it. The commander-in-chief of his army, Mardonius, was defeated at Plataea. At Mycale, the Persian commanders decided not to fight at sea and had their soldiers disembark to engage in a land-based battle, which was a further defeat. "Hearing the news of the double rout of his armies at Plataea and at Mycale," wrote Diodorus, "Xerxes left some of his troops in Sardis to continue the war against the Greeks; he himself, excessively troubled, set off for Ecbatana with the rest of his army."

2

The Development of the Persian Empire (479–404)

Persian defeats and consequences for the Phoenicians

The Persian defeats at Salamis, Plataea, and Mycale were magnified by Greek propaganda and minimized by Persian propaganda. The reality is more difficult to identify. The scale of these defeats and the territorial setbacks for the Persians should not be underestimated, no more than the errors committed by Xerxes I and his military advisors. He had lost the major part of the Aegean islands conquered in 490, but the cities of Asia Minor remained under his control. When he got back to Persia, he was welcomed triumphantly, as he deposited the spoils brought back from Greece in the major towns of his empire as a symbol of his "victory." The outbreak of a Babylonian revolt, which he had to suppress, reminded him, however, of the fragility of the Persian Empire, but at the same time of its resilience through reconquest. Even though the defeats suffered on the western front represented an undeniable narrowing of Darius I's imperial territory, Xerxes I considered this setback temporary and never gave up on campaigns of reconquest on his western border. In the palace of Persepolis, the construction of which was initiated by Xerxes I and completed by Artaxerxes I, the frieze of donor tributaries shows 300 delegates compared with 138 in the Apadana, clear evidence of the unprecedented extension of the Persian Empire. Based on practical knowledge collected in Asia Minor, Xerxes I tried to establish his domination more firmly by enlarging the imperial diaspora and by calling on the Greeks who had rallied to him. There was nothing comparable in the Phoenician cities, based on the meagre documentation available to us on this subject.

After a few years of reconstruction, the Phoenician fleets returned to the Persian fleet, along with Cilician and Cypriot fleets, as the island of Cyprus had been reconquered. In the 470s, the Athenian general Cimon organized some maritime expeditions to collect plunder so as to be able to pay his crews, and he took back cities of Lycia from the Persians. In a naval battle that he won against them, he captured more than one hundred war galleys with their crews. In 466, he emerged victorious from the Battle of the Eurymedon in Pisidia, both on land and at sea, thanks to a ruse in which he disguised his soldiers as Persian soldiers. Immediately after these defeats, the Phoenician shipyards were again working flat out, as the Persians planned to rebuild a large number of galleys. However, Xerxes I was assassinated in 465, the outcome of a bloody conspiracy, about which several differing accounts circulated among the Greek authors. Excluding his illegitimate sons, he apparently had three legitimate ones: Darius; Hystaspes; and Artaxerxes, the youngest, who eliminated his two brothers. Artaxerxes I took power for a long reign of forty-one years. Without uttering a word about settling these scores, he exalted the values of truth and dynastic loyalty, just like his predecessors. Court propaganda was also swift in adorning him with all the traditional royal virtues.

Various disturbances broke out in the western part of the Persian Empire. The Egyptians rose up in revolt, under the leadership of Inaros, who brought the nationalist forces together and allied with the Athenians. During the Egyptian revolt that took place between 464 and 454, the Phoenicians suffered the repercussions of the Persian military actions. For the first time, Phoenicia was directly attacked and ravaged by the Athenians in 459. The Samians captured seventeen Phoenician galleys, probably during the Egypt campaign. The Athenian fleet, commanded by Cimon, supported Inaros's revolt and, in 460 at Memphis, defeated the Persian fleet, comprised then of Phoenician and Cilician ships. The Phoenician fleet only won one victory, in 454, at the end of the Egypt campaign. Artaxerxes eventually restored order in Egypt, had Inaros executed, and appointed the Persian Arsames at the head of the satrapy of Egypt, leaving the competing dynasties in place in the Delta region. Maintaining Persian domination in Egypt was highly dependent on its naval power, which still relied to a large extent on the Phoenician fleets. In 450, Cimon took the Cypriot cities of Kition and Marion, and defeated the Phoenician and Cilician fleets of the Persian fleet at Salamis of Cyprus. It was also in 450 perhaps that the revolt of the satrap Megabyzus occurred in Syria. Artaxerxes I opened peace talks with the Greeks, which led to an agreement, perhaps in 449, known as the "Callias Peace."

During this succession of Persian defeats, Phoenician naval potential suffered heavy losses. According to classical sources, the number of Phoenician galleys within the Persian fleet at the time of the Second Persian War totaled three hundred. In 480, at Salamis, the Persian fleet was reported to have lost two hundred ships, not counting the ships captured. In 479, at Cape Mycale, two hundred Phoenician and Cypriot ships were burned. In 466, at the Eurymedon, two hundred Phoenician ships were destroyed and in 450, at Salamis of Cyprus, some one hundred ships. Even if these figures are not to be taken literally, they still reflect the very heavy losses of the fleets of Arwad, Tyre, and especially Sidon, which was always the most highly rated, and hence on the front line. Maintaining a substantial war fleet was very expensive in itself. On top of which came the huge costs for repairing all the damaged galleys and the rebuilding of those destroyed during the successive defeats. The pace of naval construction in the Phoenician shipyards could not keep up with demand precipitated by the loss of ships. Sidon, Tyre, and Arwad were therefore in great economic difficulty in the middle of the fifth century. Their situation had deteriorated compared to the previous period; their fleets no longer dominated the eastern Mediterranean. Only Byblos remained unscathed.

The inauguration of Phoenician coinages

The Phoenician cities started to mint coins around 450, at least a century and a half later than the Greek cities, which inaugurated their coinage in the seventh century. Why so late? In fact, they had no need for coins because, in the Near East, payments were made mainly in weighed silver, and the system had worked perfectly well since the second millennium. It was so efficient that the Babylonians were to prefer it to coins up until the Seleucid period.

Byblos, the least powerful of the Phoenician cities, was nonetheless the first to mint coins, a little before 450. Exempt from participating in the Persian wars, it benefited from a long period of peace and prosperity. Around the same time, King Yehawmilk had a stele erected in honor of Baalat, his dynastic divinity. He identifies himself as the grandson of King Urimilk II and the son of Yeharbaal, who may not have reigned, as he did not carry the royal title. Yehawmilk describes the prestigious works carried out in the temple of Baalat: a bronze altar, a gold sculpture, a winged disc in gold, and a covered portico lined with a colonnade.

The temple must still have benefited from the offerings of devotees of Baalat, even if the Egyptian objects discovered in Byblos and elsewhere in Phoenicia became rare after the Persian conquest of Egypt. The first coins from Byblos bore the Egyptian royal symbol of the recumbent sphinx, and a double lotus flower. As they were not inscribed, it is not certain that King Yehawmilk inaugurated the coinage of Byblos. Were these first coins, in very pure silver, used in commercial exchanges? They consisted of a flexible system of six different denominations, which in theory would have enabled them to be. Also, they would have had to be issued in sufficient quantities, and their users, accustomed to payments in weighed silver, would have had to change their way of thinking. It may be that the king of Byblos simply wanted to take advantage of the right to mint coins, granted by the Persians, to assert his autonomy within the empire, and to project a impressive image of his kingship to his citizens.

The reasons for the inauguration of coinages were not the same for the other cities. The heavy costs of war are sufficient to explain the appearance of coinages in Sidon, Tyre, and Arwad. These cities tried to gain a tax benefit from the difference between the value of raw silver and the legal rate of coins. For example, Athens made a profit of 5 percent on its coins in the same period: in other words, the nominal value of the coin was 5 percent higher than its intrinsic value as a metal. The Phoenician cities had another good reason to mint coinage: as their image had been tarnished in their successive defeats, coinage could help to restore it as it constituted an excellent instrument of political propaganda.

Tyre imitated Byblos and started to mint coinage around 450. Its first standard, called Phoenician, was heavier than that of Byblos: 13.56 grams instead of 9.42. The motifs chosen were the winged dolphin leaping over the waves, symbolizing the Tyrian galley, and the owl bearing Egyptian-style royal attributes. These first coins carried indications of value, but not the name of the king who issued them. Sidon was the third city to mint coinage, a little after 450, based on the Phoenician standard. It started by issuing half-shekels of 6.94 grams, followed by double shekels weighing 28.02 grams. The symbols chosen were the Sidonian galley as an expression of its martial strength, and the processional chariot carrying the city's protective deity. These first coins were not inscribed, so it is impossible to know to which king to attribute them. Arwad inaugurated its coinage slightly after Sidon, modestly with one-third shekels weighing 3.35 grams, then with 10.51 gram shekels, a weight close to the Persian standard. As symbols, it chose its galley and its protective deity of seafaring. Its first coins bore an inscription that signified "king of Arwad" in abbreviated form without, however, specifying his name.

The militarization of Byblos

During the first millennium, Byblos had become a minor and not very powerful city, as it no longer had a war fleet as it had in the second millennium. But the role of a maritime city on the political chessboard of the Near East was necessarily dependent on its military power. First, it had to possess a fleet made up of galleys, as many and as well-equipped as possible, and second, sturdy and carefully trained land forces. Byblos was the opposite of the cities of Sidon, Tyre, and Arwad, all powerfully militarized in this period and capable of playing a leading role on the international scene. Within the narrow confines of its territory, hemmed in between sea and mountains, it was a small, peaceful city, isolated, closed, inward-looking; one could say forgotten by history. Unlike the other Phoenician cities, it had been absent from all the battles of the Persian Empire since the conquest of Egypt by Cambyses II.

Byblos could have carried on like this longer still, in this state of quasi-nonexistence which, having lasted for five centuries, was a comfortable position on the whole. Yet, it suddenly decided to regain the place it had occupied on the political scene of the Near East during the third and second millennia, by militarizing itself again. To attain this ambitious objective, it was vital for it to reconstruct a war fleet and establish an army. A whole host of questions come to mind in relation to this surprising decision: Who wanted it? When? Why? How did this militarizarion work in practice? What were its consequences? As always in Phoenician history, the sources are limited and difficult to exploit, and the answers to the questions do not succeed in clarifying all the gray areas. Our knowledge of the militarization of Byblos is obtained through the architectural changes and through the evolution of its coinage. The city's first types of coins, with a recumbent sphinx and double lotus, then seated sphinx and falcon, had disappeared, replaced by new martial symbols: galley, soldiers, helmets, and animal fights.

The king who made the decision to militarize Byblos played a fundamental role in the history of the city. It was a successor of King Yehawmilk, in power around 450, but the frustrating thing is that his name does not appear in any of the surviving documents, not even on his coins. Was it through modesty? Possibly, but nothing could be less certain. So, for us, he remains the "anonymous king." On the other hand, we do know the approximate date of the militarization of Byblos: around 435–425. After this crucial decision was made by the anonymous king, forming an army and especially constructing a war fleet must have been phased over several years. Byblos called on the services of its carpenters

A Byblos coin.

who were specialized in shipbuilding and who had spent all their time in the shipyards working on merchant ships.

The representation of the galley on the coins of Byblos was remarkably detailed and precise, even though it measured no more than 2 centimeters in length. The engravers of the monetary dies had carefully observed the brand-new galleys moored in the harbor of Byblos, but they were obliged to introduce some conventional elements due to the restricted space available. The galley was probably a trireme with three rows of oars, but they only represented one row, with the portholes and without the oars. The prow ended in a three-pointed ram, aimed at ripping open enemy ships. To complete the threatening appearance of the galley, the figurehead on the prow was a roaring lion's head. On each side of the front forecastle was painted a huge eye to ward off bad luck, based on a custom still followed. The mast and sails were not represented, unlike on the coins of Sidon whose engravers were more skilled than those of Byblos. The stern ended in a curve to which two large rudder oars were fixed. A line of shields covered the guardrail of the bulwark to protect the soldiers on the deck in the event of a naval battle. The first three soldiers are shown in large scale relative to the ship.

The king of Byblos began by creating a body of infantry, also mobilized on the galleys once the war fleet had been built. These soldiers wore a helmet, which constituted a full mask for the face, with holes for the eyes, a long neck cover, a short-stripped crest, and a buoyant plume. This helmet resembled the Corinthian helmet worn by the Greeks. As protection, the soldiers of Byblos had small round-edged shields. A second body of troops, less prestigious than the previous one, was also created, whose soldiers wore leather helmets with raised edges like those of Bactrian soldiers.

The militarization of Byblos at the end of the fifth century is also reflected in the strengthening of the city's defensive system. An imposing fortified surrounding wall was built to defend the upper city situated on the tell, overhanging the sea from a height of some 30 meters. It has still not been excavated completely by archaeologists, but we know that it consisted of at least seven watch towers. Two ramps were also fitted in around the same period to facilitate access to the town's gateways.

In what context was the militarization of Byblos carried out? While there are numerous uncertainties surrounding the history of the city, one thing is certain: it was going through a period of exceptional prosperity in comparison with the other Phoenician cities. After the brilliant reign of Yehawmilk, its wealth was such that the anonymous king took the liberty of increasing the standard of his silver coins from 9.42 to 13.66 grams. He clearly had all the necessary funds to be able to undertake this fundamental military reform, which was to enhance the prestige of his city. However, the reform would also have its negative consequences. As a militarized city, Byblos had to strengthen the power of the Persian Empire by participating in all its military campaigns, just like the other Phoenician cities. Even if its army and its fleet were relatively small-scale, they supplemented the numbers of Phoenicians from Sidon, Tyre, and Arwad in the Persian fleet. This new situation implied additional constraints for the city, including having to obey the orders of Persian admirals and generals, and seeing its expenditure rise in order to equip the galleys and to maintain its fleet and land army. The constraints and the costs, already heavy in times of peace, were multiplied when the king of Persia went to war.

The Phoenician fleets in post-450 Persian policy

The Phoenician fleets of Sidon, Tyre, and Arwad were still at the disposal of Persia after 450. Unlike the previous period, they never became involved in military action, yet they still played an important role in Persian policy in the eastern Mediterranean, being either brandished as a threat or promised as an unexpected aid. Despite the "Callias Peace" agreement, a border conflict broke out in 441 between Miletus and Samos; the Miletians were defeated and appealed to Athens for a democratic regime to be set up in Samos. The Samian exiles took refuge alongside Pissuthnes, satrap of Sardis, who concluded an alliance with them to help them regain power in Samos. Pissuthnes wanted to send the Phoenician fleets to support them against Athens, but while there was a lot of talk, the fleets were not visible. The Phoenician ships allegedly advanced towards Caria and Kaunos, in breach of the second clause of the "Callias Peace," with the intention of providing assistance to the Samians against the Athenian fleet of Pericles. The Athenians and the Samians were on the look-out for them for very different reasons, both unsuccessfully. Why did they fail to intervene? Maybe it was false information propagated by the Persians as an attempt at brainwashing, even though the Samos affair, while critical for Athenians, must have been very marginal for the Persians. During this period, the Phoenician cities do not appear to have suffered any naval defeat or the resulting burden of having to rebuild their fleets, merely the usual maintenance costs.

According to Ctesias, the Greek historian and personal physician to Artaxerxes I, the king of the Persians and his wife died the same day. Xerxes II, their only legitimate son, ascended the throne in 424, though not for long as his illegitimate brothers plotted against him and assassinated him forty-five days later. The leader of the conspiracy, Sogdianos, took power for six months and fifteen days. He in turn was eliminated by Ochos, his half-brother, who seized power in 423 under the name of Darius II, for a long reign of nineteen years. Once on the throne, the new king made every effort to proclaim his legitimacy and to send out a positive image of himself, in accordance with the custom of his predecessors.

During the events of 412–409 in Samos, the main players were Darius II, through his intermediary satraps (Tissaphernes and Pharnabazus) and the Greek cities (especially Athens and Sparta). The king of the Persians made use of the divisions between Athens and Sparta to support one or the other city depending on his interests. Even more than in the earlier events, the Phoenician fleets played the enigmatic role of "ghost fleets," hoped for by one and dreaded by the other. These events are related in the accounts of Thucydides and Diodorus. According to Diodorus, an initial treaty of alliance was signed between Sparta and Darius II in summer 412; Darius II dispatched the Phoenician fleets to assist the Spartans in Miletus. However, they did not reach their destination because Alcibiades, who had become advisor to the satrap Tissaphernes, advised him the following winter to send them back in order to facilitate his return to Athens. A further treaty was concluded between the Spartans and Darius II in summer 411: the issue once again was the arrival of the Phoenician fleets that had been promised and which Tissaphernes promised yet again, even though he intended to follow Alcibiades's advice once again and break that promise. Despite the reciprocity expressed in the wording of the treaties between Sparta and Darius II, Sparta had concluded a fool's bargain as it had to hand over Ionia in exchange for Persian subsidies and naval assistance that was never provided.

The account of these events was completed by Thucydides. People came to Athens to be present at the fall of democracy and the establishment of the "Four Hundred." Dissensions reared up among the Spartans in Miletus as they started to doubt whether the Phoenician fleets promised by Tissaphernes would arrive. Alcibiades changed his speech when addressing the Athenian assembly in Samos: Tissaphernes had supposedly promised that the Phoenician fleets would come to the assistance of the Athenians. In reality, he invented this story to get himself appointed as general, to discredit Tissaphernes in the eyes of the Spartans, and thereby to force him to support the Athenians. The Phoenician fleets, consisting of 147 galleys according to Thucydides and of 300 according to Diodorus, were anchored during this time in the harbor of Aspendos in Pamphylia. The newly built Byblos fleet had joined them. The deceptive speech given by Alcibiades yielded half the expected results: Tissaphernes was totally discredited with the Spartans, but he tried to restore his position by again promising to send the Phoenician fleets to help them. On hearing the news, Alcibiades hastily made his way to Aspendos to bring the Phoenician fleets back into his camp or, at least, to prevent them assisting the Spartans.

However, for the Spartans hope that the Phoenician fleets would arrive was stronger this time, knowing for certain that they were at Aspendos and that Tissaphernes had gone to find them. Yet, once again their hope was dashed by the Athenian victory over Tissaphernes at Kynossema, following which the fleets were sent back to Phoenicia. The autumn of 411 saw the triumphant return of Alcibiades to Samos, claiming to have contributed to the departure of the fleets. Tissaphernes attempted to explain to the Spartans that the Phoenician fleets had not come because they had to deal with the threats posed by the king of the Arabs and by the Egyptians. It is true that Darius II preferred the Phoenician fleets to concentrate their efforts on monitoring Egypt. The unrest in Egypt and Judea worried him a lot more than the conflict between the Athenians and the Spartans, which was altogether marginal for the Persian Empire, and he appears to have waited for the Greeks to become exhausted fighting among themselves.

Tissaphernes issued coinage in Tarsus, modelled on that of Tyre, probably aimed at paying for the Phoenician fleets. Despite the role played by the satraps, it would be inexact to talk about the weakening of the Persian Empire. Darius II had not got involved directly in these events simply because he had no reason to do so. Even though the objectives of his strategy in Asia Minor were not always clear, maybe he had considered that inter-satrapic competition was a clever way of preventing one satrap from gaining excessive importance. In any event, Persian policy became a lot more energetic from 407, when Darius II sent his son Cyrus to Asia Minor, vested with full powers and the necessary financial resources. The satraps Pharnabazus and Tissaphernes were no longer the decision makers; from now on they were his subordinates.

Brief news of Tyre and Arwad

Tyre went along with Persian policy, providing its fleet and its land forces. The archives of the Murashu, a family of Babylonian business-men, which date from 455 to 403, give a list of foreign garrisons used in the Persian Empire. One of them, made up of Tyrians, was assigned a tenure in Babylonia. Even though times had moved on since Tyre reaped the benefits of the riches coming from its western colonies, it still main-tained links with its Cypriot colonies. A rectangular-shaped sarcopha-gus, which has been preserved for a long time in the museum of Nicosia, bears the inscription of a certain Eshmunadon, a minister from Tyre in the fourth century. Its origin is unknown, but it could have come from Kition, a well-known Tyrian colony. In any event, the colony in question still depended politically on Tyre at this time.

Tyre's relations with Cyprus are attested in classical sources by other accounts that are not always easily understandable. Three individuals are mentioned that may refer to one and the same person: Abdemon of Tyre, Abdemon of Kition, and an anonymous Phoenician exile. The general framework of the story is the same, involving Kition, Salamis on Cyprus, and King Evagoras I, who ruled in Salamis from 411 to 374. His dynasty claimed to descend from Teukros, a mythical character, hero of the Trojan War and son of Telamon of Salamis in Greece. On his return from the Trojan War and after having been exiled by his father, he set off wandering, ending up in Sidon, whence he went on to found Salamis on Cyprus. Several traditions of population movements in the Mediterranean covering several centuries are tied to his name.

The anonymous Phoenician exile appears in a story related by the Athenian orator Isocrates, a contemporary of these events. It is not specified how this exile arrived in Salamis on Cyprus. This exile gained Evagoras's confidence and became very influential. Without deference to his benefactor, he chased him from the throne of Salamis and took his place. To cut a good image with the Persians, he handed the city and the whole island of Cyprus over to them. His descendants continued to govern Salamis until Evagoras came back to expel and retake power. The coinage of Salamis actually shows that it first minted coins bear-ing a Cypriot syllabic inscription, then coins bearing Phoenician letters, in particular, the initial of the name of Tyre. Then, after 411, followed the coinage of Evagoras I, with the name of the king, again written in Cypriot syllabic script.

After that, two traditions existed, one involving Abdemon of Kition, the other Abdemon of Tyre. The name Abdemon was common in

Phoenician and it may have referred to two different people. However, as Kition was a Tyrian colony, the name may also have referred to the two cities. In the tradition concerning Abdemon of Kition, the Greek historian Theopompus recounts that Evagoras captured Abdemon of Kition and acquired sovereignty over the island of Cyprus. According to the tradition concerning Abdemon of Tyre, followed by Diodorus, King Evagoras of Salamis, descendant of the founders of his city, had to go into exile in the wake of political unrest. After a while he returned. With the help of a few men, he chased Abdemon of Tyre, a friend of the king of the Persians, from the throne and retook power. So, the episode of a period of Phoenician power in Salamis during the second half of the fifth century is genuine, albeit not well known. We do not know whether the Phoenician exile that Isocrates talks about was the same Abdemon of Kition mentioned by Theopompus, and the same Abdemon of Tyre that Diodorus talks about. It is possible, but it may also refer to different phases of Phoenician control over Salamis, which lasted several generations. These accounts do however point to there having been a strong Tyrian presence in Cyprus during this period.

Even though we have no Phoenician inscription or classical text about Arwad, we know that it was a prosperous city in this period. Indeed, the sculpture workshops of Arwad and Amrit, its large mainland town, produced remarkable anthropoid sarcophagi at that time. As for the coroplast workshops, they invented a new and highly original artistic form, anthropoid sarcophagi made of terracotta.

The dynasty of Baalshillem I of Sidon

The history of the kings of Sidon during the second half of the fifth century was known from their coinage and from a Phoenician inscription, discovered in 1925 and only published forty years later. In the site of Bostan esh-Sheikh, 2 kilometers north of Sidon, a pit was unearthed adjoining the temple of Eshmun, where the Sidonians used to throw statues that had become obsolete from the temple, having first smashed them in order to desacralize them. Among them was the marble statue of a young child, playing with a bird and a tortoise. The pedestal of the statue bore the following inscription: "This is the statue offered by Baalshillem, son of King Baana, king of the Sidonians, son of King Abdamun, king of the Sidonians, son of King Baalshillem, King of the Sidonians, to his lord Eshmun, at the Ydlal Spring: may he bless him!" This inscription gives the genealogy of four kings of Sidon, to which needs to be added the fifth king represented by the statue of the young child. The coinage of Sidon helps clarify details about these kings. Baalshillem II, the last king quoted in the inscription, reigned from 401 to 366. Retrospectively, we can date the earlier kings within a time span of some twenty years.

Baalshillem I, the first king of this dynasty, had founded it around 425, in unknown circumstances. He had his name, abbreviated to *B* or *BM,* inscribed on his coins, where a galley defending the fortifications of Sidon was represented. Underneath the galley was inscribed the Phoenician word "commander," the title of the king commanding his war fleet. The magnificent sarcophagus, the so-called sarcophagus "of the satrap," now in the Istanbul Museum, dates to around 425–420. The sculptured scenes represented an audience, followed by a departure scene, then one of horsemen hunting a panther. The main character, seated on his throne, was not the Persian satrap, but the king of Sidon, probably Baalshillem I. The sarcophagus, whose master builder was a Sidonian trained in the Greek sculpture workshops, is proof of the wealth of the new dynasty, of its interest in Greek art and its encouragement to create high-quality pieces of work in the Sidonian sculpture workshops.

The son of Baalshillem I, Abdamon, succeeded him. He had the first two letters of his name inscribed on his coins. To legitimize his son, crown prince Baana, Abdamon associated his own name, in the last phase of his coinage, with that of his son, also abbreviated with the first two letters. Baana succeeded him and reigned for a few years until 402. His coins were inscribed with his name, always abbreviated with the first two letters. It was under his reign that the statue of the young child, his grandson, was dedicated to the god Eshmun. It was offered to him by his son Baalshillem, who was not yet king. The style of the statue, influenced by Greek art, confirmed that Baalshillem I's descendants also had a taste for Greek culture. When Baalshillem II offered the statue of his son, he was about twenty years old and was to ascend to the throne in 401, around the age of twenty-five, for a very long reign of thirty-six years. His son, the young child of the statue, must then have been about five or six months old because his hair had not yet grown, he did not know how to sit, and only managed to rise by leaning on his arm. This small child was the future Abdashtart I, who was to reign over Sidon from 365 to 352.

What did the offering of the young Abdashtart statue signify? It was one of forty or so broken statues of children, discovered in the pit close to the temple of Eshmun. The children were almost all boys, who were represented naked or with their garment lifted to show their sex. Parents consecrated their sons, perhaps only their firstborn, to Eshmun, the healer-god and protector of childhood. They had to occupy the infants while the rites around the temple were being performed, around the basins using the holy water from the Ydlal Spring. This explains why games were discovered around the basins together with a whole range of glass beads and dice. The statues represent the children playing with animals such as pigeons, ducks, tortoises, and dogs. The offering of the statue of the small child Abdashtart was aimed at invoking Eshmun's protection, either to cure the child of an illness, or to keep him in good health. His father had him go through a protection ritual, with ablutions in the basins. There is no proof that on this occasion the child underwent a rite of passage, such as circumcision, which was attested in Phoenician culture. The anonymous character of the child is significant: the child was probably not given a name at birth because infant mortality was high at this time. The first priority was to ensure divine protection and wait for the child to get through the difficult phase of early childhood. A similar sort of custom for the Persians was recounted by Herodotus: "Before a child is five years old, he is not presented before the eyes of his father, but stays with the women; this is done so that, should the child die while being fed, his death causes the father no sorrow."

Under the dynasty of Baalshillem I, Sidon was still the preeminent Phoenician city, powerful and prosperous. Its kings, lovers of art and Greek culture, encouraged the Sidonian sculpture workshops. Its monetary workshop issued the largest Phoenician silver coins, which were exported as precious metal throughout the whole of the Near East, Asia Minor, Egypt, and as far as Mesopotamia and Iran. During the first part of this dynasty, before 404, there were no Persian wars in which the kings of Sidon had to take part, meaning a lot less expense and more tranquility. So, there was not yet any reason for their relations with the kings of Persia to deteriorate.

3

The Persian Empire in Turmoil (404–333)

The usurpation of Ozbaal, a priest's son, in Byblos

The end of the fifth century was marked by major upheavals. For the Greeks, it was the end of the Peloponnesian War and Athenian thalassocracy, with the establishment of the government of the "Thirty Tyrants" in Athens in 404. The Persian Empire was in the throes of a bloody crisis of succession after the death of Darius II, who left numerous sons, both legitimate and illegitimate. The Persian court was dominated by two women who hated one another: Parysatis, mother of Artaxerxes II, and Stateira, his daughter-in-law, whom Parysatis poisoned to death. It was in this period that a lot of Greek historians situate a purported Persian decadence, already referenced on several occasions and perhaps, in the end, a simple misrepresentation of reality. A fratricidal struggle broke out between Cyrus and Artaxerxes, which threatened the heart of the empire. It ended with Cyrus's death on the battlefield at Cunaxa in 404 and Artaxerxes II's accession to the throne. The new king hastened to claim legitimacy and to ensure that court propaganda did its job, as usual. These internal Persian events gave the Phoenician cities a period of respite, as they were not called on to take part in any new military campaigns.

Byblos, only just militarized, was a prosperous city then. King Elpaal inaugurated his reign ostentatiously. In line with a custom followed by many other Near Eastern kings, he decided to differentiate himself from his predecessor by striving to enact deeds that, in the eyes of his subjects, would stand out. This desire for recognition led him, first, to have his name and royal title inscribed on his silver coins: "Elpaal king of Byblos." This was the first time a Phoenician king had proclaimed his royalty in this manner on his coinage, but his initiative was not followed by the kings of Tyre, Sidon, and Arwad. To further enhance his prestige,

252

he chose to revalue his coins by increasing the weight of the silver shekel from 13.66 to 14.21 grams—a rash initiative that assumed he had sufficient reserves of silver. After overdrawing on those reserves for several years, he was forced to back-track. He therefore reduced the shekel's quantity of silver by about 1 gram, as had happened under the previous king: All of this he carried out discretely so that the inhabitants of Byblos did not notice anything. Secretly, he asked the person in charge of his minting workshop to replace the gram of silver being removed with copper. Copper was easy and cheap to buy on the neighboring island of Cyprus, whereas silver was an expensive metal that had to be sought in Anatolia or in far-off Iberia, modern-day Spain. However, the craftsmen responsible for preparing the coin blanks, who were skilled in metallurgy, warned him that if the quantity of silver was reduced too much and replaced with copper, the coins would turn yellowish, hence attracting users' notice. However, by maintaining a percentage of silver above 90 percent, Elpaal's coins forestalled any suspicion: they kept the shine of silver while retaining their weight. Hence, the king managed to save face during the final years of his reign, but his excessive spending still cut into the city's prosperity.

Even though the secret of the falsified coinage had been well kept by the monetary workshop and the inhabitants of Byblos remained unaware, Elpaal's poor management of public finances was highlighted by some members of the clergy who understood the negative impact his reign was having on their city. Around year 400 they were to take the destiny of Byblos into their own hands, initiating a coup d'état that brought Elpaal's decades-long dynasty to a brutal conclusion. However, they remained cautiously in the background as their grip on political power was not direct. The usurper was the son of a priest, and Byblos, unlike Sidon, did not have a tradition whereby the functions of king and priest could be held by the same person. Ozbaal, the usurper, was not a priest himself, but only the son of the priest Paltibaal and of Batnoam. The insurgency did not come from the clergy of Baalat, the city's supreme deity and protector of the Elpaal dynasty then. It was fomented by the clergy of Baal, god of the storm and of heaven, lord of the local pantheon at the beginning of the first millennium, who had been overshadowed by the divine patron of the ruling dynasty.

The new queen mother, Batnoam, whose name means "girl of delights" succeeded in imposing herself through her personality, just as had other Phoenician women, despite her common origins and the low-profile role that women played in society. She was to obtain the royal standing that was held by the mothers of legitimate kings and would be buried in a beautiful white marble sarcophagus imported from Greece, dressed in royal ceremonial garments. As for Ozbaal, whose name means "my strength is Baal," he inaugurated a new dynasty—an illegitimate one—and began a long reign on the throne of Byblos. In the interests of legitimization, he kept exactly the same types of coins as his predecessor and, like him, proclaimed his kingship ostentatiously by having inscribed on his coins: "Ozbaal king of Byblos." In the very first year of his reign, he put a stop to Elpaal's trick of falsified coins, by taking the weight of the shekel back from 14.21 to 13.18 gram and by reestablishing a silver standard that was practically pure, of more than 99 percent.

The clergy had always had a prominent role in the city of Byblos, much moreso than in the other Phoenician cities, even though politics and religion were always more or less interrelated in this period. Byblos was a different city, a "sacred city": it was known by Greek authors under this name, which, by the way, was to figure on its coinage during the Hellenistic and Roman periods. It benefited from a high moral reputation, which is reflected in a text of the Greek author Aelianus: "An inhabitant of Byblos who finds an object in the street will not steal it unless he had left it there himself." After Ozbaal's coup d'état, the clergy of Byblos was in a position of control over the city, through the new dynasty it had installed on the throne. However, the reign of Ozbaal, which was partially coterminous with that of Artaxerxes II, was a difficult period, both for the Persian Empire and for the Phoenician cities.

Sidon, the main architect of the Persian victory at Knidos

After the death of Baana, king of Sidon, the crown prince Baalshillem II ascended to the throne in 401 without any difficulty, as the succession was a continuation of the same dynasty. It was still a prosperous and calm period for this city. In his coinage, he retained the same types as his father to mirror dynastic continuity. He only had a few changes made: on the obverse of the coins, the galley was no longer represented in front of the city's fortifications, but by itself, larger and better engraved, with its three rows of oars, representing a trireme. On the reverse, the procession of the chariot transporting the protector god of Sidon was followed by the king performing a religious ritual. He had the initial of his name inscribed above the galley. In this way, his military function was expressed on the obverse of the coins, and his religious function on the reverse. The magnificent sarcophagus "of the Lycian," so-called because it was inspired by the Lycian style of pitched-roof sarcophagi, is dated around 390–380. It could have been sculpted on the request of Baalshillem II, king of a dynasty that was patron of the arts.

Unlike Darius II, who had a passive attitude and a lax policy, Artaxerxes II displayed great determination and undertook to restore order in the western part of the Persian Empire. He had to intervene in Asia Minor and to deal with the Egyptian front, as the pharaoh Amyrtaeusa had founded the Twenty-Eighth Dynasty in 404 and Nepherites the Twenty-Ninth Dynasty in 399. Egypt had freed itself from Persian domination, yet Artaxerxes II did not intervene immediately. In 398, he ordered the satrap Pharnabazus to start naval preparations for an Asia Minor campaign. Pharnabazus began by going to Cyprus where he asked the Cypriot kings to prepare a hundred or so galleys. He ordered the Athenian Conon, who had taken refuge alongside Evagoras I of Salamis after the Athenian defeat, to head up the Persian fleet. He then left for Cilicia to continue the preparations. On his return from Phoenicia, a merchant from Syracuse alerted Sparta about the preparations being made by the Phoenicians who, he had been told, were equipping three hundred galleys for the satrap Tissaphernes. Among them there were galleys from the cities of Tyre, Arwad, and also Byblos, which, once they had been fitted out by their respective cities, had rejoined the Phoenician fleets' assembly point at Sidon. Probably for the first time, the Byblos galleys fought a naval battle. But it was no longer Tissaphernes who directed the naval operations, as he had just been executed on orders from Artaxerxes II due to a tactical error he had committed at Sardis. Conon and Pharnabazus led the Persian fleet, including the Phoenician fleets, to Knidos, where the Spartan fleet, commanded by Peisandros, was waiting for them.

The Battle of Knidos was brilliantly won by the Persian fleet in 394. The king of Sidon Baalshillem II, nicknamed Sakton, the "shipowner," by the Greeks, played a key role at the head of the Sidonian fleet of eighty galleys. The bulk of the fleet had to remain in Phoenicia to keep an eye on Egypt. The Sidonian fleet's major advantage was the presence of quinqueremes, galleys with five rows of oars instead of the three of the triremes. Designed under the government of Denys of Syracuse, they had probably then been passed on to Cyprus, then to Sidon. After Knidos, the Persian fleet took to the sea again in spring 393, freed the Cyclades, captured Cytherus, and landed in the Isthmus of Corinth. Then Conon returned to Athens with the eighty galleys of the Phoenician fleet. Accompanied by the Sidonians, the main architects of the victory, he was welcomed warmly by the Athenians who erected a statue in his honor. This battle represented an important date for Athens because it stimulated a revival of Athenian imperialism and put a stop to the expansion of the Spartans in the Aegean Sea. They were chased out of the coastal cities of Asia Minor and the islands, with the exception of Abydos. Baalshillem II was still loyal to Artaxerxes II and the valiant Sidonian fleet continued to constitute the main support for the Persian fleet. The political situation was however substantially different from what it had been at the time of the Persian Wars when the Persians were fighting against the Greeks, brought together under the leadership of Athens. All the cards had been shuffled. In 394, the king of Sidon fought against the Greek city of Sparta, under the orders of the Athenian admiral Conon; he no longer received his orders directly from the king of the Persians, but from the satrap Pharnabazus.

The taking of Tyre by Evagoras I of Salamis

After solving the problems in Asia Minor, Artaxerxes II was preoccupied with events in Cyprus and Egypt. However, the reconquest of Egypt, his prime objective, would be unlikely to succeed without taking control of the island of Cyprus. Evagoras I had reclaimed power in Salamis after expelling the Phoenician dynasty, and he pursued a specific goal: extending his power over all the Cypriot cities. Up until 394, he made it appear that he was collaborating with the Persians against the Spartan forces. Then, however, he opposed Persian domination and conquered most of the island. After that, he wanted to extend his domination towards the Near East, starting with Phoenicia. During the preparatory phase, he sought all possible sources of external assistance. He started by dispatching ambassadors to Athens, which sent him ten galleys in 390—a complete waste as they were intercepted by the Spartans. Later, in 388, Athens sent another ten galleys and eight hundred foot soldiers, under the command of Chabrias. Evagoras I also sent ambassadors to the pharaoh Achoris, who had only sent him a quantity of silver. He considered this to be insufficient in light of the help he had provided to help him ascend to the throne of Egypt. These alliances were in fact inconsistent, as Athens, the ally of Artaxerxes II, supported Evagoras I's war against him, while Sparta, in conflict with Artaxerxes II, seized the Athenian galleys that went to fight him. In total, Artaxerxes II had at his disposal ninety galleys (seventy from Cyprus and twenty supplied by Tyre), six thousand soldiers recruited in Cyprus, allied troops, soldiers sent by the king of the Arabs, and numerous mercenaries recruited thanks to the abundance of silver he possessed.

The date of Evagoras I's military operations in Phoenicia was situated around 385. According to Diodorus, he landed in Phoenicia, and took Tyre and a few other towns. Confident in his resources, he attacked the Persians, starting with their fleet, part of which was made up by the Phoenician fleets. The apologetic account given by the Athenian orator Isocrates is even more dubious: "Surely Egypt and Cyprus rebelled against the king of the Persians, Phoenicia and Syria devastated by war, Tyre, the object of his pride, occupied by its enemies?" Supposedly, Evagoras I with his allies even conquered most of the towns in Cilicia.

Over and above this Greek pro-Evagoras I propaganda, what was the exact scope of this expedition? He could not have captured the island of Tyre, which throughout its history had victoriously resisted the sieges of several Assyrian and Babylonian kings, who were a lot more powerful than the Cypriot king. The Tyrians had always shown that they were jealous of their independence and conscious of the strength of their insular position. Tyre certainly had not submitted spontaneously to Evagoras I, even if he did come from an island with a partially Phoenician population. What is more, Salamis was in conflict with Kition, Tyre's colony, whose king Milkyaton had defeated Evagoras I and his allies in around 392. At best, Evagoras I had captured the mainland town of Ushu (Palaetyros), which was to submit itself spontaneously to Alexander the Great. Or maybe the Tyrians adopted the same policy with him as they would adopt later on with the Macedonian conqueror, namely, a warm welcome with a demonstration of submission, but in Ushu and not on the island of Tyre. For Tyre, perhaps it was a way of evading Persian tutelage without succumbing to that of the Cypriot king.

Nevertheless, Evagoras I knew perfectly well that he did not have sufficient forces to capture the island of Tyre and in addition that he did not need to make this conquest. The partial and symbolic occupation of a town in Tyre's mainland territory might have sufficed. He probably had no intention of extending his conquest in the Near East, but wanted to send the message to the Tyrians that henceforth he was master of the Tyrian colonies on Cyprus. His aim was also to make a show of force towards Artaxerxes II to dissuade him from reconquering the island of Cyprus. It is doubtful whether Evagoras I devastated Phoenicia and occupied other Phoenician towns, even symbolically. In any event, he certainly did not attack the powerful city of Sidon, which housed a Persian garrison besides. Nor did he take any towns in Cilicia, but he might have had the support of the ancient Cypriot colonies in that region.

When did Evagoras I succeed in his symbolic taking of Tyre? The only possibility is during the Egypt campaign around 385, as the Persians were too busy to oppose him. The majority of the Tyrian fleet was mobilized in the Egypt campaign. It was probably also during this period, when Persian surveillance was at a low ebb, that the Athenian strategist Iphicrates made an attack on the Phoenician coasts without being challenged, according to the Greek tactician Polyaenus. The twenty Tyrian galleys taken by Evagoras I only represented a small proportion of this city's fleet. They may have been supplied to him spontaneously by a Tyrian anti-Persian faction.

Since the Battle of Knidos, there had again been a reversal in the alliances. Artaxerxes II, worried about the resurgence of Athenian imperialism and on the advice of the satrap Tiribazus, had promulgated the "Peace of Antalcidas" in 386, which was favorable to the Spartans. The policy of the Persian kings, like that of their predecessors, still consisted of using the rivalry between neighboring cities, in this case Athens and Sparta, weakening the city that had become over-powerful and supporting the weakened one. Consequently, did the Phoenicians break off their relations with Athens to align their foreign policy with that of the Persians? In principle they had to, but perhaps Sidon and Tyre did not align with the same policy. Political agreements at this period were so changeable and paradoxical that we do not really know how each Phoenician city reacted to Evagoras I's expedition. In fact, he had the support of the Athens strategists who also helped the pharaoh Achoris, whose policy was supported by the satrap Pharnabazus.

In any event, on his return from his Egypt campaign, Artaxerxes II was obliged to react against the incursion of Evagoras I in his empire. For him, this campaign had been a disaster and the Phoenician fleets of Sidon, Tyre, Arwad, and Byblos had suffered heavy losses—to such an extent that they were no longer immediately operational for the Cypriot expedition. In addition, the king of the Persians had to think twice about using them against the ancient Phoenician colonies of Cyprus, preferring to keep them in reserve for the next Egypt campaign that he was already contemplating. A Persian fleet of three triremes was fitted out in Phocaea and in Kyme in Ionia, and placed under the command of the Persian satraps Tiribazus and Orontes. It was to secure the operating bases in Cilicia, where Tiribazus minted coinage at Issus, Mallos, Soli and Tarsus in order to pay his crews.

The Persian fleet, exceptionally without the Phoenicians, won a naval victory at Kition while the Persian army besieged Salamis, capturing it in around 383. The island of Cyprus returned to Persian control. Against all expectations, Evagoras I was authorized to hold on to the throne of Salamis, subject to paying tribute and obeying the king of the

Persians. Tyre and the whole of Phoenicia returned to the hands of the Persians. The end of Evagoras I's uprising and the signing of the Peace of Antalcidas meant that the policy of Artaxerxes II had paid off. The cities of Asia Minor and the Cypriot cities were reincorporated into the Persian Empire. The Greek cities of Europe determined not to intervene in Persian policy in the eastern Mediterranean any more. However, the outstanding issue remained the conquest of Egypt.

The difficulties of Baalshillem II of Sidon

Following a prosperous period at the beginning of his reign and his victory at Knidos in 394, Baalshillem II of Sidon began to come up against difficulties in the new Persian wars that he had to take part in, especially in the first Egypt campaign around 385. He faced financial difficulties relating to the reconstruction and maintenance of his war fleet, and political difficulties inherent in making the right choices in the repeated upheavals in alliances. He therefore felt the need to strengthen his dynasty by appointing his son Abdashtart as crown prince. He associated him with his reign through his coinage: on the sixteenth shekel, which was issued in great quantities. The obverse bore the initial of his name, and on the reverse he had added the initial of the name of his son, who at that time was more than twenty years old.

Artaxerxes II temporarily established closer ties again with Athens. He succeeded in recalling the Athenian general Chabrias who was responsible for defense for the new pharaoh Nectanebo I, and for sending Iphicrates to Asia to prepare a new expedition against Egypt with the satrap Pharnabazus. Baalshillem II of Sidon took part in the Persian preparations for the second Egypt campaign, even though they were carried out mainly on Tyre's territory. They were centralized in the Tyrian town of Akko, closer to Egypt. According to Diodorus, the Persians assembled 200,000 men and 20,000 mercenaries, and equipped a fleet of 500 ships, including 300 triremes. The second Persian attempt to reconquer Egypt in 373 failed as miserably as the first, although the pharaoh Nectanebo I had been deprived of Chabrias's help. The failure of the Phoenician fleets, primarily that of the powerful fleet of Sidon, was inexplicable since they were facing the Egyptian fleet alone.

On his return from the second Egyptian disaster, Baalshillem II had to confront further economic difficulties to reconstruct his fleet. Beginning with the thirtieth year of his reign, in 372, he adopted the Tyrian practice of dating his coinage by inaugurating dating by year of reign. This annual dating, which Sidon was to maintain up until the end of the Persian Empire, has given us a precise chronology of events. In 372, Baalshillem II was approximately fifty-five years old and his son around thirty-five. He was forced progressively to reduce the percentage of silver in his coins, which was decreased to 72 percent by the end of his reign. As the weight remained constant, he benefited from this reduction in silver.

The second Persian failure in Egypt was perhaps the phenomenon that triggered the initial satrap revolts against Artaxerxes II in around 369. The two protagonists were Datames (Tarkumuwa), satrap of Cappadocia, and Ariobarzanes, satrap of Phrygia or of Dascylium. Datames, after having prepared the second Egypt campaign with Pharnabazus in Akko, was then dispatched to Cappadocia to put an end to the disturbances. As soon as he returned to Akko, he changed sides, joining the revolt of his colleague Ariobarzanes. Artaxerxes II first sent Autophradates to quell Datames's revolt. He then sent an army led by Autophradates and a fleet commanded by Mausolus against the rebel satrap Ariobarzanes. Ariobarzanes was executed in around 364. The Phoenician fleets had probably remained loyal to the king of the Persians and helped him to suppress these satrap revolts. For the time being, the Phoenicians must not have felt overly concerned by these localized revolts in Asia Minor.

The Greek authors all exaggerated the scale of these disturbances, either to convince their compatriots to take advantage of the weakness of the Persians and to launch a new offensive in Asia Minor, or simply through their taste for the spectacular. Revolts really did occur in the western part of the Persian Empire, but they were not all concurrent or coordinated in a vast common front. Even though contacts existed between the Phoenician cities and Cyprus, and with Egypt, as is indicated by the discovery of two altars in the name of the pharaoh Achoris in Sidon and in Akko, there is nothing to suggest that there were organized networks. Despite his increasing difficulties, Baalshillem II of Sidon probably remained loyal to the Persians until the end of his reign in 366.

Abdashtart I of Sidon: A king between East and West

After the long thirty-six-year reign of his father, Abdashtart I succeeded Baalshillem II at around the age of forty, a relatively advanced age at this period of short life expectancy. In the reign of his father he had acquired maturity and experience, which prepared him for rule. He may even have replaced his aging father in certain royal functions. Through him, Baalshillem II had already established relations with the Greek cities, especially Athens, in the framework of the Persian alliances.

When he ascended to the throne in 365, Abdashtart I's first decision was to devalue Sidon's coinage. He reduced its weight by 12 percent, equivalent to a loss of 2.35 grams for the 28.02 gram double shekels. At the same time, he increased the percentage of silver from 72 to 99 percent, a return to the almost pure silver coins in circulation at the start of his father's reign. The increase in the percentage of silver was compensated by the loss in weight, the result being that this monetary reform cost Sidon nothing. Abdashtart I was a man of experience and did not take this measure lightly, but rather through necessity: He was probably forced to do it in order to preserve confidence in Sidon's coinage. When the percentage of silver was reduced too much, coins started to take on a yellowish color, which would not go unnoticed and could lead to a crisis of confidence among users. This consequence would have been serious within the city, but even more so outside, as Sidon exported substantial quantities of its coins as silver metal. If the silver was no longer pure, Sidon's coins would no longer be bought, representing a substantial loss of revenue. The city's financial resources must have been sufficiently dented by the costs of war to justify such a radical devaluation of coinage. However, even if the Sidonians started to manifest their resentment against Persian domination, Abdashtart I, like his father, showed himself, first of all, to be loyal towards Artaxerxes II.

At the beginning of his reign, he rendered a service to an embassy sent by Athens to the king of the Persians, by helping him to obtain safe conduct. That meant that he was still on good terms with Artaxerxes II. To thank him, and in response to a request of his envoy, the Athenians issued a decree in his honor, engraved on a marble stele placed on the Acropolis, next to the Parthenon. The date is missing, the start of the inscription being broken, but it was in the 360s, possibly 364. The decree refer to Abdashtart I using the Greek name of Straton: "Being a good man in his relations with the Athenian people, the king of Sidon shall never be refused anything he asks of the Athenian people." We do not know what his envoy requested, but maybe he was already in search of an ally in the event of a problem with the Persians. During this period, Athens had supported the revolt of the satrap Ariobarzanes, the city was very closely linked with Tachos of Egypt who was to rebel against the Persians, and it was involved in a struggle against the Thebans, the Persians' new friends.

The Athenian decree granted Abdashtart I the title of proxenos of the Athenians, both to him and to his descendants: in other words, he would protect Athenian merchants arriving in Sidon. In addition, the Athenians granted tax advantages to citizens of Sidon coming to trade in Athens. Under this decree, the Sidonians became privileged commercial partners of the Athenians, and as a result it was easier for them to settle in Attica. Moreover, in the fourth century, imports of Attic vases into central Phoenicia, where Sidon was situated, increased, whereas in the neighboring regions they decreased. In the first part of his reign, Abdashtart I sought to develop an exceptional reconciliation with Athens, politically, diplomatically, and economically.

Thanks to the Athenian decree, in the contemporary Greek world Abdashtart I enjoyed the positive image of a philhellenic king, a friend and ally of the Athenians. He also established excellent relations with the Greek king Nikokles of Salamis on Cyprus, for both personal and political reasons. He competed with him for the reputation of his refined and lavish banquets, where he feasted in the company of his friends, musicians, singers, dancers, and courtesans whom he invited from the Peloponnese and Ionia. According to the sources, however, his image rapidly degenerated to project a model of luxury, perverse refinement, and debauchery that should not be imitated. In reality, Abdashtart I had a rich and complex personality: refined, cultivated, aesthete, and eclectic. He followed the family tradition in his taste for Hellenism, as is reflected in the Greek way of life he seems to have introduced within his palace, his interest in sculptures influenced by Greek art, and the Greek name he was given by the Athenians. Yet, above all, he remained a traditional Phoenician king in the eyes of the Sidonians. That was the image he chose to present to them on his coinage: dressed in Sidonian costume and carrying out his function as military commander and officiating in civic worship. His official and public image in Sidon was traditionally Phoenician, whereas his Hellenized image was his secret face, known only to his Hellenized entourage and his Greek friends. It is through this double imagery that his dual culture—eastern and western at one and the same time—expressed itself.

The magnificent Sarcophagus of the Weepers now in the Museum of Istanbul, which dates to around 360–355, was probably commissioned by Abdashtart I. Its manufacture took several months, if not several years. He must have had it made during the first part of his reign, when he was at the height of his power and prosperity, as it was a work of great expense and an ambitious artistic achievement. The sarcophagus assumes the appearance of an Ionian temple with engaged columns, a double-sloping roof, and triangular pediments on the short sides. Between the columns, eighteen professional weepers are sculpted, either women from his entourage or personifications of mourning in general. The frieze of the plinth represents Phoenician hunting scenes in

Sarcophagus of the Weepers in the Istanbul Museum.

which the king must have taken part, and a funeral procession, probably his own. The master craftsman of this sarcophagus must have been a Sidonian trained in the Greek sculpture workshops, inspired by the Greek formal style with a few traces of clumsiness, in order to give it an oriental touch.

Either Abdashtart I or one of his successors is responsible for the carving of the "Tribune of Eshmun," a beautiful marble monument decorated in bas-relief that was discovered near the temple of the god Eshmun in Bostan esh-Sheikh. Following in the footsteps of his dynastic ancestors, Abdashtart I encouraged the unprecedented growth of funerary sculpture in the workshops of Sidon, which made dozens of anthropoid sarcophagi. The production of these sarcophagi, imitating the Egyptian "mummy box," started around the beginning of the fifth century. Sidonian sculptors, inspired initially by Egyptian art, were more and more influenced by Greek art during the fourth century. These sarcophagi were reserved for the wealthy Sidonians who had acquired a taste for Greek culture. Abdashtart I probably also initiated the construction of a marble temple on the podium of the temple of Eshmun, in Bostan esh-Sheikh. The style of the exterior is Attic-Ionian while the interior is of Phoenician style, with a ceiling of cedar wood and animal sculptures. This temple of dual inspiration was the mirror image of the dual cultured king of Sidon.

Although the end of Artaxerxes II's reign was fraught with conspiracies, against all odds he died of old age in 359. He had three legitimate sons and 115 illegitimate sons, if Justin can be believed. The eldest of the legitimate sons, Darius, was appointed crown prince, but he plotted against his father and was executed. The youngest, Ochos, drove his brother Ariaspes to commit suicide and ascended to the throne under the name of Artaxerxes III. Classical sources paint an appalling picture of him, claiming that he massacred his whole family.

According to Diodorus, "the great satraps' revolt" began in 362, with all the rebels, including the Phoenicians, concluding an agreement to act jointly. In reality, from the 360s onwards, a series of revolts, some of them concerted, took place, thereby destabilizing the western part of the Persian Empire. The Phoenicians did not all defect because there was still a considerable Persian naval power. In 360, the pharaoh Tachos headed off towards Phoenicia, traveling overland and by sea, and his campaign was on the verge of success. However, when Necktanebo II was proclaimed king during his absence, Tachos was forced to abandon his conquest; he fled and took refuge in Sidon before going to Susa. That was the last attempted conquest in the Near East by an Egyptian pharaoh.

Meanwhile, around 360, Abdashtart I of Sidon was influenced by the wind of revolt blowing through the western part of the Persian Empire. He broke his treaty of alliance with the king of the Persians, believing his city to be sufficiently rich and powerful to be able to win its independence. Persian domination had weighed more heavily on Sidon due to the repeated attempts to reconquer Egypt. In 356, following the example set by the kings of Kition and of Salamis of Cyprus, Abdashtart I inaugurated a bronze coinage to assist with his military preparations, coins bearing his effigy, which is a first among Phoenician coinages and which must have been inspired by his Greek sympathies. This was probably his way of asserting his independence from the Persians. His revolt was crushed by Artaxerxes III in October 355, according to a Babylonian tablet, which mentions prisoners being sent from Sidon to Babylon and Susa, and Sidonian women entering the Persian royal palace.

Abdashtart I was not, however, deposed by Artaxerxes III, who thought he could still obtain services from him, but the last three years of his reign, between 355 and 352, proved to be very difficult. He submitted unconditionally, was placed under close surveillance, and had to acknowledge defeat in the eyes of his fellow citizens. He was an energetic king, innovative and courageous, because he had been the first Phoenician to put up opposition to Persian imperialism. However, he committed a serious political error by entering into an alliance with Tachos against Nectanebo II and by thinking that his small city was powerful enough to hold out against the immense Persian Empire without even possessing the refuge of a large island like Tyre. His error had serious consequences for Sidon. He disappeared in 352, at the age of about fifty-five. According to classical sources, he may have suffered a violent death, like his friend Nikokles of Salamis. They present a negative image of him, in sharp contrast with the powerful, rich, and ostentatious king they had described prior to the revolt. It is impossible to know whether Abdashtart I suffered an accidental death, or whether he had been discretely eliminated in a settling of scores within his dynasty, or by a Persian initiative to be rid of figure who had become an inconvenience.

The appointment of Mazday as governor of Transeuphratene

After the suppression of Abdashtart I's revolt in 355, Artaxerxes III decided to place Sidon, and, more broadly, the whole of Phoenicia, under close surveillance. For this purpose, he appointed Mazday (Mazaios) as satrap of Transeuphratene. Mazday was a Persian nobleman: He is known from Greco-Roman sources and from his coinage, which he issued successively in several cities. His long career was spent in the service of four Persian kings: Artaxerxes II at the end of his reign, Artaxerxes III, Arses, and Darius III, and to conclude, he entered the service of Alexander. Mazday's title has been much debated, in fact it evolved and changed in his various coinages. The first issue was made in Tarsus, using the city's monetary types, with several series. The first two bore only his name. On the third, there was a long legend: "Mazday, in charge of Transeuphratene and Cilicia." He was appointed satrap of Cilicia, possibly when Artaxerxes III came to power in 359. Such a decision marked a departure from the earlier management of Cilicia and a strengthening of Persian control. Maybe it was justified by the fact that Cilicia had taken part in the revolt. Quite quickly, Mazday was made responsible for controlling Transeuphratene in addition to Cilicia.

The revolt of Abdashtart I of Sidon, put down in 355, changed the situation. Artaxerxes III needed closer surveillance of Transeuphratene, whose satrapic capital during this period might have been Sidon. He relieved Mazday of the government of Cilicia, entrusting Transeuphratene exclusively to him. He sent him to take up residence in Sidon where he authorized him to mint coinage in his own name. Just as he did in Tarsus, Mazday adopted the practices of the Sidon workshop—the types, the standard, the denominations, the annual dating system—and he even employed the services of certain Sidonian engravers. The obverse of his double shekels bore the Sidonian galley and a figure, and the reverse bore the Sidonian religious procession scene and the name

Mazday. The only differences with the city's own coinage were the writing of the name in full, rather than abbreviated form, the Aramaic way of expressing the date, the Aramaic writing, and the use of a few non-Sidonian engravers. The dates indicated on Mazday's coinage correspond to his years of government over Transeuphratene. It was the first time that a Persian satrap used this dating system, complying with local Sidonian practice, so this was something new. The satrapic coinage was parallel to that of the kings of Sidon between 353 and 333. Mazday minted coins in Sidon for twenty-one years, from 353 up until the arrival of Alexander in 333. He does not appear to have minted coins during the difficult years, that is, in 347 and 348 when Tennes was replaced by Evagoras II; in 342 and 341 at the start of Abdashtart II's reign; and in 338, the year when Artaxerxes III was assassinated.

One particular event involving Mazday remains unclear. According to Diodorus, in 351 the king of the Persians was said to have sent a military expedition to crush the revolt of the king of Sidon. This expedition, led by "Belesys, satrap of Syria, and Mazday, archon of Cilicia," was repelled by the army of Sidon. However, Diodorus made several mistakes, starting with the date: In 351, the first year of Tennes's reign, there was no revolt in Sidon. He also got the title of the two men wrong: Belesys was an ordinary Persian official in Syria, whereas Mazday was already in charge of Transeuphratene, and his intervention in Sidon was therefore justified. It was probably between 358 and 356 that King Abdashtart I of Sidon won a victory over the Persians Mazday and Belesys, who were charged with suppressing his revolt.

After 333, Mazday's career was not over. In 331, he would in charge of Babylonia, a satrapy that he may have received from Darius III after the Battle of Gaugamela. He was to rally to Alexander's cause by spontaneously handing Babylon over to him. He was also to be the first Iranian satrap appointed by the Macedonian conqueror, with the exceptional privilege of being allowed to mint coinage in his name in the Babylon workshop.

The slave revolt in Tyre

Just like the neighboring city of Sidon, Tyre had to face serious difficulties during the first half of the fourth century, from the 360s especially. In its coinage issued between 393 and 358, which aligned with the Phoenician standard of 13.56 grams, Tyre invented a system to date its coins, although it was not used on a regular basis. Tyrian coinage of this period progressively deteriorated in terms of manufacturing technique and style. Originally made using very pure silver, around 99 percent, the percentage decreased, falling to 68 percent at the end of this period. As the density of the copper used to replace it was lower than that of the silver, the weight of the coins also decreased. As in Sidon in 366, coins started to take on a yellowish color, hence prompting a crisis of confidence among users. The export of shekels from Tyre for the value of the metal became problematic insofar as the quality of the silver had deteriorated. One king of Tyre, whose name has not been preserved, reacted in 357 in the same manner as Abdashtart I of Sidon a few years earlier, in 365. There was only one solution: to devalue it in order to regain user confidence. The percentage of silver was taken back up from 68 percent to 99 percent. At the same time, the weight of the coins was reduced by the difference, dropping from 13.56 to 8.77 grams. Much more than simply a reduction in weight, this was an outright change of standard. Tyre moved from the Phoenician standard to one close to the Attic standard, which was 8.66 grams in the reign of Philip II of Macedonia. This measure facilitated trade between Tyre and the Greek cities and, above all, restored confidence in the Tyrian coinage, both in Tyre and abroad.

The multiplication of wars undertaken by the Persians in which Tyre was forced to take part led to a substantial increase in military costs, particularly the naval defeats, which necessitated the reconstruction of the war fleet. Compared to Sidon, Tyre also had to endure the expedition of Evagoras I of Salamis, and the Persian military preparations for the Egypt campaigns, which took place mainly in its territory. However, it was another event that occurred during the same period that was the main cause of Tyre's difficulties, namely, a bloody revolt of slaves. The episode is related in detail by Justin. Although this Latin historian lived several centuries after the event, his account contains precise details that tend to prove its authenticity. In addition, it is confirmed by a Greek oracle, a Phoenician inscription, and legends on coins. The revolt broke out during the first half of the fourth century, at a time when the Tyrians were weary after having had to fight for the Persians for so long. There were a lot of slaves in the city, and they were trained fighters since they probably followed their masters to war. They took advantage of the weariness of their masters and proceeded to massacre them. Once they were free, they lost no time in getting married and in having children, something that they were not allowed to do while slaves. Those who previously had no property of their own took possession of their masters' houses.

Just one master, named Abdashtart (Straton), together with his young son, was spared and was kept in hiding by his slave. After the revolt, the slaves decided to choose as their new king the first one to catch sight of sunrise. Thanks to the shrewd advice of his slave, Abdashtart, unlike all the others, did not look in an easterly direction where the sun would normally appear, but he looked westwards where the sun would first be reflected off the tops of the tallest houses. This ingenuity resulted in him being appointed king of Tyre by the slaves. This revolt was not spontaneous; rather it was a concerted action. The Tyrians may have promised to meet their slaves' demands, for example, emancipation, if they helped them in their battles. If the masters had failed to keep these promises, the slaves may have taken their revenge. A similar scenario played out when Nebuchadnezzar II besieged Jerusalem in 588, the Judeans had promised to emancipate all the slaves who were willing to combat alongside them: once the danger was over, they forgot their promise and recovered their slaves. The episode of the revolt of Tyre's slaves and of Abdashtart's election probably occurred between 354 and 350, according to the monetary legends.

The Phoenician confederation of Tripoli

The Lebanese town of Tripoli had kept its ancient Greek name of Tripolis. Yet, it was not a Greek city but a Phoenician city with a unique character. The Greek historian Eusebius of Caesarea dates its foundation to 761, while Diodorus puts it in the Persian period. Based on the excavations carried out on the hill of Abu Samra, the Crusaders' ancient Pilgrims' Mount, Tripoli was inhabited since at least the fourteenth century. Excavations in its harbor of Al-Mina have reached the Persian levels, which are now underwater as the sea level has risen. The Phoenician name of Tripoli, Atri, is inscribed on two coins: one from the Persian period, the other Hellenistic. Atri is also mentioned in the account of a campaign carried out by the Assyrian king Shalmaneser III in 841. The Greek form Tripolis can be explained as the transformation of the Phoenician name Atri into Tri-, Greek "three," because the Greeks had noticed three towns, to which they appended the word *polis*, "town."

According to classical sources, Tripoli was founded in the Persian period by three Phoenician cities, Arwad, Sidon, and Tyre, and comprised three towns, each one politically dependent on these three cities. Each town had its own walled enclosure to protect itself, and probably its own government too, controlled by the city it depended on. The three towns were only about 200 meters apart and only one of them had a harbor. Tripoli is described in the Periplus of Pseudo-Scylax, a nautical document that provides valuable information about the harbors and coastal shelters, which was drawn up on the request of Philip II of Macedonia, who reigned from 359 to 335. Its author marvels before the tripartite configuration of Tripoli and the juxtaposition of the three forti-fied towns, and describes it at greater length than the other Phoenician cities. Tripoli was an unusual city, as much for the Greeks as it was for the Phoenicians, raising a lot of questions. Why did Arwad, Sidon, and Tyre possess towns in the same location? It may have been in their in-terests for economic or strategic reasons to control maritime access from the Homs Gap. The presence of fortifications around these towns may be interpreted in two ways: they either sheltered rich commercial ware-houses that needed to be defended against looting, or they represented a strategic site that needed to be occupied. Why was Byblos, which was the closest city, excluded from the founding of Tripoli by the larger Phoenician cities? We should probably infer from this that at the time of the founding, Byblos was of little importance, having not yet revived its military power, thus, before the middle of the fifth century.

The precise location of the three towns at Tripoli has been the sub-ject of several assumptions, some of them fanciful. Tripoli retained its tripartite configuration until the seventh century CE, per the account given by two Arab historians, Al-Baladuri and Ibn al-Athir. They recount the taking of Tripoli on the orders of Muawiyah I, governor of Syria after 641. The Tripolitans of the three towns assembled in the harbor town and fled by sea with the help of the emperor of Byzantium. The harbor town was clearly located at Al-Mina where part of the ancient fortifica-tions has been unearthed. An area excavated some 200 meters southeast of Al-Mina probably corresponds to the second town. Yet, where was the third town sited, which was also located 200 meters away accord-ing to classical sources? The hill of Abu Samra, which was inhabited during the Persian period, held a strategic position at the entrance of the Qadisha Valley. However, being located more than 3 kilometers from the other towns means that it is unlikely that it can be pinned down as the third town, other than in the eyes of an observer looking at Tripoli from the sea (such as in the case of the author of a nautical document), from which vantage point the hill of Abu Samra can give the illusion of being close to the other two towns.

Tripoli was the seat of a sort of pan-Phoenician council. According to Diodorus, "Tripoli occupied the highest rank of all the cities of Phoenicia, because it so happened that the Phoenicians held a gen-eral assembly there and debated the most important matters." It was a federal council, like the confederation of Delos or the second Athenian confederation. However, the council of Tripoli does not appear to have been a permanent body. Only the very important issues, that is, those that went beyond local interest and required joint decisions, fell under its jurisdiction. This council was a deliberative body, but the decisions made were possibly enacted by another council. General assemblies were held episodically, there being no permanent or regular sittings at which all the Phoenician cities were represented. Byblos, which played no part in the founding of Tripoli, was probably included in the widened Phoenician circle and attended the general assemblies. Each city had to send its king and a restricted representative body, such as Sidon's Council of One Hundred. If the situation was deemed insecure, the delegation was entitled to be accompanied by a military escort. No precise details are known about how this pan-Phoenician council operated, as it was the only one of its kind. Nevertheless, it was tolerated by the Persian occupiers, unless, of course, the subject of a revolt against them was on the general assembly's agenda.

The Tennes revolt and the decline of Sidon

On his death in 352, Abdashtart I left Sidon reeling in serious difficulties, but the worst was yet to come. Tennes succeeded him and held power for a short period, between 351 and 347. Tennes was his Greek name; his Phoenician name is unknown. He probably belonged to the same dynasty as Abdashtart I; he may even have been his son. He retained exactly the same monetary types as his predecessor, only replacing the abbreviation of the name of Abdashtart I with his own. After the revolt of Sidon, Artaxerxes III, through the intermediary of Mazday who was settled locally, must have supported a king coming to power who was favorable to the Persians.

Sidon's economic situation was in a bad state in 351 owing to a further Persian failure in Egypt in that year. As Sidon's fleet still made up the mainstay of their fleet, the city was obliged rapidly to reconstitute its naval potential, which had been destroyed, in preparation for the next campaign against Egypt. These economic difficulties were reflected in Tennes's coinage: his engravers economized in their work by reusing several dies from previous years, and the number of denominations was reduced from seven to two: double shekels and sixteenth shekels. Lastly, the export of double shekels from Sidon as silver metal, which had already started to decline at the end of Abdashtart I's reign, was halted.

Sidon's political situation was hardly any better than its economic one, as they were interrelated. Sidonian discontent increased owing to the intensification of the Persian presence in the city, as it made new military preparations to attack Egypt. According to Diodorus, the situation became intolerable: "Now that the satraps and the generals reside in the city of Sidon, and behave arrogantly and contemptuously towards the Sidonians, the victims of this treatment, aggravated by their contempt, have decided to rebel against the Persians." Moreso than King Tennes, it was the Sidonians, or only an anti-Persian Sidonian faction, that took up the relay of Abdashtart I's earlier revolt in radicalizing it. In Diodorus's account, they appear to be the leaders, as it was they who benefited from Sidon's hegemonic position in convening a general assembly in Tripoli and pushing all the Phoenicians to rise up against the Persians. The other Phoenician cities decided to participate in the revolt, and were joined by the Cypriot cities. Pumiyaton, king of Kition, Idalion, and Tamassos, went in person to the Sidonian temple of Eshmun where he offered objects made of gold, probably at the beginning of Tennes's reign. The Sidonians also reached an agreement with the pharaoh Nectanebo II, who came to repel the Persian offensive of 351. Compared with Abdashtart I's revolt, this new so-called "Tennes" rebellion represented a sea change. It was no longer the revolt of a king who was involving his city, it was the revolt of a city carrying along its king, the other Phoenician cities, and other states with it.

After the search for allies, military preparations began. According to Diodorus, they were very rapid and the resources assembled considerable, as Sidon was still an opulent city, its citizens having amassed a lot of wealth from maritime trade: "A lot of triremes were fitted out and a multitude of mercenaries assembled and, in addition, weapons, projectiles, food, and all types of equipment needed in war was collected and prepared." The well-trained Sidonian citizen-soldiers were mobilized. The pharaoh supplied Tennes with four thousand Greek mercenaries under the command of Mentor of Rhodes. Sidon's fleet totaled more than one hundred galleys—the triremes and quinqueremes that were in use since the days of Baalshillem II and constituted one of its major assets. The Sidonians benefited from all the military equipment stocked in their territory and from the fleet that had been fitted out for the Persians with a view to the next Egypt campaign. The military preparations of the other Phoenician cities appear to have been less spectacular and enthusiastic than those of Sidon.

While the first two stages of planning, the search for allies and the preparations, lasted for quite a while and remained discreet, when the actual revolt did break out, it was brutal and provocative. The Sidonians carried out three spectacular measures: destroying the Persian "royal park"; setting fire to the supply of fodder for the horses that were to be used in the war against Egypt; and meting out punishment to the Persians who had behaved badly. On hearing this news, Artaxerxes III prepared a large-scale offensive against the Phoenicians, especially against the city of Sidon, the initiator of the revolt. He arrived and set up camp close to the city. Diodorus recounts the treason of King Tennes, who had been drawn into this revolt involuntarily and did not believe it would succeed. He came to an agreement with Mentor, the leader of the mercenaries, and sent Thettalion as an envoy to Artaxerxes III, to propose handing over Sidon to him in exchange for sparing his life, and emphasizing that he would be able to guide the Persian army in the campaign against Egypt. Then, as a pretext to his fellow citizens, he said he had to attend a Phoenician general assembly in Tripoli. He took with him the Council of the Hundred, comprising the most illustrious citizens, and an escort of five hundred mercenaries, the only ones he informed about his plan. Artaxerxes III had these one hundred citizens executed, considering them to be the instigators of the revolt. In the wake of this execution, the Sidonians decided to capitulate and sent a delegation to the Persian king consisting of the five hundred top-ranking citizens, possibly the members of a People's Assembly, all brandishing supplicant branches. Artaxerxes had them executed immediately, along with King Tennes. As it turned out, the treason of this pacific and pragmatic king did not succeed in saving him and his reign ended abruptly in 347.

Before the Persians entered the city, the Sidonians were said to have burned all their ships to prevent anyone from fleeing, according to Diodorus, but more likely probably to weaken the Persian fleet. Sidon was destroyed by a fire that claimed a lot of victims, as the Sidonians had barricaded themselves in their homes. A large quantity of gold and silver, which had melted in the heat of the fire, constituted a tremendouns haul for the Persians. Artaxerxes III had wanted to crush this revolt ruthlessly in order to terrorize the other rebels. His aim was achieved because all the Phoenician cities immediately submitted. He had no intention of destroying his best naval bases, however, he had eliminated a political regime that to him was unacceptable with citizens involved in the power-sharing, and he implemented the political changes that to him appeared necessary in order to subjugate the city. He probably cut off part of Sidon's territory, Sarafand in particular, which he gave to the king of Tyre.

Artaxerxes III then asked Idrieus, dynast of Caria, to send a fleet of forty galleys carrying infantry troops against the Cypriot rebels. They were under the command of the Athenian Phocion and Evagoras II, the former king of Salamis. The Persian forces assembled in front of Salamis. Frightened by the repression of Sidon, the Cypriot kings submitted, probably in 346. The king of the Persians then appointed Evagoras II, who was totally loyal to him, as the new king of Sidon, where he reigned from 346 to 343. He probably thought that the Sidonians would readily accept this Cypriot king as he was the brother or the son of Nikokles, the friend of their former king, Abdashtart I. Evagoras II continued the same monetary types as Tennes, just adding his name. However, he had himself represented dressed in Greek costume, behind the processional chariot, and he dated his coinage not by year of reign but by term, following the Greek custom. To better assert his authority, he minted a large quantity of coins, especially in the first year of his reign in 346. Sidon was going through its darkest hour, as it struggled to recover from the massacres and destructions. The local dynasty had been replaced by a Greek king and the official bodies representing the Sidonians had been abolished.

Artaxerxes III then undertook a new campaign in Egypt, using significant resources. According to Diodorus, he assembled a 300,000–strong army and enlisted Mentor, the leader of the mercenaries who had worked for King Tennes of Sidon. He is also said to have assembled 30,000 horsemen, 300 galleys and 500 transport ships. In fact, he must have reconstituted the full military potential that had been prepared in Sidon prior to the Tennes revolt and destroyed by the Sidonians. Nectanebo II, with his 100,000 men, was beaten and forced to flee southwards. This was the end of Egypt's independence and the beginning of the second Persian domination. With the reconquest of Egypt, Artaxerxes III fulfilled all his objectives and strengthened his power and prestige.

The hieroglyphic inscription on the "satrap" stele recounts the mysterious Egyptian episode of Khabbabash. He is alleged to have proclaimed himself pharaoh after the Persian conquest, between 342 and 336. Khababash went to the marshland area of the Egyptian Delta and inspected all the branches of the Nile in order to repulse the Asiatic, possibly Phoenician, ships from Egypt. This episode apparently took place during the second Persian occupation, which was highly contested by the Egyptians.

The last Phoenician kings

The ascendancy of the power of Macedonia under Philip II had not escaped the attention of Artaxerxes III. There had been talk of an agreement of friendship and alliance between the king of the Persians and the Macedonian kings. Anyway, there were probably contacts between the courts of Susa and Pella. However, it was not until after Philip II's victory against the Athenians at Cheronia in 338 and his founding of the League of Corinth in 337 that his plan for conquest in Asia became clear. In the interim, Artaxerxes III had disappeared, assassinated in a conspiracy led by Bagoas, his special advisor. His youngest son, Arses, relied on Bagoas to take power in 338, under the name of Artaxerxes IV. All of Arses's brothers were physically eliminated. Arses was also planning to get rid of Bagoas when he himself fell victim to poisoning in 336. Darius III succeeded him at around the age of 45. He was a close relative of Artaxerxes III and of Artaxerxes IV, and possibly the leader of the conspiracy. Just like his predecessors, he endeavored to demonstrate his legitimacy and promote a positive image of himself.

In Sidon, things were going badly for King Evagoras II. After a short time, in 343, the Sidonians chased him out because he defended the interests of the Persian Empire instead of those of the city. They took advantage of the moment when Artaxerxes III was occupied with his new Egypt campaign. Evagoras II was forced to flee to Cyprus where he was executed—the victim of an anti-Persian movement. He was replaced in Sidon by Abdashtart II, called Straton by the Greek authors. Obviously, he was favorable to the Persians, as he had the support of Mazday, who was still resident in Sidon, and of the new Persian king, Darius III. Nevertheless, he represented an improvement compared to Evagoras II as he was a Sidonian king, judging by his name, and possibly a grandson of Abdashtart I. In any event, the former political regime was not reestablished by the Persians, as the Sidonians were still excluded from power. Abdashtart II continued to mint coins with the same monetary types as his predecessors, adding his own abbreviated name.

In Tyre, the consequences of the slaves' revolt gradually waned. In 349, King Ozmilk, possibly the son of King Abdashtart who had been chosen by the slaves, ensured the succession. He reigned for seventeen years until 332, as indicated by the annual dating of his coinages. He minted no coins in the first two years of his reign, in 349 and 348, but minted a large quantity in year 3, 347. This date corresponds with the crushing of the Sidonian revolt of Tennes. Participation in the revolt and the expenses thereby incurred may have justified minting a lot of money in order to be able to pay them. Having suppressed the revolt of Sidon in 347, Artaxerxes III helped Tyre by extending its territory. Tyre regained its prosperity in the reign of Ozmilk as it started to export its shekels on a wide scale for their silver value, at a time when Sidon had virtually ceased to export its double shekels. It probably became the most prominent Phoenician city again, as the Persian authority would have wanted, per its policy of weakening Sidon in order to strengthen the position of Tyre.

In Byblos, the long reign of Ozbaal was followed by the short reign of Urimilk III around the year 350. He still belonged to the dynasty founded by Ozbaal, a priest's son, who had helped the clergy to maintain their grip on political power. He was replaced by Aynel (Enylos), a king of the same dynasty, who kept the same monetary type as his predecessors, and added his name written in full. His reign, probably quite long, terminated in 333. His coinage revealed that Byblos experienced a number of difficulties towards the end of this period. The style of the coins deteriorated, as though Aynel had resorted to the services of die engravers who were less meticulous or who were pressed for time. Byblos's monetary workshop worked economically, using bad quality dies until they broke and reusing dies of the previous king, whose name they simply scraped off. The last series only carried the abbreviation of the king's name without his customary royal title, or merely the name of the city, which is a reflection of the weakening of royal power in favor of the representative bodies of Byblos's citizens.

In Arwad, the last king's name was Gerashtart (Gerostratos). He inscribed the initial of his name on his coinage and the date by year of reign. He held power for seven years before the arrival of Alexander, from 339 to 333. Just like the other Phoenician cities, he put his fleet at the disposal of the Persians and commanded it personally in the Persian expeditions. During his absence, he entrusted the government of his city to his son Abdashtart (Straton).

All the Phoenician cities participated, to varying degrees, in the Tennes revolt in Sidon against Artaxerxes III in 347. Sidon suffered enormously as a result, whereas Tyre mainly benefited. The participation of Byblos and Tyre appears to have had minimal consequences for these cities.

4

The Fall of the Persian Empire (333–330)

The challenge posed by Alexander's conquest of the Phoenician cities

In 336, King Philip II of Macedonia launched his first Asiatic offensive by sending an armed force commanded by Attalus, Amyntas, and Parmenion to Asia Minor in order to prepare his landing. These operations appear to have gone wrong for the Persians. Meanwhile, Philip II was assassinated and his son Alexander III, "the Great," took power in 336, when he was twenty years old. He inherited a kingdom that had expanded, was unified, and was served by a well-trained army and a war fleet. This pupil of Aristotle had been involved in administrative and military activities through his father since the age of sixteen. He started by following the program traced by Philip II: to wage war against the Persians in order to free the Greeks of Asia Minor.

Darius III reacted as soon as he understood the threat. Whereas Alexander's resources were limited, the incredible treasures belonging to the king of the Persians enabled him to recruit more than 50,000 mercenaries, to buy allies such as King Agis III of Sparta, and to fit out a huge war fleet. He also prepared a large army, choosing the best strategists such as the Greek Memnon of Rhodes. The Phoenician fleets of Sidon, Tyre, Arwad, and Byblos were part of the fleet equipped by the king of the Persians. They still played a key role in his strategic approach, such as the core recruitment base with their shipyards and supplies of timber from nearby Lebanon. According to the Greek historian Arrian, "the fleet which was the best and the strongest within the Persian fleet, was that of the Phoenicians." Early in the spring of 334, Alexander set out with his army towards the Hellespont, which he then crossed. Incomprehensibly, the Persians did not intervene to try and stop him. The explanations put forward—the effect of surprise, the sluggishness of the Persian army, an absence of strategy—are not really convincing.

Also, perhaps the Persians were busy with the revolt of Khabbabash in Egypt. In any event, Alexander claimed a series of impressive victories in Asia Minor. In 334, it was the victory against the Persians at the Battle of the Granicus, then the taking of Miletus by the Macedonian fleet, commanded by Nikanor, and the capture of Sardis. The Persian fleet arrived while Alexander already occupied Miletus. It consisted of 400 warships, manned by well-trained crews who had come mainly from Phoenicia and Cyprus. At the time, Alexander's fleet only possessed 160 triremes and transport ships.

Darius III retained naval supremacy by a wide margin, all the more so as Alexander had dismissed his fleet at Miletus, with the exception of the Athenian fleet and a few transport ships. During summer 334, the king of the Persians appointed Memnon as supreme commander of the fleet of Lower Asia, the western fringe of the Persian Empire. The Persian fleet could have cut off Alexander's communications with Europe. According to Arrian, Alexander was conscious of his inferiority at sea, but he was short of money. Yet, he still considered that he was capable of conquering Asia with his army, and that he would no longer need his fleet. However, prior to pressing on inland, he needed to conquer the Phoenician cities so as to remove any rearguard threat. At the same time, this conquest would enable him to be rid of the Persian fleet, which would no longer have a place from which to recruit its crews or make a landing in Asia. Alexander's plan was an extremely risky one as could already be confirmed in Asia Minor, where the Persians controlled several harbors in Lycia and Caria, and the island of Kos whence the strategist Memnon had set sail. He eventually realized his strategic error in 333 and therefore set about reassembling a new war fleet.

In the spring of 333, Memnon launched a vigorous diplomatic and military campaign with a plan to invade Greece, which could succeed because Greek opinion was favorable towards him. During the summer of 333, Darius III left Babylon at the head of an enormous army. He was in Syria when he learned that Memnon had died through illness. This unexpected setback dealt a severe blow to the Persian forces. Darius III replaced him with the two satraps Pharnabazus and Autophradates. They regained Mytilene and, despite a few setbacks, the Persian fleet still retained its superiority. Fully aware of the danger that the Macedonian offensive represented, Darius III established a two-pronged strategy, maritime and land-based: while the two satraps were busy reconquering the coasts of Asia Minor, he himself confronted the Macedonian army. The decisive battle was fought near Issus on the Syrian coast. The Persian cavalry, superior in number, had difficulty maneuvering on this narrow plain and scattered after incurring heavy losses. The Greek mercenaries fled by sea. The Persian forces were not wiped out, but Darius III fled, abandoning his camp, his family and his treasure left in Damascus. It was a magnificent symbolic success for Alexander, who continued his advance southwards. From now on, nothing would prevent him from achieving his objective: capturing the Phoenician cities before driving inland.

The allegiance of Arwad, Byblos, and Sidon to Alexander

After the Battle of Issus, Alexander reached Phoenicia via the north of the Syrian coast. Most Greek authors describe how he was welcomed eagerly, even enthusiastically, by the inhabitants of the Phoenician cities, receiving their spontaneous submission. Arrian's account is the most detailed and nuanced. The first Phoenician territory that Alexander encountered was that of Arwad, the northern city. King Gerashtart, then in the seventh year of his reign, was at sea at the head of Arwad's fleet. He was sailing in the company of the other Phoenician and Cypriot fleets, led by their respective kings, under the command of the Persian Autophradates. In his absence, Gerashtart had entrusted the government of the city of Arwad and of all his mainland cities to his son, the crown prince Abdashtart, who might have been co-regent. He must have received full powers from his father, since he took the initiative of going to meet Alexander. He placed a gold crown on his head, similar to the one carried by Baal, the god of Arwad, on his city's coinage. He gave allegiance to him, handing over the island of Arwad, although it was even better protected than the island of Tyre. Knowing the difficulties that Alexander would face in order to capture the island of Tyre, one wonders how his Asian expedition would have turned out had Arwad refused to give up its island. In addition to the island of Arwad, the king's son gave over to Alexander all the vast territory belonging to the city, including Amrit (Marathos), the large and wealthy town located on the mainland opposite the island; the stronghold of Sigon, possibly Qalaat Sahyun, to the northeast of Jeble; and the town of Mariamme, possibly Mariamim on the eastern slope of the Jebel el Ansariye.

Alexander and his army stopped over in the coastal plain of Amrit, which possessed the necessary resources to maintain them, at the expense of the city of Arwad. According to Arrian, he wrote a propaganda letter advocating voluntary rallying, and promising his protection to all those who were prepared to abandon the king of the Persians and come fight alongside him, in total freedom. It was also in Amrit that it is said that he received a letter from Darius III, asking him to free his family which was held captive in Damascus and proposing a friendship and alliance agreement. The opening of diplomatic negotiations between the two camps is plausible, but the authenticity of the information handed down on this subject by the Greek authors cannot be guaranteed.

After Arwad's spontaneous and enthusiastic submission, Alexander received that of Byblos, which was spontaneous, but no more than that. Between Arwad and Byblos, on Alexander's route, was the city of Tripoli, made up—as we have seen—of three fortified towns founded by Arwad, Sidon, and Tyre. To get to Byblos with his army, he had to take the coastal route, even though there were numerous natural obstacles along the way. He probably avoided these obstacles by going inland rather than boarding his troops on transport ships where he would have run the risk of coming face to face with the powerful Persian fleet. He must have skirted round the city of Tripoli, as it was occupied by Persian forces. In fact, after the Battle of Issus, a few contingents of Darius III's mercenaries, under the orders of Macedonian exiles, managed to reach Tripoli where they reorganized themselves and strengthened their troops. From this naval base, Amyntas apparently even attempted an unsuccessful attack against Egypt as a personal initiative. Alexander did not want a confrontation with Greek mercenaries commanded by his compatriots. As it happened, the conquest of the three founding cities, Arwad, Sidon, and Tyre, was enough to ensure him Tripoli's submission.

After Byblos, Alexander received the enthusiastic submission of Sidon. By the time Sidon surrendered, the satrap Mazday, his family and other Persian residents must have already left. He stayed there as long as he could because in 333 he still minted coinage, for his twenty-first year of government in Transeuphratene, coinciding with the civic issues representing year 10 of Abdashtart II's reign. According to Arrian, it was the Sidonians themselves who had invited Alexander to come, through their hatred of the Persians and of Darius III. His bloody repression of the Tennes revolt was probably still very much in their minds, similarly the exclusion of Sidonians from political power and the damaging consequences for the city. However, the king of Sidon was favorable towards the Persians, and when he was to go to Alexander, he would do so not of his own volition but in response to the demand of his people.

How did the kings of Arwad, Byblos, and Sidon, at the head of their fleets with Autophradates, react on learning that their cities had thrown open their gates to Alexander? Kings Gerashtart of Arwad and Aynel of Byblos immediately abandoned the Persian fleet and rallied to Alexander with their respective fleets. They were followed by a few

Sidonian triremes, probably manned by anti-Persian crews, who abandoned their king Abdashtart II. In total, around eighty Phoenician galleys deserted the Persian fleet to join the Macedonian fleet. Alexander willingly welcomed these initial enemy fleets because he knew that they were not in Persian service of their own free will, according to Arrian's explanation. In reality, he welcomed them because he needed them, his aim being to retrieve all the Phoenician fleets. King Abdashtart II of Sidon remained at the head of the Sidonian fleet which had only lost a few galleys. It was still powerful, as there were still probably a hundred or so galleys. When Alexander was welcomed by the Sidonians, the major part of the Sidonian fleet was still in the service of the Persians, who retained supremacy of the sea. Abdashtart II remained loyal to Darius III to the very end and only abandoned him when the Persian fleet no longer existed, deserted by all the Phoenician, Cypriot, and Cilician fleets.

The siege of Tyre by Alexander

When Alexander headed towards Tyre, the southern Phoenician city, his conquest of Phoenicia was far from a foregone conclusion, as the largest Phoenician fleets, that of Tyre and almost all that of Sidon, were still on the side of the Persians. King Ozmilk of Tyre, then in the seventeenth year of his reign, was with his fleet alongside Darius III. Meanwhile, a delegation from the island of Tyre welcomed Alexander on his arrival in Ushu, on the coast facing the island. Arrian specified the composition of this delegation: "Most of the delegates were Tyrian dignitaries and with them, in particular, was the son of Ozmilk, king of Tyre, himself being at sea with Autophradates." The son of Ozmilk was not vested with the same powers as the son of the king of Arwad, he was a delegate, like the others, whose name was not even mentioned. Kingship in Tyre's political regime appears to have been restricted by representative bodies, a council of dignitaries in particular. The Tyrian delegation gave symbolic submission to Alexander, considering him more as an ally than an overlord. In response, Alexander asked the delegates to inform the Tyrians that he wished to offer a sacrifice to the god of Tyre, Milqart, the equivalent of the Greek god Heracles. The Tyrians understood that he wanted to capture the island and replied by saying that he could just as well perform his sacrifice in the temple Milqart in Ushu. This sent Alexander into a violent rage and he threatened the Tyrians: "Your position gives you assurance, and, because you live on an island, you despise my army of infantrymen. However, I want you to know that you will let me enter your city, willingly or by force!"

The siege of Tyre is described in most of the classical sources. These accounts were written to the glory of Alexander, who succeeded in taking the city where all previous conquerors had failed, even Nebuchadnezzar II who had laid siege to it for thirteen years. The Tyrians, friends of the Persians, were inevitably vilified in these accounts and no Phoenician source has been preserved to correct any misjudgment. However, we do know that the siege was very difficult for them, based on the evidence of Ozmilk's coinage. In the fifteenth year of his reign, in 335, the king of Tyre minted an immense quantity of coins, probably in order to pay for the war preparations for the Persians. In 334 and 333, years 16 and 17, he minted virtually no coinage and their percentage of silver was reduced.

How can Tyre's resistance to Alexander, contrary to the attitude adopted by the other Phoenician cities, be explained? The island-based town wanted to remain independent in line with Tyrian tradition and possibly to save the democratic regime introduced after the slaves' revolt. The Tyrians had always had absolute confidence in the impregnability of their island, protected by the sea, by huge fortifications, and by a powerful war fleet. They were encouraged by the Carthaginian delegation, which came to Tyre to celebrate the annual Milqart festival, which guaranteed them the support of Carthage's formidable fleet. They were viewed favorably by the Persians, to whom they owed the prosperity of their city ever since the decline of Sidon in 347. Darius III encouraged them to resist and they were probably convinced of his victory. The king of the Persians might even have promised them total independence in the event of success. The traditional rivalry between Tyre and Sidon is evidenced by the fact that Sidon served as a naval base for Alexander and its fleet helped him to capture Tyre.

What was Alexander's ultimate aim in laying siege to Tyre? He wanted to conquer all the Phoenician cities before driving inland and to gain control over their fleets to prevent the Persians from going to war in Greece. He also intended to maintain his reputation as an invincible conqueror. At the outset of the siege, the fleet of Tyre, under the command of King Ozmilk, was allowed to leave the Persian fleet to come and defend its city. Initially, its power impressed the Macedonian army. Alexander nevertheless succeeded in convincing his officers to carry out the siege, based on a dream in which Heracles (Milqart) promised him victory, at the end of a difficult siege. He had the ingenious idea of having a causeway built that would link the island to the mainland, choosing the narrowest and shallowest part of the strait. The Macedonians used blocks of stone from the houses in Ushu to construct this causeway. To begin with their task was easy, but when they got within shooting distance of the Tyrian archers posted on the ramparts of the island town, they were plagued by volleys of arrows. To protect themselves, they built two mobile towers on the causeway, covered with leather hides, while archers protected them against the Tyrian attacks, and they continued their construction work under the protection of the towers. The Tyrians then launched a huge cargo ship loaded with flammable materials against the towers. They succeeded in destroying the towers then, from the sea, went on to taunt the workers who had not abandoned their construction work.

However, seeing that the work was progressing despite all this, the Tyrians decided to provide a safe refuge for the women, the children, and the old people by sending them to Carthage. They then organized the defense of the fortifications, preparing their eighty triremes for a naval battle and blocking the entrance to their harbors. The Macedonian fleet came to anchor in the shelter of the causeway. Alexander mobilized all the Phoenician and Cypriot engineers to build a vast number of technically advanced siege engines. The Tyrians, meanwhile, assembled their defensive engines, equally as sophisticated. Several naval battles were engaged, which turned to Alexander's advantage. This meant he could then take his siege engines on to the causeway, which had been completed—rams, catapults, siege towers, and bridges—to attempt to breach Tyre's fortifications. The Tyrians counterattacked with arrows, harpoons, scythes, and all sorts of missiles, of white-hot sand and fishing nets.

Alexander finally ordered an all-out assault: The infantry entered via the breaches opened up in the fortifications and the galleys forced their way into the harbors. The island town of Tyre was taken for the first time by Alexander during summer 332, after seven months of siege. The Tyrians were massacred or sold as slaves, their galleys sunk or seized. The Sidonians, suddenly remembering their close relationship with the Tyrians, are said to have secretly saved 15,000 on their ships. King Ozmilk of Tyre, the magistrates, and the members of the Carthaginian delegation had taken refuge in the temple of Milqart. Alexander granted them his pardon and left Ozmilk on the throne. His clemency towards the king could be explained because he was not party to the delegation that had refused him access to the island and because the Tyrian political regime had not really left him with any other option. The island town of Tyre was not destroyed because it was under the protection of Heracles (Milqart), to whom Alexander offered the sacred Tyrian ship, dedicated to this god. He presided over the lavish sacrifices made to

Heracles, paid his men, and organized the funerals for those among his forces who had been killed.

The fall of Tyre marked the submission of Phoenicia as a whole to Alexander, but it did not spell the end of the Persian Empire, which was to continue until 330. Alexander refused Darius III's proposal—handing over the conquered territories to him—which his advisors deemed a favorable solution nonetheless. He marched towards Egypt where the survivors of the Persian defeat at Issus were prompting disturbances. Before that, he had to spend another couple of months besieging and overcoming Batis and then taking Gaza, the gateway to Egypt. He understood that he could only establish himself sustainably in Egypt by claiming to be the successor to the pharaohs. He therefore carried out all the necessary rituals and pilgrimages, and founded Alexandria. In spring 331, he came back up towards Syria and met Darius III's army in northern Mesopotamia, at Gaugamela, not far from Erbil. He crushed the army of the king of the Persians, who took refuge in Media. The Persian capitals fell one after the other. Babylon, held by the satrap Mazday, welcomed Alexander as a liberator. He took Susa, but clashed violently with the satrap of Persis, Ariobarzanes, whom he massacred in January 330. Irritated by this resistance and anxious to destroy the symbol par excellence of the Persian Empire, he pillaged and burned the prestigious capital of Persepolis. In forced marches, he pursued Darius III, who ended up being assassinated by one of his eastern satraps in 330. That was the end of the Persian Empire. Alexander remained a legendary figure, famous everywhere, even in Persian and Arabo-Persian traditions. Darius III, the last Achaemenid Persian king, became one of history's forgotten, reduced to the unfortunate identity of "the one who was vanquished by Alexander."

Conclusion

The End of Phoenician history

Arwad, Byblos, and Sidon were conquered in 333, Tyre in 332. This is the conventional end of the history of Phoenicia. It did not disappear overnight though, and the Phoenicians continued to live in the coastal towns of the Near East. However, one indisputable phenomenon transformed Phoenicia, namely, Hellenization, even though its qualities are hard to define. A Hellenizing cultural tendency had already touched the Sidonian ruling elites from the beginning of the fourth century, but we lack information about the other Phoenician cities. In the wake of the historical accident of Alexander's conquest, the ground was fertile for a cultural transformation in Phoenicia. This is the explanation for the rapid Hellenization of the urban areas along the Phoenician coastline during the Hellenistic period. On the other hand, the more remote villages in the mountainous areas of Lebanon experienced a period of change that was extremely slow. Even recently, some of them were virtually unaware of the civil war that shook Lebanon at the end of the twentieth century.

Other than the damage Alexander inflicted on Tyre, which rapidly recovered its prosperity, his reign did not disrupt the organization of Phoenicia from the very outset. The same kings appear to have been maintained on the throne of their cities: Gerashtart in Arwad, Aynel in Byblos, and Ozmilk in Tyre. Only Abdashtart II of Sidon was replaced by Abdalonym (Abdalonymos). The political institution of kingship survived right up until the start of the third century, when the ancient Phoenician cities were to adopt partially Hellenized institutions alongside local magistracies. The construction of gymnasiums and stadiums, along with the organization of competitions, originated from Greek custom and practice. Numerous religious syncretisms were made: Milqart, for example, was assimilated with Heracles, Ashtart with Astarte, and Baal with Zeus.

On his return from Egypt, Alexander celebrated Greek games in Tyre. He probably left garrisons in Tyre and Amrit, a town belonging to Arwad, and he appointed one or two satraps to control the whole of the Near East, with the possible exception of Phoenicia, where Coiranos of Beroia was made responsible for collecting taxes. In the main, he implemented the same principles and organization of the Achaemenid Persian Empire, hence him often being referred to as the "last of the Achaemenids." The improvement hoped for by the Phoenician cities that had warmly welcomed Alexander did not happen. Their obligations at a financial, military, and political level, far from disappearing, became even more burdensome. The cities that were autonomous under the Persian Empire, rapidly saw this autonomy shrink. Previous conquerors had never tried to assimilate the conquered countries culturally. For the first time, the Greek occupiers were to jeopardize Phoenician cultural pluralism by blatant attempts at controlled acculturation, periodically prompting anti-acculturation reactions. Civic coinage was interrupted, the Phoenician workshops had to mint Alexander-type coins. The Phoenician cities had a different position and a different role from the standpoint of conquerors who, this time, had come from the west, and who had ambitions that were more land than sea based, together with significantly different economic aims.

In 323, the death of Alexander ushered in an unprecedented crisis, not so much because he left no adult successor, but more because his political program remained unfinished. The Hellenistic world was a new creation, where armies built kingdoms, where Greek and non-Greek cities sought, for better or worse, to find their place. In the ensuing conflict, from 323, between Alexander's generals, the possession of Syria-Phoenicia was one of the issues at stake. For Ptolemy I, who had been established in Egypt, it was the necessary extension of his kingdom. For his opponents, Syria-Phoenicia was not an end in itself, but a starting point from which to be able to reconquer the whole of Alexander's Empire. Even though the attitude of the new occupiers had changed, Phoenicia was still at the heart of the confrontation between the major powers. Ptolemy I ruled over Phoenicia from 319 to 315, then Antigonus the One-Eyed and his son Demetrius I took hold of Tyre and exacted contributions from the ancient Phoenician cities, with the except of Arwad.

The second century was punctuated by the Syrian wars, recurrent conflicts between the two rival dynasties: the Lagids (Ptolemies) of Egypt and the Seleucids of Syria. The political division separated the Phoenician cities into two very different politico-economic worlds. Arwad and the northern towns were under Seleucid domination, with extensive autonomy: Arwad was the first city to receive the privilege of enjoying an autonomous period, from autumn 259. Conversely, the other cities, from Tripoli to Akko, were integrated into the Lagid administration, with was a lot more constrictive. Tyre only received autonomous status in 126, then it was Sidon's turn in 112, followed by Tripoli in around 105 and Ashkelon in 103. These four towns benefited from a general movement toward the emancipation of cities, in line with the declining authority of the Seleucids and the Lagids. Greek domination over the ancient Phoenician cities did not quell their intercity rivalries though. Hence, Arwad was in permanent conflict with Amrit, and this carried on relentlessly until Amrit was subjugated in around 145. Tyre and Sidon were permanently vying with each other to gain supremacy: the legends on their coins proclaimed that each was the metropolis of the other. Each city attempted to hold its own in a waning Hellenistic world, in order to meet the rising power of Rome. Arwad stood out yet again by trying to resist Mark Antony's Roman fleet in 38, but starving and plagued by epidemics, the city was forced to surrender.

Use of the Phoenician language receded as the Greek language became more generalized. The last bilingual inscription in Phoenician and Greek is dated to 25. It is a dedication to the Greek gods Heracles and Hermes, placed in the gymnasium in Arwad. The Phoenician text is a rough translation of the Greek, indicating that by then Phoenician was no longer written correctly. Nevertheless, ancient scholars still understood it as a dead language, as evidenced by Philo of Byblos who translated Sanchuniathon's *Phoenician History* at the beginning of the second century CE. Phoenician also receded quite rapidly as a spoken language in favor of Greek and Aramaic, the international language of the Near East since the seventh century. The multiculturalism of the Phoenician harbor cities meant having the ability to speak the languages that were widely used at that period. When Pausanias, the second century CE Greek writer, recounted his meeting with a Sidonian in Aegion, they spontaneously spoke Greek. At the beginning of the first century CE the Phoenician language saw a resurgence, but it was limited to monetary legends and proper names, probably due to a phenomenon of resistance to Greek acculturation and a temporary return to Semitic tradition.

A common yet separate destiny

A strange and contradictory impression emerges at the end of this history of Phoenicia: the Phoenicians undeniably had a common destiny and yet it varied from one city to the next. Geography was instrumental in forging their destiny. The Phoenician cities found themselves on the border between Asia and the western world, between Egypt and Anatolia, a privleged location in terms of contact and passage. They were sited between the safe haven of the mountains and the adventure of the sea. The mountains offered them the exceptional resources of its lush forests. The sea opened up the Mediterranean and Atlantic routes for them towards a multitude of riches and conquests. Although the Phoenician cities were small in terms of territorial size, they had all the advantages in their favor to become large, rich, and powerful cities. The other side of the coin was that, for the very same reasons, they attracted the greed of all kinds of predators. In an Orient dominated by mainland empires, for successive conquerors the Phoenician cities had always represented a major focal point, both economically and strategically—economically with their local resources and their trading networks, and strategically with their naval bases, their war fleets, and their experienced crews.

The Phoenicians were aware of the limits of their territories and of their military forces in the face of vast empires that had colossal armies at their disposal. They also realized that Phoenicia, given its central location in the Near East, was used as a zone of confrontation between the major powers to the south (Egyptians), west (Assyrians, Babylonians, and Persians), and north (Mitannians and Hittites). Yet, at the same time, they could not prevent themselves from conjuring up unceasing dreams of independence. They knew exactly what this independence meant because they had had more than three centuries' experience of it, between 1200 and 883. That was the time when the Near East was overwhelmed by the invasions of the Sea Peoples and endured the consequences thereof: the ancient powers were weakened and the new powers had not yet succeeded in asserting themselves.

The Phoenicians' desire for independence and their hope of succeeding were strong enough to drive them to revolt against the occupier periodically, even if these revolts always had a similar outcome, namely, repression and intensification of the earlier oppression. The Phoenician cities all possessed an amazing capacity for reconstruction and recovery, even after the worst reprisals. In truth, all the successive conquerors, be they Assyrians, Babylonians, or Persians, never succeeded in truly integrating these cities into their empires. In point of fact, it was always out the western territories of these empires that their main challenges emerged that caused them to falter. While the conquest of the West was their main objective, it was also one of the major causes of their disappearance.

The Phoenician cities were mere pawns on the chessboard of the major powers and, at the same time, grains of sand disrupting the gears of conquest. Yet, taken individually, they had very different destinies. Key issues brought them together or kept them apart, such as the solidarity between Byblos and Beirut, or the rivalry between Sidon and Tyre.

Arwad, the large Phoenician city of the north, always occupied a unique position. Culturally close to northern Syria, it tended to maintain relations with southern Turkey and Cyprus. In the conflicts between the major powers, it was pulled into the orbit of the northern states, from the Hittites to the Seleucids. Close to the main access route towards Mesopotamia via the Orontes and the Euphrates, it was the first Phoenician city reached by the expeditions from the oriental empires, as it was to be by Alexander's army. Most of the time, the Aradians adopted a flexible and pragmatic attitude towards the various conquerors. However, it sometimes happened that a king of Arwad considered himself invincible on his island, well away from coast.

Tripoli was characterized by its originality. Consisting of three towns founded by Arwad, Sidon, and Tyre, it was the seat of a pan-Phoenician Council, whose unparalleled political status has always remained very mysterious.

Byblos, in the very heart of Phoenicia, was a small city in terms of its territorial size but important by virtue of its history. It was probably the most ancient of the Phoenician cities. It was located on the dividing line between two different cultural zones, that of the north oriented towards Syria, and that of the south oriented towards Palestine, and between two zones of influence for the major powers. From the outset, its destiny was closely linked with that of Egypt, which got its timber supplies from Byblos's forests and practiced the same cult of Baalat Gubal. It was a high-ranking city up until the end of the second millennium, which later faded from the regional scene and had folded back on itself, until the middle of the fifth century when it remilitarized itself. Above all, it was a sacred city, somewhat in isolation from the world with its conservatory of traditions, which benefited from a special moral status and probably privileges compared to the other Phoenician cities. Out of caution, it avoided committing itself to any type of conflict as its population was small, it did not have an island to help defend itself, it was not well-equipped as regards the harbor, and it lacked practical access to the hinterland.

Then there were the two large neighboring cities of the south, Sidon and Tyre, which everything bound together and separated at the same time. They both sought to exert supremacy over the other Phoenician cities. In near-permanent rivalry, they fought for this supremacy, encouraged by the successive occupiers who alternately weakened one to strengthen the other. The expansionist ideology of Sidon pushed it to extend its territory, cramped in between those of Byblos and Tyre, towards the north and the south of central Phoenicia. In reality, its expansion did not involve direct conquest, which in principle was impossible because it was incorporated within an empire. Rather, it was achieved thanks to subtle political ploys with the Assyrian, Babylonian, and Persian kings, who granted it territories at Tyre's expense. Sidon appears to have missed out on the colonization phenomenon, at least for the most part, because at the time it could have gone down this path, it was under Tyre's dominion. However, it did participate indirectly as a town in the territory of Tyre, whose colonizing force was therefore strengthened. Even without possessing the defensive position of a large island like Tyre and Arwad, Sidon did not hesitate to rebel on several occasions against Assyrian and Persian domination, accepting the grave consequences of its decisions, to the point of disappearing altogether, transformed into an Assyrian province in 677. Simyra suffered the same fate around 743–738 but, unlike Sidon, it never recovered. Sidon maintained relations with Egypt, but looked mainly towards the Greek world, particularly towards Salamis of Cyprus and Athens in the fourth century. The city even experienced a stunning period of Hellenization prior to the arrival of Alexander.

Tyre was able to develop freely to the south where no large Phoenician city stopped it. It maintained relations with Egypt and with Cyprus. At the zenith of its power at the end of the ninth century, when Sidon did not overshadow it, it took the lead in the incredible colonization phenomenon in the western Mediterranean. A long while after Carthage had acquired its independence and founded its own colonies, symbolic links remained between the motherland and its colony, until the second century when Hannibal, defeated by the Romans, was to take refuge in Tyre, which appears to have been the most rebellious of the Phoenician cities. Strengthened by their insular position, the Tyrians rebelled several times against the Assyrian, Babylonian, and Persian kings. The longest-known siege was that of Nebuchadnezzar II around 586–573, which lasted for thirteen years. Among all the Phoenician cities, only Tyre refused to submit to Alexander. In 332, he put an end once and for all to the myth of the island's invincibility, connecting it to the mainland with a causeway. This was the end of the history of Phoenicia, against a backdrop of differing reactions—Sidon which surrendered enthusiastically to the Macedonian conqueror; Arwad and Byblos, which surrendered spontaneously; and Tyre, which resisted to the end. Yet, the outcome was the same, such was their common destiny: all the Phoenician cities were gradually absorbed into the Hellenistic world and its powerful domineering culture, regardless of the degree of resistance expressed.

Through the documentation that has been preserved, several Phoenician figures who left their mark on the history of Phoenicia have come down to us. Among them, King Yakinlu of Arwad, that clever merchant, undisciplined and rebellious, who taunted two Assyrian kings, Esarhaddon and Ashurbanipal. King Zakerbaal of Byblos, literate and well-educated, cunning and generous, proved able to deal with the Egyptian pharaoh, no longer as a vassal but on an equal footing. King Ozbaal, brought to power by the clergy, succeeded in masterfully reestablishing his city's economic standing. The history of Sidon is marked by several exceptional figures, starting with Abdimilkot, who revolted against the Assyrian king Esarhaddon. A woman, Amoashtart, succeeded in imposing herself in this world of men: energetic, responsible, and endowed with immense political acumen, she exercised royal functions for many years. King Bodashtart, who ousted her from power, will be remembered as a great builder. The most famous Sidonian king was Abdashtart I, Straton for the Greeks, cultivated and refined, with a dual eastern and western culture; he too was a rebel. A great patron of Sidonian sculptors, he was able to redress the economic situation of his city by carrying out the first known monetary devaluation. The history of Tyre, finally, was marked by King Hiram I: peaceable and politically astute, he developed his city's trading activities and its international influence. A woman, the Tyrian princess Elissa, played a leading role in founding the prestigious Tyrian colony of Carthage. King Baal I, who jealously guarded his island independence, courageously rebelled on two successive occasions against the Assyrian kings Esarhaddon and Ashurbanipal, with whom he succeeded in skillfully negotiating his surrender. For thirteen years, King Ithobaal III resisted the siege of the famous Babylonian King Nebuchadnezzar II, making enormous sacrifices, but finally doomed to failure.

In addition to these towering figures, elements of Phoenician civilization have survived to our own days. Despite the successive occupiers of ancient Phoenicia after Alexander's conquest, Greeks, Romans, Byzantines, Turks, and the French, its history has not been erased from memory and it has even left material traces that are still visible. For example, the ribbed-wall building technique has been passed on, from generation to generation, in the families of stonemasons in the village of Aqura, in the upper Nahr Ibrahim Valley. The ceramic forms used in everyday life have still been preserved there too, with no significant change since antiquity. However, the main contribution of the Phoenicians remains the alphabet, which, paradoxically, was not used to pass on to us the core of their writings.

Phoenicia before 1200

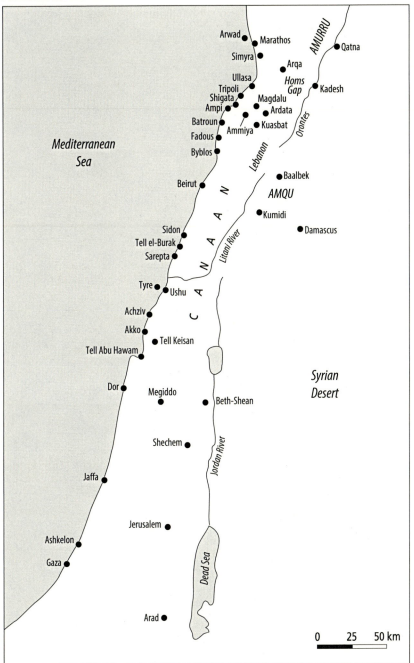

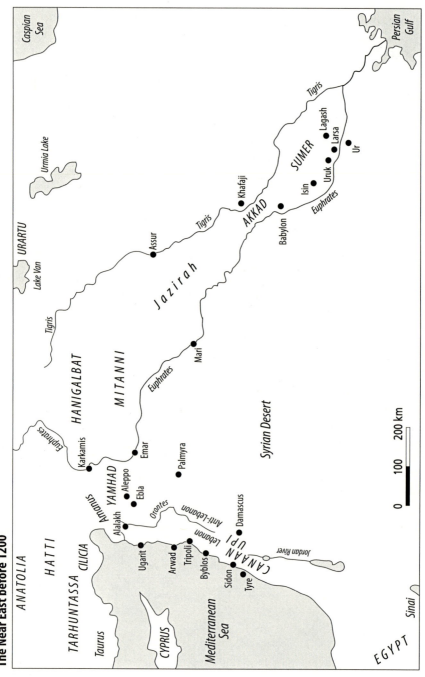

The Near East before 1200

Phoenicia from 1200 to 332

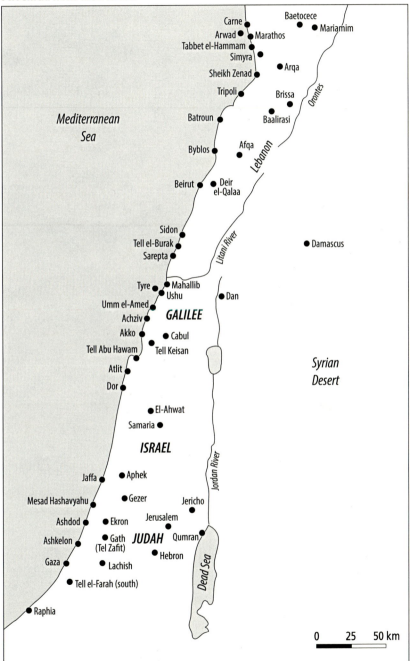

Baetocece
Carne
Arwad • Marathos • Mariamim
Tabbet el-Hammam
Simyra
Sheikh Zenad • Arqa
Tripoli
Brissa
Batroun
Baalirasi
Mediterranean
Sea
Byblos • Afqa
Beirut • Deir
el-Qalaa

Sidon
Tell el-Burak
Sarepta
Damascus
Tyre • Mahallib
Ushu
Umm el-Amed • Dan
Achziv
GALILEE
Akko • Cabul
Tell Abu Hawam
Tell Keisan
Atlit
Syrian
Dor
Desert
El-Ahwat
Samaria
ISRAEL
Jaffa • Aphek
Mesad Hashavyahu • Gezer
Jericho
Ashdod • Ekron
Jerusalem
Ashkelon • Gath
(Tel Zafit)
JUDAH • Qumran
Gaza • Hebron
Lachish
Tell el-Farah (south)
Raphia

Orontes
Lebanon
Litani River
Jordan River
Dead Sea

0   25   50 km

The Near East from 1200 to 332

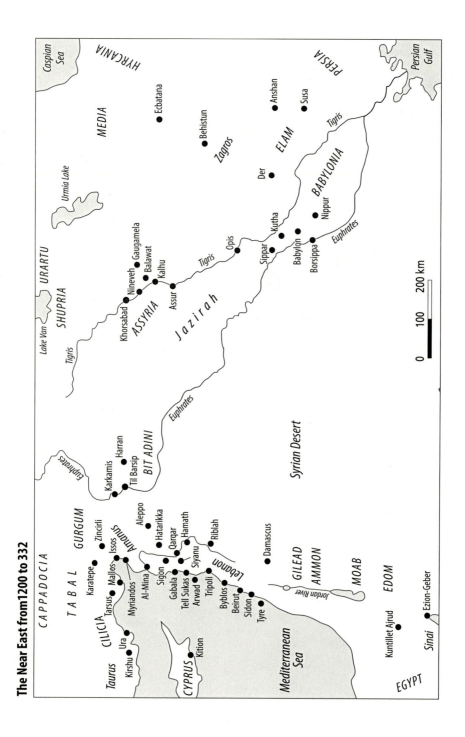

Table 1. Chronology of the proto-Phoenician kings

Dates	Kings of Byblos	Kings of Beirut	Kings of Sidon	Kings of Tyre
ca. 2600–2300	Baalat-rum?			
ca. 2046–2038	Ibdati			
ca. 1818–1773	Abishemu I			
ca. 1772–1764	Ibshemuabi			
ca. 1737–1733	Reyen (Yakin-Ilu)			
ca. 1721–1710	Inten (Yantin-Ammu)			
ca. 1721–1710	Ilimma-yapi			
late 17th–early 16th century	Abishemu II			
end 17th–early 16th century	Yapa-Shemuabi			
end 17th–early 16th century	Akery			
end 17th–early 16th century	Akay (Egliya)			
16th century	Kain			
16th century	Rynty	Yapah-Hadda		
ca. 1360–1330	Rib-Hadda	Ammunira	Yabni-…	Baal-Shiptu I
	Ili-Rapih		Zimredda	Abimilku
ca. 1300–1200			Addu-Yashma	Baal-Shiptu II
ca. 1213–1203			Addumu	Baal-Targumu
			Anniya?	
			Yapa-Addu	
			Addu-…	

295

Table 2. Chronology of the Phoenician kings

Dates	Kings of Arwad	Kings of Byblos	Kings of Sidon	Kings of Tyre
ca. 1090		Zakerbaal	Weret or Mekmer	Weret or Mekmer
1050–1000		Ahiram (ca. 1000)		
1000–950		Ithobaal (ca. 1000–970)		Abibaal (< 970)
		Yehimilk (ca. 970–950)		Hiram I (ca. 970–936)
950–900		Abibaal (ca. 943)		Baleazoros (ca. 935–918)
		Elibaal (ca. 922)		Abdastratos (ca. 918–909)
				Methusastratos (ca. 909–897)
900–850		Shipitbaal I (ca. 900)		Astharymos (ca. 897–889)
				Phelles (ca. 889–888)
	Mattanbaal I (853)			Ithobaal I (ca. 888–856)
850–800				Balezoros (ca. 848–830)
				Mattan I (ca. 830–821)
800–750				Pumiyaton (ca. 821–774)
				Milkiram? (ca. 750)
				Ithobaal II (ca. 740)
750–700	Mattanbaal II (ca. 734–732)	Shipitbaal II (ca. 737–732)		Hiram II (ca. 739–730)
				Mattan II (ca. 729)
	Abdileti (ca. 701)	Urimilk I (ca. 701)	Ithobaal (ca. 701)	Luli (ca. 728–695)
700–650	Mattanbaal III (ca. 673)	Milkyasap (ca. 673)	Abdilmilkot (ca. 677)	Baal I (ca. 677–671)
	Yakinlu (ca. 670–660)			
	Ozbaal I (> 660)		*Assyrian*	
650–600			*Province*	
600–550			*(677–610)*	Ithobaal III (ca. 591–573)
				Baal II (ca. 572–563)

Table 2, *continued*. Chronology of the Phoenician kings

Dates	Kings of Arwad	Kings of Byblos	Kings of Sidon	Kings of Tyre
			Eshmunazar I (ca. 575–550)	*Period of the judges* (563–556) Eknibal/Chelbes/Abbar (ca. 563–562) Matta /Gerashtart (ca. 561–556) *Return of the kings* Balazor (ca. 556) Maharbaal (ca. 555–552)
550–500			Tabnit (ca. 550–540) Amoashtart (ca. 539) Eshmunazar II (ca. 539–525) Bodashtart (ca. 524–515) Yatonmilk? (after 515)	Hiram III (ca. 551–533) Ithobaal IV? (> 532)
500–450	Ozbaal II? (< 480) Maharbaal (480)	Shipitbaal III (ca. 500) Urimilk II Yeharbaal?	Anysus? (before 480) Tetramnestus (480)	Hiram IV? (< 480) Mattan III (480)
450–400		Yehawmilk (ca. 450)	Baalshillem I (ca. 425) Abdamon Baana	
400–350		Elpaal Ozbaal (ca. 400)	Baalshillem II (401–366) Abdashtart I (365–352)	
350–333	Gerashtart (339–333)	Urimilk III Aynel Aynel?	Tennes (351–347) Evagoras II (346–343) Abdashtart II (342–333)	Abdashtart (after 354–350) Ozmilk (349–333)
After 333	Gerashtart Abdashtart?		Abdalonym	Ozmilk

Bibliography

Chronology

The dates are often approximate. For the various states studied in this book, they have been selected from the following works:

Beckman, G., "Hittite Chronology," *Akkadica* 119–120 (2000): 19–32.
Briant, P., *Histoire de l'Empire perse: de Cyrus à Alexandre*. Paris: Fayard, 1996.
Elayi, J., "An Updated Chronology of the Reigns of the Phoenician Kings during the Persian Period (539–333 BCE)," *Transeuphratène* 32 (2006): 13–43.
Freu, J., *Histoire politique du royaume d'Ugarit*. Collection Kubaba 11. Paris: Harmattan, 2006.
Garelli, P. et al., *Le Proche-Orient Asiatique*. Volume 1: *Des origines aux invasions des peuples de la mer*. Paris: Nouvelle Clio, 1997.
Garelli, P. and Lemaire, A., *Le Proche-Orient Asiatique*. Volume 2: *Les empires mésopotamiens. Israël*. Paris: Presses universitaires de France, 1997.
Hornung, E. et al., *Ancient Egyptian Chronology*. Leiden: Brill 2006.
Sagona, C. (ed.), *Beyond the Homeland: Markers in Phoenician Chronol-ogy*. Leuven: Peeters, 2008.
Singer, I., "A Concise History of Amurru." Pp. 135–95 in *Amurru Akkadian: A Linguistic Study*. Edited by S. Izreel. Atlanta: Society of Biblical Literature, 1991.

General studies

Baurain, C. and Bonnet, C., *Les Phéniciens, marins des trois continents*. Paris: Colin, 1992.
Belmonte, J. A., *Cuatro estudios sobre los dominios territoriales de las ciudades-estado fenicias*. Barcelona: Bellaterra, 2003.
Bondi, S. F. et al., *Fenici e Cartaginesi. Una civilta mediterranea*. Rome: Istituto poligrafico e Zecca dello Stato, 2009.
Krings, V. (ed.), *La civilisation phénicienne et punique. Manuel de recherche*. Leiden: Peeters 1995.
Lipinski, E. (ed.), *Dictionnaire de la civilisation phénicienne et punique*. Turnhout: Brepols, 1992.
Markoe, G., *The Phoenicians*. Berkeley: University of California Press, 2000.
Renan, E., *Mission de Phénicie*. Paris: Imprimerie impériale, 1864.

Zamora, J. A. (ed.), *El Hombre fenicio. Estudios y materiales.* Rome: Escuela Española de Historia y Arqueología en Roma, 2003.

Introduction

Acquaro, E. et al. (eds.), *Biblo. Una città e la sua cultura.* Rome: Consiglio nazionale delle ricerche, 1994.

Aubet, M.E., *The Phoenician Cemetery of Tyre-Al Bass: Excavations 1997–1999.* Beirut: Ministère de la Culture, Direction Générale des Antiquités, 2004.

Baurain, C., "Portées chronologique et géographique du terme 'phénicien.'" Pp. 7–28 in *Studia Phoenicia IV: Religio Phoenicia.* Namur: Société des études classiques, 1985.

Baurain, C. et al., *Phoinikeia grammata: lire et écrire en Méditerranée. Actes du colloque de Liège, 15–18 novembre 1989.* Studia Phoenicia XIII. Namur: Société des études classiques, 1991.

Bunnens, G., "Le luxe phénicien d'après les inscriptions royales assyriennes." Pp. 121–33 in *Studia Phoenicia* III. Leuven: Peeters, 1985.

Culican, W., "Quelques aperçus sur les ateliers phéniciens," *Syria* 45 (1968): 275–93.

Doumet-Serhal, C. (ed.), *Decade: A Decade of Archaeology and History in the Lebanon.* Beirut: Lebanese British Friends of the National Museum, 2004.

Dubuisson, M., "L'image du Carthaginois dans la littérature latine." Pages 159–67 in *Studia Phoenicia* II. Leuven: Peeters, 1983.

Echt, R., "Les ivoires figurés de Kamid el-Loz et l'art phénicien du IIe millénaire." Pages 69–83 in *Studia Phoenicia* III, Leuven: Peeters, 1985.

Elayi, J., *Nouvelles découvertes sur les usages funéraires des Phéniciens d'Arwad.* Paris: Gabalda, 1996.

Ferron, J., *Sarcophages de Phénicie: sarcophages à scènes en relief.* Paris: Geuthner, 1992–1993.

Gibson, J. C. L., *Textbook of Syrian Semitic Inscriptions. III, Phoenician Inscriptions.* Oxford: Clarendon, 1982.

Gubel, É., *Phoenician Furniture,* Studia Phoenicia VII. Leuven: Peeters, 1987.

—— (ed.), *L'art phénicien. La sculpture de tradition phénicienne.* Paris: Réunion des musées nationaux, 2002.

Lebrun, R., "La place du phénicien en Anatolie au premier millénaire av. J.-C.," *Res Antiquae* 5 (2008): 451–54.

Lipinski, E., *Dieux et déesses de l'univers phénicien et punique.* Studia Phoenicia XIV. Leuven: Peeters, 1995.

—— (ed.), *Phoenicia and the Bible.* Studia Phoenicia XI. Leuven: Departement Oriëntalistiek, 1991.

Morhange, C. and Saghieh-Beydoun, M., *La Mobilité des Paysages Portuaires Antiques du Liban.* Beirut: Ministere de la Culture, Direction Generale des Antiquites, 2005.

Moscati, S., *The World of the Phoenicians.* London: Phoenix Giant, 1968.

Röllig, W., "On the Origins of the Phoenicians," *Berytus* 31 (1983): 79–93.

Bibliography

Sader, H., *Iron Age Funerary Stelae from Lebanon*. Cuadernos de Arqueología Mediterránea 11. Barcelona: Publicaciones del Laboratorio de Arqueología, Universidad Pompeu Fabra, 2005.

Seefried, M., *Les pendentifs en verre sur noyau des pays de la Méditerranée antique*. Rome: École française de Rome, 1982.

Wathelet, P., "Les Phéniciens et la tradition homérique." Pages pp. 235–43 in *Studia Phoenicia* II. Leuven: Peeters, 1983.

Phoenicia before 1200

Arnaud, D., "Une bêche-de-mer antique: la langue des marchands de Tyr à la fin du XIIIe siècle," *Aula Orientalis* 17–18 (1999–2000): 143–66.

———, "Les ports de la "Phénicie" à la fin de l'âge du Bronze Récent (XIVe–XIIIe siècle) d'après les textes cunéiformes de la Syrie," *Studi Micenei ed Egeo-Anatolici* 30 (1992): 179–94.

Badre, L., "Tell Kazel-Simyra: a contribution to a relative chronological history in the eastern Mediterranean during the late Bronze age," *Bulletin of the American Schools of Oriental Research* 343 (2006): 65–95.

Belmonte, J. A., "Presencia Sidonia en los circuitos del Bronce Final," *Rivista di Studi Fenici* 30 (2002): 3–18.

Bottéro, J., *L'épopée de Gilgamesh. Le grand homme qui ne voulait pas mourir*. Paris: Gallimard, 1992.

Carayon, N. Les ports phéniciens et puniques. Géomorphologie et infrastructure. PhD Thesis, Université Marc-Bloch, Strasbourg, 2008.

Doumet-Serhal, C. et al., "Sidon Holy of Holies: the Late Bronze Age Underground Cella," *Archaeology & History in the Lebanon* 34–35 (2011–12): 297–388.

Dunand, M., *Fouilles de Byblos*. Volume V. *L'architecture, les tombes, le matériel domestique, des origines à l'avènement urbain*. Paris: Geuthner, 1973.

Espinel, A. D. "The Role of the Temple of Baalat Gebal as Intermediary between Egypt and Byblos during the Old Kingdom," *Studien zur altägyptischen Kultur* 30 (2002): 103–19.

Freu, J. "La correspondance d'Abimilki, prince de Tyr et la fin de l'ère amarnienne," *Annales de la Faculté des Lettres et Sciences humaines de Nice* 50 (1985): 23–60.

Gassia, A. "L'ensemble funéraire de Byblos: étude de la nécropole énéolithique," *BAAL* 9 (2005): 223–47.

Giveon, R., *The Impact of Egypt on Canaan: Iconographical and Related Studies*. Göttingen: Vandenhoeck & Ruprecht; Freiburg, Switzerland: Universitätsverlag, 1978.

Liverani, M., "Rib-Adda, Righteous Sufferer." Pages 97–124 in *Myth and Politics in Ancient Near Eastern Historiography*. Ithaca, NY: Cornell University Press, 2004.

Montet, P., *Byblos et l'Égypte*. Paris: Geuthner 1928.

Schiestl, R. "The Coffin from Tomb I at Byblos," *Egypt and Levant* 17 (2007): 265–71.

Sollberger, E., "Byblos sous les rois d'Ur," *Archiv fur Orientforschung* 19 (1959–60): 120–22.

Thalmann, J.-P., "Tell Arqa," *BAAL* 4 (2000): 5–74.

Vidal, J., "El enfrentamiento entre Tiro y Sidôn durante los reinados de Abi-Milki y Zimredda: ensayo de reconstrucción," *Aula Orientalis* 24 (2006): 255–63.

———, "The Men of Arwad, Mercenaries of the Sea," *Bibliotheca Orientalis* 65 (2008): 5–15.

Virolleaud, D., "Découverte a Byblos d'un hypogée de la douzième dynastie égyptienne," *Syria* 3 (1922): 273–306.

Youngblood, R. F., "The Amarna Correspondence of Rib-Haddi, Prince of Byblos (EA 68–96)." PhD diss., Dropsie College, 1985.

The period of Phoenicia's independence (1200–883)

Aubet, M. A., *The Phoenicians and the West: Politics, Colonies and Trade.* Cambridge: Cambridge University Press, 1993.

Bondi, S. F., "Note sull' economia fenicia - 1. 1mpresa privata e ruolo dello Stato," *Egitto e Vicino Oriente* 1 (1978): 139–50.

Bonnet, C., *Melqart. Cultes et mythes de l'Héraclès tyrien en Méditerranée.* Leuven: Peeters, 1988.

Bunnens, G., *L'expansion phénicienne en Méditerranée. Essai d'interprétation fondé sur une analyse des traditions littéraires.* Brussels and Rome: Institut historique belge de Rome, 1979.

———, "La mission d'Ounamon en Phénicie: point de vue d'un non-égyptologue," *Rivista di Studi Fenici* 6 (1978): 1–16.

Gitin, S., Mazar, A. and Stern, E. (eds.), *Mediterranean Peoples in Transition, Thirteenth to Early Tenth Centuries BCE.* Jerusalem: Israel Exploration Society, 1998.

Ikeda, Y., "Assyrian Kings and the Mediterranean Sea: The Twelfth to Ninth Century B.C.," *Abr-Nahrain* 23 (1984–85): 22–32.

Lemaire, A., "La datation des rois de Byblos Abibaal et Élibaal et les relations entre l'Égypte et le Levant," *Comptes rendus de l'Académie des Inscriptions et Belles-Lettres* (2006): 1699–1716.

Scandone, G., "Testimonianze egiziane in Fenicia dal XII al IV sec. a.c.," *Rivista di Studi Fenici* 12 (1984): 143–63.

Ward, W. A. and Joukowsky, M. S. (eds.), *The Crisis Years: The 12th Century B.C. From beyond the Danube to the Tigris.* Dubuque, IA: Kendall/Hunt, 1992.

Phoenicia under Assyrian domination (883–610)

Botto, M., *Studi storici sulla Fenicia. L'VIII e il VII secolo a.c.,* Pisa: Università degli Studi di Pisa, 1990.

Briquel-Chatonnet, F., *Les relations entre les cités de la côte phénicienne et les royaumes d'Israël et de Juda.* Leuven: Peeters, 1992.

Elayi, J., *Byblos, cité sacrée (VIIIᵉ–IVᵉ s. av. J.-C.)*. Paris: Gabalda, 2009.

———, "Les cités phéniciennes et l'Empire assyrien à l'époque d'Assurbanipal," *Revue d'Assyriologie* 77 (1983): 45–58.

———, "Les cités phéniciennes entre liberté et sujétion," *Dialogues d'Histoire Ancienne* 16 (1990): 93–113.

———, "Les relations entre les cités phéniciennes et l'Empire assyrien sous le règne de Sennachérib," *Semitica* 35 (1985): 19–26.

Fantar, M., *Carthage: approche d'une civilisation* 1–11. Tunis: Alif, 1993.

Ferjaoui, A., *Recherches sur les relations entre l'Orient phénicien et Carthage.* Fribourg: Editions Universitaires; Göttingen: Vandenhoeck & Ruprecht, 1993.

Katzenstein, H. J., *The History of Tyre*, 2nd, rev. ed. Beer Sheva: Ben Gurion University of the Negev Press, 1997.

Lipinski, E. (ed.), *Phoenicia and the Eastern Mediterranean in the First Millennium B.C.* Studia Phoenicia V. Leuven: Peeters, 1987.

Naaman, N., "Esarhaddon's Treaty with Baal and Assyrian Provinces along the Phoenician Coast," *Rivista di Studi Fenici* 22 (1994): 3–8.

Noureddine, I., "Phoenician Jetty at Tyre," *BAAL* 12 (2008): 161–69.

Oded, B., *Mass Deportations and Deportees in the Neo-Assyrian Empire.* Wiesbaden: Reichert, 1979.

———. "The Phoenician Cities and the Assyrian Empire in the Time of Tiglath-Pileser III," *Zeitschrift des Deutschen Palàstina-Vereins* 90 (1974): 38–49.

Pettinato, G., "I rapporti politici di Tiro con l'Assiria alla luce del 'tratatto tra Asarhaddon e Baal,'" *Rivista di Studi Fenici* 3 (1975): 145–60.

Ponchia, S., *L'Assiria e gli stati transeufratici nella prima metà dell'VIII sec. a.C.* Padua: Sargon, 1991.

Salamé-Sarkis, H., "Matériaux pour une histoire de Batrun," *Berytus* 35 (1987): 101–19.

———. "Le royaume de Sidon au VIIe siècle av. J.-C.," *Syria* 82 (2005): 139–48.

Phoenicia under Babylonian domination (610–539)

Corral, M. A., *Ezekiel's Oracles against Tyre. Historical Reality and Motivations.* Rome: Pontificio Instituto Biblico, 2002.

Da Vita, R. "The Nebuchadnezzar Twin Inscriptions of Brisa (Wadi esh-Sharbin, Lebanon)," *BAAL* 12 (2008): 299–333.

Elayi, J., "L'exploitation des cèdres du Mont Liban par les rois assyriens et néobabyloniens," *Journal of the Economic and Social History of the Orient* 31 (1988): 14–41.

Joannès, F., "Trois textes de Surru à l'époque néo-babylonienne," *Revue d'Assyriologie* 81 (1987), 147–58.

Maïla-Afeiche, A.-M., *Le Site de Nahr el-Kelb.* Beirut: Ministère de la Culture, Dir. Générale des Antiquités, 2009.

Yoyotte, J., "Sur le voyage asiatique de Psammétique 11," *Vetus Testamentum* 1 (1951): 110–44.

Zawadski, S., "Nebuchadnezzar and Tyre in the Light of New Texts from the Ebabbar Archives in Sippar," *Eretz Israel* 27 (2003): 276–81.

Phoenicia under Persian domination (539–332)

Elayi, J., *Abdashtart 1ᵉʳ/ Straton de Sidon: un roi phénicien entre Orient et Occident.* Paris: Gabalda, 2005.
———, "Byblos et Sidon, deux modèles de cités phéniciennes à l'époque perse," *Transeuphratène* 35 (2008): 89–114.
———, *Économie des cités phéniciennes sous l'Empire perse.* Naples: Istituto universitario orientale, 1990.
———, "Gerashtart, King of the Phoenician City of Arwad in the 4th Century BC," *Numismatic Chronicle* (2007): 99–104.
———, "La présence grecque dans les cités phéniciennes sous l'Empire perse achéménide," *Revue des Études Grecques* 105 (1992): 305–27.
———, "The Role of the Phoenician Kings at the Battle of Salamis (480 B.C.E.)," *Journal of the American Oriental Society* 126 (2006): 411–18.
———, "Tripoli (Liban) à l'époque perse," *Transeuphratène* 2 (1990): 59–71.
Elayi, J. and Elayi, A. G., *The Coinage of the Phoenician City of Tyre in the Persian Period.* Leuven: Peeters, 2009.
———, *Monetary and Political History of the Phoenician City of Byblos (5th–4th century BCE).* Winona Lake: Eisenbrauns, 2013.
———, *Le monnayage de la cité phénicienne de Sidon à l'époque perse (Vᵉ–IVᵉ s. av. J.-C.)* 1–11. Paris: Gabalda, 2004.
———, "Quelques particularités de la culture matérielle d'Arwad au Fer III/ Perse," *Transeuphratène* 18 (1999): 9–27.
Elayi, J. and Sayegh, H., *Un quartier du port phénicien de Beyrouth au Fer III/ Perse* 1–11. Paris: Gabalda, 1998–2000.
Lemaire, A., "Le royaume de Tyr dans la seconde moitié du IVe siècle av. J.-C.." pp. 131–50 in *Atti del II Congresso Internazionale di Studi Fenici e Punici.* Rome: Consiglio Nazionale delle Ricerche, 1991.
Stern, E., "Dor à l'époque perse," Pages 77–115 in *Actes du IIᵉ Colloque International "La Syrie-Palestine à l'Époque Perse: Continuités et Ruptures à la Lumière des Périodes Néo-Assyrienne et Hellénistique."* Edited by E.-M. Laperrousaz and A. Lemaire. Transeuphratène 8. Paris: Gabalda, 1994.
Stucky, R. and Mathys, H.-P., "Le sanctuaire Sidonien d'Echmoun. Aperçu historique du site, des fouilles et des découvertes faites à Bostan ech-Cheikh," *BAAL* 4 (2000): 123–48.
Weiskopf, M., *The So-Called "Great Satrap's Revolt," 366–360 B.C.: Concerning Local Instability in the Achaemenid Far West.* Stuttgart: Steiner, 1989.
Xella, P. and Zamora, J.-A., "L'inscription phénicienne de Bodashtart in situ à Bustan esh- Sheikh (Sidon) et son apport à l'histoire du sanctuaire," *Zeitschrift des deutschen Palästina-Vereins* 121 (2005): 119–29.
Yon, M., *Kition dans les textes.* Paris: Editions Recherche sur les civilisations, 2004.

Index of Persons, Deities, Peoples, and Ancient Authors

Amasis: pharaoh, 201, 210, 213, 215,
223–24
Amaziah: king of Judah, 137
Amel-Marduk (Evil-Merodach): king
of Babylon, 209–210
Amenemhat I: pharaoh, 52
Amenemhat II pharaoh, 52–53
Amenemhat III: pharaoh, 55, 63
Amenemhat IV: pharaoh, ix, 56, 62
Amenhotep II: pharaoh, 62
Amenhotep III pharaoh, 63, 66–67,
70, 90
Amenhotep IV (Akhenaten): pha-
raoh, 67, 70, 73, 78
Ammishtamru III: king of Ugarit, 64
Ammonites: population of
Transjordan, 193
Ammunira: king of Beirut, 73–75,
295
Ammurapi: king of Ugarit, 64–65
Amoashtart: co-regent of Sidon, 230,
232, 290, 297
Amun: Egyptian deity, 61, 67, 78, 82,
93, 101–3, 194
Amorites: semi-nomadic population,
8, 9, 38, 47–51, 93
Amos: biblical prophet, 142, 149
Amyntas: officer of Alexander, 276,
279
Amyrtaeus: pharaoh, 255
Androsthenes: explorer of Alexander
the Great, 7
Anniya: king of Sidon?, 83, 295
Antalcidas: Spartan general, 258–59
Antigonus the One-Eyed: Macedonian
general, 285
Anu: Assyrian deity, 106
Anysus: king of Sidon?, 237, 297
Apiru (Habiru): migrant populations,
70–71, 77, 80–81, 85, 94
Apis bull, 224
Appuashu: king of Pirindu, 209–10
Apries (Hophra): pharaoh, 195–96,
200–201
Arameans, 95–96, 105–7, 118, 187,
193, 211
Ariaspes: son of Artaxerxes II, 264
Ariobarzanes: satrap of Persis, 283
Ariobarzanes: satrap of Phrygia or of
Dascylium, 260–61
Aristagoras: tyrant of Miletus, 235
Aristotle: Greek philosopher, 97, 276

Arrian: Greek historian, 276–80
Arsames: Persian satrap of Egypt, 240
Arses. *See* Artaxerxes IV
Artaxerxes I: king of the Persians,
239–40, 246
Artaxerxes II (Mnemon) king of the
Persians, 252, 254–61, 263, 265–66
Artaxerxes III (Ochos): king of the
Persians, 264–66, 270, 272–75
Artaxerxes IV (Arses): king of the
Persians, 274
Artobarzanes: eldest son of Darius
I, 236
Aryandes: Persian satrap of Egypt,
224
Asher: Israelite tribe, 117–18, 121
Ashtart (Astarte): Phoenician deity,
13, 120, 131, 138, 213, 230–33, 284
Ashtart-name-of-Baal: Phoenician
deity, 230
Ashurbanipal: king of Assyria, 173–
82, 290
Ashur-bel-kala: king of Assyria,
107–9, 112
Ashur-dan II: king of Assyria, 108
Ashur-dan III: king of Assyria, 141
Ashur-etil-ilani: king of Assyria, 181
Ashur-nadin-shumi: king of Babylon,
166
Ashur-nirari V: king of Assyria, 141,
144
Ashurnasirpal II: king of Assyria,
129–31, 144
Ashur-uballit II: king of Assyria, 182
Astarte. *See* Ashtart
Astharymos: king of Tyre, 122, 296
Astyages: king of the Medes, 215
Athaliah: queen of Judah, 132
Athenaeus: Greek author, 17
Aten: Egyptian deity, 67
Atossa: daughter of Cyrus II and wife
of Darius I, 234, 236
Attalus: officer of Alexander, 276
Augustine (Saint): Latin author, 5
Autophradates: Persian satrap, 260,
277–80
Avienus: Latin author, 17
Ay: pharaoh, 647
Aynel (Enylos): king of Byblos, 275,
279, 284, 297
Azaryahu: king of Judah, 142
Azaryahu: king of Samal?, 146

Denys: Tyrian of Syracuse, 255
Dido. *See* Elissa
Diodorus (of Sicily) Greek historian,
16, 141, 195–96, 221, 238, 246–49,
265, 274, 257, 259, 266, 268–69,
271–73
Djed-kheper-re: Egyptian, 59
Djoser: pharaoh, 35, 38
Dorians: Indo-European people set-
tled in Greece, 90

Egliya. *See* Akay
Eknibal: son of Baslech, judge of
Tyre, 206, 297
Ekwesh, 89
Elamites: population of ancient Elam,
105, 156–57, 162, 181
Elibaal: king of Byblos, 113–15, 296
Elimilk: Assyrian dignitary, 131
Elissa (Dido): Tyrian princess, 138–
39, 290
Elulaios. *See* Luli
Elpaal: king of Byblos, 252–54, 297
Enkidu, 49
Enmerkar: Sumerian king of Uruk, 50
Enylos. *See* Aynel
Esarhaddon: king of Assyria, 15,
165–74, 176–77, 179–80, 290
Esdras: Judean priest and scribe, 222
Eshmun: Phoenician deity, 6, 11–12,
212, 231–34, 249–50, 263, 271
Eshmunadon, Cypriot minister of
Tyre, 248
Eshmunazar I: king of Sidon, 213,
230, 232, 237, 297
Eshmunazar II: king of Sidon, 18,
213, 230–33, 297
Etruscans: population of pre-Roman
Italy, 89
Euboeans, 123
Eusebius of Caesarea: Greek histo-
rian, 268
Evagoras I: king of Salamis of
Cyprus, 248–49, 255–59, 267
Evagoras II: king of Salamis, then of
Sidon, 266, 272–74, 297
Evil-Merodach. *See* Amel-Marduk
Ezekiel: biblical prophet, 1, 16,
196–99, 212

Fenkhu: Egyptian name for the
Phoenicians, 4

Flavius Josephus: Greek author, 60,
62, 119–20, 122–24, 131, 133, 135,
137, 142, 160–61, 188–89, 196,
199–200, 206, 208, 209–10, 212,
229–30
Florus: Latin historian, 2

Gaumata: Persian, Magian, 226
Gerashtart: son of Abdelim, judge of
Tyre, 207, 209, 297
Gerashtart: king of Arwad, 275, 278–
79, 284, 297
Gerashtart. Gerastratos. *See*
Gerashtart
Gersaphon: Assyrian dignitary, 180
Gilgamesh: legendary king of Uruk,
49–50
Gobryas (Gubaru): Persian satrap,
222
Gobryas (Ugbaru) Babylonian gover-
nor of Gutium, 215–16
Gedaliah: Babylonian governor of
Judah, 196
Gudea: king of Lagash, 49
Gubaru. *See* Gobryas

Habiru. *See* Apiru
Hadad: Aramean/Edomite king, 122
Hadadezer: Aramean king of Zoba,
118
Ham: son of Noah, 7
Hannibal: Carthaginian leader, 289
Hannon: Carthaginian navigator, 17
Hanun: Babylonian official, 205
Hanun: king of Gaza, 150, 156
Harasphes. *See* Herishef
Hatshepsut: pharoah, 61
Hathor: Egyptian deity, 38–40, 45–47,
57
Hattusili III: Hittite king, 64, 82–83,
92
Hazael: king of Damascus, 135–37
Hebrews. *See* Israelites
Henenu: majordomo of the pharaoh
Mentuhotep II, 52
Heracles: Greek deity, 60, 138, 187,
280–83, 284, 286
Herihor: priest of Amun, 101, 103
Herishef (Harasphes): Egyptian deity,
187
Hermes: Greek deity, 286